SEX DISCRIMINATION LAW

SEX DISCRIMINATION LAW

DAVID PANNICK

*Barrister; Fellow of All Souls College,
Oxford*

CLARENDON PRESS · OXFORD

1985

Oxford University Press, Walton Street, Oxford, OX2 6DP
Oxford New York Toronto
Delhi Bombay Calcutta Madras Karachi
Kuala Lumpur Singapore Hong Kong Tokyo
Nairobi Dar es Salaam Cape Town
Melbourne Auckland
and associated companies in
Beirut Berlin Ibadan Nicosia

Oxford is a trade mark of Oxford University Press

Published in the United States
by Oxford University Press, New York

British Library Cataloguing in Publication Data
Pannick, David
Sex discrimination law.
1. Sex discrimination against women——
Law and legislation——Great Britain
I. Title
344.102'878   KD734
ISBN 0-19-825481-4

Library of Congress Cataloguing in Publication Data
Pannick, David.
Sex discrimination law.
Includes index.
1. Sex discrimination——Law and legislation——
Great Britain.   2. Sex discrimination against women——
Law and legislation——Great Britain.
3. Equal pay for equal work——Law and legislation——
Great Britain.
I. Title.
KD4103.P36   1985   346.4101'3   85-15573
ISBN 0-19-825481-4   344.10613

Set by Hope Services, Abingdon
Printed and bound in Great Britain by
Biddles Ltd, Guildford and King's Lynn

To my wife,

DENISE,

and to my parents,

MAURICE AND RITA PANNICK

PREFACE

MR JUSTICE FRANKFURTER of the US Supreme Court explained that the 'function of an advocate is not to enlarge the intellectual horizon. His task is to seduce, to seize the mind for a predetermined end, not to explore paths to truth' ('Mr Justice Jackson' 68 *Harvard Law Review* 937, 939 (1955)). In the chapters which follow, I attempt to explore paths to truth in sex discrimination law. But I do so conscious of the fact that my thinking on many of the issues and cases here discussed has been vitally influenced by my efforts to persuade courts and tribunals towards a predetermined end on behalf of complainants and alleged discriminators.

I am very grateful to all those—friends, colleagues, and clients—who have directed me along these paths to truth: especially Anthony Lester QC (the father and mother of sex discrimination law in the United Kingdom), the Hon. Michael Beloff QC, Judith Beale, Hester Blanks, David H. J. Cohen, Elaine Donnelly, Tess Gill, Steve Grosz, Brenda Hancock, Alan Lakin, Nicola Jones, Anthony Julius, Denise Kingsmill, Anne Saxon, Frank Spencer, Elizabeth Whitehouse, and all the staff of the Equal Opportunities Commission whose hard work to combat sex discrimination does not always receive adequate recognition. All Souls College provided a stimulating environment in which to consider and discuss many of the issues.

I want also to thank Adam Hodgkin of the Oxford University Press. His encouragement and advice mean that I have no wish to echo the view of George Orwell that 'writing a book is a horrible, exhausting struggle, like a long bout of some painful illness' (*Collected Essays, Journalism and Letters* (Penguin edn., 1970), vol. 1, p. 29).

Most of all, I have cause to thank my wife, Denise. She has, during the writing of this book (as before, and, I fear, after), resisted the temptation to charge me with hypocrisy: while I spent evenings and weekends drafting chapters and articles on equal opportunities law, she (in addition to pursuing her own career as a barrister) carried out more than her fair share of family duties. In addition, she has contributed much to the pages of this book by providing information and argument on central issues.

Sex discrimination law makes otherwise sensible people react in unpredictable ways. Eradicating sex discrimination in society was never going to be an easy task. Endemic prejudice and traditional conceptions of the 'proper' role of women and men are not going to be swept aside by a tide of reason. In his essay *The Subjection of Women* (1869), Chapter 1, John Stuart Mill explained that 'so long as an opinion is strongly rooted in the feelings, it gains rather than loses in stability by having a preponderating weight of argument against it . . . [T]he worse it fares in argumentative contest, the more persuaded its adherents are that their feeling must have some deeper ground, which the arguments do not reach . . .'. The object of this book is to describe how sex discrimination is not merely contrary to reason, but also contrary to law, and to suggest ways in which the law should be strengthened to accord with reason.

Some of the following chapters have previously been published, in whole or in part:

Chapter 1: Some paragraphs from section IV were published in the *Times Literary Supplement* on 12 August 1983.

Chapter 2: Some paragraphs from sections II and III were published in 132 *New Law Journal* 885–7, 903–5 (1982).

Chapter 3: Some paragraphs from section IV were published in 133 *New Law Journal* 451–3 (1983).

Chapter 6: Published in 3 *Oxford Journal of Legal Studies* 1–21 (1983).

Chapter 7: Section II was published in (1982) *Public Law* 42–7.

Chapter 8: Published in (1983) *Public Law* 279–302.

Chapter 9: Published in 4 *Oxford Journal of Legal Studies* 198–234 (1984).

Chapter 10: Section V was published in 10 *New Community* 16–26 (1982).

Chapter 11: Some paragraphs from section VII were published in *The Listener* on 3 December 1981.

I am grateful to the Editors of these journals for their permission to reprint this material.

The Temple,   DAVID PANNICK
London EC4
7 March 1985

CONTENTS

TABLE OF CASES

ABBREVIATIONS

A 2d	Atlantic Reporter (USA).
AC	Law Reports: Appeal Cases (UK).
AIR P & H	All India Reports, Punjab and Haryana.
AIR SC	All India Reports, Supreme Court.
ALJR	Australian Law Journal Reports.
All ER	All England Law Reports.
ALR	Australian Law Reports.
BFOQ	Bona Fide Occupational Qualification.
Cal Rptr	California Reporter.
Ch	Law Reports: Chancery Division (UK).
Ch D	Law Reports: Chancery Division (UK).
CMLR	Common Market Law Reports.
CRE	Commission for Racial Equality.
DLR	Dominion Law Reports (Canada).
D & R	Decisions and Reports (European Commission of Human Rights).
EAT	Employment Appeal Tribunal (UK).
ECJ	European Court of Justice.
ECR	European Court Reports.
EEC	European Economic Community.
EEOC	Equal Employment Opportunity Commission (USA).
EHRR	European Human Rights Reports.
EOC	Equal Opportunities Commission (UK).
F 2d	Federal Reporter (USA).
FEP Cases	Fair Employment Practice Cases (USA).
F Supp	Federal Supplement (USA).
GOQ	Genuine Occupational Qualification.
HC	House of Commons (UK).
HL	House of Lords (UK).
ICJ	International Court of Justice.
ICR	Industrial Cases Reports (UK).
Imm AR	Immigration Appeals (UK).
IR	Irish Reports.
IRLR	Industrial Relations Law Reports (UK).
KB	Law Reports: King's Bench Division (UK).
LR CP	Law Reports: Common Pleas (UK).
LR QB	Law Reports: Queen's Bench (UK).
NE 2d	North Eastern Reporter (USA).

NI	Northern Ireland Reports.
NW 2d	North Western Reporter (USA).
NYS 2d	New York Supplement.
NZLR	New Zealand Law Reports.
OJ	Official Journal of the European Communities (EEC).
OR (2d)	Ontario Reports.
P	Law Reports: Probate, Divorce and Admiralty Division (UK).
P 2d	Pacific Reporter (USA).
QB	Law Reports: Queen's Bench Division (UK).
QBD	Law Reports: Queen's Bench Division (UK).
SALR	South African Law Reports.
SCR	Supreme Court Reports (Canada).
SCR	Supreme Court Reports (India).
S Ct	Supreme Court Reports (USA).
SE 2d	South Eastern Reporter (USA).
Sh Ct	Sheriff Court (Scotland).
SI	Statutory Instrument (UK).
SLT	Scots Law Times.
Sol J	Solicitors' Journal (UK).
SW 2d	South Western Reporter (USA).
TLR	Times Law Reports (UK).
US	United States Reports.
WLR	Weekly Law Reports (UK).
WWR	Western Weekly Reports (Canada).

1

INTRODUCTION

I

BOSWELL reports that in 1778 Dr Johnson had no doubts that equality between the sexes was neither a desirable nor a realizable goal. 'It is plain', said Dr Johnson, that 'one or other must have the superiority. As Shakespeare says, "If two men ride on a horse, one must ride behind".'[1] Of course, Dr Johnson, and others of like views, assumed that it should be the woman who must ride behind. Man, naturally, was more important and valuable than woman. Little had changed in this respect since God told Moses that a man aged 20 to 60 was worth 50 silver shekels but a woman of that age was worth only 30 shekels.[2]

Nearly two hundred years after Dr Johnson's pronouncements, Parliament made it unlawful, in certain contexts and with defined exceptions, to discriminate against an individual on the ground of his or her sex. The Sex Discrimination Act 1975 came into effect, together with the Equal Pay Act 1970, on 29 December 1975. Government spokesmen described it as 'the most comprehensive and far-reaching legislation of its kind in the world'.[3] They asserted that it would remedy a widespread injustice and help to ensure that society efficiently and fairly used its human resources. Opponents of the legislation condemned it as lawmaking by 'dedicated cranks . . . embodying their prejudices' in a statute which was 'silly . . . ridiculous . . . petty and in the end it gets us nowhere'.[4]

This book considers many of the problems posed by our commitment to equal treatment of the sexes. It discusses the nature and the scope of our anti-discrimination law. It analyses the successes and the failures of that law. It proposes improvements to remedy the defects in the substance and the procedure of the law.

[1] Boswell, *Life of Johnson*: 15 Apr. 1778.   [2] Leviticus 27: 1–8.
[3] Lord Harris of Greenwich (Minister of State at the Home Office), 362 HL 96 (1 July 1975; Second Reading). See also Roy Jenkins (Home Secretary), 889 HC 512 (26 Mar. 1975; Second Reading).
[4] Ronald Bell, 889 HC 589–94 (26 Mar. 1975; Second Reading).

It tackles some of the more difficult questions raised by the concept of sex discrimination. What is discrimination? To what extent should we take into account, when considering whether discrimination has occurred, that there are (and presumably always will be) biological differences between men and women? Only women can give birth. Women tend to live longer than men and to be less physically strong than men. What relevance (if any) do these (and similar) facts have to the application of the concept of discrimination, particularly in the contexts of insurance and pensions? Should we take into account (and if so to what extent) cultural and social distinctions between the sexes; what does equal treatment mean in the context of grooming codes at work; how can personal privacy be reconciled with anti-discrimination principles; when is sex a genuine occupational qualification for a job?

Even a cursory consideration of sex discrimination law reveals that the problems it raises (and the answers we reach) are of fundamental importance to the nature of our society. The genesis and the application of sex discrimination law tell the historian, the philosopher, the politician, the social scientist, and the anthropologist much of value about our developing attitudes to equality. Although this book will, I hope, therefore be of interest to the non-lawyer, my main concern is to discuss the legal content of sex discrimination law. But before doing so, I need briefly to explain the background to that law.

II

Blackstone concluded that the legal disabilities to which a woman was subjected by the common law of the eighteenth century 'are for the most part intended for her protection and benefit. So great a favourite is the female sex of the laws of England.'[5] Slowly and reluctantly, women have been admitted to full citizenship with the right to sign contracts and to own property (irrespective of marital status)[6] and with the right to vote.[7] The Sex Disqualification (Removal) Act 1919 provided that a woman should not be

---

[5] William Blackstone, *Commentaries on the Laws of England* (1765), i. 433.

[6] See the Married Women's Property Acts 1870 and 1882.

[7] Universal suffrage was introduced in 1918 for men over the age of 21. Certain women over the age of 30 were also entitled to vote. The voting age for women was reduced to 21 (and other eligibility criteria for men and women were made the same) in 1928: Representation of the People (Equal Franchise) Act 1922.

disqualified by sex or marriage from the exercise of any public function or from holding any civil or judicial office or post or from entering or carrying on any profession or vocation.[8] More recently, legislation has recognized a deserted wife's legal interest in the family home,[9] a wife's right to a share in the matrimonial property on divorce,[10] and a woman's right to choose a domicile (for legal purposes) different from that of her husband.[11] The Domestic Violence and Matrimonial Proceedings Act 1976 has given women greater protection against molestation by their husbands. The Sexual Offences (Amendment) Act 1976 gives greater anonymity to complainants in cases where the defendant is charged with rape and it gives some protection (albeit still inadequate protection) to such complainants from being asked questions concerning their previous sexual experience by way of prurient cross-examination. Working women have been guaranteed a number of rights in connection with maternity, including maternity pay and a right to return to work after confinement.[12] These are significant and welcome advances in the status of women. Medical advances, and the provisions of the Abortion Act 1967, have resulted in greater control over fertility. All these legal and social developments have helped to ensure that, in many respects, women enjoy equality with men.

However, some overt sex discrimination remains in public law. Social security and tax law often treat the married woman as an

[8] In *Hugh-Jones* v. *St John's College, Cambridge* [1979] ICR 848, 855–7, the Employment Appeal Tribunal (EAT) held that the exclusion of women from membership of the college under the college statutes was not inconsistent with the 1919 Act: a research Fellowship was not a civil post; nor did exclusion from a particular college amount to discrimination in entering a civil profession or vocation; in any event, the 1919 Act applied only to remove a disqualification in the case of an existing right and here there was no such right. See also *Viscountess Rhondda's Claim* [1922] 2 AC 339 where the House of Lords Committee for Privileges held, by a majority of 22–4, that a peeress of the United Kingdom in her own right was not entitled by virtue of the 1919 Act to receive a writ of summons to Parliament. The Lord Chancellor, Viscount Birkenhead, said, at 375, that the legislature 'cannot be taken to have departed from the usage of centuries or to have employed such loose and ambiguous words to carry out so momentous a revolution in the constitution of this House'. Viscount Cave, at 389, said that the 1919 Act, 'while it removed all disqualifications, did not purport to confer any right'. Similarly Lord Dunedin at 390. The argument is far from compelling: but for her sex, the Viscountess would have received the writ of summons relevant to holding a public function or civil office.

[9] Matrimonial Homes Act 1967.   [10] Matrimonial Causes Act 1973.
[11] Domicile and Matrimonial Proceedings Act 1973.   [12] See ch. 6 n. 1.

appendage of her husband.[13] The immigration rules contain a number of provisions which discriminate on grounds of sex. For example, they less favourably treat a man seeking to enter the United Kingdom or to remain here for the purposes of marriage with a woman who is settled here compared with the treatment of a woman who seeks to enter the United Kingdom or to remain here for the purposes of marriage with a man settled here. The woman is entitled to enter or remain here if her husband or fiancé is settled here. A man is entitled to enter or remain here only if his wife or fiancée is settled here and is a British citizen. This is irrespective of whether the husband or the wife is the family breadwinner.[14] A woman is entitled to receive a State pension at the age of 60. A man must wait until he is 65. Legislation governing health and safety at work still acts on the stereotyped assumption that women are less capable than men of working long hours, or performing certain job duties, irrespective of the ability of any individual woman to carry out the relevant task.[15] The first in line to succeed to the throne is the eldest son of the monarch, not the eldest child.[16]

The White Paper, *Equality for Women*, which preceded the Sex Discrimination Act 1975, recognized the existence of pockets of such sex discrimination for which the State was responsible. It stated that '[t]he status of women in relation to social security, taxation, nationality and matrimonial and family law is governed by separate legislation and will be so dealt with in the future.'[17]

---

[13] See Susan Atkins and Brenda Hoggett, *Women and the Law* (1984), ch. 9; and see Isobel M. Brougham, 'What Women Need from the Next Budget' (1983) *Law Society's Gazette* 2342.

[14] HC 169, paras. 41, 44, 48, 54, 124, 126. In May 1983, the European Commission of Human Rights unanimously held that similar sex discrimination under the previous immigration rules, HC 394, was contrary to the European Convention on Human Rights because it breached the right to respect for family life without sex discrimination: *Abdulaziz* v. *United Kingdom* 6 EHRR 28 (1983). The European Court of Human Rights heard argument on the case in Sept. 1984, and upheld the Commission's decision on 28th May 1985.

[15] See, for example, the Hours of Employment (Conventions) Act 1936, the Mines and Quarries Act 1954, and the Factories Act 1961 restricting aspects of the employment of women. Such restrictions are summarized in the report of the Equal Opportunities Commission, *Health and Safety Legislation: Should We Distinguish Between Men and Women?* (1979).

[16] See Bel Mooney, 'Nothing Succeeds Like Succession' *The Times* 30 Nov. 1981 commenting on an unsuccessful Private Member's Bill to change the law.

[17] Cmnd. 5724 (1974), para. 77.

Separate legislation to remove sex discrimination is still awaited in the fields mentioned above.

The removal of most arbitrary, State-imposed barriers to women and men carrying out their plans irrespective of their sex was one of the arguments used by those who opposed the 1975 Act. 'There are no legal impediments to women doing what they want or becoming what they wish.'[18] However, the gradual erosion of obstacles to the progress of women for which the State was responsible did not, and could not, ensure equality of treatment for the sexes in the distribution of society's valuable resources. No legislation required non-discrimination by employers or educational institutions or those who provided the public with goods, services, facilities, or premises. The common law had given very few indications that it could be of use to assist women who were denied benefits, or who suffered detriments, in these contexts on the ground of their sex.

At common law, an employer was entitled to refuse to employ a worker 'from the most mistaken, capricious, malicious, or morally reprehensible motives that can be conceived, but the workman has no right of action against him'.[19] Prior to the enactment of the first Race Relations Act in 1965, the common law 'was that people could discriminate against others on the ground of colour etc. to their hearts' content'.[20] The judiciary was, to say the least, not in the forefront of those concerned to secure equal treatment of the sexes. Indeed, '[f]or those accustomed to revere the common law as a bulwark of individual freedom and fundamental right, it must come as somewhat of a shock to discover that it was in fact the common law which was used to effect the judicial exclusion of women from public life.'[21]

The record of the judiciary on issues concerning sex discrimination prior to 1975 is not distinguished. In 1868, the Court of Common Pleas held that women were not entitled to vote at the

---

[18] Ronald Bell, above, n. 4 at col. 588.

[19] *Allen* v. *Flood* [1898] AC 1. 172 per Lord Davey.

[20] *Applin* v. *Race Relations Board* [1975] AC 259, 286 per Lord Simon. See similarly *Dockers' Labour Club and Institute Ltd* v. *Race Relations Board* [1976] AC 285, 296 per Lord Diplock.

[21] Rose Pearson and Albie Sachs, 'Barristers and Gentlemen: A Critical Look at Sexism in the Legal Profession' 43 *Modern Law Review* 400, 402–3 (1980). See also Albie Sachs and Joan Hoff Wilson, *Sexism and the Law: A Study of Male Beliefs and Judicial Bias* (1978), esp. ch. 1.

election of a Member of Parliament, despite the fact that the Representation of the People Act stated that every 'man' (excluding those who were 'subject to legal incapacity') was so entitled and despite the fact that an earlier statute provided that in all legislation words importing the masculine gender should be deemed and taken to include females unless the contrary was expressly provided. Willes J. explained that the denial to women of a right to vote 'is referable to the fact that in this country, in modern times, chiefly out of respect to women, and a sense of decorum, and not from their want of intellect, or their being for any other such reason unfit to take part in the government of the country, they have been excused from taking any share in this department of public affairs'.[22]

Similarly in 1889, in *Beresford-Hope* v. *Lady Sandhurst*, the Court of Appeal held that women were incapacitated from being elected members of a County Council. The male complainant had received less votes than Lady Sandhurst, who had been elected. The court agreed with the disappointed male candidate that, although women were eligible to vote, they were not entitled to stand for office. The votes cast for Lady Sandhurst were held to be votes 'thrown away' and so the male complainant was declared to be duly elected.[23]

In 1872, in *The Queen* v. *Harrald*, the court considered a statute which entitled women to vote at the election of local councillors, auditors, and assessors. It held that despite this provision, despite the absence of any provision in the legislation excluding the rights of married women, and despite the passing of the Married Women's Property Act (entitling such women to own property), the statute was not intended 'by a side wind' to alter the status of married women who had hitherto been unable to exercise public

---

[22] *Chorlton* v. *Lings* LR 4 CP 374, 392 (1868). He added, at 388, that he 'must protest against [the exclusion of women from voting] being supposed to arise in this country from any underrating of the sex either in point of intellect or worth. That would be quite inconsistent with one of the glories of our civilization—the respect and honour in which women are held.'

[23] 23 QBD 79 (1889). Lord Coleridge CJ, who had unsuccessfully argued *Chorlton* v. *Lings* ibid. as counsel for the women, noted at 91–2 that 'in the twenty years which have run since 1869, the questions of the rights and privileges of women have not been, as in former times they were, asleep. On the contrary, we know as a matter of fact that the rights of women, and the privileges of women, have been much discussed, and able and acute minds have been much exercised as to what privileges ought to be conceded to women.'

functions. Mellor J. explained that the statute entitling women to vote 'only removes the disqualification by reason of sex, and leaves untouched the disqualification by reason of [marital] status'. He did not seem to appreciate that, by comparison with a married man, a married woman was disqualified from voting by reason of her sex.[24] Again in 1909, in *Nairn* v. *University of St Andrews*,[25] the House of Lords held that five women graduates were not entitled to vote at the election of a Member of Parliament for the university. A woman was not, said the House of Lords, a 'person . . . of full age and not subject to any legal incapacity'.

If one moves out of the field of election law to consider the treatment of women in professions, the picture is a similar one of judicial intolerance to equal opportunity and judicial eagerness to adopt narrow and artificial constructions of legislation in order to defeat the reasonable claims of female litigants. The Solicitors Act 1843 provided that any 'person' who complied with certain conditions was entitled to be admitted to the profession. The Act specifically provided that words importing the masculine gender were to apply to a female. Nevertheless in 1913 the Court of Appeal held that the Law Society were entitled to refuse to admit a woman to their preliminary examination on the ground of her sex.[26] The reasoning of the court was that prior to 1843 women had no right to become solicitors and there was nothing in the 1843 Act

---

[24] LR 7 QB 361 (1872). A more liberal approach was adopted by the Judicial Committee of the Privy Council in *Edwards* v. *A.-G. for Canada* 46 TLR 4 (1929): women may be 'qualified persons' eligible for membership of the Senate of Canada.

[25] [1909] AC 147.

[26] *Bebb* v. *Law Society* [1914] 1 Ch. 286. See similarly *Bradwell* v. *Illinois* 83 US 130, 141–2 (1872) where Mr Justice Bradley, in an opinion joined by two other Justices, concurred in the decision of the US Supreme Court that a woman had no constitutional right to practise law without being rejected on the ground of her sex: '. . . the civil law, as well as nature herself, has always recognised a wide difference in the respective spheres and destinies of man and woman. Man is, or should be, woman's protector and defender. The natural and proper timidity and delicacy which belongs to the female sex evidently unfits it for many of the occupations of civil life. The constitution of the family organisation, which is founded in the divine ordinance, as well as in the nature of things, indicates the domestic sphere as that which properly belongs to the domain and functions of womanhood. The harmony, not to say identity, of interests and views which belong, or should belong, to the family institution is repugnant to the idea of a woman adopting a distinct and independent career from that of her husband . . . It is true that many women are unmarried and not affected by any of the duties, complications and incapacities arising out of the married state, but these are exceptions to the general rule. The paramount destiny and mission of woman are to fulfil the noble and benign offices

to suggest that Parliament had intended to remove such a disability.[27]

The courts also had no difficulty in finding that discrimination against married women, compared with married men, in the field of employment was consistent with public policy. In 1925 in *Short* v. *Poole Corporation*, a local authority had decided that the retention of married women teachers in public elementary schools was inadvisable. It therefore gave the plaintiff, a married woman teacher, notice to terminate her contract after satisfying itself that her husband was able to maintain her. The Education Committee stated its reasons for adopting such a policy. First, it believed that 'the duty of the married woman is primarily to look after her domestic concerns' and they regarded it as 'impossible for her to do so and to effectively and satisfactorily act as a teacher at the same time'. Secondly, they were of the view that 'it is unfair to the large number of young unmarried teachers who are at present seeking situations that the positions should be occupied by married women, who presumably have husbands capable of maintaining them.'[28] In the Court of Appeal, Pollock MR held that 'there is no proof that the Council have taken into account matters other than those which belong to their educational sphere . . . [T]he Council dealt with the matter from an educational standpoint.'[29] The court was, therefore, unconvinced by the complainant's argument that she employed someone to attend to her domestic affairs, she had no children, that her mother lived with her and supervised the house in her absence at work, and the council had not considered her fitness to be a teacher on her individual merits. In 1923, in *Price* v. *Rhondda Urban District Council*, Eve J. held that it was

of wife and mother. This is the law of the Creator. And the rules of civil society must be adapted to the general constitution of things, and cannot be based upon exceptional cases.'

[27] Lord Robert Cecil KC, counsel for the woman complainant, pointed out, at 287, that '[w]omen have filled many public offices; for instance, there have been Queens of England, and women have been regents; Queen Eleanor acted as Keeper of the Great Seal . . .'. Cozens-Hardy MR said, at 294: 'We have been asked to hold, what I for one quite assent to, that, in point of intelligence and education and competency women—and in particular the applicant here, who is a distinguished Oxford student—are at least equal to a great many, and, probably, far better than many, of the candidates who will come up for examination, but that is really not for us to consider.'

[28] [1926] 1 Ch 66, 84.

[29] Ibid. at 86.

not contrary to public policy for the Education Committee of the council to terminate the contracts of married women teachers.

It would [he concluded] be pressing public policy to intolerable lengths to hold that it was outraged by this Authority expressing a preference for unmarried women over married women as teachers, in view of the fact that the services of the latter are frequently not continuous but are liable to be interrupted by absences extending over several months.[30]

He did not seem to understand that the discrimination was against married women as compared with married men and that while it may be permissible to exclude those who were not able to guarantee continuous service, one should not assume that this applied to all married women and only to married women.

These cases show, quite conclusively, that sexual equality in employment and other fields was not going to be achieved through the common law. Indeed, in 1925 Lord Atkinson concluded that it was unlawful for a local council to provide equal pay for men and women doing like work. He asserted that the council had 'become such ardent feminists as to bring about, at the expense of the ratepayers whose money they administered, sex equality in the labour market'.[31] He believed that the

council would . . . fail in their duty if, in administering funds which did not belong to their members alone, they put aside all [usual] aids to the ascertainment of what was just and reasonable remuneration to give for the services rendered to them, and allowed themselves to be guided in preference by some eccentric principles of socialist philanthropy, or by a feminist ambition to secure the equality of the sexes in the matter of wages in the world of labour.[32]

As late as November 1975, on the eve of the coming into force of sex discrimination legislation, Mr Justice Caulfield indicated that sex equality would not be furthered by the common law in the context of the provision of goods, services, facilities, and premises to the public. A firm of solicitors were held to have acted in a negligent manner in proceeding with the sale of a flat owned by a husband and wife without first obtaining the usual 10 per cent deposit from the purchasers. Caulfield J. disbelieved the contention of the solicitors that the wife had given instructions to proceed

---

[30] [1923] 2 Ch 372, 391.
[31] *Roberts* v. *Hopwood* [1925] AC 578, 591–2.   [32] Ibid. at 594.

without the deposit (a contention which the wife disputed). But, said the judge, 'even if she had given instructions to proceed, the solicitors should not have taken instructions from her when the husband was available, for a sensible wife did not generally make major decisions.'[33]

By 1966 the common law had sufficiently developed for the Court of Appeal to hold that it was arguable that the Jockey Club acted in an unlawfully arbitrary and capricious manner in breach of public policy by refusing to grant women licences to train racehorses. The Court said that the Jockey Club rule was arbitrary and capricious. Lord Denning said that there seemed no reason to exclude women.[34] Danckwerts LJ described the attitude of the Jockey Club as 'arbitrary and entirely out of touch with the present state of society in Great Britain . . . The practice of the stewards is out of date and no longer justified by present conditions.'[35] Lord Justice Salmon said that to refuse a licence to a woman solely on the ground of her sex 'would be as capricious . . . as to refuse a man a licence solely because of the colour of his hair'.[36] However, the Court of Appeal was unsure whether monopolistic associations (which control a trade or sphere of human activity in which no man or woman can earn a living unless admitted to membership) owe a duty not to act arbitrarily or capriciously. Because the case came before the court only on a motion to strike out the claim as disclosing no cause of action, and because the claim did disclose such an arguable cause of action, it was not necessary for the court to decide whether the complainant did have a legal right to be considered for a licence irrespective of her sex.

Despite the hope of progress in judicial attitudes indicated by the Jockey Club case, the common law was, by 1975, a long way

---

[33] *Morris* v. *Duke-Cohan & Co.* 119 *Sol J* 826 (1975) cited in Michael Beloff *Sex Discrimination—The New Law* (1976), 50. See similarly In *Re Agar-Ellis* 10 Ch D 49, 55 (1878) (Malins V.-C., deciding a family dispute between the mother and the father concerning the religious education of the children): '. . . by the laws of England, by the laws of Christianity and by the constitution of society, when there is a difference of opinion between husband and wife, it is the duty of the wife to submit to the husband.' (The decision was upheld by the Court of Appeal at 69.) Cf. the advice of St Paul in Ephesians 5: 'Wives, be subject to your husbands, as to the Lord; for the man is the head of the woman, just as Christ also is the head of the Church . . . just as the Church is subject to Christ, so must women be to their husbands in everything.'

[34] *Nagle* v. *Feilden* [1966] 2 QB 633, 647.
[35] Ibid. at 651.   [36] Ibid. at 655.

from guaranteeing women the right to equal treatment irrespective of their sex in the distribution of the major resources of society.[37] Nor could one have predicted that English courts would have held that a Minister or a statutory authority exercised powers arbitrarily, and therefore unlawfully, by discriminating on grounds of sex where the empowering statute did not expressly validate such discrimination. By contrast, in *Van Gorkom* v. *Attorney-General* Cooke J. in the Supreme Court of New Zealand held that a Minister did not lawfully exercise his power to lay down conditions governing the payment of removal expenses to teachers when the conditions applied by him treated married female teachers less

[37] See also *R* v. *Surrey Coroner ex parte Campbell* [1982] 2 WLR 626 where the Divisional Court considered a coroner's practice of selecting only men for his jury. A woman specifically requested that she be allowed to serve, to which request the coroner acceded. She was the only woman on a ~~jury~~ of ten people. The court held that 'the practice of excluding, by prior decision or custom, women from a coroner's jury is nowadays wrong . . . misguided and incorrect in law . . .'. However, the court said that the practice did not invalidate the decision of the jury since 'there is nothing to suggest that this particular jury was otherwise not composed of a random selection of local people'. The court did not explain how coroners are to be encouraged to change such unlawful selection procedures unless the decisions of an improperly constituted jury are to be held to be null and void. On jury service, see also *de Burca* v. *A.-G.* [1976] IR 38, where the Irish Supreme Court held unconstitutional the provision of the Juries Act 1927 which exempted all women from jury service whilst entitling any woman, on her own special application, to serve if she wished. In *Jaulim* v. *DPP and A.-G. of Mauritius* 1976 Mauritius Reports 96, the Supreme Court of Mauritius rejected the argument of a defendant charged with murder that the exclusion of women from the jury was a violation of the fundamental freedoms guaranteed by the Constitution. The Court decided that the sex discrimination was lawful and added that, in any event, there was no disability imposed on women by their exclusion. The Court said, at 101–2: 'The framers of those laws may have thought and may still think that the Mauritian woman's status, her place and role in the home and family, and social conditions prevailing in this country are incompatible with a service which, as our law has stood and still stands, may require that they be kept away from home for sometimes long periods, sleeping in hotels, and unable to move about except under the vigilant eyes of court ushers. It seems unquestionable to us that such an obligation would cause much distress to many Mauritian women, and arouse a deep resentment among many of their male relatives. Those circumstances would provide, in our judgment, an objective and reasonable justification, if any was needed, for the distinction made by the impugned legislation.' There are similarities between this decision and that of the US Supreme Court in *Hoyt* v. *Florida* 368 US 57, 61–2 (1961) validating a State law which included men on a jury list unless they asked to be exempted, but excluded women unless they asked to be included. The Court reasoned that, notwithstanding the 'enlightened emancipation of women from the restrictions and protections of bygone years' the State had made a reasonable classification given the fact that 'woman is still regarded as the centre of home and family life'. See now, for a non-stereotyped view of women and jury service, *Taylor* v. *Louisiana* 419 US 522 (1975).

favourably than married male teachers. The judge said that the wording of the statutory power gave no hint that it authorized 'discrimination on the ground of sex alone . . . In modern times discrimination on the ground of sex alone is so controversial, and so widely regarded as wrong, that I would not be prepared to infer authority to introduce it from' the general language giving the Minister power to state general conditions.[38]

Cooke J. gave as one reason for his decision that the statutory power 'should not without compelling reason be taken to allow the introduction of a policy conflicting with the spirit of international standards proclaimed by the United Nations documents'.[39] The commitment of the United Kingdom to equality for men and women is clearly stated in a number of international charters of human rights to which we are signatories. Sex discrimination is prohibited by the United Nations Charter, by the Universal Declaration of Human Rights adopted by the UN General Assembly in 1948, by the UNESCO Convention Against Discrimination in Education 1960, by the International Covenant on Economic, Social and Cultural Rights 1966, and by the International Covenant on Civil and Political Rights 1966. The United Kingdom is also party to the European Convention on Human Rights, the International Labour Organisation Convention on Equal Remuneration for Men and Women Workers for Work of Equal Value 1951, and Article 119 of the EEC Treaty on equal pay for equal work without sex discrimination. Since 1975 the United Kingdom has acquired further international obligations to secure equal treatment of men and women. The EEC Equal Pay Directive,[40] which came into force in February 1976, provides that the principle of equal pay in Article 119 of the EEC Treaty requires equal pay for work of equal value without sex discrimination. The EEC Equal Treatment Directive came into force in August 1978.[41] It requires equal treatment for men and women as regards access to employment, promotion, vocational training,

---

[38] [1977] 1 NZLR 535, 541.

[39] Ibid. at 542–3. On the content of the relevant international standards see Jack Greenberg, 'Race, Sex, and Religious Discrimination in International Law' in *Human Rights in International Law: Legal and Policy Issues* (ed. Theodor Meron, 1984), ii. 307–43.

[40] Council Directive 75/117/EEC of 10 Feb. 1975.

[41] Council Directive 76/207/EEC of 9 Feb. 1976. The scope and effect of EEC law on sex discrimination in the United Kingdom is considered in ch. 5.

and working conditions (including the conditions governing dismissal). In *Defrenne* v. *Sabena (no. 3)* the European Court of Justice said that 'respect for fundamental personal human rights is one of the general principles of Community law' and that '[t]here can be no doubt that the elimination of discrimination based on sex forms part of those fundamental rights'.[42] In 1979 a United Nations Convention on the Elimination of all Forms of Discrimination Against Women was adopted. However, it has not yet been ratified by the United Kingdom.

On 29 December 1975, the Equal Pay Act 1970 and the Sex Discrimination Act 1975 came into effect. 1975 was International Women's Year. There is no doubt that, by reason of its international obligations and agreements, the UK Government was obliged to take action to prohibit sex discrimination in employment, education, and the provision of goods to the public.

III

When Title VII of the US Civil Rights Act was passed in 1964, prohibiting discrimination in employment on racial and other invidious grounds, 'sex' was added to the Bill as one such ground at the eleventh hour. Representative Howard Smith, the principal opponent of the Bill, successfully proposed an amendment to include 'sex' as a prohibited ground of action. He did so on the floor of the House of Representatives on the day before the passage of the Act. He claimed to be serious about the issue, but his argument that '[t]his Bill is so imperfect, what harm will this little amendment do?', lends support to the theory that the ban on sex discrimination in employment in the USA is the fortuitous consequence of a wrecking amendment which was passed but which failed to achieve its purpose of destroying the legislation. Some supporters of the Bill voted for Representative Smith's amendment because of fears that in its absence black women would be given an advantage over white women.[43]

By contrast, the Sex Discrimination Act 1975 was a deliberate,

---

[42] [1978] ECR 1365, 1378 (Judgment at paras. 26–7).

[43] On the origins of the US Civil Rights Act see Robert Stevens Miller Jr. 'Sex Discrimination and Title VII of the Civil Rights Act of 1964', 51 *Minnesota Law Review* 877, 880–2 (1967); Note 'Developments in the Law—Employment Discrimination and Title VII of the Civil Rights Act of 1964' 84 *Harvard Law Review* 1109, 1167 (1971).

considered social reform. Prior to 1975 women suffered from an undeniable pattern and practice of sex discrimination in areas of crucial importance to their welfare.

The White Paper of 1974 correctly stated[44] that those women in work tended to do low-grade jobs in a narrow range of industries for lower rates of pay than comparable men. Women tended to be segregated into 'women's work'. They were denied training for and promotion to jobs of a higher status carrying more pay. A higher proportion of boys than of girls took up apprenticeships. Most of the girls who did take up apprenticeships were in cosmetic services, such as hairdressing. Women had traditionally been excluded from certain trades, businesses, and occupations. Few women reached the top levels of the professions. In education, the curriculum tended to differ for boys and girls. This fostered expectations of different occupational roles for the sexes. Fewer girls than boys obtained scientific qualifications. Fewer girls went to university. Women tended to be denied goods, facilities, and services—for example in banking, insurance, mortgages, and loans—on equal terms with men. In general, then, the opportunities of the female half of the population were fettered by the reluctance, and often the refusal, of the male half to allow them to enter what was still very much a 'man's world'. Women were not treated on their individual merits, irrespective of their sex. They had no legal remedy against what Simone de Beauvoir described as man's definition of woman 'not in herself but as relative to him; she is not regarded as an autonomous being . . . She is defined and differentiated with reference to man and not he with reference to her; she is the incidental, the inessential as opposed to the essential. He is the Subject, he is the Absolute—she is the Other.'[45]

Discrimination against women had long been defended as the inevitable consequence of biological distinctions between the sexes. After all, men are stronger, taller, fitter than women; it is women who bear and rear children and who therefore should stay at home while men go to work. However, by 1975, such arguments had long been revealed as unconvincing rationalizations for discriminatory practices.

[44] Above, n. 17 at paras. 8–15.
[45] Simone de Beauvoir, *The Second Sex* (trans. and ed. by H. M. Parshley, 1972), intro.

Although males are, on average, heavier and taller than females at birth, and thereafter, sex is no more accurate an indicator of physical attributes than social factors, such as class and occupation.[46] Many women possess greater physical strength than many men. The White Paper, *Equality for Women*, explained that there was 'insufficient recognition that the variations of character and ability within each sex are greater and more significant than the differences between the sexes'.[47] Medical developments in contraception and in the artificial feeding of babies freed women who wished to work from the constraints of motherhood. Even if most women are unable to perform jobs requiring certain physical attributes, it is, as John Stuart Mill carefully explained in 1869, wrong to apply a general presumption of inferiority or incompetence that excludes consideration of the skills which the individual woman may possess. To deny women the chance to be considered on their individual merits for the relevant opportunity 'is both an injustice to the individuals and a detriment to society' since it places artificial 'barriers in the way of their using their faculties for their own benefit and for that of others'. When women are unable to perform the relevant task, they will be denied the chance to do so by the application of the ordinary criteria for the job. Sex discrimination, therefore, is neither necessary nor justifiable. 'What women by nature cannot do, it is quite superfluous to forbid them from doing. What they can do, but not so well as the men who are their competitors, competition suffices to exclude them from . . .'[48]

Biological differences between the sexes play a less important part in the development of social roles than the differences of gender.[49] Each society attributes to the two sexes distinct roles which are expected of men and women. That these roles are primarily the consequence of social or cultural, and not biological, characteristics is demonstrated by the fact that each society attributes different characteristics to men and women. Margaret Mead, the anthropologist, described this phenomenon:

Some peoples think of women as too weak to work out of doors, others

---

[46] See *Sex Differences in Britain* (ed. Ivan Reid and Eileen Wormald, 1982) for the facts as to what the differences between men and women are.

[47] Above, n. 17 at para. 16.

[48] John Stuart Mill, *The Subjection of Women* (1869), i.

[49] See Ann Oakley, *Sex, Gender and Society* (1972).

regard women as the appropriate bearers of heavy burdens, 'because their heads are stronger than men's' . . . In some cultures women are regarded as sieves through whom the best-guarded secrets will sift; in others it is the men who are the gossips. Whether we deal with small matters or with large, with the frivolities of ornament and cosmetics or the sanctities of man's place in the universe, we find this great variety of ways, often flatly contradictory one to the other, in which the roles of the two sexes have been patterned . . .

Nevertheless, it remains the case that '[h]owever differently the traits have been assigned, some to one sex, some to the other, and some to both, however arbitrary the assignment must be seen to be . . . it has always been there in every society of which we have any knowledge.'[50]

For these reasons, we cannot, as was once thought, assert that the differences in treatment of men and women customary in our society are the natural and inevitable consequence of physical distinctions. If anyone were in any doubt as to the ability of women to perform work traditionally associated with men, the Second World War demonstrated the capacity of women. While men were fighting the war, women took over the industrial and other work hitherto performed by men. In the USA, as in the United Kingdom,

women manoeuvred giant overhead travelling cranes and cleaned out blast furnaces . . . women ran lathes, cut dies, read blueprints, and serviced airplanes. They maintained roadbeds, greased locomotives, and took the place of lumberjacks in toppling giant redwoods. As stevedores, blacksmiths, foundry helpers, and drill-press operators, they demonstrated that they could fill almost any job, no matter how difficult or arduous.[51]

Women's wartime experience gave them a new self-confidence and assertiveness.

The case for unequal opportunity for the sexes was never intellectually or morally or practically strong. It 'could be defended only by resort to dark biblical rumblings and invocations of the order of nature, or by examples and theories that were in continuous process of being disproved.'[52] As theories of female incapacity were disproved by medical developments, by wartime

[50] Margaret Mead, *Male and Female* (1949), i.

[51] William H. Chafe, *The American Woman: Her Changing Social, Economic and Political Roles 1920–70* (1972), 137–8.

[52] J. R. Pole, *The Pursuit of Equality in American History* (1979), 320.

experience, and by individual women showing that their female sex was not incompatible with political, sporting, intellectual, or other achievement, so it became clear that the 'inferiority' of women had no more than a customary status. John Stuart Mill explained that '[t]he subjection of women to men being a universal custom, any departure from it quite naturally appears unnatural.'[53] He pointed to the absurdity of the English refusing to allow women to work in certain jobs, to obtain an education in certain universities or to vote, yet being quite prepared to live under a female monarch.

Why then did sex discrimination continue to exist, and why did it take until 1975 for the denial of equal opportunities for the sexes in the distribution of the major resources of society to be made unlawful? John Stuart Mill was well aware of the problem: 'So long as an opinion is strongly rooted in the feelings, it gains rather than loses in stability by having a preponderating weight of argument against it . . . [T]he worse it fares in argumentative contest, the more persuaded its adherents are that their feeling must have some deeper ground, which the arguments do not reach . . .'[54] Lord Monson opposed the Sex Discrimination Bill in 1975 on the ground that 'there is no logical reason why women should not dig ditches or mend roads . . . but in this country we feel that it just is not right . . . [F]or a man to be unemployed is a threat to his masculinity, but for a woman to be unemployed is not a threat to her femininity. It will hit her purse but not her sex life.'[55] This instinctive feeling that, in some indefinable, intangible way, women are different from men in relevant respects and that it is therefore justifiable to deny them opportunities on the ground of their sex, was undeniably furthered by the peculiar status of women as an oppressed group.

Women form a majority, not a minority, in society. They live in intimacy with their oppressors, often in units of one male and one female plus children. Indeed, prior to the industrial revolution this unit was economic as well as social: 'among artisans, shopkeepers, smallholders and unskilled labourers . . . husband, wife and children tended to form a single economic unit, like the crew of a

---

[53] John Stuart Mill, above, n. 48.
[54] Ibid.
[55] 362 HL 141–2 (1 July 1975: Second Reading).

ship, in which the role of the wife was critical'.[56] Furthermore, '[i]t would be difficult to find another group whose history reveals such a pattern of discriminatory treatment, but whose members divide so vehemently over the quest for equality.'[57] This is partly because so many women live in intimate contact with men, who inevitably influence their perception of sexual equality. But it is also because there are undeniable benefits to those women from a social structure that so differentiates between men and women. Men pay for their different social role in the greater incidence of heart-disease, ulcers, and other stress illnesses. A large number of women share (albeit unequally) in the superior social status of men by reason of the enhanced standard of living those men bring to their families compared to the standard they could hope to achieve if the men had to compete for their jobs on equal terms with women. Religious suggestions of female subservience have further contributed to women's preparedness to tolerate social inequality.[58] Women who fought to achieve social equality for the sexes could not even be confident of the support of those liberals and socialists (with notable exceptions, such as Mill) whose values were egalitarian in other respects.[59]

IV

Equality is the goal of socialists. It is a topic of debate among liberals. Too often it is a matter of ridicule for conservatives. The denial of equal rights has, according to Tom Paine, 'been the cause of all the disturbances, insurrections and civil wars that ever happened'.[60] What, then, does this provocative concept of equality mean?

[56] Lawrence Stone, *The Family, Sex and Marriage in England 1500–1800* (1977), 199.

[57] William H. Chafe, *Women and Equality* (1977), 173.

[58] For example, Paul teaches that 'man is the image of God and the mirror of his glory, whereas woman reflects the glory of man. For man did not originally spring from woman, but woman was made out of man; and man was not created for woman's sake, but woman for the sake of man': 1 Corinthians 11. See also above, n. 33.

[59] Socialist feminists 'knew they would have a job on their hands to make male socialists recognize the importance of feminism . . .': Anna Coote and Beatrix Campbell, *Sweet Freedom: The Struggle for Women's Liberation* (1982), 31. See also the views of Proudhon ch. 7 n. 41. On women and trade unions see Elizabeth M. Meehan, *Women's Rights at Work* (1985), 22–4.

[60] *Works* (1878, ed. J. P. Mendun), i. 454–5, cited in Warwick McKean *Equality and Discrimination under International Law* (1983), 2.

The proclamation in the American Declaration of Independence that it is a self-evident truth that 'all men are created equal' cannot mean that we all have equal intelligence, strength, or moral character. Such a proposition is untenable. What we do have is an equal right to respect as human beings in the distribution of benefits and detriments, a right to be treated like others to the extent that we share their characteristics. Equality requires that different treatment should not be accorded unless there are valid and relevant reasons for distinguishing between persons. Like is to be treated with like; unlikes should not be treated in the same way.[61] Such a principle is fundamental to rationality as well as to equality. But it begs the question of what constitute valid and relevant reasons for particular purposes so as to justify disparate treatment. That question can only be answered by reference to our conceptions of justice and fairness.[62]

If equality is the treating of like with like, discrimination is the failure to accord such equal treatment to people. In ordinary usage, 'to discriminate' may mean simply to differentiate. But in legal contexts, it is a pejorative term, meaning to distinguish on unfair or unreasonable grounds, to fail to treat like with like. We have in civilized societies come to recognize that certain grounds of different treatment, for example race and sex, are usually not relevant to the distribution of benefits. Unequal treatment on these grounds has, therefore, been prohibited in defined contexts. Our concept of equality has developed in these respects. In 1896, the US Supreme Court held that a State law prohibiting blacks and whites from sitting together in public transport did not breach the constitutional guarantee of equal protection of the laws.[63] Half a century later, in *Brown* v. *Board of Education*, the Supreme Court held that separate educational facilities for different races are inherently unequal and unlawful.[64] Such developments in society's understanding of equality are inevitably influenced by the character and the personality of those who sit in judgment. Prior to the final hearings in *Brown*, the conservative Chief Justice Vinson died of a heart attack at the age of 63 and was replaced by the liberal Chief

---

[61] See the dissenting opinion of Judge Tanaka in the *South West Africa Cases (Second Phase)* [1966] ICJ Reports 4, 305.

[62] See Isaiah Berlin, 'Equality' in *Concepts and Categories: Philosophical Essays* (1978), 81–102.

[63] *Plessy* v. *Ferguson* 163 US 537 (1896).   [64] 347 US 483 (1954).

Justice Warren. Mr Justice Frankfurter, who abhorred race discrimination and was determined to see it declared unlawful, said that this change of personnel on the court was 'the first indication I have ever had that there is a God'.[65]

The ambiguities in the concept of equality are the subject of contention between rival schools of philosophers and opposing political parties. In those legal systems which guarantee equality, either as a constitutional right or in defined statutory contexts, judges have the duty to decide what equal treatment connotes in concrete cases. In those legal systems, the courts have the duty to protect the essence of equality as identified by Bernard Williams: for any difference in treatment, a sufficient reason must be given.[66] All laws differentiate between persons. They classify and generalize by rules, subjecting defined classes to specific treatment. That is the merit of law compared with unfettered discretion. The importance of the principle of equality is that it ensures that the distinctions inherent in law are not drawn in an arbitrary manner. Because the anti-discrimination principle derives from central moral values widely shared in our society,[67] the principle of equality before the law 'has been recognized as one of the fundamental principles of modern democracy and government based on the rule of law'.[68] The principle of non-discrimination connotes a commitment to judging people on their merits, rather than by reference to irrelevant characteristics over which they have no control. It suggests that people will be assessed according to open criteria which offer them a chance for self-improvement.[69]

What then are relevant and valid differences between individuals which justify disparate treatment? Men with blue eyes are unlike men with brown eyes in one respect. Yet it would undoubtedly be a denial of equality to make entitlement to a State pension dependent on that distinction. Similarly, men differ from women in obvious physical respects, but those differences are not

[65] Richard Kluger, *Simple Justice* (1977), 656.

[66] Bernard Williams, 'The Idea of Equality' in *Philosophy, Politics and Society—Second Series* (ed. Laslett and Runciman, 1962), 110–31.

[67] See Paul Brest, 'In Defence of the Anti-Discrimination Principle' 90 *Harvard Law Review* 1, 5 (1976).

[68] Judge Tanaka, above, n. 61 at 304. For a discussion of the concept of equality in constitutional law see Polyvios G. Polyviou, *The Equal Protection of the Laws* (1980).

[69] See Owen M. Fiss, 'A Theory of Fair Employment Laws' 38 University of Chicago Law Review 235, 241–2 (1971).

necessarily relevant to the distribution of benefits and burdens. Principles of equality are not automatically violated where different treatment is based on the physical differences between men and women. Men do not necessarily have a valid complaint of inequality where women are given specially beneficial treatment by reason of pregnancy or pre-menstrual tension.[70] What the principles of equality reject is the idea that these physical differences are automatically relevant in all circumstances to justify the different treatment of men and women or that they necessarily outweigh the essential similarities between men and women.

The Sex Discrimination Act 1975 recognizes that men and women are alike in vital respects. It therefore proceeds on the premiss that the difference of sex does not automatically excuse different treatment. It attempts to define the circumstances in which the differences between the sexes are relevant and valid in considering the distribution of resources.[71] In effect, the Act recognizes what is stated in the preamble to the UN Convention on the Elimination of All Forms of Discrimination Against Women 1979: that, with very few exceptions, each of which must be independently justified,

discrimination against women violates the principles of equality of rights and respect for human dignity, is an obstacle to the participation of women, on equal terms with men, in the political, social, economic and cultural life of their countries, hampers the growth of the prosperity of society and the family and makes more difficult the full development of the potentialities of women in the service of their countries and of humanity.

[70] See Janet Radcliffe Richards, 'PMT—An Obstacle in the Fight for Female Equality?' *The Listener* 29 Apr. 1982. See ch. 6 for a discussion of pregnancy and sex discrimination.

[71] Similarly, the jurisprudence of the US Supreme Court under the equal protection clause of the fourteenth amendment to the US Constitution: gender-based classifications will be valid if they bear a 'fair and substantial relationship' to legitimate State ends or to important Governmental objectives. See, for example, *Michael M* v. *Superior Court of Sonoma County* 450 US 464 (1981). There is a need for an 'exceedingly persuasive justification' for a gender-based classification, and this will not exist where the objective itself reflects archaic and stereotyped notions of male and female roles: *Mississippi University for Women* v. *Hogan* 458 US 718 (1982). An Equal Rights Amendment to the US Constitution (providing that 'Equality of rights under the law shall not be denied or abridged by the United States or by any State on account of sex') proposed by Congress in 1972 failed to secure ratification by a sufficient number of States to become law.

The White Paper, *Equality for Women*, stated the objectives of an anti-discrimination law. It adopted the summary of the law's aims stated by the Race Relations Board set up under the Race Relations Acts of 1965 and 1968 to combat race discrimination. The role of the law here is to give an unequivocal declaration of public policy; to give support to those who do not wish to discriminate but who would otherwise feel compelled to do so by social pressure; to give protection and redress to victims of discrimination; to provide for the peaceful and orderly adjustment of grievances and the release of tensions; and to deter prejudice and the behaviour in which such prejudice is manifested. The White Paper acknowledged the common features of race and sex discrimination: the adverse treatment of someone on grounds irrelevant to their intrinsic qualities; the morally unacceptable and socially harmful nature of such conduct; and the pressures of prejudice and custom which encourage such behaviour.[72]

When the US Supreme Court held in 1896 that it was not unconstitutional for a State to require blacks and whites to use separate seating in public transport, the majority judgment concluded that '[l]egislation is powerless to eradicate racial instincts or to abolish distinctions based upon physical differences, and the attempt to do so can only result in accentuating the difficulties of the present situation'.[73] By 1975, it had been recognized, in the USA and in the United Kingdom, that the law could serve a deterrent, a remedial, and an educative function in

[72] Above n. 17 at paras. 19–20. Para. 24 stated that the 'Government's ultimate aim is to harmonise the powers and procedures for dealing with sex and race discrimination so as to secure genuine equality of opportunity in both fields.' See *Sail'er Inn Inc.* v. *Kirby* 485 P 2d 529, 540–1 (1971) where the Supreme Court of California stated that 'Sex, like race and lineage, is an immutable trait, a status into which the class members are locked by the accident of birth. What differentiates sex from nonsuspect statuses, such as intelligence or physical disability, and aligns it with the recognised suspect classifications, is that the characteristic frequently bears no relation to ability to perform or contribute to society . . . The result is that the whole class is relegated to an inferior legal status without regard to the capabilities or characteristics of its individual members . . . Another characteristic which underlies all suspect classifications is the stigma of inferiority and second class citizenship associated with them . . . Women, like Negroes, aliens and the poor have historically laboured under severe legal and social disabilities. Like black citizens, they were, for many years, denied the right to vote and, until recently, the right to serve on juries in many States. They are excluded from or discriminated against in employment and educational opportunities . . .' See also ch. 2 n. 11.

[73] *Plessy* v. *Ferguson*, above, n. 63 at 551.

this context. The exercise of those functions was widely perceived to be justified by the morally unacceptable and the socially harmful nature of discrimination against women and against blacks. Arguments relying on the liberty of the discriminator to act in an anti-social or unfair manner were met by confining the scope of the law. In providing employment, education, or goods, services, facilities, or premises to the public or to a section of the public, discriminators were acting in the public domain, not in private. They therefore could not legitimately claim that personal privacy or autonomy should make them immune from legal regulation of their conduct in these respects. The White Paper explained that '[t]he status of women in society, the disabilities and disadvantages imposed upon women, and their consequences, are social questions. They are legitimate subjects of the public interest and are appropriate matters for Government action.'[74]

The unjust exclusion of people on the grounds of their sex 'from the opportunities, facilities, and services of modern life is at least as substantial an injustice as the breach of a contract, the defamation of someone's reputation, or a damaging act of negligence'.[75] There is, therefore, no reason why the law should not redress the wrong of sex discrimination as it does these other wrongs. It was undoubtedly true, as the opponents of the 1975 Act argued, that the law could not ensure the eradication of sex discrimination. But this was no reason for Parliament to abstain from action. The law prohibits theft and driving one's car above the speed limit despite, indeed because of, the fact that those practices will continue to occur. The law exists to educate, to deter, and to provide remedies. Anti-discrimination law is no anomaly. As Lord Simon said of the Race Relations Act 1968, Parliament has contemplated that 'the law might perform in this field one of its traditional functions—an educative one—namely, to raise moral standards by stigmatizing as henceforward socially unacceptable certain hitherto generally condoned conduct'.[76]

The Sex Discrimination Act 1975 and the Race Relations Act 1976 (which applies very similar principles to prohibit race

---

[74] Above, n. 17 at para. 3.
[75] Anthony Lester and Geoffrey Bindman, *Race and Law* (1972), 87–8, where the authors are considering the analogous problem of race discrimination.
[76] *Charter* v. *Race Relations Board* [1973] AC 868, 900.

discrimination) do not make discrimination a criminal offence.[77] They provide civil law remedies for what had hitherto been moral wrongs with adverse consequences to individual victims and to society generally. Anti-discrimination law is far from a British idiosyncrasy. In seeking to understand the scope and the effect of the 1975 Act (and the Equal Pay Act 1970) we will need to compare and contrast UK law with its cousins in other jurisdictions, for example in the USA, Canada, Australia, New Zealand, and Ireland.[78] The statutory and constitutional prohibition of sex discrimination in these and many other jurisdictions indicates that anti-discrimination law is a phenomenon widely recognized as necessary to the maintenance of a harmonious society in the developed nations of the world. The United Kingdom's commitment to equal opportunity for the sexes under the Treaty of Rome of the European Economic Community, under the European Convention on Human Rights of the Council of Europe, and under international treaties, ensures that sex discrimination law is here to stay. The extent to which the 1975 Act (and the Equal Pay Act 1970) have materially improved the condition and the status of women can only be analysed after discussion of the content and the application of that legislation. What specific protection against sex discrimination does the law give to women and how have the courts applied the law?

[77] Cf. the erroneous statement of Lord Templeman in *Mandla* v. *Dowell Lee* [1983] 2 AC 548, 568: 'The fields of activity in which discrimination is made a criminal offence are employment, education and the provision of goods, facilities, services and premises.'

[78] The relevance to the 1975 Act of US case-law under Title VII of the US Civil Rights Act 1964 (which prohibits discrimination by employers on grounds of sex or on other invidious grounds) has been recognized by English courts and tribunals: see, for example, *Skyrail Oceanic Ltd* v. *Coleman* [1981] ICR 864, 870 (Court of Appeal); *Steel* v. *Union of Post Office Workers* [1978] ICR 181, 188 (EAT); *Clarke* v. *Eley (IMI) Kynoch Ltd* [1983] ICR 165, 171 (EAT). US courts appear to be afflicted with more than their fair share of frivolous cases in this context. See, for example, *Osei* v. *Old Time Gospel Hour* 35 FEP Cases 1504 (US District Court: 1984): an employee who was dismissed for abusive language on learning that his employer had used for commercial purposes a photograph of his feet in shackles does not have a Title VII claim, since the use of an employee's photograph for profit does not involve a right protected by Title VII. See also *Hand* v. *Briggs* discussed in ch. 9 n. 67.

2

THE SEX DISCRIMINATION ACT 1975:
THE CONCEPT OF DISCRIMINATION

I

The Sex Discrimination Act 1975 applies in three main contexts: employment, education, and the provision of goods, services, facilities, and premises.[1] In these contexts, the 1975 Act makes it unlawful to discriminate against a person on the ground of his or her sex. The Act provides civil remedies such as damages and injunctions. The 1975 Act prohibits sex discrimination against men, as well as against women.[2] As Lord Denning explained, in this respect '[w]hat is sauce for the goose is sauce for the gander . . .'.[3]

In the contexts which it covers, the 1975 Act makes unlawful four separate types of discrimination: direct sex discrimination, indirect sex discrimination, discrimination against married persons, and victimization. The case law applying the 1975 Act establishes that '[s]ex discrimination is a sensitive and complex branch of our law. The cases invariably arouse strong feelings on one side and sometimes on both, for it is often difficult to say which is more hurtful: to feel oneself the victim of discrimination or to be charged with having practised it. The governing statute, moreover, is complex in scheme . . . Any industrial tribunal [or court] therefore confronted with a complaint of sex discrimination . . . may expect troubled waters ahead.'[4]

II

A person directly discriminates against a woman if they treat her less favourably on the ground of her sex than they treat or would

---

[1] See ch. 3 for discussion of the scope of the 1975 Act.
[2] S. 2(1). See also ss. 3(2) and 4(3).
[3] *Ministry of Defence* v. *Jeremiah* [1980] ICR 13, 24.
[4] *Creagh* v. *Speedway Sign Service Ltd* (EAT, 7 Feb. 1984).

treat a man.[5] This is the common understanding of discrimination. It has two elements. The woman complainant must show, first, that she was less favourably treated than a comparable man was or would be treated and, secondly, that this was on the ground of her sex. The 1975 Act gives little guidance on who is a comparable man for this purpose. It says that a comparison of the cases of persons of different sex must be such that 'the relevant circumstances in the one case are the same, or not materially different, in the other'.[6] In other words, like must be compared with like.

If a woman proves that she has been less favourably treated on the ground of her sex, then it is no defence that the defendant acted in good faith or with a good motive, unless the defendant can bring itself within one of the specific exceptions stated in the Act.[7] In deciding whether the less favourable treatment was on the ground of sex, it is not necessary for the complainant to show that her sex was the sole reason for the difference in treatment; it is enough that it was a substantial or important reason.[8]

There is direct sex discrimination only if the less favourable treatment was on the ground of 'her' sex, that is the sex of the complainant. This is in contrast to the concept of direct discrimination under the Race Relations Act 1976 which covers the less favourable treatment of the complainant on the ground of another person's race (for example that of a customer served by the complainant employee in breach of the employer's instructions not to serve blacks).[9] The 1975 Act is further to be distinguished from the concept of direct discrimination in the Race Relations Act in that the latter expressly declares in section 1(2) that 'segregating a person from other persons on racial grounds is treating him less

---

[5] S. 1(1)(a).

[6] S. 5(3). S. 1(2) adds that if a person treats or would treat people differently according to their marital status, then for the purpose of s. 1(1)(a) the treatment of a woman should be compared with the treatment of a man 'having the like marital status'.

[7] *Grieg* v. *Community Industry* [1979] ICR 356, 360 (EAT). See similarly *Din* v. *Carrington Viyella Ltd* [1982] ICR 256, 259 (EAT), and *R.* v. *CRE ex parte Westminster City Council* [1984] ICR 770, 776-7 (Divisional Court) (cases under the Race Relations Act 1976).

[8] *Owen & Briggs* v. *James* [1982] ICR 618, 623, 625-6 (Court of Appeal), again under the 1976 Act.

[9] *Showboat Entertainment Centre Ltd* v. *Owens* [1984] ICR 65 (EAT). See also *Zarczynska* v. *Levy* [1979] ICR 184 (EAT) and *Applin* v. *Race Relations Board* [1975] AC 259, 289-90 per Lord Simon on the Race Relations Act 1968.

favourably than they are treated'.[10] There are, of course, many differences of principle between race discrimination and sex discrimination.[11] But standards applicable in the one context are often useful in analysing issues in the other context. The factors which suggest that separate facilities for different races may be inherently unequal are relevant to a determination of whether separate facilities for the sexes are ever equal. Separate facilities for different races fail to be equal because facilities for one race will possess 'to a far greater degree those qualities which are incapable of objective measurement but which make for greatness', that is to say qualities such as reputation, prestige, and tradition.[12] The 1975 Act contains provisions to deal with cases where privacy and decency require separate facilities for the sexes, for example in the provision of lavatories.[13] The equivalent of section 1(2) of the Race Relations Act 1976 should, therefore, be included in the 1975 Act.[14]

[10] See *FTATU* v. *Modgill* [1980] IRLR 142 where the EAT held that the failure by employers to take positive steps to prevent employees voluntarily establishing working groups in different parts of the factory, according to race, does not constitute segregation by the employers where no worker has been denied a job in a particular department by reason of his or her race.

[11] See *Frontiero* v. *Richardson* 411 US 677, 685–6 (1973: US Supreme Court); *Regents of the University of California* v. *Bakke* 438 US 265, 303 (1978) per Powell J. in the US Supreme Court; *Michael M.* v. *Superior Court of Sonoma County* 450 US 464, 478 (1981) per Stewart J. in the US Supreme Court; G Myrdal *An American Dilemma* (2nd ed. 1962), 1073–8; Richard A. Wasserstrom 'Racism, Sexism and Preferential Treatment: An Approach to the Topics' 24 *University of California at Los Angeles Law Review* 581, 589–90 (1977). See also ch. 1 n. 72.

[12] *Sweatt* v. *Painter* 339 US 629, 634 (1950: US Supreme Court). The constitutional jurisprudence of the US Supreme Court evolved from upholding separate facilities for blacks and whites as compatible with equal protection of the laws (*Plessy* v. *Ferguson* 163 US 537 (1896)) to assessing, with ever-increasing strictness of scrutiny, the equality of the separate facilities provided (*Missouri ex rel. Gaines* v. *Canada* 305 US 337 (1938), *Sweatt* v. *Painter* above, *McLaurin* v. *Oklahoma State Regents* 339 US 637 (1950)), to the eventual conclusion that separate facilities for different races are inherently unequal and therefore unconstitutional. In *Brown* v. *Board of Education* 347 US 483, 493–5 (1954), Chief Justice Warren for an unanimous Supreme Court announced that '[s]eparate educational facilities are inherently unequal'. See Richard Kluger *Simple Justice* (1977) for a compelling account of the case.

[13] For example, s. 7(2)(b) (on which see ch. 9 s. V) and ss. 35(1)(c) and 35(2) (on which see ch. 3 nn. 89–92).

[14] The US federal courts have yet to accept that when segregation is by sex it is therefore unconstitutional as when segregation is by race. See *Vorchheimer* v. *School District of Philadelphia* 532 F 2d 880 (1976) where the US Court of Appeals held that the Constitution does not forbid the maintenance by a public school board of a limited number of single-sex schools in which enrolment is voluntary when the

Because direct discrimination depends on establishing that, on the ground of her sex, a woman was less favourably treated than a man was or would have been treated, sex discrimination may exist where one woman is preferred to another for a job vacancy, for example. The issue is not whether a man or a woman receives the benefit in question, but whether the woman complainant would have been better treated had she been male.[15] Direct discrimination concentrates on individual rights, not on group entitlements.

In applying the concept of direct discrimination, as the EAT wisely recognized in an early case, 'no guidance can be got from instinctive feelings; rather the reverse. Such feelings are likely to be the product of ingrained social attitudes, assumed to be permanent but rendered obsolete by changing values and current legislation.' The EAT acknowledged that

in the case of a reforming Act of this kind, deliberately introducing new ideas and policies, preconceived ideas of what is fit are at best an uncertain guide, and the only sure course is to follow the words of the Act in accordance with what appears to be its policy. Occasionally, no doubt, it will produce odd results, but they are the price which will have to be paid for such a sweeping reform . . .[16]

The very different approach of the Court of Appeal in the same case, the first to be decided under the 1975 Act at that level, demonstrates the perennial problems of enforcing civil rights legislation in courts whose judges may be unaware of the mischief which Parliament aimed to eradicate or unsympathetic to the aims of that legislation.

The case of *Peake* v. *Automotive Products Ltd* concerned an employer's practice of allowing female workers to leave the

general educational opportunities offered to males and females in the separate institutions are essentially equal. In a *per curiam* decision, the Supreme Court divided 4–4, and so the Court of Appeals decision was upheld: 430 US 703 (1977). In *Mississippi University for Women* v. *Hogan* 458 US 718, 720 n (1982), the Supreme Court expressly declined to consider the issue of 'whether States can provide "separate but equal" undergraduate institutions for males and females'. See also *Kirstein* v. *Rector and Visitors of the University of Virginia* 309 F Supp 184 (1970: US District Court) and *Williams* v. *McNair* 316 F Supp. 134 (1970: US District Court), affirmed on appeal 401 US 951 (1971) (US Supreme Court).

[15] See *Skelton* v. *Balzano* 424 F Supp 1231, 1235–6 (1976: US District Court) and *Welch* v. *University of Texas* 659 F. 2d 531, 533 n. (1981: US Court of Appeals) on Title VII of the US Civil Rights Act 1964 which prohibits sex discrimination in employment.

[16] *Peake* v. *Automotive Products Ltd* [1977] ICR 480, 483, 489.

factory five minutes earlier each day than the men so as to avoid being jostled in the rush. The male complainant said that, because of his sex, he had to stay on the premises longer than a woman employee. Over a year the extra time added up to about two and a half working days. The Court of Appeal allowed an appeal from the finding of the EAT that this constituted unlawful sex discrimination. Lord Denning held that

[a]lthough the Act applies equally to men as to women, I must say it would be very wrong to my mind if this statute were thought to obliterate the differences between men and women or to do away with the chivalry and courtesy which we expect mankind to give womankind. The natural differences of sex must be regarded even in the interpretation of an Act of Parliament.[17]

Lord Justice Shaw concluded that the 1975 Act was not 'designed to provide a basis for capricious and empty complaints of differentiation between the sexes. Nor was it intended to operate as a statutory abolition of every instinct of chivalry and consideration on the part of men for the opposite sex.'[18]

The Court of Appeal did not appreciate the irony: a statute introduced to make unlawful gender-based classifications, which had often been rationalized by reference to chivalry or the alleged need to protect frail women, was being frustrated by judicial reliance on precisely those factors of chivalry and paternalism. In *Peake*, the Court of Appeal decided that different treatment of each sex was not discrimination when based on 'the interests of safety' or 'sensible administrative arrangements' or when the maxim *de minimis non curat lex* (the law does not concern itself with trifles)[19] applies.

The court's willingness to imply broad exceptions into the 1975 Act would have seriously impeded the utility of the statute. However, the *Peake* approach was soon renounced. In *Ministry of*

---

[17] [1977] ICR 968, 973.

[18] Ibid. at 975. A similar principle appears to have been suggested by the Supreme Court of Washington in *McLean* v. *First Northwest Industries of America Inc.* 635 P 2d 683 (1981). It was there held that a 'Ladies' Night' ticket pricing policy entitling women to be admitted at half-price to certain baseball games was not contrary to State anti-discrimination law because '[t]he discount on ticket prices for women was not calculated to nor is it contended that it did cause the [male complainant] to feel unwelcome, unaccepted, undesired or unsolicited'.

[19] On that maxim see *Maxwell—The Interpretation of Statutes* (12th edn., ed. P. St. J. Langan, 1969), 103–4 and *Broom's Legal Maxims* (10th edn. 1939), 88–90.

Defence v. *Jeremiah*, male employees who volunteered for overtime had to work in the 'colour bursting shops', where the work was dirty, protective clothing had to be worn, and vigorous showers were necessary after the work had been completed. Women employees were not required to work there. The Court of Appeal held that this was unlawful sex discrimination against the men. Lord Denning said of *Peake* that the court was there 'under a disadvantage, because Mr Peake appeared in person: and we were not referred to some of the relevant parts of the statute'. He confessed that

on reconsideration, I think the only sound ground [for the decision in Peake] was that the discrimination was *de minimis*. Mr Lester [counsel for the complainant] told us that, on a petition to the Appeal Committee of the House of Lords, they refused leave to appeal for that very reason. They thought that the decision was correct on the *de minimis* ground. In these circumstances, the other ground (about chivalry and administrative practice) should no longer be relied upon . . .[20]

Lord Justice Brandon said that certain matters relied upon by the employers were irrelevant to liability under the 1975 Act: that women objected to working in the colour-bursting shops; that facilities, such as lavatories and showers, were not available for women in these areas; that to require women to work in those areas would be unreasonable and likely to lead to industrial unrest; and that there was no evidence that any male employee, other than the complainant, objected to the difference in treatment between men and women. He declined to rule on whether the Court of Appeal was correct in *Peake* to imply an exception into the statute for action taken in the interests of safety and good administration, because there was no finding of fact in the case before him that the difference of treatment arose out of any such consideration.[21] The third judge, Brightman LJ, did not expressly consider *Peake*. But his judgment suggests that 'he was in substance intending to agree with Lord Denning' that the implied exceptions recognized in *Peake* were not a defence under the 1975 Act.[22]

The *de minimis* argument has also been affected by subsequent case law. In *Gill* v. *El Vino Co Ltd*[23] the Court of Appeal held that

---

[20] Above, n. 3 at 25.   [21] Ibid. at 28–9.
[22] See *Page* v. *Freight Hire (Tank Haulage) Ltd* [1981] ICR 299, 303 (EAT).
[23] [1983] QB 425.

a wine bar unlawfully discriminated against women by refusing to serve them standing at the bar and by requiring women (but not men) to sit at a table if they wanted to be served. The wine bar had, for several years after the enactment of the 1975 Act and despite several legal challenges to its practice, continued to conduct this sex discrimination. The practice was clearly unlawful, falling within the Act's prohibition of sex discrimination in the context of providing goods, services, or facilities to the public. If such a blatant discriminatory practice should survive legal challenge, one could only be deeply pessimistic about the value of the 1975 Act in deterring and remedying less publicized and less blatant sex discrimination.

Yet a county court judge found in favour of the wine bar. Judge Ranking held that only a handful of people would find, or had found, the practice to be objectionable and that the policy now challenged had existed for many years. It should not need to be explained to a judge that Parliament has, by the 1975 Act, decided that the less favourable treatment of women on the ground of their sex in specified contexts is unlawful, whatever the 'reasonable man' may think and however long established the practice. Judge Ranking also held that the sex discrimination was, in any event, of minimal importance and so not unlawful.[24] The obvious answer is that the female complainants and the owners of the wine bar (who had fought long and hard to preserve the house rules) did not see it that way. In any event, judges should be hesitant to dismiss as of minimal importance a legal right otherwise guaranteed by Parliament. Perhaps it may even be taken as an indication of the progress towards equality of opportunity for the sexes that endemic discriminatory practices that were once loudly applauded as essential to the preservation of society are now defensively found to be of minimal importance.

In the Court of Appeal it was held that the maxim *de minimis* had no application in the circumstances. Lord Justice Eveleigh

---

[24] Cf. the decision of a Northern Ireland County Court judge under the analogous provisions of the Sex Discrimination (Northern Ireland) Order 1976 in *Evason* v. *P. & F. McGlade Ltd* (1979, unreported): the refusal of a Belfast establishment to serve women in the public bar was held unlawful when a woman was with male and female companions and all the other rooms in the establishment (where women could be served) were full. The court rejected the arguments that it was a long-established practice to reserve the bar for men and that to serve women at the bar might cause embarrassment to male customers. See ch. 3 n. 93.

said that he found it 'very difficult to evoke the maxim *de minimis non curat lex* in a situation where that which has been denied to the plaintiff is the very thing that Parliament seeks to provide, namely facilities and services on an equal basis'.[25] Griffiths LJ said that he could not 'regard this as *de minimis*; women are denied a facility which may be of particular importance to a journalist'[26] (since the bar was in Fleet Street in London and was frequented by journalists). The Court of Appeal judgment is of especial importance for its refusal to do other than apply the plain words of the statute.[27] The *El Vino* case is a clear, and correct, statement that courts will not be impressed by attempts to imply exceptions and limitations into the 1975 Act to excuse sex discrimination. Eveleigh LJ emphasised that the correct way to approach the issues

is to take the simple words of the statute and try to apply them . . . Now this is not a technical statute and, therefore, is not of a kind where one should or need go for the meaning of words to other decided cases. It is a simple statute seeking to deal with ordinary everyday behaviour and the relative positions of men and women.[28]

The approach adopted by the Court of Appeal is in sharp contrast to the attitude of some county court judges to sex discrimination law. Another example of the failure of county courts to understand the objectives of the legislation is the decision of Judge Lord in Manchester County Court in *Twambley* v. *Jamal Nouri Fattah trading as Jamal's Wine Bar*.[29] Mr Twambley, the plaintiff, had been charged £1 to enter a wine bar; women were admitted free. Judge Lord reluctantly recognized that this was unlawful sex discrimination, however 'admirable' the motives of the wine bar owner. The defendant had not charged women to enter the wine bar 'since they are more ladylike' (hardly a controversial proposition) and 'did not get drunk or come to his premises inebriated'. While there is nothing to prevent a wine bar

---

[25] Above, n. 23 at 431.

[26] Ibid. at 432. He commented at 431–2: 'is she being treated less favourably than men? I think that permits of only one answer: of course she is'.

[27] See Sir Roger Ormrod, ibid. at 432: he said it was 'impossible to say, where one sex has an option and the other has not, that there is not a differentiation between them and, prima facie, a differentiation which results in less favourable treatment'.

[28] Ibid. at 429.   [29] *The Times* 2 Oct. 1982.

owner from charging an entry fee, or refusing entry, to drunks, male or female, the 1975 Act prohibits the owner from acting on the assumption that all men are potential drunks and no women have such a potential.[30] Although Judge Lord gave a declaration that the wine bar had acted unlawfully, he awarded 'nominal, contemptuous and derisory' damages of 1 penny and refused to award costs against the defendant. He announced that it was 'frivolous and foolish litigation', 'an absolute farce' and 'a scandalous waste of public money' (the complaint having been supported by the Equal Opportunities Commission).[31]

It is, of course, entirely a private matter whether a judge sympathizes with the purposes of a statute. However, one would hope that the Court of Appeal decision in *El Vino* will encourage judges to remember that, in public, their duty is to administer the law and not to diminish its chances of deterring blatantly unlawful conduct by expressing idiosyncratic views on the wisdom of litigation. The approach of Judge Lord can be usefully contrasted with that of the New Zealand Human Rights Commission. It has held that the practice of night-clubs, cabarets, and bars of charging men, but not women, for admission constitutes 'a widespread practice of discrimination on the ground of sex [which is] not only a breach of the law but . . . is (by reason of extensive advertising) a very obvious public notice that the principle of equality between the sexes is not being observed'.[32] The hostility of Judge Lord's remarks reminds one that, however sensible the interpretation of the law by appeal courts, the vast majority of cases will be decided by lower courts or tribunals with no appeal. If the 1975 Act is to achieve its objectives, County Court judges need to control their emotions and restrict themselves to applying the 'simple words of the statute' in the manner indicated by the Court of Appeal.

The policy of applying the 'simple words of the statute' to decide whether a practice amounts to less favourable treatment of women (or men) on the ground of their sex will not always suffice. The concept of direct discrimination has raised a number of complex analytical problems. Is it less favourable treatment of women on the ground of their sex to dismiss workers for becoming pregnant, but not for any other temporary incapacitating condition?[33] Or to

[30] See below, nn. 39–44.
[31] Under their powers pursuant to s. 75 of the 1975 Act: see ch. 10 n. 6.
[32] 8 *Commonwealth Law Bulletin* 1214 (1982).   [33] See ch. 6.

dismiss women workers for refusing to comply with an employer's sexual demands? Or for refusing to comply with a grooming code that allows male employees, but not female employees, to wear trousers at work? What does equal treatment of the sexes without discrimination require in the context of insurance?[34] Does such equal treatment prohibit discrimination against homosexuals or transsexuals on the ground of their sexual preferences?[35]

In considering whether direct sex discrimination has occurred courts need to ask whether the sex of the complainant was 'the activating cause' of the less favourable treatment of which she complains.[36] On occasions, whether there has been an act of sex discrimination will depend on the application of section 5(3) of the 1975 Act: what are the 'relevant circumstances' in deciding who is the appropriate male comparison for testing whether the treatment of the female complainant was less favourable?[37] The potential problems are well illustrated by *Roberts* v. *Tate & Lyle Food and Distribution Ltd*. The employers operated a retirement pensions scheme with a normal retirement age of 65 for men and 60 for women. On a mass redundancy, the employers allowed all workers to take a pension five years early, that is men at 60 and women at 55. However, they then decided that this was unfair to the men: since women aged 55–9 were given a pension, the

---

[34] See ch. 7 on these three issues.   [35] See ch. 8.

[36] *Seide* v. *Gillette Industries Ltd* [1980] IRLR 427, 431 (EAT), approved by the Court of Appeal in *Kingston* v. *British Railways Board* [1984] ICR 781, 792 (both cases under the Race Relations Act 1976). See similarly *Din* v. *Carrington Viyella Ltd* above n. 7. In *Record Production Chapel, Sogat* v. *Turnbull* (16 Apr. 1984, unreported), the EAT in Scotland held that a trade union chapel directly discriminated in 1983 by refusing membership to women cleaners expelled from the chapel in 1980 on the ground of their sex albeit those women would not have been readmitted to the chapel in 1983 if they were male.

[37] See *Grieg* v. *Community Industry* above, n. 7 where the EAT said, at 361, that 'section 5(3) is principally although not exclusively talking about the personal circumstances of the applicant for employment and the personal circumstances of the person alleging discrimination'. In *Grieg*, a woman was refused employment in a team of six on the ground that she would be the only woman on the team. The EAT rejected the employers' argument that this was not sex discrimination because, if a man had applied to join a team of five women, he too would have been rejected. The EAT held that 'the relevant employment to consider is not some hypothetical employment with the personnel concerned totally different, but is the employment for which the applicant applied . . .'. See also *Peake* above, n. 16 at 488 where the EAT said that 'in deciding whether the circumstances of the two cases are the same, or not materially different, one must put out of the picture any circumstances which necessarily follow from the fact that one is comparing the case of a man and of a woman'.

employers decided that men of those ages should be similarly treated. Miss Roberts, aged 53, did not receive a pension as one of the workers made redundant. She claimed that if men aged ten years below the normal retirement age for men were given a pension (which they were), so women aged ten years below the normal retirement age for women should also be given a pension (which they were not), which would have resulted in Miss Roberts receiving a pension. The employers replied that they had treated Miss Roberts, aged 53, in exactly the same way as they had treated a man aged 53: neither received a pension. Whether there was less favourable treatment of Miss Roberts on the ground of her sex depended on whether the 'relevant circumstances' under section 5(3) included the actual age of the complainant and the male comparable, or the age-off normal retirement and pension age of Miss Roberts and the male comparable. If the treatment of Miss Roberts were to be compared with that of a man of the same age as her, she was not discriminated against: neither of them received a pension. If, however, the treatment of Miss Roberts were to be compared with that of a man whose age-off pension age was the same as hers—that is seven years off pension age—she was discriminated against: a man aged 58 received a pension but she did not. The EAT concluded that it was unable to state when section 5(3) required reference to actual age and when it required reference to age-off pension age.[38]

Important examples of direct sex discrimination occur when a person acts on a stereotyped assumption about the abilities or qualities of the sexes and declines to consider the abilities or qualities of the individual man or woman. The White Paper, *Equality for Women*, stated that the unequal status of women 'has been caused less by conscious discrimination against women than by the stereotyped attitudes of both sexes about their respective roles'. Therefore, it would 'not generally be permissible' under the proposed law 'to seek to justify discrimination on grounds of sex . . . on the basis of assumptions or evidence about the general differences between the sexes'.[39] Recognizing this principle,

---

[38] [1983] ICR 521, 526–7. The claim failed under the 1975 Act in any event because it concerned provision in relation to retirement, which is excluded from the scope of the Act by section 6(4): see ch. 3 n. 19. The Court of Appeal referred the issues raised by *Roberts* to the European Court of Justice: see ch. 5 n. 81.

[39] Cmnd. 5724 (1974), paras. 16 and 71. See *Stanton* v. *Stanton* 421 US 7, 15

Lawton LJ said in the Court of Appeal in *Noble* v. *David Gold &
Son (Holdings) Ltd* that the 1975 Act provides, subject to a few
exceptions, that 'employers when offering jobs must not assume
that women are less capable of doing them than men, and vice
versa'.[40]

This approach was applied by the Court of Appeal in *Skyrail
Oceanic Ltd* v. *Coleman* where the employer was found to have
committed unlawful sex discrimination by sacking a female
employee because it assumed that her husband, and not her, was
the family breadwinner.[41] The EAT applied this principle in
Horsey v. *Dyfed CC*. A woman was refused a job opportunity
because her employer assumed that, as a married woman, she
would choose to follow her husband to live close to his work and so
would have to give up her employment. Mr Justice Browne-
Wilkinson, for the EAT, accepted that the concept of direct sex
discrimination does not only cover cases where the sole factor
influencing the decision complained of is the sex of the victim. It
also covers cases where

the reason for the discrimination was a generalised assumption that
people of a particular sex . . . possess or lack certain characteristics, e.g. 'I
like women but I will not employ them because they are unreliable' . . .
Most discrimination flows from generalised assumptions of this kind and
not from a simple prejudice dependent solely on the sex . . . of the
complainant. The purpose of the legislation is to secure equal opportunity
for individuals regardless of their sex . . . This result would not be
achieved if it were sufficient to escape liability to show that the reason for
the discriminatory treatment was simply an assumption that women . . .

(1975) where the US Supreme Court referred to 'the role-typing society has long
imposed' on women.

[40] [1980] ICR 543, 551.

[41] [1981] ICR 864. The complainant was a female employee dismissed because
her husband worked for a rival firm. Her employer and her husband's employer
agreed that as the man was presumably the breadwinner, it would be better if the
wife were dismissed, given that one of them had to be dismissed. In fact Mrs
Coleman's husband earned a modest wage. The dissenting opinion of Lord Justice
Shaw is noteworthy for its strength of feeling. He found the case 'trivial and banal
. . . artificial and pretentious'. He said that he had heard, in the case, 'execrating
noises about sex discrimination' and that the 'promotion of such claims can only
have the consequence of bringing the laudable aims of the legislation against sex
discrimination into disrepute': 872–4. It is unclear what Lord Justice Shaw thought
those aims were if not to give a legal remedy to a woman subjected to less
favourable treatment on the ground of her sex.

possessed or lacked particular characteristics and not that they were just women . . .[42]

The House of Lords has expressed similar views on how acting on sex-based stereotyped assumptions amounts to sex discrimination under the 1975 Act. Special vouchers for entry to the United Kingdom for settlement were made available for a 'head of household' who satisfied certain other immigration criteria. It was assumed by the State that a woman was not a head of household unless she was widowed or single, or unless she took on the responsibilities of a head of household due to her husband's long-term medical disability. The House of Lords held that this less favourable treatment of women amounted to direct sex discrimination under the 1975 Act.[43]

Women (and men), therefore, are entitled to be treated as individuals, by reference to their own qualities and defects, and not by reference to characteristics commonly associated with persons of their own sex.[44] An employer must not ask whether women are reliable employees, but he may, of course, ask whether this woman is likely to be a reliable employee. It is irrelevant to the issue of direct sex discrimination whether the stereotyped assumption relied upon is true or false of women in general. A female applicant is entitled to be considered for a job vacancy according to her abilities to perform the job duties whether or not it is generally true, as the employer believes, that most women

---

[42] [1982] ICR 755, 760. See also *Hurley* v. *Mustoe* [1981] ICR 490, 493 (EAT) and *Secretary of State for Scotland* v. *Henley* (EAT, Scotland, 19 May 1983, unreported, transcript at 6).

[43] *R.* v. *Entry Clearance Officer, Bombay ex parte Amin* [1983] 2 AC 818, 833 per Lord Fraser who accepted that enquiries as to whether or not the wife was the head of a household 'would be impracticable. The practice therefore is that the husband is assumed to be the head of household in a normal case. Accordingly I consider that there was sex discrimination in this case.' See also Lord Scarman at 841. The decision of the House of Lords is closely analogous to two decisions of the European Court of Justice in *Sabbatini* v. *European Parliament* [1972] ECR 345 and *Chollet* v. *Commission of the European Communities* [1972] ECR 363. Staff regulations for those in the service of the Parliament and the Commission stated that officials who married forfeited their right to an expatriation allowance unless the official thereby became the head of a household. The regulations provided that 'head of household' normally meant a married male official, whereas a married female official was considered to be a head of a household only in exceptional circumstances. The ECJ held that this sex discrimination was unlawful.

[44] As Lord Denning put it in *Shields* v. *E. Coomes (Holdings) Ltd* [1978] ICR 1159, 1171, '[h]e may have been a small, nervous man, who could not say "boo to a goose". She may have been as fierce and formidable as a battle-axe.'

would be incapable of performing the job duties. Perhaps one can say that the more universally true of women in general is the stereotyped assumption upon which the employer relies, the more willing a court would be to accept that a rudimentary consideration of a female applicant's individual merits suffices. But still, in all cases, individual consideration is required. In *City of Los Angeles Department of Water and Power* v. *Manhart* the US Supreme Court held that it was unlawful sex discrimination contrary to Title VII of the US Civil Rights Act 1964 for an employer to require female employees to make larger pension contributions than male employees to receive the same monthly benefits. The Court rejected the argument that such disparate treatment was non-discriminatory because women, on average, live longer than men and hence cannot demand the same monthly benefits for equal contributions since this would result in them receiving, in total, more than men. The Court in *Manhart* said that Title VII prevents employers from basing decisions 'on mere "stereotyped" impressions about the characteristics of males or females . . . This case does not, however, involve a fictional difference between men and women. It involves a generalisation that the parties accept as unquestionably true: women, as a class, do live longer than men.'[45] Nevertheless, the Court concluded that Title VII focuses on the individual, precluding less favourable treatment on the basis of a class characteristic which is not shared by all members of the class. An individual woman—denied equal benefits for equal contributions with men—does not necessarily share the class characteristic of longevity. Her less favourable treatment is by reason of her sex, not by reason of her individual attributes irrespective of sex. Section 45 of the Sex Discrimination Act 1975 contains a special exception in the field of insurance where men and women are treated differently.[46] But that does not affect the important principle that the 1975 Act, like Title VII, in rejecting direct sex discrimination prohibits the application of sex-based stereotypes even if they are true of women in general. It entitles people to be considered as individuals irrespective of their sex. By

---

[45] 435 US 702, 707-11 (1978). *Manhart* was cited with approval by Lawton LJ in the Court of Appeal in *Skyrail* above, n. 41 at 870. Note that the White Paper, above n. 39, saw the mischief as stereotyped attitudes based on 'assumptions *or* evidence' about general differences between men and women.

[46] See ch. 7 s. IV.

contrast, the concept of indirect sex discrimination under the 1975 Act seeks to ensure equality of opportunity from a different perspective: it proceeds from the premiss that women, considered as a group, are entitled to a fair share of benefits.

III

When the Labour Government published its White Paper, *Equality for Women*, in September 1974, it proposed that sex discrimination should be made unlawful only where the defendant had an 'intention (or inferred intention) to treat one person less favourably than another on grounds of sex . . .'. The White Paper suggested that 'to understand the meaning of unlawful discrimination, it is essential not to confuse motive with effect'.[47] This is, indeed, what we commonly understand by 'discrimination': a refusal to grant a benefit to X, or the imposition of a detriment on Y, because of his or her sex (or race). This concept of discrimination was at the heart of the Race Relations Acts 1965 and 1968.

During Parliamentary consideration of the Sex Discrimination Bill 1975, the Government amended its definition of discrimination. In addition to direct discrimination, it decided to make unlawful as indirect discrimination those practices which, while neutral on their face as between men and women, have a disproportionate adverse impact on women and which cannot be justified. The change was made after the Home Secretary, Roy Jenkins, visited the USA (with his special adviser, Anthony Lester). He learnt that in a race discrimination case, *Griggs* v. *Duke Power Co.*, the US Supreme Court had unanimously interpreted Title VII of the US Civil Rights Act 1964 (which prohibits discrimination in employment on the ground of race or sex, amongst other invidious grounds) to prohibit 'not only overt discrimination, but also practices that are fair in form but discriminatory in operation. The touchstone is business necessity. If an employment practice which operates to exclude Negroes cannot be shown to be related to job performance, the practice is prohibited.'[48]

[47] Above, n. 39 at para. 33.
[48] 401 US 424, 431 (1971). The US Supreme Court applied the disparate impact theory of indirect discrimination to sex discrimination in *Dothard* v. *Rawlinson* 433

The concept of indirect discrimination recognizes that the problem is not merely isolated acts of malevolence but also systems which, often unintentionally, result in disadvantage to women (or blacks).[49] Disparate impact theory attempts to reach beyond the individualized nature of isolated acts of prejudice 'and to provide a basis for intervening against the present effects of past and other types of institutional discrimination'.[50] The US Supreme Court in *Griggs* adopted a liberal approach to the words of Title VII, which provides that it is an unlawful employment practice to deprive an individual of employment opportunities 'because of such individual's race . . . sex . . .'. The Court found that by these words Congress had intended to ensure

that tests or criteria for employment or promotion may not provide equality of opportunity merely in the sense of the fabled offer of milk to the stork and the fox. On the contrary, Congress has now required that the posture and condition of the job-seeker be taken into account. It has—to resort again to the fable—provided that the vessel in which the milk is proferred be one all seekers can use.[51]

In the United Kingdom, Parliament wisely did not leave it to the judiciary to imply into the concept of discrimination the prohibition of practices which have a disparate impact on one sex and which cannot be justified. The 1975 Act (like the Race Relations Act 1976) defines the concept of indirect discrimination in detail. However, so vague is the terminology adopted that the effective use of the concept still depends on sympathetic judicial interpretation.

US 321 (1977). A similar process of judicial development of the concept of discrimination occurred in the law of the European Economic Community. Art. 48 of the EEC Treaty prohibits 'discrimination based on nationality between workers of the Member States as regards employment, remuneration, and other conditions of work and employment'. In *Sotgiu* v. *Deutsche Bundespost* [1974] ECR 153, 164 (para. 11) the ECJ held that art. 48 'forbid[s] not only overt discrimination by reason of nationality but also all covert forms of discrimination which, by the application of other criteria of differentiation, lead in fact to the same result . . .'. Those other criteria are not in breach of art. 48, said the Court, if they are justified by 'objective differences' (judgment at para. 12). See similarly *Commission of the European Communities* v. *Ireland* [1978] ECR 417, 450 (judgment at para. 78) and *CRAM* v. *TOIA* [1979] ECR 2645, 2654 (judgment at para. 14).

[49] See ch. 10 n. 62.

[50] Christopher McCrudden, 'Institutional Discrimination' 2 *Oxford Journal of Legal Studies* 303, 345 (1982).

[51] Above, n. 48.

Section 1(1)(b) of the Sex Discrimination Act 1975 defines the concept of indirect discrimination.[52] A person may be liable for indirect sex discrimination even if they did not intend to treat the complainant unfavourably on the ground of sex.[53] When the Sex Discrimination Bill was being considered by Standing Committee B in the House of Commons, Ian Gilmour (for the Conservative Opposition) explained that one of the reasons why they wished to delete clause 1(1)(b) from the Bill was that 'we do not know what it means. Secondly, we do not think the Government know what it means; and, thirdly, if we did know what it meant we do not think we would like it, but we cannot be sure.'[54] A decade later, it remains the case that few people understand the concept of indirect discrimination. If anti-discrimination law is to help guarantee equal opportunity in the employment and other contexts covered by the 1975 Act, it will be essential for practices fair in form but discriminatory in impact to be more widely understood and more strenuously challenged. The decisions hitherto of courts and tribunals, while not uniformly constructive, show that much can be achieved.

There are four elements of indirect discrimination. There must be a requirement or condition applied equally to men and to women. It must have a disparate impact on women (or men). It must be unjustifiable irrespective of sex. It must impose a detriment on the complainant.

There is little authority on what constitutes a 'requirement or condition' in this context, although the EAT has emphasized that 'it is necessary to define with some precision the requirement or

---

[52] S. 1(1)(b) provides that a person indirectly discriminates against a woman if 'he applies to her a requirement or condition which he applies or would apply equally to a man but:

  (i) which is such that the proportion of women who can comply with it is considerably smaller than the proportion of men who can comply with it, and

  (ii) which he cannot show to be justifiable irrespective of the sex of the person to whom it is applied, and

  (iii) which is to her detriment because she cannot comply with it.'

See ch. 4 nn. 75–83 for a discussion of indirect discrimination and the Equal Pay Act 1970.

[53] That is made clear by s. 66(3) of the 1975 Act. It provides that there is to be no award of damages for an act of unlawful indirect discrimination if the defendant proves that the requirement or condition was not applied with the intention of treating the complainant unfavourably on the ground of her sex. On remedies for sex discrimination see ch. 3 nn. 152–8.

[54] Standing Committee B (22 Apr. 1975), col. 36.

condition which is called in question'.[55] In *Steel* v. *Union of Post Office Workers*, Phillips J. for the EAT referred to *Griggs* and suggested that section 1(1)(b) is concerned with 'a practice' that has a disparate impact on women and is unjustifiable.[56] In *Clarke* v. *Eley (IMI) Kynoch Ltd*, the EAT said the words 'requirement or condition' should not be given 'a narrow construction. The purpose of the legislature in introducing the concept of indirect discrimination . . . was to seek to eliminate those practices which had a disproportionate impact on women . . . and were not justifiable for other reasons.' Mr Justice Browne-Wilkinson for the EAT noted that the concept was derived from *Griggs*. He said that the words of section 1(1)(b) should, if at all possible, be given a meaning consistent with the elimination of the mischief at which the subsection was aimed.[57]

Parliament intended by section 1(1)(b) to prohibit discriminatory practices having a disparate impact on women. It is unfortunate that it did not say so in clear terms rather than use the words 'requirement or condition'. Perhaps this was because Parliament wanted to cover the isolated decision which was not a settled policy but was applied on only one occasion. There are two main types of practice covered by section 1(1)(b). First, there is the practice having a disparate impact on women due to existing social or other conditions. For example, in *Price* v. *Civil Service Commission* the Civil Service rule that job applicants had to be under the age of 28 had a disparate impact on women because women tend to rear children before commencing or re-commencing a career.[58] In *Home Office* v. *Holmes* the refusal of an employer to provide part-time work for a woman employee returning to work after time off to rear her children had a disparate impact on

---

[55] *Price* v. *Civil Service Commission* [1978] ICR 27, 30 (EAT). See also *Francis* v. *British Airways Engineering Overhaul Ltd* [1982] IRLR 10 (EAT) where a claim under s. 1(1)(b) failed because no requirement or condition had been identified.

[56] [1978] ICR 181, 188.

[57] [1983] ICR 165, 171. See also *Watches of Switzerland Ltd* v. *Savell* [1983] IRLR 141, 146, where the EAT said that the statutory words 'requirement or condition' should be given 'a liberal interpretation in order to implement the object of the legislation'. Note also s. 37 of the 1975 Act (on which see ch. 3 n. 98) which entitles the EOC in certain circumstances to bring proceedings in respect of a 'discriminatory practice', which covers a breach of s. 1(1)(b).

[58] Above, n. 55. See also *Price* v. *Civil Service Commission (no. 2)* [1978] IRLR 3: when the case was returned to the industrial tribunal by the EAT the employers conceded that s. 1(1)(b)(i) was satisfied.

women because part-time work is almost entirely a female phenomenon: over 90 per cent of part-time workers are women and 44 per cent of women who are in employment work on a part-time basis.[59] This is undoubtedly because most family care responsibilities continue to be borne by women. Secondly, section 1(1)(b) covers the practice which has a disparate impact on women because of past direct sex discrimination. For example, in *Steel* a seniority rule had such an impact: prior to 1975 women were not allowed to attain the status necessary to achieve seniority.[60]

In *Perera* v. *Civil Service Commission*, a race discrimination case, the Court of Appeal suggested that there is no requirement or condition for the purposes of section 1(1)(b) unless the factor relied on by the defendant is 'an absolute bar' to appointment or promotion. If the employer only takes the factor into account as one amongst others, then it cannot be challenged under section 1(1)(b).[61] This is unfortunate. To focus solely on absolute barriers to the employment of women is to ignore the impact in practice of non-absolute criteria which may have a considerable adverse impact and be totally unjustifiable. Indirect discrimination is

---

[59] [1984] ICR 678 (EAT). The figures on part-time work are from the *EOC Annual Report* (1983) at 86 and from the EAT decision in *Jenkins* v. *Kingsgate (Clothing Productions) Ltd* [1981] ICR 715, 719–20. See also *Wright* v. *Rugby Borough Council* 26 Oct. 1984): a Birmingham Industrial Tribunal held that an employer indirectly discriminated by refusing to allow a woman to work flexible hours so that she could perform her job duties and perform her family care responsibilities. But see *Fulton* v. *Strathclyde Regional Council* (EAT, Scotland, 15 Jan. 1985) declining to apply *Holmes* to part-time workers who wanted their employers to provide a job-sharing arrangement. The Scottish EAT there said it would be reluctant to act on alleged social trends as to the prevalence of part-time work among working women without evidence being presented. See similarly *Kidd* v. *DRG (UK) Ltd* (EAT) *The Times* 19 Feb. 1985.

[60] Above, n. 56; and see *Steel* v. *Post Office (no. 2)* [1978] IRLR 198 (industrial tribunal). Similarly *Sun Alliance and London Insurance Ltd* v. *Dudman* [1978] ICR 551 (EAT). This provides a method of challenging the continuing effects of directly discriminatory acts which occurred prior to the introduction of the 1975 Act, or are now time-barred (on which see ch. 3 nn. 121–6). But see *Record Production Chapel, Sogat* v. *Turnbull* above n. 36 where the EAT in Scotland accepted that such a case was one of direct sex discrimination.

[61] [1983] ICR 428. It was there held that it was not a 'requirement or condition' under s. 1(1)(b)(i) of the Race Relations Act 1976 for the employer to specify that candidates for a job should be able to speak English (which the complainant said had a disparate impact on persons of non-British nationality and was not justifiable by reference to the nature of the job) because, according to Lord Justice Stephenson at 437–8, the employer was prepared to consider 'a brilliant man whose personal qualities made him suitable' for the job despite his low standard of English.

concerned with the impact in practice of criteria for receiving employment and other benefits.[62] It seems clearly contrary to the purpose of section 1(1)(b) if the employer can validly say that it will, other than in exceptional circumstances, only appoint persons over six feet tall (a criterion having a disparate impact on women), when this is unjustifiable in the circumstances, although there is no absolute bar and it is prepared to consider persons under that height. The important issue of whether indirect discrimination exists, in practice, should not be avoided by a narrow construction of what constitutes a 'requirement or condition'. *Perera* was argued before the Court of Appeal by the complainant on his own behalf. This inevitably reduces the authority of the general comments of the Court on the meaning of indirect discrimination.

If the requirement or condition is not applied equally to men and women—in other words there are different criteria applied to each sex—then the claim is one of direct sex discrimination, not indirect sex discrimination. The case is potentially one of indirect sex discrimination only where men and women have the same criteria applied to them but the impact of the criteria hits disproportionately at women.[63]

The complainant must show under section 1(1)(b)(i) that the impugned requirement or condition is such that the proportion of women who can comply with it is considerably smaller than the proportion of men who can comply with it. In *Price*, the EAT held that it would be 'wholly out of sympathy with the spirit and intent of the Act' if the employer could argue that women 'can comply' with an age requirement because they are not obliged to have or to rear children. The EAT held that

It should not be said that a person 'can' do something merely because it is theoretically possible for him to do so: it is necessary to see whether he can do so in practice. Applying this approach to the circumstances of this case, it is relevant in determining whether women can comply with the condition [that applicants for a job vacancy be under the age of 28] to take into account the current usual behaviour of women in this respect, as observed in practice, putting on one side behaviour and responses which are unusual or extreme.[64]

[62] See below, nn. 64 and 66 on this approach to s. 1(1)(b).

[63] See *Wong* v. *Greater London Council* (15 Oct. 1980, unreported judgment of the EAT) on the indirect discrimination provisions of the Race Relations Act 1976.

[64] Above, n. 55 at 31. A 35-year-old woman there applied for a job with the Civil Service. She was rejected because she was unable to satisfy the maximum age

This approach is consistent with the statement of Mr John Fraser, Under-Secretary of State for Employment, during the Standing Committee debates on the 1975 Bill. In response to the concern of Mr David Lane MP that 'can comply' might not cover women who could physically comply with a requirement (for example to go on a three months' residential course) but who would find it much more difficult to comply than would men, because they were rearing young children, Mr Fraser explained that the phrase 'will be understood by the courts and tribunals' to mean 'can reasonably be expected to comply'.[65] The House of Lords, in a race relations case, approved the approach to 'can comply' taken by the EAT in *Price*.[66]

Section 1(1)(b)(i) poses difficult questions of proof. When is a requirement or condition such that a considerably smaller proportion of women than of men can comply with it? In *Price*, the EAT said that one should look at the relevant pool of men and women, which may be less than the total male and female population, and, in that case, probably consisted of 'qualified men and qualified women'.[67] The 1975 Act does not require statistical proof of the facts relevant to section 1(1)(b)(i). But that will be the usual method of proof. The EAT has indicated that 'it is most undesirable that, in all cases of indirect discrimination, elaborate statistical evidence should be required before the case can be found proved',[68] especially given the time and expense which that would involve. Some passages in *Price* indicate a broad and generous approach to the issue of proof. The scheme of the indirect discrimination provision 'is to define in sub-paragraph (i) in fairly wide terms activities which are prima facie discriminatory . . . Thus sub-paragraph (i) proscribes a wide range of activity . . .' The filter mechanism, said the EAT, is that the defendant may

requirement of 28. She claimed that the age bar had a disproportionate adverse impact on women because they tended to return to work, or to commence a career, after bearing and rearing children. Her claim succeeded, see nn. 58 and 81.

[65] Standing Committee B, (24 Apr. 1975), cols. 60 and 73.

[66] *Mandla* v. *Dowell Lee* [1983] 2 AC 548, 565–6: Lord Fraser said that, in the context of s. 1(1)(b)(i), the word 'can' must 'have been intended by Parliament to be read not as meaning "can physically", so as to indicate a theoretical possibility, but as meaning "can in practice" . . .'.

[67] Above, n. 55 at 32. This was approved by the Court of Appeal in *Perera* above n. 61 at 437.

[68] *Perera* v. *Civil Service Commission* [1982] ICR 350, 359 (EAT). For the similar approach of the US Supreme Court see *Dothard* v. *Rawlinson* above n. 48 at 330–1.

seek to justify the requirement or condition under section $1(1)(b)(ii)$.[69]

In *Clarke*, the female complainants challenged as indirectly discriminatory a company policy of selecting for redundancy part-time workers prior to full-time workers. The EAT accepted that the relevant time for assessing the ability of women and men to comply with the requirement or condition was the date when the detriment was suffered.[70] The EAT did not interfere with the finding of fact of the industrial tribunal[71] that the proportion of women who could comply with the requirement (that to rank in selection for redundancy by virtue of length of service in the unit on the principle of last-in, first-out, one had to be employed full-time and not part-time) was considerably smaller than the proportion of men who could comply, given the current or usual behaviour of women in working part-time in greater proportions than men.

In asking whether the proportion of women who could comply with the condition or requirement was 'considerably smaller' than the proportion of men who could comply, Parliament presumably meant to exclude cases where the disparity was of no statistical significance. Some US courts have applied an 80 per cent rule, finding disparate impact contrary to Title VII of the Civil Rights Act if the success rate for women is less than four-fifths that for men.[72]

Indirect discrimination principles could be concerned with challenging policies which, in general, have a disparate impact on women: for example, height and age barriers. Alternatively, the principles could be concerned with practices that, in the specific work-place (or other relevant establishment), have a disparate impact on the women affected. Of course, there will often be no conflict between these two approaches: an employer's policy of refusing to promote part-time workers has a disparate impact on women in general, and it may also have a disparate impact on women working in the relevant factories because most part-time workers employed there are women. But what if an employer who refuses to promote part-time workers shows that, in its factory,

---

[69] Above, n. 55 at 29.   [70] Above, n. 57 at 172.

[71] [1982] IRLR 131.

[72] See Schlei and Grossman *Employment Discrimination Law* (Bureau of National Affairs, Washington DC, 2nd edn., 1983), 98–9.

exceptionally, most of the part-time workers are men? Can there
be disparate impact under section 1(1)(b)(i) against the women
part-timers who do work there? Can there be such a disparate
impact against the men part-time workers there, given that,
exceptionally, most of the men in that factory work part-time but,
in the country at large, part-time work is predominantly a female
phenomenon?

Section 1(1)(b)(i) and the principle of disparate impact do not
intend to make one's rights dependent on the arbitrary factors of
where one works, and the number of men and women who do
particular jobs there. The law is concerned with men and women
generally and it gives rights to people by reference to their
membership of a group defined by reference to sex. The disparate
impact of a practice on that sex generally is what matters. The
alternative is an unprincipled and arbitrary position causing
uncertainty to the disadvantage of all parties and hindering the
removal of barriers to the equal treatment of the sexes. The
concept of indirect discrimination inevitably has a degree of
flexibility according to the different justifications for the impugned
practice which may be presented by each employer under section
1(1)(b)(ii). But in order to require the employer to justify its
practice, it is desirable to rely on general truths about men and
women, and not on the fortuitous circumstances of a particular
factory.[73]

A further difficult issue raised by section 1(1)(b)(i) is whether
we consider in isolation the disparate impact on women of the

[73] This was the approach taken by the majority of the EAT in Scotland in *Record
Production Chapel, Sogat* v. *Turnbull* above n. 36: 'Section 1(1)(b) applies to men
and women generally and not to the accidental fact that at any particular time
within a limited pool of equally qualified persons there happen to be considerably
more men than women'. One difficulty with the general approach to indirect
discrimination is to know whether to ignore regional variations: suppose women
tend to be taller or heavier in certain parts of the country? Could that be relevant to
an issue of disparate impact in appropriate circumstances? The alternative
approach to s. 1(1)(b)(i)—concentrating on the specific impact of the requirement
or condition in the specific work environment, regardless of general truths about
men and women in the country at large—can best be supported by arguing that
indirect discrimination is a supplement to the concept of direct discrimination; that
it is concerned with employers, and others, who cannot be shown to have
distinguished between men and women by reference to sex, but who have adopted
a practice that in the establishment controlled by them has that effect.
This alternative approach appeared to be adopted by the Scottish EAT in *Fulton*
above, n. 59.

specific requirement or condition challenged by the complainant, or whether we adopt a 'bottom-line' approach and ask whether the relevant criteria adopted by the defendant in general have a disparate impact on women with regard to this particular benefit. In *Price*, the EAT said it was not 'significant' that a higher number of female applicants than of male applicants were appointed to the job. The issue, said the EAT, is whether the specific requirement or condition challenged in the case is 'more disadvantageous to women than to men'.[74] It is no defence for the employer to say that, considered as a whole, its appointment or promotion criteria do not discriminate against women. The US Supreme Court considered a similar issue in *Connecticut* v. *Teal*. There promotion to a specific job was dependent on passing a written examination. This excluded blacks in a disproportionate number. However, the result of the entire promotion process reflected no such disparate impact. The employers argued that the Court should adopt a 'bottom-line' approach, looking not at the written examination results in isolation, but at the results of the promotion procedure as a whole. The Court rejected this conclusion by a 5–4 majority, finding that there was a breach of Title VII of the Civil Rights Act. The dissenting judges argued that there was no unfavourable disparate impact on blacks. The majority replied that Title VII is concerned with the opportunity to compete on equal terms, not with equality of results. Therefore, they said, Title VII should not be read 'as requiring the focus to be placed instead on the overall number of minority or female applicants actually hired or promoted'.[75] Arbitrary barriers to equality of opportunity are unlawful irrespective of how many women (or blacks) manage to reach the goal.

The drafting of section 1(1)(b)(i) of the 1975 Act does not make easy the recognition and furtherance of its statutory purposes: to promote equality of opportunity for men and women generally by making 'unlawful practices and procedures which are fair in form but discriminatory in operation and which are not justifiable'.[76] During the Standing Committee stage of the 1975 Bill, Mr David Lane said of the drafting of the subsection that there were 'degrees of narrowness and width here and we ought to have some

---

[74] Above, n. 55 at 30.   [75] 457 US 440, 450 (1982).
[76] John Fraser, Under-Secretary of State for Employment, Standing Committee B, (22 Apr. 1975), col. 45.

clarity'.[77] Those degrees of narrowness and width remain to be fully determined by the courts.

IV

If the complainant proves that the impugned requirement or condition has a disparate impact on women, the burden shifts to the respondent to 'justify' the practice irrespective of the sex of the person to whom it is applied. In *Steel*, the EAT imposed a strict test that the employer, or other respondent, had to show that the practice was necessary, not merely convenient, and for this purpose it was relevant whether the employer could find some other, non-discriminatory method of achieving its objective.[78] The EAT said it gained assistance from the judgment in *Griggs* where the US Supreme Court held that the employer had to show that a practice which hit disproportionately at blacks was justified by reference to 'a genuine business need'.[79] The EAT remitted *Steel* to an industrial tribunal which held that to allocate postal walks by reference to seniority was not justifiable since, prior to 1975, many women had been placed at a permanent seniority disadvantage to their male colleagues by reason of direct sex discrimination.[80] In *Price*, the industrial tribunal to whom the EAT remitted the case held that the maximum age of 28 for certain jobs was not justifiable as other methods existed to enable the employer to further its aim of a balanced career structure.[81]

An industrial tribunal in *Clarke* rejected two purported justifications for an agreed redundancy procedure that provided for part-time workers to be dismissed before full-time workers. The fact that the majority of the work-force wished to apply this procedure was no justification. Nor was the fact that the procedure was commonly applied, and had been so for many years, throughout the industry.[82] The EAT upheld these findings. The concept of

[77] Standing Committee B, (24 Apr. 1975), cols. 59–60.
[78] Above, n. 56 at 186 and 188. The EAT added that 'the industrial tribunal has to weigh up the needs of the enterprise against the discriminatory effect of the requirement or condition'.
[79] Above, n. 48 at 432. [80] Above, n. 60. [81] Above, n. 58.
[82] Above, n. 71 at 138–9. The US Court of Appeals has held that avoidance of trade union pressure or agreement with a trade union cannot, of itself, justify a practice which has a disproportionate adverse impact on women or minorities under Title VII of the US Civil Rights Act: *Robinson* v. *Lorillard Corp.* 444 F 2d 791, 799 (1971).

indirect discrimination is precisely concerned with traditional practices which have long been applied without adequate regard for their disparate impact on women.[83]

The strict test of justifiability stated in *Steel* has been loosened by some later cases. In *Singh* v. *Rowntree MacKintosh Ltd* (a case under the Race Relations Act 1976 where the EAT upheld the decision of an industrial tribunal that it was justifiable in a confectionery factory for the employer to prohibit employees from wearing beards, despite the disparate impact on Sikhs), the EAT held that an employer does not need to show that the requirement or condition is 'absolutely essential'. It must be more than merely convenient; the test can be described as one of 'necessity' provided that term is 'applied reasonably and with common sense'.[84]

In *Ojutiku* v. *Manpower Services Commission*, another Race Relations Act case, the Court of Appeal considered the criterion of justifiability. Eveleigh LJ said that section 1(1)(b)(ii) does not require an employer 'to prove that the requirement is necessary for the good of his business'. He said that 'if a person produces

---

[83] However, 'to give as much reassurance as possible' the EAT indicated in *Clarke* above, n. 57 at 175, that a last-in, first-out procedure for dealing with redundancy would be justifiable under s. 1(1)(b)(ii) of the 1975 Act partly because it had for many years been the most commonly agreed criterion for selection for redundancy and partly because it would have only a 'limited discriminatory effect'. This is unconvincing. That a practice is long-standing cannot make it justifiable, as the EAT accepted in considering the practice of making part-time workers redundant before full-time workers. It is unclear how the EAT reached the conclusion that 'last-in, first-out' has only a limited discriminatory effect on women. If and when a case arises on such a point, evidence will, no doubt, be produced to show that, by reason of breaks in a career for family care reasons, women tend to have less length of service than men. It is interesting to note that during the Standing Committee debates on the 1975 Bill, John Fraser, Under-Secretary of State for Employment, gave 'last-in, first-out' on redundancy as an example of a policy which was 'justifiable' because 'it offers the fairest treatment to . . . employees': Standing Committee B, (24 Apr. 1975) at col. 71. Presumably for similar reasons, Title VII of the US Civil Rights Act 1964 specifically provides that it is not unlawful discrimination for an employer to apply a bona fide seniority system provided that it does not intend to discriminate on invidious grounds: s. 703(h) of the 1964 Act.

[84] [1979] ICR 554. However, the EAT gave no adequate explanation of why the rule was necessary, even on this weakened criterion, when the company enforced the hygiene rule in only two out of its eight factories in the United Kingdom. In a case involving very similar facts, *Panesar* v. *Nestle Co. Ltd* [1980] ICR 144, the Court of Appeal refused leave to appeal from the decision of the EAT. Lord Denning said that whether a chocolate company's rule that employees must be clean-shaven was justifiable notwithstanding its disparate impact on Sikhs was a question of fact which the industrial tribunal had decided in favour of the employer.

reasons for doing something which would be acceptable to right-thinking people as sound and tolerable reasons for so doing, then he has justified his conduct'.[85] Kerr LJ agreed that 'justifiable' is a 'perfectly easily understandable ordinary word [which] clearly applies a lower standard than the word "necessary"'. He suggested that a person justifies a practice in this context by 'advancing good grounds' for it.[86] Stephenson LJ said that the approach of the EAT in *Steel* was 'valuable as rejecting justification by convenience and requiring the party applying the discriminatory condition to prove it to be justifiable in all the circumstances on balancing its discriminatory effect against the discriminator's need for it. But that need is what is reasonably needed by the party who applies the condition . . .' He suggested that the question is whether the defendant has 'good and adequate reasons' for applying the impugned condition.[87] In *Clarke*, the EAT concluded that the Court of Appeal in *Ojutiku* was applying the same test as the EAT in previous cases: 'was it right and proper in the circumstances to adopt the requirement?'[88]

The test of justifiability under the Race Relations Act was again considered in *Mandla* v. *Dowell Lee*. A Sikh boy was refused admission to a school because he wore a turban and the headmaster declined to allow pupils to do so. The Court of Appeal held that Sikhs are not a racial group for the purposes of the 1976 Act so the indirect discrimination provisions did not apply. The court further suggested that, in any event, there was no unlawful discrimination in this case. Lord Denning said that the defendant headmaster was not 'at fault in any way. He was not unfair or unreasonable. It is for him to run his school in the way he feels best. He was not guilty of any discrimination against the Sikhs, direct or indirect.'[89] Oliver LJ gave a quite extraordinary judgment in which he described the defendant headmaster as 'entirely blameless' and attacked the use of the law against the defendant 'as an engine of oppression'. Oliver LJ, like Lord Denning, did not analyse the concept of justifiability under section 1(1)(b) but he said that he was 'far from persuaded' that the condition was not justifiable.[90] Kerr LJ criticized the Commission for Racial Equality (which had supported the case against the headmaster) for what he described as 'harassment of this head-

---

[85] [1982] ICR 661, 667–8. [86] Ibid. at 670. [87] Ibid. at 674.
[88] Above, n. 57 at 174. [89] [1983] QB 1, 13. [90] Ibid. at 17–18.

master'. His comment on the application of section 1(1)(b)—that
'[i]f persons wish to insist on wearing bathing suits, then they
cannot reasonably insist on admission to a nudist colony'—does
not significantly advance understanding of anti-discrimination law.
He declined to decide whether the headmaster's conduct was
'justifiable'. But he concluded that the headmaster 'is entitled to
decide for himself how his school should be run in relation to the
wearing of turbans by his pupils'.[91]

The House of Lords unanimously overturned this remarkably
illiberal judgment of the Court of Appeal. The Law Lords held
that Sikhs are a racial group defined by reference to their ethnic
origins and are therefore protected against direct and indirect
discrimination under the Race Relations Act 1976. They further
said that the criticisms expressed in the Court of Appeal as to the
conduct of the Commission for Racial Equality in supporting the
proceedings against the headmaster were 'entirely unjustified'.[92]
The Law Lords held that the headmaster's practice was unlawful
indirect discrimination: it had a disparate impact on Sikhs and it
was unjustifiable. Lord Fraser, with whom the others agreed,
noted that '[r]egarded purely from the point of view of the respondent [headmaster, the rule] was no doubt perfectly justifiable'.
But this did not suffice: the test is objective, not subjective. Lord
Fraser said that the explanations given by the headmaster— he did
not intend to discriminate, it was a multi-racial school, and he
would find difficulty in explaining to non-Sikh pupils why the rules
about wearing correct school uniform should be relaxed only in
favour of Sikhs—'could not, either individually or collectively,
provide a sufficient justification' under section 1(1)(b)(ii). The
headmaster could not rely on his objections to the wearing of the
turban as an outward manifestation of a non-Christian faith. This
was a purported justification incompatible with the statute which
recognizes only a justification 'irrespective' of a person's colour,
race, nationality, or ethnic or national origins. Lord Fraser added
that it is a question of fact in each case whether or not justification
has been shown.[93] Lord Templeman added that '[t]he discrimina-

---

[91] Ibid. at 21, 24–5.　　　　[92] Above, n. 66 at 567.

[93] Ibid. at 566–7. Lord Fraser said, at 566, that 'irrespective of' here meant
'without regard to'. On the meaning of this phrase under the Race Relations Act
1976 see also *Orphanos* v. *Queen Mary College* [1985] 2 WLR 703 (House of
Lords).

tion cannot be justified by a genuine belief that the school would provide a better system of education if it were allowed to discriminate.'[94]

The Appellate Committee of the House of Lords gave little general guidance in *Mandla* v. *Lee* on the application of section 1(1)(b)(ii). In *Clarke*, Mr Justice Browne-Wilkinson pointed out on behalf of the EAT that '[o]n emotive matters such as racial or sex discrimination there is no generally accepted view as to the comparative importance of eliminating discriminatory practices on the one hand as against, for example, the profitability of a business on the other'. The EAT emphasized that to leave the application of the criterion of justifiability to the unfettered discretion of industrial tribunals throughout the country in employment cases, encouraging them to treat complex issues as questions of fact, would be likely to lead only to different standards being applied in different areas of the country with arbitrary consequences. What is needed is an authoritative statement of 'how to strike the balance between the discriminatory effect of a requirement on the one hand and the reasons urged as justification for imposing it on the other'.[95]

Our courts have not adopted the approach of US courts interpreting the Civil Rights Act 1964, that to justify a practice having a disparate impact on women (or blacks) one must point to 'an irresistible demand' from business (or other) necessity.[96] During the passage of the Sex Discrimination Bill 1975, amendments to replace 'justifiable' by 'necessary' in clause 1(1)(b)(ii) were defeated in the Standing Committee[97] and in the House of

[94] Ibid. at 570.

[95] Above, n. 57 at 174–5. One cannot leave the development of the criterion of justifiability to industrial tribunals 'in an area where no consensus exists among tribunal members, even less a social consensus': B. A. Hepple, 'Judging Equal Rights' (1983) *Current Legal Problems* 71, 83. In *Home Office* v. *Holmes* above, n. 59 at 684–5, however, the EAT indicated its reluctance to state general principles. This is an unhelpful approach. It fails to provide necessary guidance to employers, employees, and industrial tribunals, and it threatens to produce inconsistent decisions.

[96] *US* v. *Bethlehem Steel Corp.* 446 F 2d 652, 662 (US Court of Appeals: 1971). See also *Robinson* v. *Lorillard Corp.* above, n. 82 at 798: 'the business purpose must be sufficiently compelling to override any racial impact; the challenged practice must effectively carry out the business purpose it is alleged to serve; and there must be available no acceptable alternative policies or practices which would better accomplish the business purpose advanced, or accomplish it equally well with a lesser differential racial impact.'

[97] Standing Committee B, (24 Apr. 1975), cols. 79–80.

Lords.[98] Still, courts should strive for an interpretation of the subsection which has 'sympathy with the spirit and intent of the Act'.[99] Parliament has placed the burden of proof on a defendant seeking to justify a requirement or condition which has a disparate impact on women, and Parliament has stated a strict test by the use of the word 'justifiable' rather than merely 'reasonable' or 'convenient'. It is clear that section 1(1)(b)(ii) requires the weighing of reasons advanced for the impugned practice against the discriminatory impact. To explain a practice is not necessarily to justify it. There is an objective, not a subjective test. In making indirect sex discrimination unlawful, Parliament intended to deal with precisely those practices which have long been continued (usually for rational reasons) without regard to their disparate impact on women and without consideration of alternative means of achieving legitimate objectives not creating such a disparate impact. Policies having such an impact are unlikely to satisfy the test of justifiability where alternative programmes could be used to achieve the same goal. Nor is a policy having a disparate impact on women likely to be justifiable unless it appreciably advances a significant goal of the respondent. To invalidate practices that do not pass these tests will not impose serious burdens on employers and other defendants. But it will play an important part in eliminating arbitrary barriers to equal opportunity for the sexes.

If the complainant proves that a requirement or condition has a disparate impact on women, and if the respondent is unable to justify the practice, it is then for the complainant to satisfy the final limb of the concept of indirect discrimination: she must show under section 1(1)(b)(iii) that the practice is to her detriment because she cannot comply with it.

As an industrial tribunal suggested in *Meeks* v. *National Union of Agricultural and Allied Workers*, by including section 1(1)(b)(iii) in the 1975 Act 'Parliament wanted to ensure that only actual victims of indirect discrimination could complain . . .'[100] Originally the definition of indirect discrimination in the Bill contained no such sub-clause. Rather it spoke of 'an unfavourable' requirement

---

[98] 362 HL 1020 (14 July 1975). Section 2(c) of the Irish Employment Equality Act 1977 prohibits requirements which have a disparate impact on women unless they can be shown to be 'essential'.

[99] *Price* above, n. 55 at 31. See also *Steel* above, n. 56 at 185 on 'the spirit of the Act'.

[100] [1976] IRLR 198, 201.

or condition. An amendment to remove those words was carried during the Standing Committee debates.[101] At the Report Stage in the House of Commons, the Government carried an amendment to add what is now section 1(1)(b)(iii). Mr John Fraser, Under-Secretary of State for Employment, explained that the addition was needed because 'there must be a particular victim of indirect discrimination'.[102]

In *Steel*, the EAT held that the time to consider whether there is a detriment 'is that at which the requirement or condition has to be fulfilled, and it is irrelevant that in the fullness of time the complainant would or might be able to' comply with it.[103] Similarly, it is irrelevant that the complainant would or might have been able to comply at an earlier date, or could have now been in a position to comply had she made a different choice at an earlier date.[104]

Section 1(1)(b)(iii) does not require the complainant to show that but for the impugned requirement or condition she would have been appointed to the job or received the other benefit (or avoided the other detriment) at issue. Section 1(1)(b) is concerned to ensure fair consideration of individuals for the relevant opportunities or disadvantages.[105] The language of 'compliance' in section 1(1)(b)(iii) is vague and unhelpful in this respect.[106] Although the complainant needs to show that she has suffered a detriment[107] under section 1(1)(b)(iii), the failure to consider her

---

[101] Standing Committee B, (24 Apr. 1975), cols. 79–80.

[102] 893 HC 1491–2.(18 June 1975).

[103] Above, n.56 at 186. In *Clarke* above, n. 57 at 172 the EAT confirmed that 'the relevant point of time at which the ability or inability to comply has to be shown is the date on which the applicant alleges she has suffered detriment. This is in fact the same point in time' as the date when the requirement or condition has to be fulfilled. See above, n. 70.

[104] See *Bohon-Mitchell* v. *Common Professional Examination Board and Council of Legal Education* [1978] IRLR 525, 530, a decision of an industrial tribunal under the Race Relations Act 1976.

[105] See Laurence Lustgarten *Legal Control of Racial Discrimination* (1980) at 51.

[106] See the complicated case of *Watches of Switzerland Ltd* v. *Savell* above n. 57 where the EAT held that the complainant had not satisfied s. 1(1)(b)(iii). 'Cannot comply' in s. 1(1)(b)(iii) must be the corollary of 'can comply' in s. 1(1)(b)(i) and should be interpreted accordingly: see above nn. 64–6 for the meaning of 'can comply'.

[107] In *Ministry of Defence* v. *Jeremiah* above, n. 3 the Court of Appeal considered the meaning of 'detriment' under s. 6(2)(b) of the 1975 Act, which makes it unlawful to discriminate against an employee by dismissing her or subjecting her to 'any other detriment'. Brandon LJ said this means 'putting under a

on fair terms suffices, whether or not she would have been selected for the relevant opportunity if considered on fair terms.

The concept of indirect sex discrimination, although complex, is of vital importance in helping to achieve equal opportunity for women in the employment and other fields covered by the 1975 Act. Its importance is due to its ability to challenge traditional practices which, in their impact, disadvantage women, whether or not the respondent intended its practices to have such an effect.[108]

V

The Sex Discrimination Act 1975 also makes it unlawful to discriminate, directly or indirectly, against a married person of either sex on the ground of his or her marital status. Parliament thought that marital discrimination, as defined in section 3 of the Act, was, intentionally or unintentionally, the cause of many of the barriers to equal opportunities for the sexes.[109]

However, there are two major limitations on the utility of this concept of discrimination under the 1975 Act. Marital discrimination is only made unlawful in the context of employment, and not in the contexts of education and the provision of goods, facilities, services, and premises. Moreover, the Act only prohibits discrimination against a married person. A woman denied a job because she is unmarried (or perhaps because she is divorced) has no protection (unless she can prove sex discrimination under section 1 of the 1975 Act).[110] The 1975 Act needs amendment to cover all the contexts included in the statute, not merely employment, and to

---

disadvantage': p. 26. Brightman LJ added that 'a detriment exists if a reasonable worker would or might take the view that the duty was in all the circumstances to his detriment': p. 31. In *Home Office* v. *Holmes* above, n. 59 at 683, the EAT said that the same disadvantage to the complainant may be relied on to found the detriment under s. 1 as to satisfy the test of detriment under s. 6.

[108] *Perera* v. *Civil Service Commission* above, n. 68 at 355–6 (EAT).

[109] Dr Shirley Summerskill, Under-Secretary of State for the Home Department, Standing Committee B (24 Apr. 1975), col. 88

[110] In *Bick* v. *Royal West of England Residential School for the Deaf* [1976] IRLR 326, an industrial tribunal held that a woman dismissed from her job because she was engaged to be married had no protection under s. 3 as it is concerned with discrimination against married persons. The complainant would have succeeded in a claim under s. 1(1)(a) read with s. 1(2) showing direct sex discrimination if she could have shown that a male employee would not have been dismissed because he was engaged to be married: see above, n. 6.

cover discrimination against any person, married or not, on the ground of any marital status.

Section 3 covers direct discrimination (treating a married person less favourably on the ground of his or her marital status than one would treat an unmarried person of the same sex) and indirect discrimination (applying a requirement or condition which has a disparate impact on married persons compared with unmarried persons of the same sex, which is to the detriment of the complainant because he or she cannot comply with it, and which the employer cannot show to be justifiable). In *Hurley* v. *Mustoe*, the EAT held that an employer had indirectly discriminated contrary to section 3 by refusing to employ persons with small children. The employer could not justify the policy (which had a disparate impact on married persons compared with unmarried persons) by reference to its wish only to employ reliable people. This was because '[t]here are other means whereby the reliability of any applicant can be tested'.[111]

VI

The 1975 Act also makes it unlawful to discriminate by way of victimization. Section 4 defines victimization to mean treating someone less favourably in one of the contexts covered by the 1975 Act because he or she has asserted a right contained in or otherwise acted by reference to the provisions of the 1975 Act or the Equal Pay Act 1970. Victimization is prohibited where the less favourable treatment is by reason of the fact that the person victimized has brought proceedings against the discriminator or any other person under the 1975 or 1970 Acts; or has given evidence or information in connection with proceedings under those Acts; or has otherwise done something under or by reference to those Acts; or has alleged that the discriminator or any other person has committed an act which (whether or not the allegation so states) would amount to a breach of those Acts; or by reason of the fact that the discriminator knows the victimized

---

[111] Above, n. 42 at 495. See similarly *Thorndyke* v. *Bell Fruit (North Central) Ltd* [1979] IRLR 1 (industrial tribunal). See above, nn. 39–44 on such stereotyped assumptions and direct sex discrimination.

person intends to do any of these things or suspects that he or she has done or intends to do any of them.[112]

Section 4 only makes it unlawful to victimize someone by adverse treatment of them in the contexts of employment, education, or the provision of goods, services, facilities, and premises covered by the 1975 and 1970 Acts. So section 4 gives no protection against general abuse or detriments inflicted because a person has acted under or by reference to the 1975 or 1970 Acts. This seriously reduces the value of section 4.[113]

In *Kirby* v. *Manpower Services Commission*, a case under the Race Relations Act 1976, the EAT adopted a narrow approach to the concept of victimization. The complainant was employed at a job centre. He received confidential information in the course of his employment showing that prospective employers were discriminating on racial grounds against potential employees. He reported this to the local Council for Community Relations. He was moved to another job within the job centre, away from confidential information, by reason of making these disclosures. The EAT held that he had not been unlawfully victimized since he had been treated in the same way as the employers would treat anyone else in their employment who disclosed confidential information.[114]

The victimization provisions are presumably intended to give special statutory protection to persons who take action under or by

---

[112] A person is not protected against victimization if they suffer the treatment complained of 'by reason of any allegation made by him if the allegation was false and not made in good faith': s. 4(2) of the 1975 Act. On the concept of victimization see *British Airways Engine Overhaul Ltd* v. *Francis* [1981] ICR 278. A female employee was reprimanded by the employers for making a public statement about company affairs in breach of staff regulations. The EAT held that she had no claim under s. 4 because there was no suggestion in her statement that the company or her trade union had breached the 1975 or 1970 Acts.

[113] Section 94 of the Sex Discrimination Act 1984 (Australia) prohibits victimization, which consists of subjecting, or threatening to subject, a person 'to any detriment' for reasons related to action under the Act, unless he or she made a false allegation in bad faith. See similarly s. 50 of the New South Wales Anti-Discrimination Act 1977 which makes it unlawful to subject another person 'to any detriment in any circumstances on the ground that' he or she has acted by reference to anti-discrimination law, unless he or she made a false allegation in bad faith. The problem with broadening the victimization provision is to avoid making it unlawful for people to treat another adversely in wholly private or personal contexts, for example one person declining to remain on friendly terms with another because the latter has made a complaint against that person under anti-discrimination law.

[114] [1980] ICR 420.

reference to anti-discrimination law. Those provisions are not merely intended to ensure that a person who so acts is treated as favourably as an employee who acts in a similar way in a context where there is no statutory protection. If *Kirby* is correct, an employer does not breach the 1975 Act (though there would be a strong claim for unfair dismissal assuming the employee had served the appropriate qualifying period) if it dismisses an employee for bringing proceedings under the 1975 Act so long as it can show that it would so dismiss any employee who brings legal action against the employer. If that is the law, section 4 needs amendment to give protection to those who are subjected to a detriment because they act (or threaten to act or are believed to act) by reference to the 1975 and 1970 Acts.

3

THE SCOPE OF THE SEX DISCRIMINATION ACT 1975: SUBSTANCE AND PROCEDURE

I

Discrimination, as defined in sections 1–5 of the 1975 Act, is only unlawful if it occurs in one of the fields covered by the Act.[1] The 1975 Act prohibits discrimination in the fields of employment, education, and the provision of goods, services, facilities, and premises.

II

Section 6 of the Act makes it unlawful for a person to discriminate in relation to employment by it at an establishment[2] in Great Britain. It may not discriminate against applicants for jobs[3] in the arrangements[4] made for the purpose of determining who to employ, in the terms on which it offers employment, or by refusing or deliberately omitting to offer someone the employment. As the Employment Appeal Tribunal stated in *Brennan* v. *J. H. Dewhurst Ltd*, '[t]he policy of section 6 is to ensure that at all stages in

---

[1] *R.* v. *Immigration Appeal Tribunal ex parte Ahluwalia* [1979–80] Imm AR 1,7 per Eveleigh LJ for the Divisional Court, cited with approval by the Court of Appeal in *R.* v. *Immigration Appeal Tribunal ex parte Kassam* [1980] 1 WLR 1037, 1041 (per Stephenson LJ) and 1043 (per Ackner LJ) and approved by the House of Lords in *R.* v. *Entry Clearance Officer, Bombay ex parte Amin* [1983] 2 AC 818, 833 (per Lord Fraser) and 841 (per Lord Scarman). See ch. 2 on the definitions of discrimination in ss. 1–5.

[2] See s. 10 of the 1975 Act for guidance on the meaning of an 'establishment in Great Britain'. See also ch. 4 n. 8 and ch. 9 p. 252.

[3] S. 6(1).

[4] In *Brennan* v. *J. H. Dewhurst Ltd* [1984] ICR 52, the EAT held that s. 6(1) covers arrangements made for the purpose of determining who should be offered an employment vacancy if they discriminate against a woman even though they were not made for that purpose. However, s. 6(1) does not cover in 'arrangements' an *ad hoc* decision by a person conducting an interview to ask particular questions or to approach the matter in a particular way. Expressions to the contrary in the industrial tribunal decision in *Roadburg* v. *Lothian Regional Council* [1976] IRLR 283 were disapproved. On questions asked at an interview see also below, n. 151.

applying for and obtaining employment the woman is on an equal footing with a man in her ability to obtain the job'.[5] Nor may the employer discriminate against a woman employed by it[6] in the way it affords her access to opportunities for promotion, transfer, or training, or to any other benefits, facilities, or services,[7] or by refusing or deliberately omitting to afford her access to them, or by dismissing her or subjecting her to any other detriment.[8]

The 1975 Act broadly defines 'employment'.[9] It covers employment under a contract of service (or apprenticeship), the standard definition of an employee adopted in employment protection legislation.[10] But it also covers employment under a contract personally to execute any work or labour. Parliament thereby prohibited discrimination by the employer not only against employees but also against independent contractors engaged personally to carry out specific work or labour.[11]

---

[5] *Brennan* v. *J. H. Dewhurst Ltd* [1984] ICR 52, 57.   [6] S. 6(2).

[7] A refusal to investigate complaints of unfair treatment may amount to a refusal of access to a benefit, facility, or service: *Eke* v. *Commissioners of Customs and Excise* [1981] IRLR 334, 336 (EAT on the Race Relations Act 1976). Note *Hishon* v. *King & Spalding* 104 S Ct 2229 (1984) where the US Supreme Court held that if an employer refused to promote an employee to a partnership because of her sex, this could amount to unlawful sex discrimination in relation to the 'terms, conditions or privileges of employment' contrary to Title VII of the US Civil Rights Act 1964.

[8] On 'subjecting her to any other detriment' see the Court of Appeal decision in *Ministry of Defence* v. *Jeremiah* [1980] ICR 13 at 26 where Brandon LJ said it means 'putting under a disadvantage' and at 31 where Brightman LJ said 'a detriment exists if a reasonable worker would or might take the view that the duty was in all the circumstances to his detriment'. See, similarly, *Kirby* v. *Manpower Services Commission* [1980] ICR 420, 428–9 (EAT). In *BL Cars Ltd* v. *Brown* [1983] ICR 143, the EAT held that the circulation of instructions to security officers to question black employees before allowing them off the premises (because the employers believed that a black employee was responsible for a theft) could amount to a detriment under the analogous section of the Race Relations Act 1976. The EAT said that the question depended upon all the facts and circumstances and could not be decided by a preliminary hearing on a point of law. In *De Souza* v. *Automobile Association* (*The Times* 27 Oct. 1984) the EAT held that for a manager to use a term of racial abuse in relation to a black employee did not, of itself, amount to 'any other detriment' under the Race Relations Act 1976.

[9] S. 82(1) of the Sex Discrimination Act 1975. There are similar definitions in s. 1(6) of the Equal Pay Act 1970 and in s. 78(1) of the Race Relations Act 1976.

[10] S. 153(1) Employment Protection (Consolidation) Act 1978.

[11] See *Hugh-Jones* v. *St John's College, Cambridge* [1979] ICR 848 (EAT); *Knight* v. *A.-G.* [1979] ICR 194 (EAT); *Tanna* v. *Post Office* [1981] ICR 374 (EAT on the Race Relations Act 1976); *Daley* v. *Allied Suppliers Ltd* [1983] ICR 90 (EAT on the Race Relations Act 1976); *Quinnen* v. *Hovells* [1984] ICR 525 where Waite J. for the EAT said, at 531, that the 'concept of a contract for the

Discrimination by an employer is not covered by the 1975 Act where it concerns benefits such as the payment of money where the provision of those benefits is regulated by a contract of employment. This is because of a series of complicated provisions[12] designed to ensure that such matters are decided under the Equal Pay Act 1970.[13] Lord Denning described the task of construing these provisions as 'like fitting together a jigsaw puzzle. The pieces are all jumbled up together in two boxes. One is labelled the Sex Discrimination Act 1975. The other, the Equal Pay Act 1970. You pick up a piece from one box and try to fit it in. It does not. So you try a piece from the other box. That does not fit either . . . You will not find the missing pieces unless you are very discriminating.'[14]

Section 6 states some exceptions to the principle of no discrimination in employment. It is not unlawful to discriminate in employment for the purposes of a private household.[15] There is also a 'small employers' exception. It is not unlawful to discriminate where the number of persons employed by the employer (added to the number employed by any associated employer)[16] does not

engagement of personal work or labour lying outside the scope of a master–servant relationship is a wide and flexible one, intended by Parliament in our judgment to be interpreted as such . . . [T]hose who engage, even cursorily, the talents, skill or labour of the self-employed are wise to ensure that the terms are equal as between men and women and do not discriminate between them.' See also *Mirror Group of Newspapers Ltd* v. *Gunning* [1984] ICR 706, 714, where the EAT said: 'It is not . . . a matter either of saying on the one hand that the least element of personal involvement required in the execution of work or labour of any description will automatically bring a contract within the definition, or of saying on the other hand that only in cases where the contract is exclusively for work and labour which the contracting party is bound to carry out in his own person can the definition be satisfied. Every case will depend upon its particular facts.'

[12] Ss. 6(5), 6(6), 8(3), 8(4), and 8(5) of the 1975 Act. See also s. 6(7), which provides that s. 6(2) does not apply to certain benefits, facilities, or services if the employer is concerned with the provision (for payment or not) of benefits, facilities, or services of that description to the public or to a section of the public including the employee in question.   [13] See ch. 4.

[14] *Shields* v. *E. Coomes (Holdings) Ltd* [1978] ICR 1159, 1168. Bridge LJ agreed, at 1178, that '[t]he particular provisions designed to prevent overlapping between the two statutes are complex, and it may often be difficult to determine whether a particular matter of complaint falls to be redressed under one Act or the other.' On this overlap, and the necessity of bringing the claim under the correct Act, see *Oliver* v. *J. P. Malnick & Co. (no. 2)* [1984] ICR 458 (Industrial Tribunal).

[15] S. 6(3)(a). (Discrimination in this context is, however, unlawful if it amounts to victimization, on which see ch. 2 s. VI.) See *Heron Corporation Ltd* v. *Commis* [1980] ICR 713 (EAT) on the analogous provision in the Race Relations Act 1976.

[16] On the meaning of an 'associated employer' see s. 82(2) and see *EOC* v. *Robertson* [1980] IRLR 44 (Industrial Tribunal).

exceed five (disregarding any persons employed for the purpose of a private household).[17] The European Court of Justice held in 1983 that the blanket exclusion of employment in a private household or by a small employer contravened the EEC Equal Treatment Directive.[18]

It is not a breach of the 1975 Act for the employer to discriminate concerning 'provision in relation to death or retirement', for example pension benefits provided by the employer for employees.[19] Section 7 of the 1975 Act provides for exceptions to the principle of no sex discrimination by employers when sex is a 'genuine occupational qualification' for the job.[20] The 1975 Act also contains specific exceptions to the principle of no sex discrimination in employment in relation to the employment of mineworkers below ground,[21] the employment of ministers of religion (where the doctrines of the religion or the religious susceptibilities of a significant number of its followers would not accept a female, or a male, minister),[22] height requirements for male and female prison officers,[23] and height, uniform, or equipment requirements for police officers.[24] The 1975 Act originally contained an exemption validating sex discrimination in relation to the employment of men as midwives.[25] A few days before the United Kingdom was to be brought before the European Court of Justice to be charged with breaching the EEC

[17] S. 6(3)(b). (Discrimination in this context is, however, unlawful if it amounts to victimization, on which see ch. 2 s. VI.) See *Oliver* v. *J. P. Malnick & Co.* [1983] ICR 708 (EAT). The Race Relations Act 1976 does not have a small employer exception.

[18] *Commission of the European Communities* v. *United Kingdom* [1984] ICR 192. See ch. 5 n. 43.

[19] S. 6(4) of the 1975 Act. See similarly s. 6(1A)(b) of the Equal Pay Act 1970 in ch. 4 n. 112. See also ch. 7 nn. 79–81. See ch. 5 nn. 13–18 and nn. 51–55 on the impact of Community Law in this context. Similar exclusions of death and retirement benefits are contained in s. 11(4) on partnerships and s. (12)4 on trade unions and other organizations.

[20] See ch. 9.

[21] S. 21. American women have long been accepted as part of the work force in mines: see Aidan White, 'An Underground Movement' *The Guardian* 12 Mar. 1982.

[22] S. 19. In any event, note *President of the Methodist Conference* v. *Parfitt* [1984] ICR 176, where the Court of Appeal held that because of the spiritual nature of the relationship between a minister and his Church, the arrangements made between them were non-contractual, so he could not bring a claim for unfair dismissal.

[23] S. 18.   [24] S. 17(3).   [25] S. 20.

Equal Treatment Directive in this respect, the Government announced that the law would be changed. It is now unlawful for employers to discriminate against men in relation to employment as a midwife.[26] Ironically, the ECJ found that the unamended 1975 Act did not, in fact, contravene EEC law in this respect.[27]

The 'employment context' within which the 1975 Act applies covers more than employers. It also makes it unlawful for discrimination to be carried out by a firm of six or more partners;[28] by trade unions, organizations of employers (or any other organization whose members carry on a particular profession or trade for the purposes of which the organization exists);[29] by a body which confers an authorization or qualification which is needed for, or which facilitates, engagement in a particular profession or trade;[30] by vocational training bodies;[31] by employment agencies;[32] by the Manpower Services Commission;[33] or by a principal against contract workers.[34] The 1975 Act expressly

---

[26] Sex Discrimination Act 1975 (Amendment of Section 20) Order 1983 SI no. 1202. See Lawrence Stone, *The Family, Sex and Marriage in England 1500–1800* (1977), 73 on the eighteenth-century phenomenon of 'the growing profession of male midwives, whose rise in numbers and popularity was looked upon with deep suspicion both by the ignorant female midwives, whose livelihoods were threatened by their advent, and also by their professional medical colleagues, who associated the trade with that of abortionists'.

[27] *Commission of the European Communities* v. *United Kingdom* above, n. 18. See ch. 5 n. 42.   [28] S. 11.   [29] S. 12.

[30] S. 13. 'Profession' and 'trade' are defined in s. 82(1). In *British Judo Association* v. *Petty* [1981] ICR 660, 664 the EAT held that s. 13 'covers all cases where the qualification in fact facilitates the woman's employment, whether or not it is intended by the authority or body which confers the authorisation or qualification so to do'. The EAT added that s. 13 does not require the complainant actually to prove that the discriminatory term has in fact prejudiced his or her job prospects. Where there is a pre-entry closed shop, a trade union may be a qualifying body for the purposes of s. 13: *Record Production Chapel, Sogat* v. *Turnbull* (16 Apr. 1984: EAT in Scotland).

[31] S. 14.

[32] S. 15. S. 82(1) defines an employment agency to mean 'a person who, for profit or not, provides services for the purpose of finding employment for workers or supplying employers with workers'. In *CRE* v. *Imperial Society of Teachers of Dancing* [1983] ICR 473, 475 the EAT held that a school which was asked to provide a school leaver to fill an employment vacancy was an employment agency under the analogous provision of the Race Relations Act 1976. Where there is a pre-entry closed shop, a trade union may be an employment agency for the purposes of s. 15: *Record Production Chapel, Sogat* v. *Turnbull* above, n. 30. On the application of s. 15, see also *Rice* v. *Fon-A-Car* [1980] ICR 133 (EAT).

[33] S. 16.

[34] S. 9. In *Rice* v. *Fon-A-Car* above, n. 32 at p. 136 the EAT held that it was not sufficient for the purposes of s. 9 'merely that work shall be done by one person for

provides that police officers are treated as employed for the purposes of protection against sex discrimination,[35] by contrast with their treatment under general employment protection legislation.[36]

III

The second main context in which the 1975 Act applies is education. It is unlawful for a body responsible for an educational establishment to discriminate against a woman in the terms on which it offers to admit her as a pupil or by refusing or deliberately omitting to accept her application for admission. It is unlawful for such a person to discriminate against a pupil in the way it affords her access to any benefits, facilities, or services or by refusing or deliberately omitting to allow her access to them, or by excluding her from the establishment or by subjecting her to any other detriment.[37]

Local Education Authorities and other responsible bodies have similar duties in relation to educational opportunities provided by

the benefit of someone else unless there is an undertaking under the contract to supply the worker'. See also *Daley* v. *Allied Suppliers Ltd* above, n. 11 where the EAT held that the analogous provision in the Race Relations Act 1976 did not make the Manpower Services Commission liable for discrimination by a company to whom the complainant had been sent as a trainee.

[35] S. 17(1). See *de Launay* v. *Commissioner of Police of the Metropolis*, an industrial tribunal decision in 1983 that the police force had unlawfully discriminated against and unlawfully victimized a woman police officer in breach of the 1975 Act. Also in 1983 a report of the Police Studies Institute revealed that there was widespread sex discrimination within the Metropolitan Police which was operating an illegal 10 per cent quota on the entry of women into the force: see Malcolm Dean, 'Met Finds Itself with No Grounds for an Appeal' *The Guardian* 28 Dec. 1983.

[36] S. 146 of the Employment Protection (Consolidation) Act 1978.

[37] S. 22. See above nn. 7–8 on the meaning of benefits and detriment. In *Whitfield* v. *London Borough of Croydon* (unreported, Croydon County Court, 1979), Judge Perks held that a school's policy of providing a craftwork course only for boys and a home economics course only for girls was not unlawful sex discrimination contrary to the 1975 Act. This aspect of the decision would not have been upheld on appeal. The Secretary of State has power under s. 24 to designate for the purposes of para. 5 of the table in s. 22 establishments the governing bodies of which have a duty not to discriminate contrary to s. 22. See the Sex Discrimination (Designated Educational Establishments) Order 1975 SI no. 1902 and the Sex Discrimination (Designated Educational Establishments) (Wales) Order 1975 SI no. 2113 as amended by the Sex Discrimination (Designated Educational Establishments) (Amendment) Order 1980 SI no. 1860.

them.[38] Single-sex establishments are exempt from the duty not to discriminate in admissions policies. A single-sex establishment is one which admits pupils of one sex only, or whose admission of pupils of the opposite sex is 'exceptional', or which admits pupils of the opposite sex 'whose numbers are comparatively small and whose admission is confined to particular courses of instruction or teaching classes'. A school which is not a single-sex establishment may lawfully discriminate in relation to the admission of boarders, and the provision of boarding facilities, where it admits only pupils of one sex, or where the numbers of pupils of the opposite sex who are admitted 'are comparatively small'.[39] There are special transitional provisions for a single-sex establishment which turns co-educational.[40]

The 1975 Act also exempts from the provisions prohibiting sex discrimination in education any further education course in physical training or any course designed for teachers of physical training.[41]

IV

The third main context in which the 1975 Act applies is in the provision of goods, facilities, services, and premises to the public or a section of the public.

Section 29(1) of the Act makes it unlawful for any person concerned with the provision (for payment or not) of goods, facilities, or services to the public or a section of the public to discriminate against a woman who seeks to obtain or use them either by refusing or deliberately omitting to provide her with them at all or in the same manner and on the same terms as are normal in relation to men.

The reference in section 29(1) to what is 'normal' clearly indicates that the section is not intended to deal with a person who provides things on an isolated occasion, but rather with a person who holds itself out as engaged regularly, or at least recurrently, in

---

[38] Ss. 23 and 25.
[39] S. 26.
[40] S. 27.
[41] S. 28. Note also s. 36(5) which exempts most educational benefits, facilities, or services outside Gt Britain.

the activity.[42] The 1975 Act provides no definition of 'goods', 'facilities', or 'services'. These words should, therefore, be given their ordinary and natural meaning: 'goods' cover any movable property; 'facilities' include any opportunity for obtaining a benefit; 'services' refer to work done for or benefits conferred on another.[43]

Section 29(2) does give 'examples' of the facilities and services (but not the goods) covered by section 29(1); access to and use of any place which members of the public or a section of the public are permitted to enter (such as public lavatories, parks, offices, and shops); accommodation in a hotel, boarding-house, or similar establishment; banking and insurance facilities, or other facilities for grants, loans, credit, or finance (for example, mortgages); facilities for education (for example, a dancing-school or a language class);[44] facilities for entertainment, recreation, or refreshment (such as a cinema, theatre, or restaurant); facilities for transport or travel; the services of any profession or trade,[45] or any local or other public authority. Section 29(1) therefore can be seen to have a broad scope. The examples given in section 29(2) are 'self-evidently not intended to be exhaustive'.[46]

Section 29(1) has been applied in relation to credit facilities provided by a department store to its customers;[47] the refusal of a

---

[42] See *Dockers' Labour Club and Institute Ltd* v. *Race Relations Board* [1976] AC 285, 297 per Lord Diplock on the analogous provision in the Race Relations Act 1968. Similarly *Applin* v. *Race Relations Board* [1975] AC 259, 271 per Lord Reid.

[43] See *Shorter Oxford English Dictionary*. See also Anthony Lester and Geoffrey Bindman, *Race and Law* (1972), 260.

[44] Cf. s. 2(2) of the Race Relations Act 1968 which referred to 'facilities for education, instruction or training'.

[45] Cf. s. 2(2) of the Race Relations Act 1968 which referred to 'the services of any business, profession or trade . . .'.

[46] *Applin* v. *Race Relations Board* above, n. 42 at 291 per Lord Simon on the analogous provision in the Race Relations Act 1968. He said that the section was 'setting out some of the most easily envisageable and most derogatory forms of discrimination'. In *R.* v. *Entry Clearance Officer, Bombay, ex parte Amin* above, n. 1, Lord Fraser, at 834, said that 'the examples in s. 29(2) are not exhaustive, but they are . . . useful pointers to aid in the construction of subsection (1)'. Lord Scarman, at 842, said that 'section 29(2) does no more than give examples of facilities and services. It is certainly not intended to be exhaustive.'

[47] *Quinn* v. *Williams Furniture Ltd* [1981] ICR 328. The Court of Appeal held that there was a breach of the 1975 Act by the store refusing credit facilities to a woman customer unless her husband signed a guarantee form, when a comparable male customer would not have been asked to provide his wife as a guarantor. Lord Denning said, at 333, that '[b]y requiring—or even suggesting or advising—that she

wine-bar to serve women unless they were sitting at a table and not if they were standing at the bar;[48] the refusal of a friendly society to allow female members to be elected to the governing body of the society.[49]

The scope of section 29(1) has been unjustifiably restricted by two decisions in the context of immigration law: the House of Lords decision in *R.* v. *Entry Clearance Officer, Bombay ex parte Amin*[50] and the Court of Appeal decision in *R.* v. *Immigration Appeal Tribunal ex parte Kassam.*[51]

Mrs Amin was, until the coming into force of the British Nationality Act 1981, a citizen of the United Kingdom and Colonies. (By reason of the 1981 Act she became a British Overseas Citizen). Prior to the enactment of the Commonwealth Immigrants Act 1968, Mrs Amin, and others like her, enjoyed the right of unrestricted entry into the United Kingdom. The 1968 Act removed that right. Lord Fraser said this was because 'the influx became difficult to absorb'.[52] The European Commission of Human Rights described the 1968 Act in less bland terms as racial discrimination against some United Kingdom citizens on the ground of the colour of their skin.[53] In 1968 the Government introduced a special voucher scheme. A limited number of vouchers were made available to heads of households who had United Kingdom passports and who were under pressure to leave their countries of residence. Mrs Amin was refused a voucher because of the discriminatory assumption that a woman was not

should get her husband to sign the guarantee form in order to facilitate the agreement being entered into, it seems to me that there was unlawful discrimination . . .'

[48] *Gill* v. *El Vino Co. Ltd* [1983] QB 425 (Court of Appeal).

[49] *Jones* v. *Royal Liver Friendly Society* (unreported, Court of Appeal 1 Dec. 1982). Note also *Savjani* v. *Inland Revenue Commissioners* [1981] QB 458 where the Court of Appeal held under the analogous provision of the Race Relations Act 1976 that the Inland Revenue provide 'services' to the public by giving relief from tax or making repayments of tax or by giving advice about tax. See also *Bennett* v. *The Football Association Ltd* (unreported, Court of Appeal, 28 July 1978) where Lord Denning said that the Football Association came within s. 29 by providing facilities for recreation, in that they organize leagues for youth teams. Lord Justice Eveleigh expressed doubts on this point and Sir David Cairns did not mention it. They all agreed that the claim by a girl footballer refused access to the facilities by reason of her sex failed because of s. 44 of the 1975 Act; see below n. 110.

[50] Above, n. 1.   [51] Ibid.   [52] Ibid. at 827.

[53] *East African Asians* v. *United Kingdom* 3 EHRR 76 (1973). The Commission held that this race discrimination was degrading treatment in breach of art. 3 of the European Convention on Human Rights.

the head of a household other than in exceptional circumstances.

The House of Lords, by a majority of 3–2, held that this sex discrimination[54] was not in breach of section 29(1) of the 1975 Act. The majority held that the supply of vouchers was not a 'facility' or a 'service' providing access to the United Kingdom for settlement. This was despite the fact that the special voucher was recognized by those judges to be 'itself authority for entry'[55] into the United Kingdom. And it was despite the fact that, as Lord Scarman noted in his dissenting speech (joined by Lord Brandon), '[e]ntry into the United Kingdom for study, a visit or settlement is certainly a facility which many value and seek to obtain'.[56]

The majority of the House of Lords gave two reasons why such a facility is not a 'facility' under section 29(1). First, Lord Fraser (with whom Lord Keith and Lord Brightman agreed on the interpretation of the 1975 Act) said that section 29 applies 'to the direct provision of facilities or services and not to the mere grant of permission to use facilities'.[57] That is rather a fine distinction on the facts of the case. The voucher is itself a facility: if it is not, then any shop or restaurant can escape the effect of section 29 (and the similar provision in the Race Relations Act 1976) by admitting people only if they have a voucher and by refusing to distribute such vouchers to women (or blacks). In any event, section 50(1) of the 1975 Act (to which none of their Lordships referred) states that indirect access to benefits is covered by section 29.[58]

Secondly, the majority opinion of Lord Fraser contended that section 29 only applies to acts by the Government which 'are at least similar to acts that could be done by private persons'.[59] But, as Lord Scarman pointed out in his dissenting opinion, the examples of facilities and services given in section 29(2)—in particular the services of any local or public authority—are hardly confined to 'market-place activities'. Section 29(1) applies to provision 'for payment or not'. Moreover, the special exemption from liability under section 29 for sex discrimination relating to political parties and religious bodies[60] shows that section 29 covers more than market-place activities. The majority opinion placed reliance on section 85(1) of the 1975 Act.[61] This states that the Act

---

[54] The House of Lords unanimously accepted that this was sex discrimination as defined in the 1975 Act: see ch. 2 n. 43.

[55] Above, n. 1 at 831 per Lord Fraser.

[56] Ibid. at 841. [57] Ibid. at 834. [58] Below, n. 116.

[59] Above, n. 1 at 835. [60] Below, nn. 87 and 90. [61] Below n. 161.

covers State action 'as it applies to an act done by a private person'. However, it would not seem that this takes the matter any further. Lord Fraser acknowledged that it 'does not in terms restrict the comparison to an act *of the same kind* done by a private person'.[62] The crucial issue is the nature of the benefits provided, not their source, public or private.[63] All that section 85(1) does, as Lord Scarman argued, is to ensure that 'the Act applies to the public acts of Ministers, Government departments and other statutory bodies on behalf of the Crown as it applies to acts of private persons'.[64]

The House of Lords has in *Amin*, without any justification from the language or purpose of the 1975 Act, denied much of the statute's application to State action even though that action discriminates against women, even though the action concerns the provision of facilities to the public and even though the 1975 Act contains an express exception for acts done under statutory authority[65] (suggesting that State action is covered by section 29). The decision of the House of Lords in *Amin* is particularly unfortunate when so much sex discrimination in immigration, social security, and tax law directly results from Government conduct.[66] The decision in *Amin* adopted a similar approach to the earlier Court of Appeal decision in *Kassam*.[67]

A person can be liable under section 29(1) only if it is providing

[62] Above, n. 1 at 835.

[63] The Court of Appeal recognized this in *Jones* above n. 49. Lord Justice Dillon said that the 1975 Act 'is not particularly concerned with the nature of the body which discriminates, whether it is a friendly society or a club or an incorporated company or anything else. It is concerned with what the body does, in the course of which it discriminates.'

[64] Above, n. 1 at 842.

[65] Below, n. 113. That exception, in s. 51 of the 1975 Act, could not be relied upon in *Amin* because the special voucher scheme (with its sex discrimination) had no express statutory basis.

[66] See ch. 1 nn. 13 and 14.

[67] Above, n. 1. The Court of Appeal there rejected the argument that the Home Secretary is concerned with the provision of facilities under s. 29(1) in granting immigrants leave to enter and remain in the United Kingdom. It was apparently not argued in *Amin* or *Kassam* that the Secretary of State acted *ultra vires* his powers under the Immigration Act 1971 by introducing rules which discriminate between men and women on the ground of their sex. See *Van Gorkom* v. *A.-G.* [1977] 1 NZLR 535 (Supreme Court of New Zealand), discussed in ch. 1 n. 38. See also *Roberts* v. *Hopwood* [1925] AC 578, discussed in ch. 1 at n. 31: if it can be *ultra vires* to seek to further the equality of men and women in 1925, perhaps it could be *ultra vires* now to deny such equality.

the goods, facilities, or services 'to the public or a section of the public'. This phrase contains 'words of limitation' on the scope of section 29.[68] The White Paper, *Equality for Women*, suggested that the phrase ensured that section 29 would not cover provision 'to members of genuinely private social clubs, nor other personal and private relationships'.[69] In three cases under the Race Relations Act 1968, a number of Law Lords made a variety of efforts (some more successful than others) to state criteria relevant to identifying 'a section of the public'. In *Charter* v. *Race Relations Board*, the House of Lords held that a Conservative club did not offer the facility of membership to a section of the public, so it was not unlawful for it to refuse an applicant on the ground of the colour of his skin.[70] In *Applin* v. *Race Relations Board*, it was held that children in the care of a local authority constituted a section of the public to whom foster-parents provided services or facilities.[71] The case was brought not against foster-parents, but against persons who sought to induce foster-parents only to foster white children. In *Dockers' Labour Club and Institute Ltd* v. *Race Relations Board*, the Law Lords held that a working men's club (which belonged to a union of such clubs) did not act unlawfully in refusing to admit a member of another club within the union on the ground of the colour of his skin: the members of the clubs in the union did not constitute a section of the public.[72]

The Law Lords agreed in these cases that the law was 'confined to situations in which there can be said to be some public element' and where one was not concerned with 'situations of a purely private character'.[73] It was agreed that 'private' is the 'appropriate contrast to 'public' . . .'.[74] With regard to the criteria of a public provision, Lord Diplock suggested in *Dockers' Labour Club* that the test 'could be put in a way which everyone could understand by putting the question: "Would a notice 'Public Not Admitted',

---

[68] *Charter* v. *Race Relations Board* [1973] AC 868, 885 (per Lord Reid), 897 (per Lord Hodson), 900 (per Lord Simon) on the analogous provision of the Race Relations Act 1968.

[69] Cmnd. 5724 (1974), para. 66.

[70] Above, n. 68.   [71] Above, n. 42.   [72] Ibid.

[73] *Charter* above, n. 68 at 887 per Lord Reid.

[74] Ibid. at 898 per Lord Hodson. Similarly Lord Simon at 902 and Lord Cross at 906. See also *Dockers' Labour Club* above, n. 42 at 291 per Lord Reid, who emphasized that 'the sphere excluded by these words from the operation of the Act was wider than the purely domestic sphere. The true antithesis of public is not domestic but private.' Similarly *Applin* above n. 42 at 289 per Lord Simon.

exhibited on the premises on which the goods, facilities or services were provided, be true?" '[75] The defect of this approach is that even though the public may not be admitted, a section of them may be allowed in (for example all those born in Wales or all those with three 'A' levels) and this may satisfy the 'section of the public' test. The three cases under the 1968 Act were not resolved by reference to the numbers of persons eligible to receive the relevant goods, facilities, or services.

In *Charter* and *Dockers' Labour Club* the claims failed because the Law Lords decided that in determining whether members of a club are a section of the public 'an appropriate test was to see whether there was any genuine selection on personal grounds in electing candidates for membership'.[76] The test was stated to be whether entry to the club was regulated by the personal acceptability of the applicant to existing members (in which case the facility was not open to a 'section of the public') or whether membership was, in practice, made available to anyone who complied with formal conditions or criteria. In *Applin* Lord Wilberforce, in his dissenting judgment, approved the 'personal selection' test. He suggested that the words 'a section of the public' refer to 'something which is generally available to whoever wants it', that the 1968 Act applied where 'a person is concerned to provide something which in its nature is generally offered to and needed by the public at large, or a section of it, which is offered impersonally to all who choose to go through the doors or approach the counter'.[77] The other Law Lords in *Applin* disagreed with Lord Wilberforce on the application of the test on the facts of the case. Lord Simon noted, wisely, that he was 'not convinced that a process of screening or selection . . . is a touchstone in all circumstances' for determining whether the facility is offered to a

[75] Above, n. 42 at 297.
[76] Ibid. at 291 per Lord Reid. See similarly at 297 per Lord Diplock. And see *Charter* above n. 68 at 887 (per Lord Reid), at 903 (per Lord Simon), and at 909 (per Lord Cross). See also *Bateson* v. *YMCA* [1980] NI 135 where Hutton J (in the Northern Ireland High Court applying the equivalent provision to s. 29 in the Sex Discrimination (Northern Ireland) Order 1976) said that there was no 'personal selection' of persons allowed to use the facilities of a snooker room merely because members of the public allowed in had to be well behaved. Nor did it matter that the number of members of the public allowed in was small compared with proper members of the club. Still, the facility was made available to a 'section of the public'.
[77] Above, n. 42 at 277–8.

section of the public.[78] The Law Lords have expressly rejected the idea that cases in charity law, where a similar criterion concerning a section of the public is applied, are of assistance in defining what is meant by a 'section of the public' in anti-discrimination law.[79]

The 'personal selection' test seemed arbitrary in *Dockers' Labour Club* where the complainant was a member of a club affiliated to the union. Members of a club could, on payment of a small fee, become associates and enter any club in the union. The complainant was refused entry as an associate to one of the affiliated clubs because of his colour. The fact that there were over one million associates was held not to make those persons a 'section of the public'. In deciding whether a defendant provides goods, facilities, or services to a 'section of the public' courts should be prepared to lift the veil of privacy and seclusion. They should consider the numbers of those to whom the relevant benefits are offered, the nature of any common quality of the persons so treated, and the circumstances in which the customers are provided with the benefit.

Parliament responded to the Law Lords' decisions under the 1968 Act by including section 25 in the Race Relations Act 1976.[80] This brought many political and social clubs within the scope of the goods, facilities, and services provisions of the 1976 Act. The 1975 Act has no comparable provision to section 25 of the 1976 Act. It therefore seems that social and other clubs which apply an acceptability test before admitting people to membership fall outside section 29. It is therefore not unlawful for such clubs to discriminate on grounds of sex in their treatment of members and non-members in relation to the provision of goods, facilities, and services. There may well be an argument for allowing such clubs to remain outside the law in this respect in refusing to admit women, so long as the nature and the size of the club does not result in

[78] Ibid. at 289.

[79] See *Charter* above, n. 68 at 887 (per Lord Reid), 897 (per Lord Hodson), 902 (per Lord Simon), and at 907 (per Lord Cross).

[80] This makes it unlawful for an association of persons (however described, whether corporate or unincorporate and whether or not its activities are carried on for profit) to discriminate on racial grounds if it satisfies three criteria: it has 25 or more members; it is not already covered by the provision analogous to s. 12 of the 1975 Act dealing with discrimination by organizations of workers, employers' organizations etc. (see above, n. 29); and admission to membership is regulated by its constitution and it is so conducted that the members do not constitute a 'section of the public'.

them controlling access to valuable resources unrelated to the sex of individuals. Freedom of association must be balanced against freedom from sex discrimination. However, it is much more difficult to explain why (as is presently the case) a club which chooses to admit men and women should be entitled lawfully to discriminate between male and female members of the club on the ground of sex in the provision of the benefits of membership.

In *Jones* v. *Royal Liver Friendly Society*, the Court of Appeal rejected an attempt by the defendants to rely on the absence in the 1975 Act of any section comparable to section 25 of the 1976 Act. Lord Justice Dillon did 'not think it is necessary to conjecture why a section equivalent to section 25 has not been introduced into the Sex Discrimination Act . . .'. He said that the crucial issue under section 29(1) of the 1975 Act was not the nature of the body which discriminates, but what the body does. Since the defendants offered their policies 'to anyone who is prepared to apply for the policies and pay the appropriate premiums', it was held to be offering facilities to the public or to a section of the public. Its less favourable treatment of women members compared with men members was therefore a breach of section 29(1).[81]

The White Paper, *Equality for Women*, explained that section 29

will not require any change in the essential nature of the goods, services or facilities provided to the public from time to time. The supplier of goods designed or intended to meet the needs of one sex rather than the other will not be obliged to supply any corresponding goods that there may be for the other sex; and where he supplies goods designed to meet the different needs of both sexes, he will not be obliged to stock them in any particular proportions. The [Act] will not interfere with normal commercial judgment. It will simply require the supplier of goods to make his goods available to any customer regardless of the customer's sex. The same general principle applies to the provision of facilities and services.[82]

So when a person provides goods, facilities, or services designed for one sex—for example, women's clothes—it is not obliged to

---

[81] Above, n. 49. There was no doubt in *Gill* above n. 48 that customers of a wine-bar open to the public were a section of the public for purposes of s. 29. Similarly, immigrants applying for leave to enter the United Kingdom were conceded to be a section of the public in *Kassam* above, n. 1 at 1042. This was approved in *Amin* above, n. 1 by Lord Scarman at 841.

[82] Above, n. 69 at para. 66.

provide the corresponding materials for men (that is, men's clothes). But it is required to make the goods, facilities, or services available to any customer on the same terms, regardless of sex. Section 29(3) attempts to express this principle 'for the avoidance of doubt'.[83]

Sections 30 and 31 of the 1975 Act prohibit sex discrimination in relation to premises. Section 30 makes it unlawful to discriminate against a woman in relation to the disposal[84] of premises or in relation to the management of premises. An owner-occupier is not covered by the prohibition on sex discrimination in the disposal of premises unless he or she uses the services of an estate agent for the purpose of disposing of the premises or publishes (or causes to be published) an advertisement in connection with the disposal. Section 31 makes it unlawful for a landlord, or other person whose consent or licence is required for the disposal of premises in Great Britain comprised in a tenancy, to discriminate against a woman by withholding the consent or licence.

The 1975 Act recognizes a number of exceptions to liability under section 29 or under sections 30 and 31. These exceptions cover small premises[85] where the provider of accommodation (or the person withholding the licence or consent) or a near relative of that person resides, and intends to continue to reside, on the premises and shares accommodation with other residents who are not members of his or her household;[86] political parties;[87]

---

[83] Cf. s. 24(5) of the New Zealand Human Rights Commission Act 1977: 'Where the nature of a skill such as hairdressing varies according to whether it is exercised in relation to men or women, a person does not [unlawfully discriminate] by exercising the skill in relation to one sex only, in accordance with that person's normal practice.' In *Waldock* v. *Whitney and Prosser* (1984), a county court judge held that it was not unlawful sex discrimination for a hairdresser to charge a higher price for women than for men, since most women wanted a higher standard of service than most men. The judge said that the woman complainant had not expressly requested the lower standard of service—at the lower price—and so he did not need to consider whether it would be unlawful to deny her that facility or service on the same terms as men. It would certainly seem to be acting on stereotyped assumptions about men and women, and therefore sex discrimination, to deny a woman the same service as a man if she asked for it: see ch. 2 at nn. 39–44. On the subject of hair and sex discrimination law, note the comments of Lord Denning in *Jeremiah* above, n. 8 at 22: 'A woman's hair is her crowning glory, so it is said. She does not like it disturbed: especially when she has just had a "hair-do".'

[84] See s. 82(1) for a definition of 'disposal'.

[85] S. 32(2) defines 'small premises'.

[86] Ss. 31(2) and 32(1).   [87] S. 33.

voluntary bodies—that is any body not set up by any enactment and the activities of which are not carried on for profit;[88] facilities or services restricted to men (or to women) which are provided at a hospital, reception centre provided by the Supplementary Benefits Commission, or other establishment for persons requiring special care, supervision, or attention;[89] facilities or services restricted to men (or to women) which are provided at a place occupied or used for the purposes of an organized religion, with the facilities or services so restricted in order to comply with the doctrines of that religion or to avoid offending the religious susceptibilities of a significant number of its followers.[90] A further exemption covers the case of facilities or services restricted to men (or to women) when the users are likely to suffer serious embarrassment at the presence of a person of the opposite sex, or where a user is likely to be in a state of undress and might reasonably object to the presence of a user of the opposite sex,[91] or if physical contact between the user and any other person is likely and that other person might reasonably object if the user were a woman (or a man).[92] It is not clear why 'serious embarrassment' should validate sex discrimination, especially as the exemption already covers cases of undress and physical contact (for example, saunas and massage parlours).[93]

---

[88] S. 34. The term 'enactment' is not defined in the 1975 Act. It is normally construed to mean a statute, statutory instrument, by-law, regulation etc. or part thereof. See, for example, *Wakefield and District Light Railways Co.* v. *Wakefield Corporation* [1906] 2 KB 140, affirmed [1908] AC 293; *Rathbone* v. *Bundock* [1962] 2 QB 260, 273 (Divisional Court). A company is not set up 'by' an enactment for the purposes of s. 34, even though the Companies Act 1948 is an enactment. By contrast with s. 51(1) of the 1975 Act (on which see below, n. 113), s. 34(1)(b) refers to a body set up 'by' an enactment, not 'by or under' an enactment. A body is set up by an enactment if the enactment identifies and constitutes it, not where the enactment merely states a procedure, criteria, and powers to create such a body.

[89] S. 35(1)(a).

[90] S. 35(1)(b).   [91] S. 35(1)(c).   [92] S. 35(2).

[93] See a decision of a Northern Ireland county court on the analogous provision of the Sex Discrimination (Northern Ireland) Order 1976 in *Holden* v. *Department of Manpower Services* (1981): the 'serious embarrassment' clause was held to validate the refusal to allow a 26-year-old man to join a residential training course because all the other students would be young women. In *Evason* v. *P. & F. McGlade Ltd* (1979) another Northern Ireland county court judge rejected the argument that it would cause 'serious embarrassment' to male customers if women were served in a bar: 'Society is never static and social mores change. In no sense can I accept that the mere physical presence of presumably ordinary women in the bar could cause what Parliament intended to be covered by the term "serious embarrassment" to any right-thinking man'.

Section 36 of the Act states that section 29(1) does not apply to the provision of goods, facilities, and services outside Great Britain,[94] with two exceptions. First, section 29(1) does apply in relation to travel facilities outside Great Britain where the refusal or omission occurs in Great Britain (for example, at a travel agent).[95] Secondly, section 29(1) does apply in relation to any ship registered at a port of registry in Great Britain, or in relation to any aircraft or hovercraft registered in the United Kingdom and operated by a person which has its principal place of business, or is ordinarily resident, in Great Britain, or in relation to any ship, aircraft or hovercraft belonging to or possessed by Her Majesty the Queen in right of the Government of the United Kingdom, even if the ship, aircraft, or hovercraft is outside Great Britain.[96] A further exception with regard to territorial application is that section 29 does not apply to banking, loans, and other financial facilities supplied for a purpose to be carried out, or in connection with risks wholly or mainly arising, outside Great Britain.[97]

V

Part IV of the Sex Discrimination Act 1975 defines a number of ancillary unlawful acts. Section 37 deals with indirectly discriminatory practices.[98] It gives the Equal Opportunities Commission power to bring certain proceedings in respect of such acts.[99] Section 38 makes it unlawful to publish or cause to be published an advertisement which indicates, or might reasonably be understood as indicating, an intention to do any act which is contrary to the

[94] S. 36 was not mentioned in *Amin* above, n. 1, presumably because it was accepted that the relevant benefit was within Great Britain in that it consisted of being admitted to the United Kingdom for settlement through immigration control.
[95] S. 36(2).
[96] S. 36(3). S. 36(4) adds, however, that s. 36 does not render unlawful an act done in or over a country outside the United Kingdom or in or over that country's territorial waters for the purpose of complying with the laws of that country.
[97] S. 36(1)(b).
[98] It does not cover directly discriminatory practices. In *CRE* v. *Prestige Group PLC* [1984] ICR 473, 480, Lord Diplock for the House of Lords referred to the analogous provision of the Race Relations Act 1976 as 'curiously drafted'. On s. 37 see also ch. 6 s. V.
[99] See ch. 10 n. 14.

1975 Act.[100] Section 38(3) explains that the 'use of a job description with a sexual connotation (such as "waiter", "salesgirl", "postman", or "stewardess") shall be taken to indicate an intention to discriminate, unless the advertisement contains an indication to the contrary'. As Ian Gilmour pointed out for the Conservative Opposition during the Second Reading debate on the Sex Discrimination Bill 1975, this is more than slightly hypocritical in an Act of Parliament which adopts the normal statutory presumption that 'he' and 'his' refer to women as well as men, and which creates the post of 'chairman' of the EOC.[101]

Section 39 makes it unlawful to give instructions to discriminate contrary to the 1975 Act. It makes it unlawful for a person who has authority over another person, or in accordance with whose wishes that other person is accustomed to act, to instruct that other person to do any act contrary to the 1975 Act.[102] Section 40 of the 1975 Act prohibits pressure to discriminate. It is unlawful to induce, or attempt to induce, a person to do any act contrary to the 1975 Act by providing or offering to provide that person with any benefit, or by subjecting or threatening to subject that person to any detriment.[103] Section 40(2) adds that an offer or a threat does not fall outside this provision because it is not made directly to the person in question, so long as it is made in such a way that they are likely to hear of it.

Section 42 makes it unlawful knowingly to aid another person to discriminate contrary to the 1975 Act.[104] Section 41 imposes

---

[100] See *EOC* v. *Robertson* above n. 16. See also *CRE* v. *Associated Newspapers Group Ltd* [1978] 1 WLR 905 on the differently worded provision of the Race Relations Act 1968. It is not clear how s. 38 applies to advertisements indicating an intention to do an act of indirect sex discrimination.

[101] 889 HC 533 (26 Mar. 1975).

[102] In *CRE* v. *Imperial Society of Teachers of Dancing* above, n. 32 at 476–7 the EAT considered the analogous provision of the Race Relations Act 1976. The EAT said that the provision covers 'the use of words which bring about or attempt to bring about a certain course of action'. However, said the EAT, for a person to be accustomed to act in accordance with the instructions of another person 'requires that there should be some relationship between the person giving the instructions . . . and the other person . . . It does not seem to us to be possible to construe the section as meaning that it is sufficient to show that the other person is accustomed to act in accordance with the wishes of persons in the same position as the person giving the instructions.'

[103] See *CRE* v. *Imperial Society of Teachers of Dancing* ibid. at 475–6 on the differently worded provision of the Race Relations Act 1976.

[104] In *GLC* v. *Farrar* [1980] ICR 266, 271 the EAT suggested that 'aids' here means 'assisting or supporting' and does not mean 'aiding and abetting in the

vicarious liability on employers and principals for the acts of their servants done in the course of their employment (whether or not they were done with the employer's knowledge or approval)[105] and for the acts of their agents done with their authority ('whether express or implied, and whether precedent or subsequent').[106] An employer has a defence to liability for acts done by its employee if it can prove that it took such steps as were reasonably practicable to prevent the employee from doing that act, or from doing in the course of employment acts of that description.[107] It is unclear why employers should have this special defence to vicarious liability in the context of anti-discrimination law.

Part V of the 1975 Act states a number of general exceptions to liability under the main body of the Act. The onus is on a defendant to bring itself within such an exception.[108] These exceptions cover charities;[109] competitive sport;[110] insurance;[111]

---

technical sense which has been adopted in many criminal statutes'. The word 'knowingly' requires that the defendant had a guilty mind, that is knowledge of the facts which constitute sex discrimination contrary to the 1975 Act: see, generally, *R. v. Taaffe* [1983] 1 WLR 627, 629 (Court of Appeal) approved in [1984] AC 539 (House of Lords). An employee or agent for whose acts an employer or principal is liable under s. 41 (on which see below, n. 105), or would be liable but for s. 41(3) (on which see below, n. 107), is deemed by s. 42(2) to aid the doing of the act by the employer or principal.

[105] See *Seide* v. *Gillette Industries Ltd* [1980] IRLR 427, 430 where the EAT held in a case under the Race Relations Act 1976 that if an employer transfers an employee to a different department because another employee refuses to work with the first employee for racial reasons, this amounts to unlawful discrimination by the employer. This approach was approved in *Kingston* v. *British Railways Board* [1984] ICR 781, 792 (Court of Appeal).

[106] S. 41(2) seems to confine the liability of the principal to cases of express or implied authority (which derives from the principal's relationship with the agent) and to cases of ratification by the principal (before or after the act), but does not appear to cover cases of ostensible authority (which derives from the circumstances as perceived by a third party dealing with the agent and believing that the agent acts on behalf of the principal). If principals were liable for acts of an agent within the ostensible authority of the latter, one would expect to see principals, like employers, given a special defence by s. 41(3) (on which see below, n. 107). If s. 41(2) were intended to cover ostensible authority, it would, like s. 41(1) (dealing with the vicarious liability of employers), include the words 'whether or not it was done with the [principal's] knowledge or approval'.

[107] S. 41(3).

[108] *CRE* v. *Prestige Group PLC* above, n. 98 at 479 (on the equivalent Part VI of the Race Relations Act 1976).

[109] S. 43. See *Hugh-Jones* above, n. 11 at 853. There is no such exception in the Race Relations Act 1976.

[110] S. 44. See *Bennett* above, n. 49, *GLC* v. *Farrar* above n. 104, and *Petty*

communal accommodation;[112] acts done under statutory authority;[113] acts safeguarding national security (though it is difficult to think of circumstances when national security might depend on acts of sex discrimination).[114]

A limited amount of affirmative action in certain training and associated contexts, and in elective bodies in trade unions, is made lawful by sections 47–9 of the Act.[115] Indirect access to benefits is covered by the Act.[116]

Part VI of the 1975 Act concerns the powers and the duties of the Equal Opportunities Commission.[117]

VI

Part VII of the 1975 Act deals with enforcement of the law. Proceedings in respect of section 38 (discriminatory advertisements), section 39 (instructions to discriminate), and section 40 (pressure to discriminate) may only be brought by the Equal Opportunities Commission.[118]

In the employment field, cases of alleged sex discrimination are

above, n. 30 all discussed in David Pannick, *Sex Discrimination in Sport* (EOC 1983).

[111] S. 45. See ch. 7, s. IV.

[112] S. 46.

[113] S. 51. See *Hugh-Jones* above, n. 11 at 854–5; *GLC* v. *Farrar* above, n. 104 at 269–71; *Page* v. *Freight Hire (Tank Haulage) Ltd* [1981] ICR 299 (EAT). The potential width of this defence was indicated in *Farrar* at 270 where the EAT said that 'Parliament has expressly validated or excluded from the area of illegality anything which is done as a result of a requirement in [an] Act or an instrument made under it.' On the overlap between ss. 51 and 7(2)(f) of the 1975 Act, particularly with regard to 'protective legislation', see ch. 9 s. IX.

[114] S. 52. The composition of the armed forces cannot have been in Parliament's mind since that subject is excluded from the scope of the 1975 Act: see below, n. 163. Sex discrimination in the armed forces has provoked litigation in the American courts. See, for example, *Rostker* v. *Goldberg* 453 US 57 (1981) where the US Supreme Court held that the decision of Congress to authorize the registration of men, but not women, for draft into the armed services was constitutional. On the role of women in the army see John Keegan, 'Less Deadly than the Male?' *The Observer* 15 Nov. 1981. Holland has integrated its armed forces by abolishing separate women's units: *The Guardian* 17 Nov. 1981.

[115] See ch. 11 s. IV.

[116] S. 50. This deals with a case where the defendant does not itself provide benefits to others, but facilitates access for those others to benefits provided by a third person.

[117] See ch. 10.

[118] S. 72. See ch. 10 n. 7.

brought in the industrial tribunal.[119] There is an appeal on a point of law to the Employment Appeal Tribunal, and, thereafter, with leave, to the Court of Appeal. Claims of sex discrimination in the contexts of education, goods, services, facilities, or premises are brought in the county court.[120] There is an appeal on a point of law to the Court of Appeal. (In Scotland, the sheriff court performs the same function as the county court in England and Wales, and the appeal from the Employment Appeal Tribunal is to the Court of Session, which performs similar functions to the Court of Appeal in England and Wales). The provision of direct access to civil courts and tribunals for individual complainants was a welcome improvement on the unsatisfactory procedure under the Race Relations Act 1968. That statute required complaints of unlawful discrimination to be made to the Race Relations Board. If conciliation failed, the Board (but not the complainant) could initiate civil proceedings in the courts.

A claim of unlawful sex discrimination in the employment context should be brought within three months from the date of the act of which complaint is made.[121] In the county court, the limitation period for claims of sex discrimination is six months (or, in the case of a claim in the education context where it is necessary to notify the Secretary of State for Education before commencing the claim, eight months beginning from the date of the act of which complaint is made).[122] Section 76(5) states that a court or tribunal may consider a claim which is out of time 'if, in all the circumstances of the case, it considers that it is just and equitable to do so'. This requires the court or tribunal 'to do what it thinks is fair in the circumstances'.[123]

Although an act which occurred outside the limitation period cannot be a cause of action in itself, unless section 76(5) is applied,

[119] Ss. 62 and 63. There is an exception in cases alleging discrimination by a qualifying body contrary to s. 13 of the Act (see n. 30 above) when an appeal or proceedings in the nature of an appeal may be brought under any enactment: s. 63(2).
[120] Ss. 62 and 66. Before bringing a claim of sex discrimination in the field of education alleging a breach of ss. 22 or 23 by a body to which s. 25(1) applies (see above, nn. 37 and 38), the claimant must give notice of the claim to the Secretary of State for Education and give him or her two months to consider the claim: s. 66(5).
[121] S. 76(1).   [122] S. 76(2). See above, n. 120 on education claims.
[123] *Hutchinson* v. *Westward Television Ltd* [1977] ICR 279, 282. The EAT there said that cases decided under other statutes with different limitation criteria are not likely to be very helpful in deciding cases under s. 76(5).

regard may, of course, be had to such an act as evidence, if it is relevant to an act complained of within the limitation period which forms the basis of the action.[124]

Section 76(6) gives some clarification on the question of when an act is to be understood as done for the purpose of the time-limits in the 1975 Act. [125] Where the inclusion of any term in a contract renders the making of the contract an unlawful act, that act should be treated as extending throughout the duration of the contract. Any act extending over a period should be treated as done at the end of that period.[126] A deliberate omission is to be treated as done when the person in question decided upon it. In the absence of evidence establishing the contrary, a person is treated as deciding upon an omission when it does an act inconsistent with doing the omitted act or, if it has done no such inconsistent act, when the period expires within which it might reasonably have been expected to do the omitted act if it was to be done.

Section 74 of the 1975 Act establishes a procedure by which a complainant (or potential complainant) may question a person whom she thinks may have unlawfully discriminated against her.[127] The questions—and any answers—are admissible as evidence in the proceedings. If it appears to the court or tribunal that the defendants deliberately, and without reasonable excuse, omitted to reply to the questionnaire within a reasonable period, or that the reply is equivocal or evasive, the court or tribunal may draw any inference that it considers just and equitable, including an

---

[124] See *Din* v. *Carrington Viyella Ltd* [1982] ICR 256, 261 (EAT) and *Eke* above, n. 7 (both cases under the analogous provision of the Race Relations Act 1976). See also *Record Production Chapel, Sogat* v. *Turnbull* above, n. 30.

[125] See also *Lupetti* v. *Wrens Old House Ltd* [1984] ICR 348, a decision of the EAT under the analogous provision of the Race Relations Act 1976. The EAT held that where an employee claims that the dismissal was unlawfully discriminatory, the three-month time-limit runs not from the date when notice of the dismissal was given, but from the date when the employment was terminated.

[126] See *Amies* v. *Inner London Education Authority* [1977] ICR 308, 311 (EAT): where the complaint concerns a continuing rule, the time-limit of three months does not begin to run until that rule ceases to be applied; but where the complaint concerns the failure to award an applicant a particular job vacancy, the three-month time-limit runs from the date when the complainant suffered the detriment. See also *Calder* v. *James Finlay Corporation Ltd* (24 Nov. 1982, EAT in Scotland): where the employers operated a mortgage subsidy scheme for employees, any discrimination was continuing and so the three-month time-limit did not apply while the complainant remained in employment.

[127] See Elaine R. Donnelly, 'Discrimination Claims—The Questionnaire Procedure' (1983) *The Law Society's Gazette* 2340.

inference that the defendants committed an unlawful act of discrimination.

The questionnaire procedure may be used prior to the commencement of proceedings, so as to help the potential claimant to decide whether to bring a claim. Or it may be used after proceedings have been commenced.[128] 'The statutory machinery for obtaining early information . . . was not . . . intended to be a substitute for, but an addition to, the complainant's rights to discovery and inspection of documents.'[129] The questionnaire has obvious advantages over the normal procedures of seeking interrogatories or further and better particulars of the written pleadings of an opponent's case in litigation. The questionnaire can be used before litigation is started. Any relevant question can be asked: one is not restricted to seeking elucidation of the other party's written statement of their case.[130] The questionnaire procedure is most useful in obtaining from a potential or actual defendant information within its control which can help the complainant to assess the strength of her case and thereby help her to decide whether to proceed with it. If properly used, the questionnaire can work to the advantage of the defendant (as well as the complainant) by enabling it to avoid unnecessary litigation. The questionnaire has proved itself to be far removed from 'a legal provision . . . which smacks of the Star Chamber', the absurd description by Leon Brittan during the Parliamentary Debates on the 1975 Bill.[131] There is no good reason why (as is presently the case) the questionnaire procedure should not apply also to claims under the Equal Pay Act 1970.

The general principles of discovery of documents apply to sex discrimination cases. Each party to litigation is obliged to disclose to the other party for the purposes of the case any documents necessary for fairly disposing of the issues in dispute. In *Science Research Council* v. *Nassé* the House of Lords stated the following principles. First, that courts and tribunals should be aware that the

---

[128] The time-limits, the appropriate forms and provisions for service in respect of the questionnaire are contained in the Sex Discrimination (Questions and Replies) Order 1975 SI no. 2048, as amended by the Sex Discrimination (Questions and Replies) (Amendment) Order 1977 SI no. 844.

[129] *Science Research Council* v. *Nassé* [1980] AC 1028, 1069 per Lord Salmon.

[130] See *Quinn* above, n. 47 for a case where a defendant's answers to a questionnaire led to a finding of unlawful sex discrimination.

[131] 893 HC 1602 (18 June 1975: Report Stage in the House of Commons).

information necessary to prove a complaint of sex discrimination is usually in the hands of the defendants and that discovery is essential if the case is to be fairly disposed of.[132] Secondly, confidentiality, of itself, is not a reason for refusing discovery, although it is a factor to be considered by the court or tribunal.[133] In particular, the argument that disclosure of documents may inhibit candour in the compiling of records is not persuasive.[134] Thirdly, the test in industrial tribunals, as in county courts, is whether discovery is necessary for fairly disposing of the proceedings or for saving costs.[135] Fourthly, where documents are confidential, the tribunal or court should examine them before ordering discovery to see if disclosure really is necessary. Courts and tribunals should also consider whether there are any means (consistent with fairly disposing of the proceedings and saving costs) of preserving the confidence, for example by covering up irrelevant parts of the documents.[136]

An employee who alleges that unlawful discrimination was the cause of her failure to win promotion is entitled to discovery of all relevant documents from the beginning of her career with the respondent employers, unless this would be unfair or oppressive to the employers.[137] Such an employee, who has failed to gain promotion or an appointment, will normally be entitled to discovery of the relevant documents pertaining to the other candidates.[138] However, where the number of appointments complained of is substantial, and where the assembly of the relevant material would be difficult and expensive, the tribunal

[132] Above, n. 129 at 1064 (per Lord Wilberforce), 1069–70 (per Lord Salmon), 1081–2 (per Lord Fraser).

[133] Ibid. at 1065 (per Lord Wilberforce), 1071–2 (per Lord Salmon), 1085 (per Lord Fraser).

[134] Ibid. at 1070 (per Lord Salmon), 1081 (per Lord Fraser).

[135] This is the test stated in the County Court Rules 1981, Order 14, which is made applicable to industrial tribunal proceedings by Rule 4(1)(b)(ii) of the Industrial Tribunal (Rules of Procedure) Regulations 1985 SI no. 16. See above, n. 129 at 1066 (per Lord Wilberforce), 1072 (per Lord Salmon), 1089 (per Lord Scarman).

[136] Above, n. 129 at 1066 (per Lord Wilberforce), 1072–3 (per Lord Salmon), 1089–90 (per Lord Scarman).

[137] *Selvarajan* v. *Inner London Education Authority* [1980] IRLR 313 (EAT under the Race Relations Act 1976).

[138] *Oxford* v. *DHSS* [1977] ICR 884 (EAT); *Rasul* v. *CRE* [1978] IRLR 203 (EAT under the Race Relations Act 1976).

will allow discovery to the extent that it is fair to both sides.[139] How to achieve this objective will, of course, depend on the facts of the individual case.[140]

VII

Having considered pre-trial procedure, we next need to consider the procedure at the trial of a claim under the 1975 Act.

The burden of proof and the standard of proof are crucial to the outcome of many claims under the 1975 Act. Only in very rare cases will the complainant have clear proof of unlawful sex discrimination ('we do not employ women'). More often, the complainant will need to rely on equivocal evidence to create an inference that the respondent treated her less favourably on the ground of her sex. However, 'there is no doubt that, although the Act of 1975 is silent upon the burden of proof, the formal burden of proof lies upon the applicant [in direct discrimination cases]. That having been said, it should be recognised that in the course of the case the evidential burden may easily shift to the respondent . . .'[141]

While the burden of proof lies upon the applicant in direct discrimination cases (the standard of proof being on a balance of probabilities), 'it would only be in exceptional or frivolous cases that it would be right for the industrial tribunal to find at the end of the applicant's case that there was no case to answer and that it was not necessary to hear what the respondent had to say about it'.[142] The EAT has suggested that whether a claim of direct discrimination has been established will be most easily understood

---

[139] *Perera* v. *Civil Service Commission* [1980] IRLR 233 (EAT under the Race Relations Act 1976).

[140] In *British Library* v. *Palyza* [1984] ICR 504, the EAT held that the decision of an industrial tribunal on discovery in a race discrimination case may be reviewed by the EAT 'substituting our discretion for theirs' and that the jurisdiction of the EAT is here not confined to cases where the industrial tribunal exercised its discretion on wrong principles. This decision is plainly wrong: it is incompatible with the statutory jurisdiction of the EAT under s. 136 of the Employment Protection (Consolidation) Act 1978 to hear and decide appeals only on questions of law.

[141] *Oxford* v. *DHSS* above, n. 138 at 886. See also, on the burden of proof being on the complainant, *Science Research Council* above, n. 129 at 1082 per Lord Fraser.

[142] *Oxford* v. *DHSS* above, n. 138 at 887. Similarly *Owen & Briggs* v. *James* [1981] ICR 377, 384 (EAT under the Race Relations Act 1976).

'if concepts of shifting evidential burdens are avoided'. Such a legalistic approach, according to the EAT, is 'more likely to obscure than to illuminate the right answer'. The proper approach for an industrial tribunal is to look at all the evidence and

> to take into account the fact that direct evidence of discrimination is seldom going to be available and that, accordingly, in these cases the affirmative evidence of discrimination will normally consist of inferences to be drawn from the primary facts. If the primary facts indicate that there has been discrimination of some kind, the employer is called on to give an explanation and, failing clear and specific explanation being given by the employer to the satisfaction of the industrial tribunal, an inference of unlawful discrimination from the primary facts will mean the complaint succeeds.[143]

The Northern Ireland Court of Appeal adopted a similar approach to a case under the Sex Discrimination (Northern Ireland) Order 1976. Lord Lowry said that if inferences of sex discrimination could not be drawn in such cases, 'the object of the legislation would be largely defeated'.[144] There the court drew an inference of sex discrimination from the failure to promote a woman whose qualifications and experience were superior to those of the successful male candidate, when the employers could give no satisfactory explanation for preferring that male candidate. More typical are cases where the complainant can show only that she was as well qualified as the successful male candidate. In *Saunders* v. *Richmond-upon-Thames LBC*, for example, the EAT said that it did not find that the qualifications of the unsuccessful female candidate for the post of golf professional 'were, or anyhow much, superior to those of the successful [male] candidate. At all events we certainly do not accept that her qualifications were of a kind that the failure to appoint a candidate so qualified prima facie gave rise to an inference of discrimination.'[145]

---

[143] *Khanna* v. *Ministry of Defence* [1981] ICR 653, 658–9 (EAT under the Race Relations Act 1976). See similarly on the need for industrial tribunals to draw inferences of unlawful discrimination, in appropriate cases, *Chattopadhyay* v. *Headmaster of Holloway School* [1982] ICR 132, 137 (EAT under the Race Relations Act 1976) and *Science Research Council* above n. 129 at 1081 and 1084 per Lord Fraser.

[144] *Wallace* v. *South Eastern Education and Library Board* [1980] IRLR 193, 195.

[145] [1978] ICR 75, 80. On the burden of proof in direct discrimination cases under Title VII of the US Civil Rights Act 1964 see *McDonnell Douglas Corporation* v. *Green* 411 US 792 (1973) and *Texas Department of Community*

To establish unlawful direct discrimination, it is not necessary for the complainant to prove that her sex was the sole reason for her suffering the less favourable treatment. It is enough if her sex was 'an important factor' or 'a substantial reason' or a 'substantial and effective cause'.[146] It is not a defence to a claim of direct sex discrimination to show that the best candidate was appointed (though this will be important evidence that the complainant's sex was not taken into account and will be relevant to the question of remedies); the issue is whether or not the complainant's sex was, in fact, an important reason why she was unsuccessful.[147] The fact that the defendants employ many, or few, other women in relevant posts may be a relevant factor in deciding whether, on the evidence, sex discrimination has occurred: such evidence may help to establish or rebut an inference of direct discrimination.[148]

Also relevant as evidence to establish or rebut an inference of direct sex discrimination are acts or omissions by the defendant prior to the limitation period, even if they are prior to the coming into force of the 1975 Act,[149] and acts or omissions subsequent to the matters of which complaint is made in the instant proceedings.[150] It is not necessarily direct sex discrimination for an interviewing panel to ask a woman applicant questions which would not be asked of a male candidate. It depends on 'consideration of the circumstances in which, and the purposes for which, the question was asked'.[151]

Affairs v. *Burdine* 450 US 248 (1981). In a claim of indirect discrimination under the 1975 Act, the burden of proof is on the respondent to justify an impugned practice which the complainant has shown to have a disparate impact on women: see ch. 2 s. IV.

[146] *Owen & Briggs* v. *James* [1982] ICR 618, 623–4, 625–6 (Court of Appeal) and *Seide* above n. 105 at 431 (both cases under the Race Relations Act 1976). Cf. *Lewis* v. *University of Pittsburgh* 33 FEP Cases 1091 (1983): a US Court of Appeals held that to establish a claim of direct race or sex discrimination contrary to Title VII of the US Civil Rights Act 1964, the complainant had to show that but for her sex (or her race) she would have obtained the relevant benefit; it was not sufficient to show that her sex (or her race) was a substantial factor in the impugned decision.

[147] See, for example, *Conway* v. *The Queen's University of Belfast* [1981] IRLR 137 (Northern Ireland Court of Appeal): a candidate may be the victim of unlawful sex discrimination by being denied an interview even though a better candidate was appointed.

[148] *Owen & Briggs* v. *James* above, n. 142 at 382–3 and above, n. 146 at 622–3.

[149] Above, n. 124.

[150] *Chattopadhyay* above, n. 143.

[151] *Saunders* above, n. 145 at 78–9. Cf. *King* v. *TWA* 35 FEP Cases 102 (1984: US Court of Appeals) under Title VII of the US Civil Rights Act 1964.

If a complaint of sex discrimination succeeds, the remedies available depend upon whether the claim is in the industrial tribunal or in the county court. Section 65 of the 1975 Act provides that where an industrial tribunal finds that a complaint of sex discrimination is well founded, it shall give one or more of the following remedies as it considers to be just and equitable: an order declaring the rights of the parties; an order requiring the payment of compensation; a recommendation that the respondent employer take within a specified period action appearing to the tribunal to be practicable for the purpose of obviating or reducing the adverse effect on the complainant of any act of discrimination to which the complaint relates. The maximum amount of compensation which the tribunal may award in sex discrimination cases is the same as the maximum compensatory award in unfair dismissal cases. This currently stands at £8000.[152] The level of compensation, up to this maximum, is to be assessed by reference to any damages which the respondent could have been ordered to pay to the complainant if the matter had fallen to be dealt with by the county court.[153] Assessment of damages in the county court is considered below.

In *Prestcold Ltd* v. *Irvine*[154] the Court of Appeal considered the power of an industrial tribunal to make recommendations. The Court of Appeal held that it was not open to the tribunal to make a recommendation as to wages. The power to make recommendations concerns non-monetary matters. It is, however, open to the tribunal to order the payment of compensation, or to increase the

---

[152] S. 65(2). Where an applicant succeeds in claims for unfair dismissal and for sex discrimination, she cannot claim compensation under each heading for the same loss; moreover, the maximum aggregate compensation for the unfair dismissal compensatory award and for sex discrimination is £8000. See s. 76 of the Employment Protection (Consolidation) Act 1978. The limit of £8000 is with effect from 1 Apr. 1985.

[153] See *Hurley* v. *Mustoe (no. 2)* [1983] ICR 422, 424–5 (EAT): the industrial tribunal has a discretion whether or not to award any compensation, since its duty is to award such of the available remedies as are 'just and equitable'. However, the EAT added that once the industrial tribunal has decided that compensation is an appropriate remedy, 'the compensation payable for unlawful discrimination contrary to the Act of 1975 is to be computed on the basis of what damages would be recoverable in a county court and not on the basis of what an industrial tribunal thinks to be just and equitable having regard to the damages recoverable at common law.' The EAT further explained that the equitable doctrine of coming to court with 'clean hands' has no application to the assessment of damages in a county court.

[154] [1981] ICR 777.

amount of compensation ordered (up to the maximum award), if, without reasonable justification, the respondent fails to comply with a recommendation made by the tribunal.[155] The EAT in *Prestcold Ltd* v. *Irvine* held that because the respondent must know, from the time it is notified of the recommendation, the period within which it should act, the recommendation must state the precise period of its application.[156]

Section 66(1) of the 1975 Act states that sex discrimination cases brought in the county court 'may be made the subject of civil proceedings in like manner as any other claim in tort . . .'. Section 66(2) adds that 'all such remedies shall be obtainable in such proceedings as . . . would be obtainable in the High Court . . .' This suggests that the normal county court limit of damages up to £5000 does not apply in sex discrimination cases. The county court may also issue an injunction to restrain the repetition of unlawful discrimination by the defendant.

Section 66(4) makes it clear, '[f]or the avoidance of doubt', that 'damages in respect of an unlawful act of discrimination may include compensation for injury to feelings whether or not they include compensation under any other head'. Section 66(3) states that there shall be no award of damages in indirect discrimination cases 'if the respondent proves that the requirement or condition in question was not applied with the intention of treating the claimant unfavourably on the ground of his sex . . .'. Damages will, subject to these principles, be awarded to compensate for the loss suffered by the complainant as a result of the act of sex discrimination of which complaint is made. As the Court of Appeal has explained, '[c]ompensation is to be awarded for foreseeable damage arising directly from an unlawful act of discrimination. It follows that an applicant can claim for any pecuniary loss properly attributable to an unlawful act of discrimination.'[157] Damages for injury to feelings will only be available if the injury resulted 'from the knowledge that it was an

---

[155] S. 65(3). See *Nelson* v. *Tyne and Wear Passenger Transport Executive* [1978] ICR 1183 (EAT).

[156] [1980] ICR 610, 616: 'the period specified in the recommendation must be stated either by reference to an express number of years, months or days or by reference to a date itself stated in the recommendation.'

[157] *Skyrail Oceanic Ltd* v. *Coleman* [1981] ICR 864, 871 (per Lawton LJ, with whom Sir David Cairns agreed).

act of sex discrimination' which led to the less favourable treatment at issue in the case.[158]

VIII

Part VIII of the 1975 Act contains 'supplemental' provisions. Section 77 prevents attempts to contract out of the Act and deals with other contractual terms which breach the Act.[159] Sections 78 and 79 enable the trustees or other persons responsible for an educational charity to apply to the Secretary of State for the removal or modification of part of a trust deed or other instrument which restricts the relevant benefits to men (or to women). Section 80 empowers the Secretary of State, after consultation with the EOC, to amend various provisions of the 1975 Act by an order the draft of which has been approved by each House of Parliament.

Section 85 concerns the application of the 1975 Act to the Crown. Section 85(1) provides that the 1975 Act applies to an act done by or for the purposes of a Minister of the Crown or government department and to an act done on behalf of the Crown by a statutory body or a person holding a statutory office[160] as it applies to an act done by a private person.[161] Section 85(2) adds that the employment provisions of the 1975 Act apply to service for the purposes of a Minister of the Crown or government department (other than service of a person holding a statutory office) and to service on behalf of the Crown for the purposes of a

---

[158] Ibid. The Court of Appeal there considered, in 1981, that £100 was an adequate sum to compensate for injury to feelings: ibid. at 872. See also *Hurley* v. *Mustoe (no. 2)* above, n. 153 at 426 on compensation under this head: 'the mere fact that one has lived a life in conditions of some adversity does not necessarily mean that one has no feelings'. The EAT there substituted an award of £100 compensation under this head in place of the 'derisory award' of 50 pence made by the industrial tribunal.

[159] In *Commission of the European Communities* v. *United Kingdom* above, n. 18 the European Court of Justice held that s. 77 does not fully comply with the EEC Directive on Equal Treatment in Employment. This is because UK law does not nullify non-binding collective agreements or the internal rules of undertakings or the rules governing independent occupations or professions to the extent that they recognize sex discrimination. See ch. 5 n. 40 on Community Law.

[160] S. 85(10) defines 'statutory body' and 'statutory office'.

[161] In *Amin* above, n. 1 at 835 the House of Lords held that this section 'applies only to acts done on behalf of the Crown which are of a kind similar to acts which might be done by a private person'. See above, nn. 59–64.

person holding a statutory office or for the purposes of a statutory body, as they apply to employment by a private person, and shall so apply as if references to a contract of employment included references to the terms of service.[162]

Section 85(4) adds, however, that section 85 does not apply in relation to service in the naval, military, or air forces of the Crown. Furthermore, section 85(5) states that nothing in the 1975 Act shall render unlawful sex discrimination in admission to the Army Cadet Force, Air Training Corps, Sea Cadet Corps or Combined Cadet Force, or any other cadet training corps administered by the Ministry of Defence.[163]

Section 86 applies to any appointment by a Minister of the Crown or government department to an office or post where section 6 of the 1975 Act (which covers employment under a contract of service or apprenticeship or under a contract personally to execute any work or labour) does not apply. Section 86(2) provides that in making the appointment, and in making the arrangements for determining who should be offered the office or post (though not, it seems, in determining the treatment accorded to the person after appointment), the Minister of the Crown or government department shall not do any act which would be unlawful under section 6 if the Crown were the employer for the purposes of the 1975 Act.[164]

Although the 1975 Act does not apply to Northern Ireland,[165] an analogous law there has effect.[166]

---

[162] In *Knight* v. *A.-G.* above, n. 11, the EAT held that a Justice of the Peace did not fall within these provisions. In *Department of the Environment* v. *Fox* [1979] ICR 736, the EAT held that a rent officer did not fall within these provisions.

[163] On sex discrimination in the armed forces see above, n. 114.

[164] In *Knight* v. *A.-G.* above, n. 11 at 201 the EAT said that 'section 86(2) assumes that the act, if done by the Minister of the Crown, would not be unlawful under section 6. It is prohibited under section 86 of the Act itself. That, it seems to us, does not make it unlawful under Part II.' The consequence is that a remedy does not lie in an Industrial Tribunal for a breach of s. 86. A complainant would have to seek judicial review in the High Court against the impugned act of the Minister. See s. 62(2) of the 1975 Act: the statement in s. 62(1) that proceedings for a breach of the Act must be brought in the industrial tribunal or the county court (see above, nn. 119 and 120) 'does not preclude the making of an order of certiorari, mandamus or prohibition'. (It is unclear if s. 62(1) prohibits the making of a declaration, an injunction, or an order of damages in such judicial review proceedings).

[165] S. 87(2).

[166] Sex Discrimination (Northern Ireland) Order 1976 SI no. 1042 (NI 15).

4

EQUAL PAY

I

The Equal Pay Act 1970[1] aims 'in simple terms to bring into force what was loosely described as the policy of equal pay for equal work'.[2] The 1970 Act is 'only an outline and the detail has to be supplied by judicial interpretation'.[3] This has created problems in the application of the Act. Despite the contrast between the style of the 1970 Act and the detailed drafting of the Sex Discrimination Act 1975, in the sphere of employment the two statutes 'provide in effect a single comprehensive code' aimed at eliminating sex discrimination. Hence

what is abundantly clear is that both Acts should be construed and applied as a harmonious whole and in such a way that the broad principles which underlie the whole scheme of legislation are not frustrated by a narrow interpretation or restrictive application of particular provisions.[4]

The Equal Pay Act received the Royal Assent in May 1970. It was not brought into effect until 29 December 1975. This was in the vain hope that employers would voluntarily remove sex discrimination in pay and the other contractual terms of employment by that date. The 1970 Act, like many others, 'has to be applied by hundreds and thousands of ordinary people who are not lawyers, and it should therefore be kept as simple and as free from legalistic complications as is possible'.[5] However, 'legalism has started to take over'.[6] The short title to the 1970 Act states its

---

[1] The 1970 Act, as amended by the Sex Discrimination Act 1975, Section 8(1), is contained in Sched. I, Part II of the 1975 Act.

[2] *National Vulcan Engineering Insurance Group Ltd* v. *Wade* [1979] ICR 800, 808 per Ormrod LJ in the Court of Appeal.

[3] *National Coal Board* v. *Sherwin* [1978] ICR 700, 703–4 per Phillips J. for the EAT.

[4] *Shields* v. *E. Coomes (Holdings) Ltd* [1978] ICR 1159, 1178 per Bridge LJ. See similarly Orr LJ at 1174 and Lord Denning at 1168. See also *Steel* v. *Union of Post Office Workers* [1978] ICR 181, 187 (EAT).

[5] *National Vulcan* above, n. 2 at 808.

[6] *Clay Cross (Quarry Services) Limited* v. *Fletcher* [1979] ICR 1, 8 per Lawton LJ.

objective as 'to prevent discrimination, as regards terms and conditions of employment, between men and women'. In attempting to achieve this objective, the Act uses the device of an 'equality clause'. The terms of a contract under which a woman is employed[7] at an establishment in Great Britain[8] is deemed to include such a clause.[9] The equality clause applies to benefit men as well as women. The 1970 Act guarantees men equal pay with women, as well as guaranteeing women equal pay with men.[10]

Section 1(2) of the 1970 Act states the effect of the equality clause. It relates to terms (whether or not concerned with pay) of the contract of employment. Prior to the amendment of section 1(2) in 1983, the equality clause provided as follows. Where a woman is employed on like work[11] with a man in the same employment,[12] or where a woman is employed on work rated by a job evaluation scheme as equivalent[13] to that of a man in the same employment, she is entitled to terms which are not less favourable than his. Although this right extends to all contractual terms, it is convenient to concentrate on the central problem of equal pay. Section 1(3) of the Act gives the employer a potential defence to a claim that a woman employee has been denied equal pay to that received by a man doing like work or work rated as equivalent. An equality clause does not operate in relation to a variation between the woman's contract and the man's contract if the employer proves that the variation is genuinely due to a material difference (other than the difference of sex) between her case and his.[14]

Prior to the 1983 amendments to the Equal Pay Act, a woman

---

[7] Defined in s. 1(6) to include contracts personally to execute any work or labour as well as contracts of service or apprenticeship: see ch. 3 n. 9 on the similar definition of 'employment' in the Sex Discrimination Act 1975.

[8] See s. 10 of the 1975 Act, on which see ch. 3 n. 2. In *Barratt Developments (Bradford) Ltd* v. *UCATT* [1978] ICR 319, 322, the EAT said of the word 'establishment' in the Employment Protection Act 1975: 'Parliament having wisely not sought to define what an "establishment" is, it may be very difficult to say what the line is which distinguishes an establishment from something which is not an establishment, but perfectly easy to say on which particular side of the line any particular set-up falls'.

[9] S. 1(1).   [10] S. 1(13).

[11] As defined in s. 1(4). See below, s. III.

[12] S. 1(6) provides that men shall be treated as in the same employment with a woman if they are men employed by her employer or by an associated employer at the same establishment or at establishments in Great Britain which include that one and at which common terms and conditions of employment are observed either generally or for employees of the relevant classes.

[13] As defined in s. 1(5). See below, s. IV.   [14] See below, s. VI.

had a right to equal pay only if she could show that she was employed on like work or on work rated as equivalent to that of a man in the same employment. As Phillips J. explained in the first case to come before the Employment Appeal Tribunal concerning the 1970 Act, there were a number of options which were open to the draftsman of the Act in seeking 'to define the test which is to be applied in determining whether discrimination exists'. It

> would be possible to prescribe tests of varying degrees of severity. The least favourable from a woman's point of view would be to require equality of treatment when men and women are doing the *same work*. More favourable would be to require equality where the work done by the man and woman, although different, was of *equal value*.

The 1970 Act had, he observed, 'chosen a middle course' of looking for like work, or work rated as equivalent.[15]

The restriction of rights under the 1970 Act to women doing like work, or work rated as equivalent, to that of men severely limited the effect of the legislation. Like work is defined by section 1(4) to mean, in essence, work which is 'of the same or a broadly similar nature'. Because of occupational segregation between the sexes, vast numbers of women simply cannot point to a man doing like work in the same employment and therefore could not claim under the 1970 Act unless their work was rated as equivalent to that of a man in the same employment. But few employers have undertaken job evaluations. There is no compulsion under the Act for them to do so. In the absence of such a job evaluation, a woman cannot claim that her work has been rated as equivalent to that of a man.

Because of the limited scope of the 1970 Act it had little effect on pay discrimination between men and women.[16] However, in 1982 the European Court of Justice held that the United Kingdom was in breach of its obligations under EEC Directive 75/117 which guarantees equal pay for work of equal value without sex discrimination.[17] This caused the Government to amend the 1970 Act in 1983 in an attempt to bring it into line with Community law. With effect from 1 January 1984 a woman can claim equal pay to that of a man doing work of equal value in the same employment.[18]

[15] *Capper Pass Ltd* v. *Lawton* [1977] ICR 83, 87.
[16] See ch. II s. I.
[17] *Commission of the European Communities* v. *United Kingdom* [1982] ICR 578. See ch. 5 on Community law nn. 23–4.
[18] The Equal Pay (Amendment) Regulations 1983 SI no. 1794. See below,

II

In seeking to establish that she is employed on like work, work rated as equivalent or work of equal value to that of a man in the same employment, a woman complainant needs to point to a male comparable.

It is for the applicant, not the industrial tribunal, to select the male comparable.[19] If she proves that she is indeed doing like work, work rated as equivalent or work of equal value to that man, she is entitled to equal pay (unless the employer shows that the difference in pay is due to a material difference other than sex). Once the equality clause has been applied to increase the woman's pay to the level of that of the male comparable, she remains entitled to that rate of pay even if he thereafter leaves the job.[20]

In *Macarthys Limited* v. *Smith* the Court of Appeal thought that, as a matter of English law, a woman is not entitled to compare her pay with that of the man who preceded her in the job. Lawton LJ (with whom Cumming-Bruce LJ agreed) said that the language of the 1970 Act 'is consistent only with a comparison between a woman and a man in the same employment at the same time. The words, by the tenses used, look to the present and the future, but not to the past.'[21] Lord Denning dissented. The Court was not referred to decisions of US courts (applying the similar provisions of US equal pay law) which hold that a female complainant may compare her pay with that of her male predecessor.[22] However, the Court agreed that Article 119 of the EEC Treaty, which

section V. See generally Anthony Lester QC and David Wainwright, *Equal Pay for Work of Equal Value* (1984).

[19] *Ainsworth* v. *Glass Tubes & Components Ltd* [1977] ICR 347 (EAT). Cf. *Dance* v. *Dorothy Perkins Ltd* [1978] ICR 760 (EAT), wrongly suggesting that a woman complainant cannot compare her pay with that of a man doing like work if he is not representative of the group of men doing that work.

[20] *Sorbie* v. *Trust Houses Forte Hotels Ltd* [1977] ICR 55 (EAT). Note that an equality clause raises the complainant's pay to the level of the pay of the male comparable, not vice versa: see the industrial tribunal decision in *Tremlett* v. *Freemans (London SW9) Ltd* [1976] IRLR 292, and see ch. 5 n. 5 for the same principle under European Community law.

[21] [1979] ICR 785, 793.

[22] See *Hodgson* v. *Behrens Drug Co.* 475 F 2d 1041 (1973) a decision of the US Court of Appeals on the US Equal Pay Act 1963 which prohibits employers from discriminating 'between employees on the basis of sex by paying wages to employees . . . at a rate less than the rate at which he pays wages to employees of the opposite sex'. See also n. 54 below on the US legislation.

guarantees equal pay for equal work, raises the same issue.[23] The question was therefore referred to the European Court of Justice. The ECJ held that the concept of equal work 'may not be restricted by the introduction of a requirement of contemporaneity'[24] and so a woman can compare her pay with that of a man employed on equal work prior to her employment. The Court of Appeal then applied this decision,[25] as Article 119 takes priority over domestic law. Any other conclusion to this issue of contemporaneity would have meant that the 1970 Act did not apply to cases where there is only one employee doing particular work for the employer and the female occupant of this position is paid less than her male predecessor. By analogy with *Macarthys*, it would seem that a woman complainant who no longer works for an employer may bring a claim to compare her wages with those of the man who succeeded her in the job.

Can a woman claim equal pay to that of a hypothetical male worker by showing that, if she were a man, she would be paid more by her employer? In *Macarthys* the ECJ suggested that a comparison with 'a hypothetical male worker' could not be made as it would be 'indirect and disguised discrimination, the identification of which' would require 'comparative studies of entire branches of industry'. Therefore, the direct application of Article 119 is 'confined to parallels which may be drawn on the basis of concrete appraisals of the work actually performed by employees of different sex within the same establishment or service'.[26] The ECJ here seems to have confused two different concepts. It is understandable that Article 119 should not entitle a woman to compare her pay with that of a man in a different industry. But the practical difficulties there involved are not raised where the woman is able to prove that her employer would pay her more if she were male. The reference to the hypothetical male worker is merely one means of proving that she has been less favourably treated on the ground of her sex.

The notion of the hypothetical male comparison is central to the

---

[23] See ch. 5 on Community law n. 4.

[24] *Macarthys Ltd* v. *Smith* [1980] ICR 672, 690 (Judgment of the ECJ at para. 11).

[25] Ibid. at 692–4. See also *Albion Shipping Agency* v. *Arnold* [1982] ICR 22 (EAT).

[26] Ibid. at 690–1 (Judgment of the ECJ at paras. 14–15).

concept of discrimination in the Sex Discrimination Act 1975. Direct discrimination is there defined as treating the complainant, on the ground of her sex, less favourably than one treats, *or would treat*, a man.[27] The absence of this express concept in the Equal Pay Act is one indication of its lack of sophistication. Since the 1970 and 1975 Acts form an interlocking code[28] and since the mischief aimed at by the 1970 Act cannot be removed unless the statute prohibits an obvious form of sex discrimination, it may well be that the 1970 Act can be interpreted as covering this case. US courts have had similar difficulties as to whether the US Equal Pay Act 1963 entitles a woman to a remedy if she can prove that a hypothetical male employee would receive higher pay. In *County of Washington, Oregon* v. *Gunther*, the majority of the US Supreme Court held that Title VII of the US Civil Rights Act 1964 allows a claim for sex-based wage discrimination by reference to the pay of a hypothetical male worker. The majority opinion of Brennan J. explained that any other view of the scope of Title VII would render lawful discriminatory wage policies which could not be brought under the Equal Pay Act. He said that if Title VII gave no remedy, there would be no redress where 'an employer hired a woman for a unique position in the company and then admitted that her salary would have been higher had she been male . . .'.[29] The dissenting opinion of Rehnquist J. (joined by Burger CJ, Powell and Stewart JJ) argued that there was no need for such a remedy under Title VII since the Equal Pay Act already covered the situation: 'However unlikely such an admission might be in the bullpen of litigation, an employer's statement that "if my female employees performing a particular job were males, I would pay them more simply because they are males" would be' sufficient to establish a claim under the US Equal Pay Act since '[o]vert discrimination does not go unremedied' by that Act.[30]

III

There are two stages to the inquiry of whether a woman is doing like work to a man under section 1(4) of the 1970 Act.[31] First, she

---

[27] See ch. 2 s. II for a discussion of the concept of direct sex discrimination.
[28] Above, n. 4.   [29] 452 US 161, 178–9 (1981).   [30] Ibid. at 201.
[31] S. 1(4) states: 'A woman is to be regarded as employed on like work with men if, but only if, her work and theirs is of the same or a broadly similar nature, and the

must show that her work and his are 'of the same or a broadly similar nature'. In *Capper Pass Limited* v. *Lawton*, Phillips J. (for the EAT) explained that this did not mean that the work had to be 'of the *same* nature . . . It is enough if it is of a similar nature. Indeed, it need only be broadly similar.' Tribunals should, he said, apply 'a broad judgment' in deciding this issue. The case will not fail at this stage because of minute differences between the work done by the woman and the work done by the male comparable.[32] If this hurdle is successfully surmounted by the complainant, she will then need to show that the differences between her work and that of the man are not of 'practical importance in relation to terms and conditions of employment'. Here 'trivial differences, or differences not likely in the real world to be reflected in the terms and conditions of employment, ought to be disregarded.' Once it is determined that work is of a broadly similar nature, it should be regarded as being like work 'unless the differences are plainly of a kind which the industrial tribunal in its experience would expect to find reflected in the terms and conditions of employment'.[33]

This assessment of 'like work' has nothing to do with the personal skill or merit of a particular employee. It is concerned rather with the jobs, objectively considered in terms of such factors as the 'effort, skill, responsibility or decision' required to perform them.[34] An employer cannot avoid a finding of like work by introducing comparatively small differences in job content between the two jobs or by giving the work a different job description.[35] The comparison is not between the respective contractual obligations of the man and the woman 'but between the things done and the frequency with which they are done'.[36]

The fact that the job of the male comparable involves more responsibility than the job of the female complainant may justify a

differences (if any) between the things she does and the things they do are not of practical importance in relation to terms and conditions of employment; and accordingly in comparing her work with theirs regard shall be had to the frequency or otherwise with which any such differences occur in practice as well as to the nature and extent of the differences.'

[32] Above, n. 15 at 87–8. This general approach was approved in *Shields* above, n. 4 at 1179–80 per Bridge LJ. See also Lord Denning at 1169.

[33] *Capper Pass Ltd* above, n. 15 at 87–8.

[34] *Shields* above, n. 4 at 1169 per Lord Denning.   [35] Ibid.

[36] Ibid. at 1174 per Orr LJ. Similarly Bridge LJ at 1180. See also *Electrolux Limited* v. *Hutchinson* [1977] ICR 252 (EAT) and *Redland Roof Tiles Limited* v. *Harper* [1977] ICR 349 (EAT).

finding that there is not like work.[37] The fact that the woman complainant does her work at a different time to the male comparable, perhaps because he is on a night shift, does not prevent there being like work. But the employer may pay a night-shift premium or an overtime rate assessed at a reasonable level.[38]

The drafting of section 1(4) of the 1970 Act on like work has caused some anomalies. If the woman complainant is not doing like work to the male comparable, she has no legal remedy even though the difference in pay is far greater than the difference in job duties could justify. This is because 'a case is either within or without the Act: there is no half-way house'.[39] It would also seem that a woman paid less than a man in the same employment is not entitled to equal pay if the tribunal concludes that her job involves greater skill, responsibility, and effort than his: in such a case there is not like work.[40] Such a conclusion is clearly contrary to the purpose of the 1970 Act.

IV

As an alternative to showing that she is employed on like work to a man in the same employment, a woman may seek to prove that she is employed on work rated as equivalent to his. Section 1(5) of the 1970 Act states that a woman is to be regarded as employed on work rated as equivalent to that of a man if her job and his have been given an equal value in terms of the demand made on a worker under such headings as effort, skill, and decision on a study undertaken with a view to evaluating such jobs (or would have

---

[37] *Waddington* v. *Leicester Council for Voluntary Service* [1977] ICR 266 (EAT); *Eaton Ltd* v. *Nuttall* [1977] ICR 272 (EAT); *Capper Pass Limited* v. *Allan* [1980] ICR 194 (EAT).

[38] *Dugdale* v. *Kraft Foods Ltd* [1977] ICR 48 (EAT); *National Coal Board* v. *Sherwin* above n. 3; *Shields* above, n. 4 at 1170 per Lord Denning. See similarly the US Supreme Court on the analogous problem under the US Equal Pay Act: *Corning Glass Works* v. *Brennan* 417 US 188 (1974).

[39] *Electrolux* above, n. 36 at 259. See also *Maidment* v. *Cooper & Co. (Birmingham) Limited* [1978] ICR 1094, 1100 (EAT).

[40] This is suggested by the EAT decision in *Waddington* above, n. 37. The EAT noted, at 268, that '[n]ot unnaturally, [the applicant] did not take kindly to being paid less than her subordinate . . . There is no doubt . . . that in many respects the work which she did and the work which he did were similar. There were however certain differences as indeed is indicated by the fact that she asserted, and it is admitted, that she was [his] superior.' The claim was remitted by the EAT to an industrial tribunal for reconsideration in accordance with the law.

been given equal value but for the evaluation being made on a system setting different values for men and women). An evaluation study does not satisfy section 1(5) unless it is thorough in analysis and decides the position of an employee on a relevant salary scale without the need for any further decision on matters concerning the nature of the work.[41] A tribunal may not carry out its own evaluation study from the information before it.[42]

In *O'Brien* v. *Sim-Chem Ltd*, Lord Russell for the House of Lords noted that job evaluation studies with a view to determining equivalents and differences in work are not confined to the Equal Pay Act. They are 'in more general use in industry in an attempt to achieve a broadly sound pay structure'. However, a job evaluation study for the purpose of the 1970 Act 'cannot be carried out without the agreement of the relevant parties—including of course the employer—that there shall be one'.[43] The House of Lords there concluded that once a job evaluation study had been undertaken, and had decided that the woman's job was of equal value to the man's job, the woman was then entitled to the same rate of pay. It was no defence for the employer to argue that it had accepted the results of the job evaluation study but had not adjusted the pay structure because of a fear that this would conflict with government pay policy.

In *Arnold v. Beecham Group Ltd* the EAT said that the job evaluation scheme was only 'completed', and therefore effective for the purposes of the 1970 Act, where both employers and employees have accepted it as a valid study, or have adopted it as regulating their relationship.[44] Otherwise, said the EAT, employers and employees would be discouraged from entering into job evaluation studies and co-operating with them. The EAT rejected the argument that this approach puts the woman employee at the mercy of her employers and the trade union, which may prevent the application of section 1(5) by declining to accept the conclusions

---

[41] *Eaton* above, n. 37 at 277–8. The different types of job evaluation studies are explained in *Eaton* at 278. To have effect under s. 1(5), an evaluation study 'should be complete and objective and by its application enable all factors of importance in relation to the work to be taken into account making it unnecessary for the employers to make subjective judgments upon the work content': *England* v. *Bromley LBC* [1978] ICR 1, 5 (EAT).

[42] *England* v. *Bromley LBC* above, n. 41 at 7.

[43] [1980] ICR 573, 578.

[44] [1982] ICR 744, 751. See also *England* above, n. 41 at 4.

of a job evaluation study if the results are unpalatable to them. This seems contrary to the purpose of the 1970 Act which is to secure equal pay for women irrespective of employer (and trade union) willingness to support that goal.

The validity of a job evaluation study can be challenged where it contains a 'fundamental error'.[45] The ECJ has emphasized that 'where a job classification system is used for determining pay it is necessary to ensure that it is based on the same criteria for both men and women and so drawn up as to exclude any discrimination on grounds of sex'.[46] The Advocate-General, Mr Verloren van Themaat, drew attention to the danger that

the evaluation criteria are not always neutral as between the sexes. For example, certain qualities in work could be described as typically female (for instance, dexterity, meticulousness, readiness to undertake repetitive work and so on) and are valued commensurately lower than "male" qualities (ability to handle materials and machines, physical strength and so on . . .).[47]

V

With effect from 1 January 1984, a woman can compare her pay with that of a man doing work of equal value in the same employment, whether or not there has been a job evaluation study. The 1970 Act was amended to introduce this right as a result of the decision of the ECJ applying EEC Directive 75/117.

The Commission of the European Communities brought proceedings against the Government of the United Kingdom for breach of the Directive by failing to guarantee equal pay for work of equal value. The ECJ noted that the job evaluation provisions of section 1(5) of the 1970 Act did not assist workers if their employer declined to introduce a job evaluation scheme. Because there was 'no means whereby a worker who considers that his post is of equal value to another may pursue his claims if the employer refuses to introduce a job classification system', the United Kingdom was found to be in breach of the Directive. The Court

---

[45] *Greene* v. *Broxtowe District Council* [1977] ICR 241, 243 (EAT); *Arnold* above, n. 44 at 753.

[46] *Commission of the European Communities* v. *United Kingdom* above, n. 17 at 598 (Judgment of the ECJ at para. 8).

[47] Ibid. at 585.

rejected the Government's contention that 'the criterion of work
of equal value is too abstract to be applied by the courts'.[48] Most of
the other Member States of the Community had already introduced
measures to secure equal pay for work of equal value. The
criterion had there been applied by a variety of methods: works
inspectorates; a more extensive system of job evaluation; and, in
Ireland, the recommendations of an Equality Officer which have
evidentiary weight but are not legally binding in court. Evaluation
schemes have been ranking different jobs for decades.

Equal pay for work of equal value is an essential element of anti-
discrimination law in a society in which occupational segregation
of men and women persists. The anthropologist Margaret Mead
explained that all societies tend to undervalue work done by
women:

Men may cook or weave or dress dolls or hunt humming-birds, but if such
activities are appropriate occupations of men, then the whole society, men
and women alike, votes them as important. When the same occupations
are performed by women, they are regarded as less important.[49]

It is a matter of regret that it should need a decision of the ECJ to
remind the Government of its obligations on equal pay. The
repeated recommendations of the Equal Opportunities Commission,
given the statutory duty of submitting to the Government
proposals for amending the 1970 Act where necessary,[50] for
changes in the law were ignored.[51]

In an attempt to comply, belatedly, with the requirements of
Community law, the Government introduced the Equal Pay
(Amendment) Regulations 1983.[52] These provide for changes in

[48] Ibid. at 597–9.   [49] Margaret Mead, *Male and Female* (1949), ch. 7.
[50] See ch. 10 at n. 5 on this duty of the EOC.
[51] In 1974, Mr John Fraser, Under-Secretary of State for Employment, told the
House of Commons that '[i]n general the Equal Pay Act 1970 and the Equal Pay
Act (Northern Ireland) 1970 enable the United Kingdom to comply with the
directive [75/117]': 883 HC 638 (written answer 20 Dec. 1974).
[52] Above, n. 18. On 5 Dec. 1983, the House of Lords approved the Regulations
but passed an Opposition Amendment stating that 'this House believes that the
regulations do not adequately reflect the 1982 decision of the European Court of
Justice and Article 1 of the EEC Equal Pay Directive of 1975': 445 HL 929. On the
content of EEC law, see ch. 5 nn. 23–4. For discussions of the content of the
Regulations see Christopher McCrudden, 'Equal Pay for Work of Equal Value: the
Equal Pay (Amendment) Regulations 1983' 12 *Industrial Law Journal* 197 (1983);
Richard Townshend-Smith, 'The Equal Pay (Amendment) Regulations 1983' 47
Modern Law Review 201 (1984); Michael Rubenstein, *Equal Pay for Work of
Equal Value: The New Regulations and their Implications* (1984).

the 1970 Act to cover the case 'where a woman is employed on work which . . . is, in terms of the demands made on her (for instance under such headings as effort, skill and decision), of equal value to that of a man in the same employment'. Such a woman is entitled to equal pay, and other contractual terms, to that received by the man (unless the employer can establish its section 1(3) defence).

The definition of equal value in the 1983 Regulations makes clear that what matters are the 'demands' made on employees in practice, not the value of the work to the employer. It is unfortunate that Parliament merely stated effort, skill and decision as non-exhaustive examples of the criteria to be applied in assessing equal value. Presumably the working conditions in which the jobs are done will also be considered relevant to the evaluation.[53] Other relevant criteria will, no doubt, be identified by the developing caselaw.

The type of effort involved in the two jobs being compared presumably need not be the same. '"[E]ffort" is the physical or mental exertion required in performing a job. So long as the ultimate degree of exertion remains comparable, the mere fact that two jobs call for effort different in kind will not render them unequal.'[54] The criterion of 'skill' focuses attention on what the job requires, not on the individual aptitude and efficiency of the female complainant and the male comparable.[55] It is therefore irrelevant that one of those employees has greater skill than the job actually 'demands'.[56] An important guide to the skill required to perform a job is given by the training, qualifications, and experience properly required of employees. 'Decision' refers to

---

[53] See s. 3(c) of the Irish Anti-Discrimination (Pay) Act 1974 which defines work of equal value 'in terms of the demands it makes in relation to such matters as skill, physical or mental effort, responsibility and working conditions'. Similarly, s. 11(2) of the Canadian Human Rights Act 1977 states that work of equal value is to be assessed by reference to 'the composite of the skill, effort and responsibility required in the performance of the work and the conditions under which the work is performed'.

[54] *Usery* v. *Columbia University* 568 F 2d 953, 959 (1977), a decision of the US Court of Appeals on the US Equal Pay Act 1963 which entitles a woman to claim equal pay if employed on a job the performance of which requires 'equal skill, effort and responsibility' and which is performed 'under similar working conditions' to that of a man.

[55] See *Shields* above, n. 4 at 1169 per Lord Denning. See also *Shultz* v. *Kimberly Clark Corp.* 315 F Supp 1323, 1332 (1970: US District Court).

[56] *Peltier* v. *City of Fargo* 533 F 2d 374, 377 (1976: US Court of Appeals).

the responsibility involved in the job and the authority given to the employee.

In applying these criteria of work of equal value courts and tribunals should bear in mind that Parliament cannot have intended equal value to be given a narrow, mathematically exact meaning. Performing job evaluations is not a science. The concept of equality needs to be flexibly applied with reference to industrial common sense.[57] However, as with the concept of like work, a woman who is unable to establish that her work is of equal value to that of the male comparable has no legal remedy simply because the job differences do not justify the pay differential.[58] It would be contrary to the purpose of the equal value law for a woman's claim to be dismissed if the tribunal concludes that her work is of greater value than that of her male comparable who receives higher pay than her.[59]

It is unfortunate that the 1983 equal value amendments to the 1970 Act were only brought into effect from 1 January 1984.[60] EEC Directive 75/117, which entitles women to equal pay for work of equal value without sex discrimination, was adopted on 10 February 1975. Article 8(1) of that Directive required Member States to put into force the laws, regulations, and administrative provisions necessary to comply with the Directive by 10 February 1976. Under the 1983 amendments to the 1970 Act, a woman is not able to claim damages or back pay for work of equal value prior to 1 January 1984 even though she brings her claim after that date.[61] So only after 1 January 1986 does a woman claiming work of equal value have the right to claim the maximum two years' back pay under section 2(5) of the 1970 Act.

The material difference defence which employers may rely upon is different in equal value claims to claims of like work and claims

---

[57] See *Hayward* v. *Cammell Laird Shipbuilders Ltd* [1984] IRLR 463, 467, the first case to be decided under the Equal Value Regulations. The tribunal there upheld the claim of a woman cook that her work was of equal value to that of three men, a painter, a joiner, and a thermal insulation engineer, employed by the Respondents.

[58] Above, n. 39.

[59] Above, n. 40 on the similar problem under the like work criterion.

[60] Para. 1(2) of the Regulations.

[61] See *De Brito* v. *Standard Chartered Bank Ltd* [1978] ICR 650 (EAT) and *Snoxell* v. *Vauxhall Motors Ltd* [1977] ICR 700, 722–4 (EAT) on the similar problem after the coming into effect of the 1970 Act.

based on job evaluation schemes.[62] There is, furthermore, a complicated procedure for bringing an equal value claim.[63] These aspects
of the equal value law will undoubtedly reduce the practical
effectiveness of the legal right to equal pay for work of equal value.

The inadequacies of the 1983 Regulations which amended the
Equal Pay Act 1970 were at least partly due to the unsatisfactory
manner in which those amendments were made. The Government
provided only 90 minutes for debate in each of the Houses of
Parliament, using the procedure of a statutory instrument under s.
2(2) of the European Communities Act 1972 which did not enable
critics to table substantive amendments of their own. The draft
Regulations were introduced in the House of Commons on 20 July
1983 by Mr Alan Clark, Under-Secretary of State for Employment.
He left no doubt about his lack of commitment to the policy of
strengthening the Equal Pay Act. He told the House of Commons
that 'a certain separation between expressed and implied beliefs is
endemic among those who hold office'.[64] He warned the House
that there were in the draft Regulations 'certain legalistic passages
which I might have to deal with at 78 rpm instead of 33'.[65] He did
so. The Opposition spokesman, Mr Barry Jones, justifiably
complained that the Minister had 'made a frivolous speech on an
important subject'; his speech was 'damaging and even demeaning
to his Department'.[66] The quality of the speech of the Under-
Secretary of State was indicated by the fact that it was warmly
applauded by Mr Tony Marlow, a Conservative back-bencher,
whose own contribution to the debate was a criticism of the very
idea of entitling women to equal pay for work of equal value. Mr
Marlow was worried that '[a]ny trouble-maker . . . is going to
pretend that her work is of equal value. It is an open invitation to
any feminist, any harridan, or any rattle-headed female with a chip
on her bra-strap to take action against her employer.'[67]

VI

If a woman proves that she is employed on like work, or work

---

[62] See below, s. VI.

[64] 46 HC 481 (20 July 1983).

[66] Ibid. at col. 488.

[63] See below, s. VII.

[65] Ibid. at col. 479.

[67] Ibid. at col. 491. On the attitude of the House of Lords towards the
Regulations see n. 52 above.

rated as equivalent, or work of equal value to that of a man in the same employment, she is entitled to equal pay (and other contractual terms and conditions) unless the employer can show that the variation in pay is genuinely due to a material factor other than sex. Section 1(3) of the 1970 Act contains this defence.[68] In effect, once a woman has proved that she is paid less than a man in the same employment doing like work (or work related as equivalent or work of equal value) 'it is presumed that the variation between her contract and his contract is due to the difference of sex'.[69]

The onus of establishing a section 1(3) defence is on the employer. The burden of proof is on the ordinary civil standard of balance of probabilities.[70] The purpose of the section 1(3) defence is to recognize that there may well be good reasons to pay different wages to people doing similar work, irrespective of their sex. For example, length of service, special personal skills or qualifications, higher productivity may all justify a wage differential.[71]

The section 1(3) defence differs according to whether the woman complainant has established, on the one hand, like work or work rated as equivalent, or, on the other hand, work of equal value. It is convenient first to consider the section 1(3) defence in cases of like work and work rated as equivalent.

A large number of problems have arisen in the application of section 1(3). Courts have had difficulty in understanding the type of factors which employers may rely upon to establish a material difference other than sex. In *Clay Cross (Quarry Services) Limited*

---

[68] Before the amendments introduced by the 1983 Regulations, s. 1(3) provided that 'An equality clause shall not operate in relation to a variation between the woman's contract and the man's contract if the employer proves that the variation is genuinely due to a material difference (other than the difference of sex) between her case and his.' Para. 2(2) of the 1983 Regulations substitutes a new s. 1(3): 'An equality clause shall not operate in relation to a variation between the woman's contract and the man's contract if the employer proves that the variation is genuinely due to a material factor which is not the difference of sex and that factor:
(a) in the case of an equality clause falling within subsection (2)(a) or (b) above [that is, in a case of like work or work rated as equivalent], must be a material difference between the woman's case and the man's; and
(b) in the case of an equality clause falling within subsection (2)(c) above [that is, in a case of work of equal value], may be such a material difference.'

[69] *National Vulcan Engineering Insurance Group Ltd* v. *Wade* [1977] ICR 455, 458 (EAT).
[70] See the Court of Appeal decision in *National Vulcan* above, n. 2.
[71] *Shields* above, n. 4 at 1170 per Lord Denning.

v. *Fletcher* the employers argued that the male employee was paid more than the female complainant doing like work because of market forces: when he was first employed, he was the only suitable applicant and he was able to command the same high wage that he had been paid in his previous job. The employers therefore argued that the lower wage paid to the woman was nothing to do with her sex. The Court of Appeal unanimously held that this was inadequate to establish a section 1(3) defence. An employer does not satisfy section 1(3) merely because it proves that the difference in pay between the female complainant and the male comparable was for reasons other than her sex. The employer must establish that the pay variation is genuinely due to a difference in the 'personal equation' of the complainant and the male comparable, that is by reference to their respective skills, experience, qualifications. An employer cannot satisfy section 1(3) where the only difference it can point to is based upon the circumstances in which the complainant and the male comparable came to be employed, especially if those circumstances amount to the fact that the employer had to pay the man a higher salary in order to persuade him to take the job. The Court of Appeal reached these conclusions for four main reasons. First, because section 1(3) requires a material difference between the woman's case and the man's. Parliament could easily have said that there is no breach of the 1970 Act where an employer proves that the less favourable treatment of the woman is not on the ground of her sex. Secondly, the test is easy for tribunals to apply. Thirdly, it is consistent with Community law. Fourthly, in the absence of such an interpretation the 1970 Act would be a dead letter, its objectives frustrated.[72]

It is undoubtedly the case that men tend to have greater bargaining power for pay than do women. That is one reason why legislation is required to secure equal pay for men and women at work. If an employer could establish a defence to a claim for equal pay merely by showing that the man would not work for less, the 1970 Act would be useless. However, the reasoning of the Court of Appeal in *Clay Cross* does have peculiar consequences. In *Clay Cross* it was accepted by the Court of Appeal that 'there was no intention on the part of the employer to discriminate against [the

---

[72] Above, n. 6 per Lord Denning at 4–6, per Lawton LJ at 9–11 and per Browne LJ at p. 12.

woman complainant] by reason of her sex, and the reason for the difference between her pay and [that of the male comparable] had nothing to do with her sex'.[73] Yet, as Browne LJ acknowledged, the long title of the 1970 Act describes it as designed to prevent 'discrimination . . . between men and women'. Moreover, the 1970 Act 'should be construed as one with the Sex Discrimination Act 1975'.[74] How, then, can an employer be found to have breached the 1970 Act when it has proved that the pay disparity was not on the ground of sex?

The only way in which the policy of the 1970 Act can be reconciled with the decision in *Clay Cross* is to assume that the employer there indirectly discriminated against women: its practice had a disparate impact on women and was unjustifiable.[75] The disparate impact arises from the fact that work done by women has tended to be undervalued compared with work done by men, enabling men to command higher wages than similarly qualified women in the market. Adopting a pay policy which perpetuates these market forces is unjustifiable given the objectives of the 1970 Act to defeat such market forces. There is some support for this approach in the *Clay Cross* judgments. Lord Denning said that the 'result' of the employer's action was that the complainant was 'discriminated against'. Lawton LJ noted that '[t]here are more ways of discriminating against women than by deliberately setting out to do so: see section 1(1)(b) of the Sex Discrimination Act 1975', which defines indirect discrimination. Browne LJ referred to 'the effect' of the employer's policy.[76]

The market forces issue is difficult but important. The unequal pay for like work inflicted on many women is a direct consequence of market forces which undervalue the jobs which tend to be done by women. The 1970 Act was intended to attack that mischief. Its purposes would be frustrated if, by way of defence, an employer could rely on market forces as a reason for paying women less than men doing like work.[77] As we shall see, this issue is of even greater

[73] Ibid. at 12 per Browne LJ.   [74] Ibid.

[75] See ch. 2 ss. III and IV for a discussion of the concept of indirect discrimination.

[76] Above, n. 6 at 5, 9 and 12. Lord Denning at 7 referred to the indirect discrimination decision of the US Supreme Court in *Griggs* v. *Duke Power Co.* 401 US 424 (1971).

[77] Cf. *Rainey* v. *Greater Glasgow Health Board Eastern District* [1984] IRLR 88 where the EAT in Scotland in effect declined to follow *Clay Cross* on the issue of

significance, and difficulty, when one considers work of equal value.

Clay Cross should, therefore, be understood to mean that an employer cannot establish a section 1(3) defence where it has discriminated, directly or indirectly, against women in its pay policy. An example of indirect discrimination is where the employer relies only on market forces to explain the pay difference between the man and the woman doing like work. The language of the Court of Appeal decision wrongly suggests that section 1(3) covers only a difference in the 'personal equation' and that an employer may not succeed in a section 1(3) defence when it establishes that it paid the man more than the woman doing like work for an insubstantial, but non-discriminatory reason. The 1970 Act is concerned to eradicate sex discrimination. So '[i]f there is a sufficient explanation for the different wages paid which has nothing to do with the sex of the employees, the purpose of the legislature is not going to be achieved by insisting on equal wages and indeed to do so might be thought to be unfair.'[78] The factor relied on by the employer to justify the pay difference must be 'material' but this means it must be 'real'.[79] It does not mean that the tribunal must approve of the factor as a reason for paying the man more than the woman. The more flippant and insubstantial the reason presented by the employer for paying the man more than the woman doing like work, the less likely it is that the tribunal will believe that the pay difference had nothing to do with sex, directly or indirectly. That is a question of evidence and proof.

Clay Cross is one indication that a section 1(3) defence cannot be established where the employer's pay policy indirectly discrimi-

market forces and s. 1(3). The US Supreme Court has reached a similar conclusion to *Clay Cross* on the analogous issue under the US Equal Pay Act: see *Corning Glass Works* above, n. 38 at 205.

[78] *Albion Shipping Agency* n. 25 at 28. The EAT there held that where a female employee seeks to compare her pay with that of the man who preceded her in the job, the employer will have a s. 1(3) defence if it proves that she is paid less than the man was paid because of a decline in the economic circumstances of the business and that the lower pay is not linked with the employee's sex. See also *Macarthys* above, n. 24 at 690 where the ECJ stated (judgment para. 12) that a difference in pay between workers doing like work but at different periods of time 'may be explained by the operation of factors which are unconnected with any discrimination on grounds of sex'.

[79] *Navy, Army & Air Force Institutes* v. *Varley* [1977] ICR 11, 15 (EAT).

nates against women. This question was at issue in *Jenkins* v.
Kingsgate (Clothing Productions) Ltd. The employer there paid
full-time workers a higher rate per hour than part-time employees.
This had a disproportionate adverse impact on women. In industry
generally, and in that firm, the overwhelming proportion of part-
time workers were women. A substantial proportion of women
who work are employed on a part-time basis. Could the employer
show that the difference in the number of hours worked was a
material difference other than sex? In *Jenkins* the EAT referred to
the ECJ the question whether Article 119 of the EEC Treaty
prohibited indirect discrimination in this context.[80] The Advocate-
General, Mr. J.-P. Warner, said that in his view Article 119
prohibited practices which have a disparate impact on women and
which the employer cannot justify on objective grounds.[81] Unfortunately, the ECJ was less clear in its decision. It held that a

difference in pay between full-time workers and part-time workers does
not amount to discrimination prohibited by Article 119 of the Treaty
unless it is in reality merely an indirect way of reducing the level of pay of
part-time workers on the ground that that group of workers is composed
exclusively or predominantly of women.[82]

This seems to suggest that an employer could defend its pay policy
unless its motive was to discriminate: a discriminatory impact
would not make the policy unlawful even if the policy could not be
shown to be reasonably necessary.

When *Jenkins* returned to the EAT, Browne-Wilkinson J.
accepted that this appeared to be what the ECJ was deciding.
However, he concluded that domestic law, by the 1970 Act,
accorded employees greater rights than Community law. He held
that the Equal Pay Act 1970 prohibits indirect discrimination, that
is where an employer adopts a pay policy or practice which hits at a
group composed wholly or mainly of women and when that policy
or practice is not justified as reasonably necessary to achieve a
legitimate objective. This is irrespective of whether the employer
intends to treat women less favourably than men. The EAT gave
two main reasons for this conclusion. First, the language of the
1970 Act suggests that it prohibits all sex discrimination, direct or
indirect, intentional or unintentional: the Act states its concern
with the *effect* of contractual terms. Secondly, the 1970 Act is part

---

[80] [1980] IRLR 6.   [81] [1981] ICR 592, 600–1.
[82] Ibid. at 613 (Judgment of the ECJ at para 15).

of a code against sex discrimination. Therefore it should, so far as possible, be interpreted consistently with the Sex Discrimination Act 1975 which does prohibit indirect sex discrimination. For these reasons, the EAT concluded in *Jenkins* that a pay policy or practice which indirectly discriminates against women cannot satisfy section 1(3) of the 1970 Act.[83]

Similarly it will not be possible for an employer to prove a section 1(3) material difference 'when it can be seen that past sex discrimination has contributed to the variation' between the woman's pay and that of the male comparable.[84] This is because 'it is not the intention of the Act to permit the perpetuation of past discrimination in terms of pay'.[85]

It would seem from the terms of section 1(3) that it is for the employer to show that *all* the variation in pay, not merely part of it, is genuinely due to the material difference.[86] However, tribunals will not examine this with 'mathematical precision'.[87] The employer may be able to rely upon a grading system to justify the pay difference between the female complainant and the male comparable. As long as the grading system is based on factors such as skill and experience and 'is fairly and genuinely applied irrespective of sex', it will satisfy section 1(3).[88] A grading system is, therefore, not an automatic section 1(3) defence: the 1970 Act is concerned with substance, not with labelling.[89]

Particular problems have been caused in the context of section 1(3) by the practice of 'red-circling'. Employers sometimes agree to protect the existing pay levels of individual employees who are being regraded or re-employed in lower-grade work through no fault of their own, for example because of illness. Such employees then receive a red-circle rate for the new job and so are paid more

---

[83] [1981] ICR 715, 723–7. In *Rainey* above, n. 77 at 89–90 the EAT in Scotland rejected the indirect discrimination argument under the 1970 Act as 'very far-reaching'.

[84] *Snoxell* above, n. 61 at 717 approved in *Shields* above, n. 4 at 1182 per Bridge LJ.

[85] *Sun Alliance and London Insurance Ltd* v. *Dudman* [1978] ICR 551, 555 (EAT).

[86] *Sherwin* above, n. 3 at 703.

[87] *Boyle* v. *Tennent Caledonian Breweries Ltd* [1978] IRLR 321 (EAT).

[88] *National Vulcan* above, n. 2 at 808 per Lord Denning.

[89] *Snoxell* above, n. 61 at 724; *Waddington* above, n. 37 at 270–1. The employer successfully relied on a grading system which objectively assessed individuals by reference to skill and experience in *Pointon* v. *University of Sussex* [1979] IRLR 119 (Court of Appeal).

than other employees doing that work. If a woman who is not red-circled claims equal pay with a red-circled man doing like work, does the employer have a section 1(3) defence? An employer may not rely on red-circling to give it a section 1(3) defence where the red-circling itself originates in sex discrimination.[90] But 'where it can be demonstrated that there is a group of employees who have had their wages protected for causes neither directly nor indirectly due to a difference of sex, and assuming that the male and female employees doing the same work who are outside the red circle are treated alike', then a section 1(3) defence would exist.[91] In determining whether the employer has discharged the onus on it of showing that the red circling is not sex-based, 'it is relevant for the industrial tribunal to take into account the length of time elapsed since the "protection" was introduced, and whether the employers have acted in accordance with current notions of good industrial practice in their attitude to the continuation of the practice'.[92] If the original red-circling was not based on sex discrimination, then it may continue to give a section 1(3) defence to pay differences even after the original reason for the extra pay no longer exists.[93]

The factual concept of red-circling should not be erected into a proposition of law.[94] It is merely a shorthand description of a particular state of affairs. Indeed, red-circle cases fall squarely within the terms of section 1(3): the employer will only establish a defence where it can show that there is a reason, other than sex, why the female complainant is paid less than the male comparable doing like work.[95]

Section 1(3) of the Equal Pay Act, as amended by the 1983

---

[90] *Snoxell* above, n. 61 at 717.   [91] Ibid. at 720.

[92] *Outlook Supplies Ltd* v. *Parry* [1978] ICR 388, 393 (EAT).

[93] *Avon and Somerset Police Authority* v. *Emery* [1981] ICR 229 (EAT). However, if the employer admits into the red circle a man whose higher pay cannot be justified, a woman doing like work is entitled to claim equal pay with him even though red-circling may be justified for all other men doing that work: *United Biscuits* v. *Young* [1978] IRLR 15 (EAT).

[94] *Methven* v. *Cow Industrial Polymers Ltd* [1980] ICR 463, 469 per Dunn LJ in the Court of Appeal.

[95] See, for example, *Farthing* v. *Ministry of Defence* [1980] IRLR 402 (Court of Appeal). In *Clay Cross* above, n. 6, the Court of Appeal recognized that red-circling can give a s. 1(3) defence: see Lord Denning at 5 and Browne LJ at 12. To reconcile *Clay Cross* and *Farthing* one must conclude that the circumstances in which an employee came to be employed by the employer cannot give rise to red-circling, whereas the circumstances in which an employee transferred from a previous post with that employer may give rise to red-circling.

Regulations, contains a differently worded defence in cases where the woman complainant shows that her work is of equal value to that of the male comparable (as opposed to showing it is like work or work rated as equivalent). In equal value cases, as in the other cases, section 1(3) requires the employer to prove that the variation in pay is genuinely due to a material factor other than the difference of sex. But in like work and job evaluation study cases the employer 'must' prove that this factor is 'a material difference between the woman's case and the man's'. In equal value cases, by contrast, the employer 'may' prove that the factor is such a material difference. But it need not do so. The difficulty is to understand when a factor may be material and other than sex and yet not be a material difference between the man's case and the woman's case. Section 1(3), as amended by the 1983 Regulations, gives no express guidance on this problem. Indeed, it does seem unnecessarily complicated to apply a different section 1(3) test in cases where the jobs are assessed to be of equal value to cases where the jobs are rated as equivalent by a job evaluation study. The nature of the employer's justification for unequal pay should not depend on the method used to compare the work of the female complainant and the male comparable.

Presumably the draftsman of the 1983 Regulations intended to ensure that in equal value cases the employer would not be confined to differences in the 'personal equation' of the complainant and the comparable man but would be able to rely upon market forces as a justification for paying the man a higher wage.[96]

---

[96] See the comments of Alan Clark, Under-Secretary of State, introducing the Amendment Regulations in the House of Commons, above, n. 64 at col. 486: 'What we have in mind are circumstances where the difference in pay is not due to personal factors between the man and the woman, but rather to skill shortages or other market forces. If a man is paid more than a woman for work of equal value because his skills are in short supply, this is not sexually discriminatory, provided the reason is genuine and the employer can show this.' See similarly the Earl of Gowrie, the Government spokesman in the House of Lords: 'In equal value cases the regulations also allow an employer to argue that genuine economic considerations apart from sex justify unequal pay. Could I give one or two examples of this? Let us suppose that a female clerk claims equal pay with a male computer-programmer on the grounds that her work is of equal value to his. The employer might admit that the work is of equal value but might argue that he has to pay the computer programmers more in order to retain their services, otherwise they would simply leave for higher pay elsewhere. This is a perfectly valid reason for a difference in pay because it is not based on sex. Another example: local education authorities who need to attract mathematics teachers in shortage areas can offer them a lead in

As explained above, in *Clay Cross* the Court of Appeal concentrated on the words 'between her case and his' to reach the conclusion that the defence could only be established by reference to the 'personal equation' and could not be established by reference to market forces.[97] In equal value cases, the employer is not confined to pointing to a material difference between the woman's case and the man's case.

In attempting to assess whether the section 1(3) defence in equal value cases allows an employer to rely on market forces, it is important to remember that an employer cannot establish a section 1(3) defence where the factor relied on is a difference of sex, directly or indirectly. If an employer pays a female typist less than a male clerk doing work of equal value, and does so because of 'market forces' (in other words there are more typists and they will work for less pay than clerks), the employer does not necessarily have a section 1(3) defence. Its policy does not directly discriminate against the female typist: male typists, if there were any, would receive the same rate of pay. Nevertheless, the policy will fail to satisfy section 1(3) if it indirectly discriminates against women by having a disproportionate adverse impact on women (who tend to be secretaries, while men tend to be clerks, in this context) and if the policy is unjustifiable (because it is not reasonably necessary for the employer to pay secretaries less than clerks). In assessing the justifiability of a pay policy in this context, tribunals will no doubt consider whether the objectives of the 1970 Act would be frustrated if employers could deny equal pay to women doing work of equal value by relying on market forces. The approach taken by tribunals may well depend on whether the skill shortage for the jobs which tend to be done by men results from the under-representation of women in that type of work and whether this is because of sex discrimination; and whether women are here willing to work for lower pay in the job done by the female complainant because of the market forces which have traditionally undervalued work which tends to be done by women.

---

pay over other teachers starting their careers. This is to do simply with the shortage of maths teachers; it has nothing whatsoever to do with sex discrimination—and, of course, it applies to either sex': 445 HL 884 (5 Dec. 1983).

[97] Above, n. 72.

VII

Parliament introduced a complicated procedure to be followed in cases where a woman claims equal pay for work of equal value.[98] When a woman claims, in the alternative, under the like work and equal value provisions of the 1970 Act, the tribunal should hear the like work claim first and only consider the equal value claim if the like work claim fails. This is because the equal value provisions only apply where there is not like work (or work rated as equivalent under a job evaluation scheme).[99]

Before hearing an equal value claim, an industrial tribunal must invite the parties to apply for an adjournment for the purpose of seeking to settle the claim. If the parties agree, the tribunal must grant such an adjournment.[100] On hearing the equal value claim, the tribunal has three options. First, it can decide that it is satisfied that there are no reasonable grounds for determining that the work is of equal value, thereby dismissing the claim. Secondly, it can require a member of the panel of independent experts to prepare a report on whether the work is of equal value. Thirdly, on the application of a party, the tribunal may consider it appropriate (having regard to the need to conduct the hearing in a just manner most suitable to the clarification of the issues) to hear evidence and argument on the section 1(3) material difference defence before considering whether to refer the issue of equal value to the independent expert.[101] At this stage a tribunal cannot refuse to send the issue of equal value to the expert because it is satisfied that there are no reasonable grounds for the employer to deny that the work is of equal value. The tribunal cannot decide the issue of equal value in favour of the woman complainant at this stage.

No doubt it will be rare for the tribunal to put the cart before the

[98] See the Industrial Tribunals (Rules of Procedure) (Equal Value Amendment) Regulations 1983 SI no. 1807 amending the Industrial Tribunals (Rules of Procedure) Regulations 1980 SI no. 884 ('the 1980 Rules'), since replaced by the Industrial Tribunals (Rules of Procedure) Regulations 1985 SI no. 16 ('the 1985 Rules') to which I shall refer below.

[99] S. 1(2)(c) of the Equal Pay Act 1970 introduced by para. 2(1) of the Equal Pay (Amendment) Regulations 1983.

[100] Rule 12(2A) of Schedule 2 to the 1985 Rules.

[101] S. 2A(1) of the Equal Pay Act 1970 introduced by para. 3(1) of the Equal Pay (Amendment) Regulations 1983, and Rules 7A(1) and 8(2E) of Schedule 2 to the 1985 Rules. There is no justification for Parliament imposing this special preliminary hearing in equal value cases.

horse and decide the material difference defence before looking at the equal value issue. Clarification of the issues is unlikely to result from such a course. It will be difficult to separate the issues in many cases.

Usually, then, the tribunal will consider at the first hearing whether to refer the issue of equal value to the independent expert. One of the circumstances in which the tribunal may decide that there are no reasonable grounds for finding work of equal value (and that therefore this issue need not be referred to the independent expert, and the claim should be dismissed) is if a job evaluation scheme under section 1(5) of the 1970 Act has given the relevant work of the female complainant and the male comparable different values and there are no reasonable grounds for determining that the job evaluation was made on a system which discriminated on grounds of sex. For this purpose, a job evaluation study so discriminates where a difference, or coincidence, between values set by that system on job demands is not justifiable irrespective of the sex of the person on whom those demands are made.[102]

Other than in cases where a non-discriminatory job evaluation scheme has valued the relevant jobs differently, an employer will usually have great difficulty in persuading a tribunal that there are no reasonable grounds for finding work of equal value and that the issue should therefore not be sent to the expert. Parliament has clearly indicated by the creation of the office of independent expert in equal value cases that such cases raise difficult questions which will normally best be decided after expert analysis. It will require something of a special case for an industrial tribunal to avoid using the specialist procedure carefully set out by Parliament. Once an arguable claim has been presented by the female applicant, the burden of proof at this stage is on the employer to show that there are no reasonable grounds for determining that the work is of equal value. The tribunal is to send the matter to the expert unless it is 'satisfied' that no such reasonable grounds exist. At this stage, the tribunal does not need to believe that the female applicant will necessarily succeed in her claim that the work is of

---

[102] Ss. 2A(2) and (3) of the Equal Pay Act 1970 introduced by para. 3(1) of the Equal Pay (Amendment) Regulations 1983. See *Neil* v. *Ford Motor Co. Ltd* [1984] IRLR 339 (industrial tribunal) and see Rubenstein above n. 52 at ch. 6. On the criteria of a job evaluation under s. 1(5) of the 1970 Act see above nn. 41–5.

equal value. It is enough for the tribunal to think that an expert might reasonably conclude that it is work of equal value. In deciding this threshold question, tribunals should be wary of imposing their own inexpert judgment for that of the specialists: applicants should therefore be given the benefit of the doubt at this stage.[103]

When an issue of equal value is referred to an independent expert, the industrial tribunal hearing is adjourned.[104] The expert is required to take account of all information supplied and representations made. The expert is required to send to the parties for comment a written summary of all information and representations received. The expert then makes a report to the tribunal in a document which reproduces the summary and which states a brief account of representations received from the parties and the conclusions reached (with reasons) or the reasons for not reaching a conclusion on whether there is work of equal value. The expert has a duty to take no account of the difference of sex and to act fairly at all times.[105]

After the tribunal and the parties have received the expert's report, the hearing before the industrial tribunal is resumed. The report of the expert is admitted as evidence in the case unless the expert has failed to comply with his or her duties, or has formed a conclusion which, on the information supplied and the representations made, could not reasonably have been reached, or for some other material reason (other than disagreement with the conclusion or reasoning of the expert about equal value) the report is 'unsatisfactory' and the tribunal exercises its discretion not to admit the report. If the expert's report is not admitted as evidence for one of these reasons, then the tribunal must refer the issue of equal value to another expert (unless the tribunal is satisfied that

---

[103] In *Hayward* above, n. 57 at 465, a Liverpool industrial tribunal quoted with approval the comments made by the Earl of Gowrie (the Government spokesman) during the House of Lords debate on the draft Regulations: '[I]t is only the hopeless case that will be excluded by this regulation. If there is any doubt, it must be resolved in the applicant's favour and the case will proceed in the normal way.' Above, n. 96 col. 924.

[104] Rule 7A(4) of Schedule 2 to the 1985 Rules. The expert may apply to the industrial tribunal for an order that a person provide the expert with relevant written information or documents: Rule 4(1A) of Schedule 2 of the 1985 Rules. There is no power to compel the employer to allow the expert access to the workplace.

[105] Rule 7A(3) of Schedule 2 to the 1985 Rules.

there are no reasonable grounds for determining that the work is of equal value, an unlikely event as the tribunal was not so satisfied when it sent the issue to the first expert for a report).[106] A party may require the expert to attend the industrial tribunal hearing to be cross-examined on the issue of equal value dealt with in the report. A party may, at the hearing (and on giving reasonable notice), call one witness to give expert evidence on the question of equal value.[107]

A tribunal may allow a party to give evidence or call witnesses upon the question of equal value in two other circumstances. First, if the matter is relevant to and is raised in connection with a decision on the material difference defence under section 1(3). Secondly, if the expert's report does not contain a conclusion on the question of equal value and this is due to the failure of a person to provide information or documents to the expert (after being required to do so by the tribunal).[108]

Other than in these circumstances, no party to an equal value claim may give evidence or question any witness upon the issue of equal value.[109] The tribunal has power to ask the expert to explain, in writing, any matter contained in the report or to give further consideration to the issue of equal value.[110]

The expert's report is, at best, only 'evidence' of whether the relevant work is of equal value. It is for the tribunal to 'determine that question' after receiving the expert's report. Nevertheless, tribunals are likely, in most cases, to give considerable evidentiary weight to the expert's report when determining whether there is work of equal value. The expert is no ordinary witness. He is independent and he has had the opportunity to study the work done in far more detail than is possible for an industrial tribunal.[111]

---

[106] Rules 7A(7) and (8) of Schedule 2 to the 1985 Rules.

[107] Rules 7A(9), 8(2A), and 8(2B) of Schedule 2 to the 1985 Rules.

[108] Rule 8(2D) of Schedule 2 to the 1985 Rules.

[109] Rule 8(2C) of Schedule 2 to the 1985 Rules.

[110] Rules 7A(10) and (11) of Schedule 2 to the 1985 Rules.

[111] S. 2A(1) of the Equal Pay Act 1970 introduced by para. 3(1) of the Equal Pay (Amendment) Regulations 1983, and Rule 7A(7) of Schedule 2 to the 1985 Rules. See the Earl of Gowrie (Government spokesman) above n. 96 at col. 926: the report of the independent expert 'is simply evidence on the question of the value of the jobs at issue. It is for the tribunals to decide what weight to attach to all the evidence, and ultimately to decide the issue.' In *Hayward* above n. 57 at 467, the industrial tribunal concluded that '[o]nly if we considered that the expert had gone badly wrong would we feel justified in interfering'.

VIII

Like the Sex Discrimination Act 1975, the Equal Pay Act contains a number of important exceptions. The 1970 Act does not apply to provision in relation to death or retirement: so most pension schemes provided by employers are outside the scope of the 1970 Act.[112] Nor does the statute apply to contractual terms which result from the employer's compliance with the laws regulating the employment of women.[113] The Equal Pay Act does not affect terms giving special (favourable) treatment to women in connection with pregnancy or childbirth.[114]

The Equal Pay Act does apply to service in a government department (other than service by a person holding a statutory office).[115] But it does not apply in relation to service in the naval, military, or air forces.[116]

A claim that an equality clause has been breached may be presented to an industrial tribunal.[117] A claim may not be brought unless the applicant has been employed in the relevant employment within the six months prior to her application.[118] An employer also has the right to apply to an industrial tribunal for an order declaring relevant rights under the 1970 Act.[119] Similarly, the Secretary of State for Employment may refer such a matter to the tribunal.[120] Other courts are given powers (which they will, in practice, exercise) to strike out claims in respect of an equality clause, if they conclude that such claims could more conveniently be decided in an industrial tribunal, or to refer such cases to an industrial tribunal.[121] Where a woman succeeds in her claim under the 1970 Act, she is not entitled to be awarded any payment by

---

[112] S. 6(1A). The 1970 Act does cover terms relating to membership of an occupational pension scheme so far as those terms relate to any matter in respect of which the scheme has to conform to the equal access requirements of the Social Security Pensions Act 1975. Community law may give a right and a remedy to equal pay (and equal treatment) in respect of pensions and other retirement and death benefits: see ch. 5 nn. 13–18.

[113] S. 6(1)(a).

[114] S. 6(1)(b). See *Coyne* v. *Exports Credits Guarantee Department* [1981] IRLR 51 (industrial tribunal). See ch. 6 on sex discrimination and pregnancy.

[115] Ss. 1(8) and 1(10).

[116] S. 1(9). S. 7 contains special provisions relating to service pay, restricting the powers of the Secretary of State to introduce any instrument causing unequal pay due to sex discrimination.

[117] S. 2(1). [118] S. 2(4). [119] S. 2(1A).
[120] S. 2(2). [121] S. 2(3).

way of arrears of remuneration or damages in respect of a time more than two years before the date on which the claim was brought.[122]

In addition to giving remedies for sex discrimination in the individual contract of employment, the 1970 Act gives the Central Arbitration Committee power to consider complaints of sex discrimination in collective agreements and pay structures, in wages regulation orders, and in agricultural wages orders. The CAC may declare what amendments are necessary to secure equal pay in these contexts.[123] The CAC may also consider pay in the armed services if the Secretary of State or the Defence Council refers such a matter to it.[124]

The Equal Pay Act 1970 does not apply to Northern Ireland.[125]

IX

The entitlement to equal pay for equal work without sex discrimination is a fundamental human right.[126] Unfortunately the complexity and the obscurity of the Equal Pay Act 1970, and the procedure for applying it, detract from the ability of the law to achieve its purpose. This is particularly regrettable when courts have recognized that industrial tribunals were designed to give cheap and speedy remedies for injustices without the need to resort to lawyers[127] and when many cases under the 1970 Act 'directly or indirectly affect large numbers of persons other than the parties to the particular complaint'.[128]

---

[122] S. 2(5).

[123] Ss. 3, 4, 5 and 10. The powers of the CAC apply only when the impugned instrument 'contains any provision applying specifically to men only or to women only'. This may limit the possibility for challenge in cases of indirect sex discrimination. See *R.* v. *CAC ex parte Hy-Mac Ltd* [1979] IRLR 461 (Divisional Court). Browne LJ said at 464 that 'there may be cases in which the agreement is a sham, in fact containing provisions which applied specifically only to men or women, although on its face it does not'. See generally P. L. Davies, 'The Central Arbitration Committee and Equal Pay' 33 *Current Legal Problems* 165 (1980).

[124] S. 7(2).

[125] S. 11(3). But see Sched. 1 to the Sex Discrimination (Northern Ireland) Order 1976 SI no. 1042 (NI 15) which contains an analogous Equal Pay Act (Northern Ireland) 1970, as amended.

[126] See *Defrenne* v. *Sabena (no. 3)* [1978] ECR 1365, 1378 (Judgment of the ECJ at paras. 26–7). See also *Randhir Singh* v. *Union of India* AIR 1982 SC 879 (Indian Supreme Court).

[127] Above, n. 5.   [128] *Eaton* above, n. 37 at 274.

Too often when deciding claims under the 1970 Act, industrial tribunals, through no fault of their own, have resembled the High Court of Chancery as described by Charles Dickens, with lawyers 'groping knee-deep in technicalities' and pushing each other 'against walls of words'.[129] In one decision on the 1970 Act, Lord Justice Cumming-Bruce in the Court of Appeal needed to apologize for the fact that parts of his judgment were 'drafted in a kind of legal jargon which may later have to be translated into English, and I hope it is intelligible'.[130] Allowing for inflation, the Equal Pay Act is one of those legal contexts where, in the words of Jeremy Bentham, if one wants to know what the law requires, too often 'as well-grounded a guess might be had of an astrologer for five shillings as of a counsel for twice or thrice as many guineas . . .'.[131]

[129] *Bleak House*, ch. 1.

[130] *O'Brien* v. *Sim-Chem Limited* [1980] ICR 429, 432.

[131] *The Works of Jeremy Bentham* (ed. Bowring, 1843), ii, 396. Lord Denning criticized the Equal Value Regulations on the ground that '[n]o ordinary lawyer would be able to understand them. The industrial tribunals would have the greatest difficulty and the Court of Appeal would probably be divided in opinion': 445 HL 901–2 (5 Dec. 1983).

5

EUROPEAN COMMUNITY LAW

I

Whatever the political and economic benefits (and detriments) of membership of the European Economic Community for the United Kingdom, such membership has undoubtedly strengthened anti-discrimination law to the advantage of working women. In 1974, Lord Denning, in the Court of Appeal, described Community law as 'like an incoming tide. It flows into the estuaries and up the rivers. It cannot be held back.' He advised that

[i]n future, in transactions which cross the frontiers, we must no longer speak or think of English law as something on its own. We must speak and think of Community law, Community rights and obligations, and we must give effect to them. This means a great effort for lawyers. We have to learn a new system . . . We must get down to it.[1]

In giving effect to Community law, there are three main issues to be considered:

1. The content of Community law in the field of sex discrimination.
2. The application of Community law to sex discrimination in the United Kingdom.
3. The circumstances in which a British court or tribunal will refer a case to the European Court of Justice for a ruling on the meaning of Community law.

II

Article 119 of the Treaty of Rome provides that 'men and women should receive equal pay for equal work'. Article 119 broadly

---

[1] *H. P. Bulmer Ltd* v. *J. Bollinger SA* [1974] 1 Ch. 401, 418–9. See generally Lawrence Collins, *European Community Law in the United Kingdom* (3rd edn., 1984). For a different perspective see Francis Bennion, *Statute Law* (2nd edn., 1983), 68. He suggests that one consequence of the impact of Community law 'is that the careful provisions of Acts such as the Equal Pay Act 1970 and the Sex Discrimination Act 1975 are disrupted'. Mr Bennion was the Parliamentary draftsman of the 1975 Act. See ch. 11 n. 1.

defines 'pay' to mean 'the ordinary basic or minimum wage or salary and any other consideration, whether in cash or in kind, which the worker receives, directly or indirectly, in respect of his employment from his employer'.

Article 119 has a double aim: first, 'to avoid a situation in which undertakings established in States which have actually implemented the principle of equal pay suffer a competitive disadvantage in intra-community competition as compared with undertakings established in States which have not yet eliminated discrimination against women workers as regards pay'; and secondly, Article 119 'forms part of the social objectives of the Community, which is not merely an economic union, but is at the same time intended, by common action, to ensure social progress and seek the constant improvement of the living and working conditions of their peoples . . .'. This double aim, economic and social, 'shows that the principle of equal pay forms part of the foundations of the Community'.[2]

The broad scope of the concept of 'pay' in Article 119 means that it is unlawful for an employer to provide special travel facilities for the families of male employees after the worker's retirement and not so to provide for the families of female employees after such a worker's retirement. Even though there was no contractual right to such benefits, and they were provided to persons other than the worker himself or herself, the European Court of Justice held that Article 119 applied as the benefits were granted directly or indirectly in respect of employment.[3]

For the purposes of Article 119 a woman employee is entitled to compare her pay with that of a male employee who preceded her in the job. This is because the criterion of 'equal work' is 'entirely qualitative in character in that it is exclusively concerned with the nature of the services in question [and] may not be restricted by the introduction of a requirement of contemporaneity'.[4]

---

[2] *Defrenne* v. *Sabena (no. 2)* [1976] ICR 547, 565–6 (Judgment of the ECJ at paras. 8–12).

[3] *Garland* v. *British Rail Engineering Ltd* [1982] ICR 420.

[4] *Macarthys Ltd* v. *Smith* [1980] ICR 672, 690 (Judgment of the ECJ at para 11). See ch. 4 nn. 21–5. This principle would also suggest that a woman could compare her pay with that of her successor in the job. Under the Equal Pay Act 1970, a woman is entitled to bring a claim within six months of leaving the employment for pay back to two years prior to the date when she brought the claim: see ch. 4 nn. 118 and 122. See also ch. 4 nn. 26–30 on whether art. 119 entitles a woman to compare her pay with that of a hypothetical male worker.

Article 119 can only be satisfied by raising the salary of the lower-paid worker: an employer does not comply with Article 119 by lowering the salary of the more favourably treated worker.[5]

The differences in pay prohibited by Article 119 are 'exclusively those based on the difference of the sex of the workers'.[6] So, if the difference in pay between two workers occupying the same post is 'explained by the operation of factors which are unconnected with any discrimination on grounds of sex', then there is no breach of Article 119.[7] It is unclear to what extent, if at all, Article 119 prohibits indirect sex discrimination,[8] that is a policy or practice which hits disproportionately at women and which the employer cannot justify. The question was raised in *Jenkins* v. *Kingsgate (Clothing Productions) Ltd*. The employer there paid part-time workers a lower hourly rate than full-time workers. Most part-time workers there employed (and in the United Kingdom in general)[9] were women. The issue was whether it was enough to satisfy Article 119 for the employer to show that it had no intention of discriminating against women, or whether it needed also to show an objective justification for its pay policy (for example that it discouraged absenteeism) given that the pay policy had a disparate impact on women. The judgment of the ECJ pointed in each direction in different paragraphs.[10] When the case returned to the Employment Appeal Tribunal, Browne-Wilkinson J. noted the ambiguity, but assumed that the ECJ were saying that Article 119 does not apply to cases of unintentional indirect discrimination.[11] It would be surprising if Article 119 were so limited. Community

---

[5] *Defrenne* v. *Sabena (no. 2)* above, n. 2 at 566 (Judgment of the ECJ at para. 15); *Worringham* v. *Lloyds Bank Ltd* [1981] ICR 558, 565–6 (opinion of the Advocate-General J-P. Warner). On the analogous issue under the 1970 Act see ch. 4 n. 20.

[6] *Jenkins* v. *Kingsgate (Clothing Productions) Ltd* [1981] ICR 592, 613 (Judgment of the ECJ at para. 10).

[7] *Macarthys* above, n. 4 at 690 (para. 12). So art. 119 has a defence similar to that stated in s. 1(3) of the 1970 Act, on which see ch. 4 s. VI. On the application of the defence in a case raising issues under art. 119 see *Albion Shipping Agency* v. *Arnold* [1982] ICR 22 (EAT). As under section 1(3) of the 1970 Act, so under art. 119 it is for the employer to prove that the difference in pay is genuinely due to a reason other than the sex of the worker. See *Macarthys* above, n. 4 at 678–9 (per Advocate-General Capotorti).

[8] On the concept of indirect sex discrimination see ch. 2 ss. III and IV.

[9] See ch. 2 n. 59.

[10] *Jenkins* above, n. 6 at 613 (paras. 11–15).

[11] [1981] ICR 715, 725. On the similar problem of whether the Equal Pay Act 1970 prohibits indirect sex discrimination see ch. 4 nn. 80–83.

law has, in other contexts, developed a more rigorous concept of indirect discrimination.[12]

One of the most difficult problems under Article 119 concerns the extent to which pension benefits are within the scope of equal pay. In *Worringham* v. *Lloyds Bank Ltd*, the ECJ held that an employer's contribution in the name of an employee to an occupational pension scheme by way of an addition to gross salary was 'pay' for the purposes of Article 119.[13] The Court found it unnecessary to consider the broader question of whether the rights and benefits of a worker under such a pension scheme constitute 'pay' within the meaning of Article 119.[14]

Social security schemes or benefits (including pension benefits) which are 'directly governed by legislation without any element of agreement within the undertaking or the occupational branch concerned' and which are 'obligatorily applicable to general categories of workers' do not fall within Article 119.[15] More difficult is to describe what pension scheme benefits are outside Article 119 because of links with State schemes. In *Defrenne* v. *Belgium*, Mr Advocate-General Dutheillet de Lamothe,[16] in an opinion described by Lord Denning as 'not very easy for English readers to follow',[17] considered the problem. He suggested that retirement pensions paid directly by an employer to its former employees were undoubtedly within the scope of Article 119.

[12] See ch. 2 n. 48. In *Jenkins* above, n. 6 at 601 Advocate-General Warner referred to that jurisprudence as supporting the conclusion that art. 119 does prohibit indirect sex discrimination.

[13] Above, n. 5 at 588–9 (paras. 12–17).

[14] Ibid. at 589 (para. 18). Note that in *Razzouk and Beydoun* v. *European Commission* [1984] 3 CMLR 470, the ECJ held that it was unlawful for the Commission to discriminate between male and female staff in the provision of survivors' pensions. The Advocate-General, Sir Gordon Slynn, considered art. 119 at 491–2. He suggested that benefits under pension schemes are covered by art. 119 when they are 'outside a national system of social security' even if they 'replace social security legislation for the [staff] concerned'. Moreover, he said, a survivor's pension was 'pay' even though not paid to the worker concerned but to his or her spouse. See above, n. 3.

[15] *Defrenne* v. *Belgium* [1971] ECR 445, 451 (Judgment of the ECJ at para. 7). But see *Liefting* v. *Governing Board of the Amsterdam University Hospital* [1984] 3 CMLR 702, 714 (Judgment of the ECJ at para. 13): '. . . sums which public authorities are required to pay as social security payable by persons working for the authority, when such sums are included in calculating the gross salary payable to civil servants, should be considered as pay within the meaning of Article 119 in so far as they determine directly the calculation of other salary-related benefits'.

[16] Ibid. at 457–61.

[17] *Worringham* v. *Lloyds Bank Ltd* [1979] IRLR 440, 442 (Court of Appeal).

Similarly, in his view, Article 119 covered a pension payment which was not received directly from the employer but indirectly from a pension fund which manages and distributes contributions from workers and employers. He added, however, that pensions from social security schemes, or from special schemes of social security, fall outside Article 119. In *Worringham*, Mr Advocate-General Warner added that, in his view, 'where a privately established pension scheme is designed, not as a supplement to the State social security scheme . . . but as a substitute for it or for part of it', then it is outside Article 119. He therefore concluded that a private occupational pension scheme which is 'contracted out' of the State scheme by fulfilling the requirements of United Kingdom law (thereby substituting rights and benefits under the occupational scheme for rights and benefits under the State scheme) does not fall within Article 119.[18]

Article 119 defines the entitlement to equal pay by reference to 'equal work'. This concept is amplified by the Equal Pay Directive.[19] Article 1 of the Directive explains that the principle of equal pay for men and women outlined in Article 119 'means, for the same work or for work to which equal value is attributed', the elimination of sex discrimination with regard to all aspects and conditions of remuneration. Article 1 adds that 'where a job classification system is used for determining pay, it must be based on the same criteria for both men and women and so drawn up as to exclude any discrimination on grounds of sex'. The Directive 'in no way affects the concept of "pay" contained' in Article 119.[20] The Equal Pay Directive is 'principally designed to facilitate the practical application of the principle of equal pay outlined in Article 119 of the Treaty [and] in no way alters the content or scope of that principle as defined in the Treaty'.[21] It was adopted

---

[18] Above, n. 5 at 568. On art. 119 and pension schemes see Richard Plender, 'Equal Pay for Men and Women: Two Recent Decisions of the European Court' 30 *American Journal of Comparative Law* 627 (1982); Evelyn Ellis and Philip Morrell, 'Sex Discrimination in Pension Schemes: Has Community Law Changed the Rules?' 11 *Industrial Law Journal* 16 (1982). On the concept of equality in pensions for men and women see also ch. 7 s. IV, in particular the US Supreme Court decisions in *Los Angeles Department of Water and Power* v. *Manhart* 435 US 702 (1978) and *Arizona Governing Committee* v. *Norris* 103 S. Ct. 3492 (1983).

[19] 75/117/EEC of 10 Feb. 1975.

[20] *Worringham* above, n. 5 at 589 (Judgment of the ECJ at para. 21).

[21] *Jenkins* above, n. 6 at 614 (Judgment of the ECJ at para. 22).

'to hasten the full implementation of Article 119 . . . by means of a series of measures to be taken on the national level . . .'.[22]

In 1982, the ECJ held that the Equal Pay Act 1970 was in breach of the Directive because it failed to give a worker the right to claim equal pay with a person of the opposite sex doing work of equal value in the same establishment where no job evaluation had been carried out.[23] As a result, the 1970 Act was amended with effect from 1 January 1984 to entitle a worker to claim equal pay in such circumstances.[24]

Article 119, and the Equal Pay Directive, 'cannot be interpreted as prescribing, in addition to equal pay, equality in respect of the other working conditions applicable to men and women'.[25] Such matters are governed by the Equal Treatment Directive.[26] This entitles men and women to equal treatment, without sex discrimination, as regards access to employment (including promotion) and vocational training, and as regards working conditions (including the conditions governing dismissal).

The overlap between Article 119 and the Equal Treatment Directive was considered by the ECJ in *Burton* v. *British Railways Board*.[27] The employers there offered voluntary redundancy to their staff five years before normal retirement age (which was 65 for men and 60 for women). The male complainant, aged 58, was therefore not eligible for such voluntary redundancy (and the financial benefits consequent thereon). A woman employee of that age would have been so eligible. The complainant had no valid claim under the Sex Discrimination Act 1975 because of the exclusion of benefits relating to death or retirement.[28] The ECJ held that the issue concerned 'not the benefit itself, but whether the conditions of access to the voluntary redundancy scheme are discriminatory'. This, said the Court, is a matter covered by the

[22] *Defrenne (no. 2)* above, n. 2 at 569–70 (Judgment of the ECJ at paras. 53 and 60).
[23] *Commission of the European Communities* v. *United Kingdom* [1982] ICR 578.
[24] See ch. 4 s. V.
[25] *Defrenne* v. *Sabena (no. 3)* [1978] ECR 1365, 1377 (Judgment of the ECJ at para. 24).
[26] 76/207/EEC of 9 Feb. 1976.
[27] [1982] ICR 329.
[28] S. 6(4) of the Sex Discrimination Act 1975: see ch. 3 n. 19. S. 6(1A) of the Equal Pay Act 1970 contains a similar exclusion in relation to sex discrimination in pensions provided by way of contractual benefits: see ch. 4 n. 112.

Equal Treatment Directive, not by Article 119 or by the Equal Pay Directive.[29]

On the question of substance raised by the *Burton* case—whether the different age requirements for men and women to be eligible for voluntary redundancy breached the Equal Treatment Directive —the ECJ said that 'account must be taken of the relationship between measures such as that at issue and national provisions on normal retirement age'. The Court noted that there is a Directive on equal treatment for men and women in matters of social security.[30] Article 7 of that Directive states that it is without prejudice to the rights of Member States to exclude from its scope the determination of pensionable age for the purpose of granting old-age and retirement pensions and the possible consequences of this for other benefits. Therefore, concluded the Court, it could not be a breach of Community law for a State to adopt a different pensionable age for men as compared with women. Since the different ages for men and women here stated by the employers governing eligibility for voluntary redundancy were 'tied to the retirement scheme governed by United Kingdom social security provisions' (that is, the different ages adopted the five-year differential in normal retirement age of 65 for men and 60 for women under UK social security law), there was no sex discrimination contrary to the Equal Treatment Directive.[31]

In *Southampton & South West Hampshire Health Authority (Teaching)* v. *Marshall*,[32] the EAT held that *Burton* decided only that access at different ages to benefits or disadvantages in the context of social security is not sex discrimination in breach of the Equal Treatment Directive. *Burton* did not, according to the EAT, make compatible with the Directive the employer's practice here of compulsorily retiring men at 65 and women at 60 when this was objected to by a woman employee who wished to carry on working until she reached the age of 65.

---

[29] Above, n. 27 at 347–8 (paras. 7–8).

[30] 79/7/EEC of 9 Dec. 1978. Art. 1(2) of the Equal Treatment Directive notes that such a social security Directive would deal with equal treatment in social security matters.

[31] Above, n. 27 at 348–9 (paras. 10–18). See *Roberts* v. *Tate & Lyle Food and Distribution Ltd* [1983] ICR 521 (EAT) discussed in ch. 2 n. 38 on the problems posed by this approach for the concept of sex discrimination. See ch. 7 nn. 78–81 on different retirement ages for men and women.

[32] [1983] IRLR 237. See also n. 81 below.

In *Hofmann* v. *Barmer Ersatzkasse*, the ECJ held that it was not a breach of the Equal Treatment Directive for an employed father to be denied paid paternity leave by the State up to six months after the birth of his child even though an employed mother was entitled to maternity leave for such a period and even though, in this case, the parents preferred the father, rather than the mother, to enjoy the benefit. The Court referred to Article 2(3) of the Directive, which provides that the Directive is 'without prejudice to provisions concerning the protection of women, particularly as regards pregnancy and maternity'. The Court concluded that the Directive

recognises the legitimacy of the protection of two types of women's needs. On the one hand it is a question of guaranteeing protection of the woman's biological condition during and following her pregnancy until the time when her physiological and psychic functions have become normal again after delivery and, on the other hand, protection of the special relationship between the woman and her child during the period following pregnancy and delivery, by making sure that this relationship is not disturbed by the many duties resulting from the simultaneous exercise of a professional activity.[33]

The extent to which special provisions for women are compatible with the general principle of equal treatment without sex discrimination will be determined by reference to whether the special provision at issue protects the unique 'biological condition' of women after giving birth and whether it protects her 'special relationship' with her new-born child. States will be unable to justify special measures for women by reference to theories about the desirability (or not) of mothers working outside the home, or by reference to other stereotyped assumptions about the precise role of men or women as parents.[34] It is surprising that, even with the 'reasonable margin of appreciation'[35] allowed to States in

[33] Case no. 184/83. *The Times* 24 July 1984. See ch. 6 nn. 22 and 69 on art. 2(3) of the Directive. See similarly *European Commission* v. *Italy* [1984] 3 CMLR 169, 183–5 (Judgment of the ECJ at paras. 11–17): it was held not to be a breach of the Equal Treatment Directive for the State to give a mother who adopts a child of less than six years of age the right to employment leave and to a financial allowance without according similar rights to adoptive fathers because of 'the legitimate concern to assimilate as far as possible the conditions of entry of the child into the adoptive family to those of the arrival of a newborn child in the family during the very delicate initial period'.

[34] See ch. 2 nn. 39–45 on stereotyped assumptions as direct sex discrimination.

[35] *Hofmann* above n. 33.

assessing what period of special maternity leave may be given to women, the ECJ should validate special treatment for women up to six months after the birth of the child and should give no indication of what length of special leave for women would breach the principle of equal treatment in the Directive. United Kingdom domestic law recognizes that working women are (in specified circumstances) entitled to 40 weeks' maternity leave, 29 weeks of which must be taken following confinement.[36] This is the outer boundary of the period in fact necessary to allow for the mother's complete recovery and to enable her to breast-feed her child.[37] The major defect of the ECJ judgment in *Hofmann* is its failure to explain that any more than six months special leave for a mother following confinement would breach the principle of equal treatment in the Directive by accepting different treatment of men and women by reason only of stereotyped assumptions about the respective roles of the mother and the father in rearing a child.[38]

In *Commission of the European Communities* v. *United Kingdom*[39] the ECJ considered two aspects of domestic law. First, it held that domestic law breached the Directive on equal treatment in that it did not amend or make void collective agreements, rules of undertakings, and rules governing independent occupations and professions which were not legally binding but which discriminated on the ground of sex.[40] Secondly, it considered the application of Article 2(2) of the Directive, which allows States to authorize sex discrimination where the sex of a worker 'constitutes a determining factor' for the job.[41] The Court recognized that 'the principle of respect for private life' and 'personal sensitivities' are relevant factors in applying Article 2(2). These factors meant that the UK Government had not breached the Equal Treatment Directive by restricting men's occupational opportunities in the field of mid-

---

[36] Employment Protection (Consolidation) Act 1978, Part III.

[37] There is little doubt that, following *Hofmann*, s. 2(2) of the Sex Discrimination Act 1975—on which see ch. 6 nn. 22 and 69—would be interpreted to validate such a period of special treatment for a mother.

[38] See ch. 11 n. 54 on the undesirable social consequences of this decision in perpetuating sexual stereotypes of the role of men and women at home and in employment.

[39] [1984] ICR 192.

[40] Ibid. at 214–15 (Judgment of the ECJ at para. 4–11).

[41] See ch. 9 on the similar 'genuine occupational qualification' defence under s. 7 of the Sex Discrimination Act 1975.

wifery.[42] However, it was a breach of the Directive for the Sex Discrimination Act 1975 to contain a blanket exclusion of employment in a private household and of employment in undertakings where the number of persons employed does not exceed five, irrespective of whether the principle of respect for private life requires sex discrimination in the circumstances of the individual case.[43]

In *Von Colson and Kamann* v. *Nordrhein-Westphalia* the ECJ held that the Equal Treatment Directive does not require sex discrimination regarding access to employment to be remedied by a sanction imposing an obligation on the employer to enter into a contract of employment with the victim of the sex discrimination. The Directive leaves Member States to decide what sanctions should be available to achieve the objectives of the Directive. However, the sanction must ensure real and effective legal protection and must have a genuine deterrent effect on the employer. A national measure which restricts the rights of compensation of persons discriminated against to a purely nominal award (for example, the reimbursement of their costs) does not conform to the requirements of Community law for the effective implementation of the Directive.[44]

On 19 December 1984, the Directive on equal treatment for men and women in matters of social security came into effect.[45] The Social Security Directive requires equal treatment of men and women without sex discrimination, in particular as concerns the scope of schemes and the conditions of access to them, the obligation to contribute and the calculation of contributions, the calculation of benefits (including increases due in respect of a spouse and for dependents) and the conditions governing the duration and retention of entitlement to benefits. The Directive covers statutory schemes providing protection against sickness, invalidity, old age, accidents at work and occupational diseases, and unemployment. It also covers social assistance in so far as it is intended to supplement or replace such statutory schemes. However, the Directive does not apply to provisions concerning

---

[42] Above, n. 39 at 216–17 (paras. 13 and 17–20). S. 20 of the 1975 Act has now been amended to enhance such employment opportunities for men: see ch. 3 nn. 25–7.

[43] Ibid. at 216 (Judgment at paras. 12–16). On these exceptions under the 1975 Act see ch. 3 nn. 15–18.

[44] Case 14/83. *The Times* 25 Apr. 1984.   [45] Above, n. 30.

survivors' benefits or to those concerning family benefits, except in the case of family benefits granted by way of increases of benefits in respect of the risks mentioned above. The Directive also empowers Member States to exclude from its scope the determination of pensionable age for the purposes of granting old-age and retirement pensions and the possible consequences thereof for other benefits; advantages in respect of old-age pension schemes granted to persons who have brought up children; the granting of increases of long-term invalidity, old-age, accidents at work and occupational disease benefits for a dependent wife; and associated aspects of social security.

III

There are two principal ways in which Community law may be applied to a dispute on a matter concerning alleged sex discrimination.

First, Community law may be applied by the European Court of Justice in proceedings brought by the European Commission against the UK Government alleging that the Government has not fulfilled its obligations under Community law. Two such infringement proceedings[46] have been brought against the UK Government in the context of sex discrimination law: those cases concerned equal pay for work of equal value,[47] and collective agreements, rules of undertakings, rules governing independent occupations and professions, midwives, small employers, and employment in private households.[48]

Secondly, a party in proceedings before a tribunal or court in the United Kingdom may argue that its rights and duties should be defined by reference to Community law. In such cases, the tribunal or court may decide the question of Community law or it may refer the issue of Community law to the European Court of Justice for a ruling on the scope and application of Community law in the relevant context.[49]

There are two main ways in which a party may claim that Community law affects its substantive rights in a tribunal or a court. It may argue that, so far as possible, the Sex Discrimination

---

[46] Under art. 169 of the Treaty of Rome.
[47] Above, n. 23.   [48] Above, n. 39.
[49] On the circumstances in which such a reference will be made see below s. IV.

Act 1975 (and the Equal Pay Act 1970) should be interpreted consistently with Community law. Alternatively, it may contend that even when domestic law, read on its own, is unambiguous and in conflict with Community law, nevertheless Article 119, the Equal Pay Directive, the Equal Treatment Directive, and any other relevant provision of Community law create independent rights and duties which can and should be enforced in tribunals and courts.

The application of Community law in domestic courts and tribunals depends on section 2(1) of the European Communities Act 1972. This provides that all 'rights, powers, liabilities, obligations and restrictions' arising by or under Community law which, under Community law, 'are without further enactment to be given legal effect or used in the United Kingdom shall be recognised and available in law, and be enforced, allowed and followed accordingly . . .'. For this reason, in *Garland* v. *British Rail Engineering Ltd* Lord Diplock, for the House of Lords, explained that, in an appropriate case, counsel should draw attention to Article 119, the Equal Pay Directive and the Equal Treatment Directive. As Lord Diplock explained,

> even if the obligation to observe the provisions of Article 119 were an obligation assumed by the United Kingdom under an ordinary international treaty or convention and there were no question of the treaty obligation being directly applicable as part of the law to be applied by the courts in this country without need for any further enactment, it is a principle of construction of United Kingdom statutes, now too well established to call for citation of authority, that the words of a statute passed after the treaty has been signed and dealing with the subject matter of the international obligation of the United Kingdom, are to be construed, if they are reasonably capable of bearing such a meaning, as intended to carry out the obligation and not to be inconsistent with it. *A fortiori* is this the case where the treaty obligation arises under one of the Community treaties to which section 2 of the European Communities Act 1972 applies.[50]

For this reason, concluded the House of Lords in *Garland*, the exemption in section 6(4) of the Sex Discrimination Act 1975 of an employer's 'provision in relation to . . . retirement'[51] should be construed consistently with Article 119. Therefore, by reason of the decision of the ECJ in *Garland* that Article 119 prohibited sex

[50] Above, n. 3 at 438.   [51] Above, n. 28.

discrimination in the provision of post-retirement travel facilities to employees (and their families),[52] section 6(4) should be construed as not excluding from the scope of the 1975 Act sex discrimination in respect of such matters. So such sex discrimination was held by the House of Lords to breach the 1975 Act. Somewhat disingenuously, Lord Diplock asserted that this result could be reached 'without any undue straining of the ordinary meaning of the language used' in section 6(4).[53]

Three points arise from the decision of the House of Lords in *Garland*. First, that section 6(4) is not to be given 'the wider meaning' adopted by the Court of Appeal that 'provision in relation to . . . retirement' means any provision about retirement.[54] Rather, it should be given 'the narrower meaning' adopted by the Employment Appeal Tribunal that the words in section 6(4) did not cover 'a privilege [that] has existed during employment' and is allowed by the employer 'to continue after retirement'.[55]

The second issue arising from the decision of the House of Lords is whether the 1975 Act, and the Equal Pay Act 1970, are to be construed consistently with Article 119 alone, or are also to be construed consistently with the two Directives. Although the Equal Treatment Directive was adopted in 1976, after the enactment of the domestic legislation, and so does not fall directly within the principle explained by Lord Diplock, the better view is that domestic law should be construed consistently with that

[52] Above, n. 3 at 433–5.
[53] Ibid. at 438.
[54] *Roberts* v. *Cleveland Area Health Authority* [1979] ICR 558.
[55] *Garland* v. *British Rail Engineering Ltd* [1978] ICR 495, 499. The EAT there suggested that the test under s. 6(4) is 'whether what is being done is part and parcel of the employer's system of catering for retirement or whether, as here, the case is merely one where a privilege has existed during employment and has been allowed to continue after retirement'. In *Roberts* v. *Tate & Lyle* above n. 31 the EAT applied this test, and added, at 528–9, that 'the purpose of section 6(4) is fairly apparent. Parliament, in enacting the Act of 1975, was seeking to eliminate all discrimination between men and women. However, it was faced by a widespread and inherently discriminatory practice deeply embedded in the social organisation of the country, namely the differential in retirement ages between men and women. This differential treatment was blatantly discriminatory. However, the effect of such discriminatory practice percolated throughout society. State pensions reflected the differential; the vast majority of occupational pension schemes reflected the differential; normal ages of retirement maintained the differential. Accordingly, unless all this was to be swept away, the Act had to exclude claims arising out of this inherently discriminatory practice. For this reason, section 6(4) appeared in the Act.'

Directive, as well as with Article 119 and the Equal Pay Directive.[56] The Equal Treatment Directive was, as its preamble makes clear, adopted pursuant to the Treaty of Rome. In *Burton*, Mr Advocate-General VerLoren van Themaat suggested that the 1975 Act should, so far as possible, be construed in accordance with the Equal Treatment Directive in order to avoid a conflict between domestic law and Community law.[57] Given that the Equal Pay Directive is 'principally designed to facilitate the practical application of the principle of equal pay',[58] it would be strange if domestic law were to be interpreted consistently with Article 119 but inconsistently with the Equal Pay Directive. Since the Equal Pay Directive and the Equal Treatment Directive are complementary provisions of Community law covering different aspects of sex discrimination in employment, it would be equally strange if domestic law had to be interpreted consistently with the Equal Pay Directive but could be construed inconsistently with the Equal Treatment Directive.

The third, and most difficult, issue raised by the House of Lords judgment in *Garland* is what happens when domestic law cannot be interpreted consistently with Community law, but the two conflict? Section 2(4) of the European Communities Act 1972 states that 'any enactment passed or to be passed . . . shall be construed and have effect subject to' enforceable Community law. Because there was no conflict in *Garland* between the 1975 Act and Community law, that case did

not present an appropriate occasion to consider whether, having regard to the express direction as to the construction of enactments 'to be passed' which is contained in section 2(4), anything short of an express positive statement in an Act of Parliament passed after January 1, 1973, that a particular provision is intended to be made in breach of an obligation assumed by the United Kingdom under a Community treaty, would justify an English court in construing that provision in a manner inconsistent with a Community treaty obligation of the United Kingdom, however wide a

---

[56] Unless domestic law is to be construed consistently with the Equal Treatment Directive, or that directive has direct effect in English courts, on which see below, nn. 66–78, it is difficult to see why in *Garland* above, n. 3 at 437–8 Lord Diplock stated that the Equal Treatment Directive, and the Equal Pay Directive, as well as art. 119, 'should have been' drawn to the attention of the EAT and the Court of Appeal.

[57] [1982] QB 1080, 1089–90.   [58] Above, n. 21.

departure from the prima-facie meaning of the language of the provision might be needed in order to achieve consistency.[59]

Domestic law will sometimes give greater rights to a complainant in the sex discrimination field than does Community law.[60] That causes no problems of principle: the complainant relies on domestic law, and Community law has little or no relevance. Where Community law provides more extensive rights than domestic law, however, and the two cannot be construed consistently, the consequence of section 2(1) of the 1972 Act[61] is that the complainant will not be able to rely on a provision of the Community unless, as a matter of Community law, that provision has direct effect in an English court or tribunal. Where a provision of Community law does have such direct effect, and cannot be interpreted consistently with domestic law, section 2(4) of the 1972 Act suggests that the Community law rights take priority over the inconsistent provisions of domestic law.

Article 119 of the Treaty of Rome has direct effect in all cases involving overt sex discrimination which can be identified 'solely with the aid of [the] criteria of equal work and equal pay . . .'.[62] For this reason, in *Macarthys Ltd* v. *Smith* Lord Denning (with whom the other members of the Court of Appeal agreed) explained that 'the provisions of Article 119 of the EEC Treaty take priority over anything in our English statute on equal pay which is inconsistent with Article 119. That priority is given by our own law. It is given by the European Communities Act 1972 itself.'[63] The EAT asked in *Albion Shipping Agency* v. *Arnold* where industrial tribunals derive their jurisdiction to hear claims brought under Article 119, unless one treats the claim as arising under domestic law as amended by Article 119. The EAT there rightly concluded that complainants can rely on Article 119 as the basis of a claim in a tribunal.[64] Since the Equal Pay Directive clarifies what is meant in Article 119 by the concept of equal pay for equal work without sex discrimination, but does not alter the content and scope of the principle stated in Article 119, it is very

[59] *Garland* above, n. 3 at 438.
[60] See *Jenkins* above, n. 11 at 725–6 (EAT).   [61] Above, n. 50.
[62] *Jenkins* above, n. 6 at 613–14 (Judgment of the ECJ at para. 17).
[63] *Macarthys* above, n. 4 at 692.
[64] *Albion* above, n. 7 at 30. See similarly *Shields* v. *E. Coomes (Holdings) Ltd* [1978] ICR 1159, 1167 per Lord Denning in the Court of Appeal.

probable that the Equal Pay Directive has direct effect in similar circumstances to Article 119.[65]

On three occasions the EAT has held that the Equal Treatment Directive is not directly effective in an English court or tribunal against a non-State defendant and so cannot, of itself, be relied upon by a complainant as the basis of her claim against a private employer.[66]

It is well established that a Directive may have direct effect in domestic courts so that it can be invoked against a Member State if it is unconditional and sufficiently clear and precise to be capable of producing direct effects.[67] What the ECJ has yet to decide is whether a Directive such as that dealing with equal treatment for men and women may have horizontal direct effect, that is whether it may be binding and enforceable in domestic courts as against a private person or body as well as against a Member State which has failed to implement the relevant Directive into domestic law. However, there is authority suggesting that a Directive only imposes obligations on a Member State (so as to prevent a State relying on its own failure to implement the Directive if proceedings are brought against it in a national court) and not on private individuals or companies.[68]

The relevant provisions of the Equal Treatment Directive do impose unconditional and sufficiently precise obligations to permit of their application in national courts. The concepts of 'discrimination on grounds of sex' and 'working conditions, including the conditions governing dismissal' are as unconditional and precise as the concept of equal pay for equal work without sex discrimination

---

[65] This is despite the judgment of the Court of Appeal in *O'Brien* v. *Sim-Chem Ltd* [1980] ICR 429, 443–4 (Cumming-Bruce LJ) and 446 (Waller LJ) that the Equal Pay Directive does not have direct effect. The House of Lords did not deal with this point in that case: [1980] ICR 573.

[66] *Hugh-Jones* v. *St John's College, Cambridge* [1979] ICR 848; *Southampton* above n. 32; *Roberts* v. *Tate & Lyle* above n. 31.

[67] See, for example, *Van Duyn* v. *Home Office* [1975] 1 Ch 358; *Pubblico Ministero* v. *Ratti* [1979] ECR 1629, 1642 (Judgment of the ECJ at paras. 20–3).

[68] See *Pubblico Ministero* above n. 67 at 1645 (Judgment of the ECJ at para. 46) and at 1650 (Opinion of Advocate-General Reischl); J-P Warner, 'The Relationship between European Community Law and the National Laws of Member States' 93 *Law Quarterly Review* 349, 359 (1977); Pierre Pescatore, 'The Doctrine of "Direct Effect": An Infant Disease of Community Law' 8 *European Law Review* 155, 171 (1983). See also A. J. Easson, 'Can Directives Impose Obligations on Individuals?' 4 *European Law Review* 67 (1979).

which the ECJ has recognized to be directly applicable in national courts in certain circumstances.[69]

Some of the arguments presented in previous cases by the ECJ for the direct effect of Directives against a State[70] similarly suggest that a Directive may have horizontal direct effect against a private employer. First, although by reason of Article 189 of the Treaty of Rome, Regulations are directly applicable and so capable of producing direct effects, it does not follow that other measures mentioned in Article 189, such as Directives, can never produce similar effects. Secondly, where the Community authorities have imposed an obligation on a Member State to act in a certain way, the effectiveness of such a measure could be weakened if the nationals of that State could not invoke it in national courts as part of Community law against private defendants. Thirdly, Article 177, empowering national courts to refer to the ECJ all questions regarding the validity and the interpretation of all acts of Community institutions,[71] implies that individuals may invoke such acts, including Directives, before the national courts.

Whether a particular Directive has such horizontal direct effect may depend on its objectives, its content and on other relevant factors. The objectives and the content of the Equal Treatment Directive strongly suggest that it does have such a direct effect. In *Defrenne* v. *Sabena (no. 3)* the ECJ noted that 'respect for fundamental personal human rights is one of the general principles of Community law, the observance of which it has a duty to ensure. There can be no doubt that the elimination of discrimination based on sex forms part of those fundamental rights.'[72] The ECJ here recognized the crucial importance of the Equal Treatment Directive and its distinction from the generality of Directives. To achieve the purpose of protecting fundamental human rights, it is vital for the relevant parts of the Equal Treatment Directive to have horizontal direct effect. Otherwise Community law would be unable adequately to deter and to remedy sex discrimination in employment.

In *Defrenne* v. *Sabena (no. 3)* the Court and the Advocate-General suggested that the Directive, because of its special

---

[69] Above, n. 62.

[70] *Van Duyn* above, n. 67 at 376–7 (Judgment of the ECJ at paras. 11–12).

[71] See below, s. IV.

[72] Above, n. 25 at 1378 (Judgment of the ECJ at paras. 25–9).

function of protecting fundamental rights, does have horizontal direct effect. The Court stated that 'at the period under considera- tion' the Community had not, 'as regards the relationships of employer and employee . . . assumed any responsibility for supervising and guaranteeing the observance of the principle of equality between men and women in working conditions other than remuneration'.[73] The Court thus strongly implied that, once the time-limit for implementation of the Equal Treatment Directive had expired (which it had not done at the time under consideration in that case, but which it has now done), the Community *would* have such a responsibility with regard to the relationship of employer and employee. Mr Advocate-General Capotorti similarly recognized that the Directive may well have horizontal direct effect.[74]

The Equal Treatment Directive itself suggests by its language that it is intended to have horizontal direct effect. Article 6 provides that

Member States shall introduce into their national legal systems such measures as are necessary to enable all persons who consider themselves wronged by failure to apply to them the principle of equal treatment within the meaning of [the Directive] to pursue their claims by judicial process after possible recourse to other competent authorities.

This suggests that individuals are entitled to unimpeded access to national courts where they claim to be victims of a breach of the Directive. It necessarily implies that complainants are entitled to rely on the Directive in national courts to establish a claim against the responsible employer.

The denial of horizontal direct effect to the main provisions of the Equal Treatment Directive would lead to arbitrary consequences which could not be reconciled with the fundamental rights at issue in this context. If the main provisions did not have such a direct effect, it would be necessary to make a distinction between those employments for which the State is responsible (and in respect of

[73] Ibid. at 1378–9 (Judgment of the ECJ at paras. 30, 31, and 33).
[74] He said, at 1388: 'if, when the time-limit expires, the Member States do not comply with their obligation to enact the measures prescribed by the [Equal Treatment] Directive, the way would be open for the enforcement, in the Community system, of personal rights of individuals on the basis of the Directive itself; this would of course only be to the extent permitted by the structure of each provision in the Directive.'

which an employee could therefore rely on the Directive in national courts) and those employments for which the State was not responsible. In addition to the inherent difficulties posed by such an exercise, the implementation of such a distinction would result in unfair discrimination against certain employees according to the nature of their employers.

Similarly, if the Directive did not have horizontal direct effect, the distinction between pay (covered by Article 119, which does have such a direct effect) and working conditions (covered by the Equal Treatment Directive), a distinction not always easy to apply,[75] would determine whether sex discrimination by a private employer was remediable in national courts by reference to Community law. In the context of the fundamental right to employment without sex discrimination, such a distinction would be arbitrary. Article 119 (with the Equal Pay Directive) and the Equal Treatment Directive are interlocking parts of a code designed to further the economic and social goal of securing equality of treatment without sex discrimination in the field of employment.[76]

Furthermore, if the Directive did not have horizontal direct effect, this would result in unfair discrimination as between the nationals of Member States where the Directive is self-executing as a matter of domestic law and the nationals of Member States such as the United Kingdom where, by reason of section 2(1) of the European Communities Act 1972,[77] the Directive is only applicable and effective in national courts (other than as an aid to interpretation)[78] if, as a matter of Community law, it has such a direct effect. If the Equal Treatment Directive did not have horizontal direct effect, its important provisions protecting the fundamental rights of employees of non-State employers would be enforceable (in the event of a conflict with domestic law) only in infringement proceedings against the State. Such victims of unlawful sex discrimination would have no means of personally enforcing their fundamental right to employment without sex discrimination.

The content and the purpose of the Equal Treatment Directive

---

[75] See *Burton*, above, nn. 27–9.

[76] This provides a further reason why the Equal Pay Directive has direct effect: see above, n. 65.

[77] Above, n. 50.   [78] Ibid.

therefore strongly suggest that it has horizontal direct effect enabling its provisions to be relied on by a victim of sex discrimination in employment as against a private employer in national courts and tribunals.

IV

Article 177 of the Treaty of Rome confers jurisdiction on the European Court of Justice in Luxembourg to give preliminary rulings on the proper interpretation of the Treaty and of the measures, such as Directives, adopted by the institutions of the Community.

The second paragraph of Article 177 provides that any court or tribunal of a Member State *may*, if it considers that a decision on a question of interpretation is necessary to enable it to give judgment, request the ECJ to give a ruling on the relevant question. The third paragraph of Article 177 adds that, where such a question is raised in a case pending before a court or tribunal of a Member State against whose decision there is no judicial remedy under national law, that court or tribunal *shall* bring the matter before the ECJ.[79]

So, by reason of Article 177, a county court, an industrial tribunal, the EAT, the High Court or the Court of Appeal (or, in Scotland, a sheriff court or the Court of Session) may refer to the ECJ a question of law under Article 119, the Equal Pay Directive, the Equal Treatment Directive, or any other provision of Community law, where a decision on that question of law is necessary to enable the court or tribunal to decide the claim. Where such a claim is being heard by the House of Lords (or, exceptionally, a lower court which is the final court of appeal in domestic law on the relevant issue), then that final court of appeal in domestic law must refer such a question to the ECJ.[80]

[79] See generally *CILFIT* v. *Ministry of Health of Italy* [1982] ECR 3415 and J. Kodwo Bentil, 'European Court's Preliminary Ruling' 133 *New Law Journal* 617 and 721 (1983).

[80] See *Garland* above, n. 3 at 439. On the circumstances in which the Court of Appeal may be the final appeal court in domestic law for the purposes of art. 177, see *Hagen* v. *D. and G. Moretti SNC* [1980] 3 CMLR 253, 255. In *CILFIT* above, n. 79, the ECJ held, at 3431 (para. 21), that a court or tribunal (such as the House of Lords) against whose decisions there is no judicial remedy under national law is required, where a question of Community law is raised before it, to refer the question to the ECJ 'unless [the court or tribunal] has established that the question

There have been a number of references to the ECJ by English courts and tribunals on questions of interpretation of Article 119, the Equal Pay Directive and the Equal Treatment Directive.[81]

When considering whether to refer a question of Community law to the ECJ, an English court or tribunal needs to consider two main issues. First, is it necessary to obtain a ruling from the ECJ in order to decide the present case? Secondly, if the court or tribunal hearing the claim is not a final court of appeal, should it exercise its discretion to make such a reference?

English courts have accepted that the criterion of it being 'necessary' to decide the issue of Community law if the matter is to be referred to the ECJ does not mean 'unavoidable', but reasonably necessary in order to do justice, with the domestic court or tribunal having a discretion how it applies this criterion.[82] However, the Divisional Court has emphasized that it would normally be highly undesirable for a court such as a magistrates' court to refer a question of law to the ECJ before all the facts had been found, for the obvious reason that it may not be necessary to answer the question of law in order to decide the case. The time

raised is irrelevant or that the Community provision in question has already been interpreted by the Court or that the correct application of Community law is so obvious as to leave no scope for any reasonable doubt. The existence of such a possibility must be assessed in the light of the specific characteristics of Community law, the particular difficulties to which its interpretation gives rise and the risk of divergencies in judicial decisions within the Community.' See also *R.* v. *Thompson* [1980] 2 All ER 102, 105 where Bridge LJ for the Court of Appeal said that '[w]e bear in mind the warning in the opinion of the Advocate-General (Mr J.-P. Warner) delivered in *Meyer-Burckhardt* v. *European Commission* [1975] ECR 1171, 1186 that ". . . national courts should exercise great caution before reaching the conclusion, on any point of Community law, that the answer to it admits of no possible doubt" '. See also *ApS Samex* below, n. 87. In *Garland*, above, n. 3 at 439 Lord Diplock explained that the Law Lords there did not have 'any serious doubt as to what answer would be given' to the question addressed to the ECJ, but the question had to be asked as there was not 'so considerable and consistent a line of case law of the European Court of Justice . . . as would make the answer too obvious and inevitable to be capable of giving rise to what could properly be regarded as "a question" within the meaning of Article 177'.

[81] See, for the decisions to refer a question of Community law to the ECJ, *Macarthys Ltd* v. *Smith* [1979] ICR 785 (Court of Appeal); *Worringham* v. *Lloyds Bank Ltd* [1979] IRLR 440 (Court of Appeal); *Jenkins* v. *Kingsgate (Clothing Productions) Ltd* [1980] IRLR 6 (EAT); *Garland* above n. 3 at 439 (House of Lords, mentioning the reference on 19 Jan. 1981); *Burton* v. *British Railways Board* [1981] IRLR 16 (EAT); *Southampton* above, n. 32 and *Roberts* above n. 31 (both referred by the Court of Appeal in 1984).

[82] *R.* v. *Plymouth Justices ex parte Rogers* [1982] 1 QB 863, 868–70 (Divisional Court).

and the expense of referring the matter to the ECJ may, in the circumstances, prove to be wasted.[83] The usual test applied in this context is whether the question of law is conclusive of the case in the sense that certain answers would end the case.[84]

In *H. P. Bulmer Ltd* v. *J. Bollinger SA*, Lord Denning, in the Court of Appeal, suggested that when a national court or tribunal (other than a final court of appeal, which has a duty to refer to the ECJ an issue of Community law necessary to the determination of the case) has decided that it is necessary to answer a question of Community law in order to give judgment in a case, then in considering whether to exercise its discretion to refer the question of Community law to the ECJ the court or tribunal should take into account certain factors. The relevant factors are, according to Lord Denning, the length of time which may elapse before a ruling can be obtained from the ECJ; the need not to overload the ECJ; the need to formulate a precise question of Community law; the difficulty and the importance of that question; the expense; the wishes of the parties.[85] In very many cases the court or tribunal will, on considering such factors, decide not to refer the question of Community law to the ECJ, but rather to decide that question itself, enabling an aggrieved party to appeal if so advised.

An inferior court, such as a magistrates' court, should, in any event, 'exercise considerable caution' before referring a question of Community law to the ECJ. Usually such a court should itself decide the question of Community law, as 'a higher court can make the reference and frequently the higher court would be the more suitable forum to do so. The higher court is as a rule in a better position to assess whether any reference is desirable.'[86] However, where an appeal from the High Court (or a comparable body such as the EAT) to the Court of Appeal may take as long, and be as expensive, as a reference to the ECJ, and where a party

[83] Ibid. at 870–1. See also *Lord Bethell* v. *Sabena* [1983] 3 CMLR 1 (Commercial Court).

[84] *Customs and Excise Commissioners* v. *ApS Samex* [1983] 1 All ER 1042, 1054 (Commercial Court). See similarly *H. P. Bulmer Ltd* above, n. 1 at 422–3 per Lord Denning. See *CILFIT* above, n. 80 on when it is not necessary (in the case of the final court of appeal) to obtain a ruling from the ECJ because that court has already ruled on the relevant point, or the answer is clear as a matter of Community law.

[85] Above, n. 1 at 423–5. See also Stephenson LJ (with whom Stamp LJ agreed) at 430.

[86] *Plymouth Justices* above, n. 82 at 871. See also *R.* v. *Henn* [1981] AC 850, 904 (Lord Diplock for the House of Lords).

is likely, in any event, to ask the Court of Appeal to refer the matter to the ECJ, there may be no point in the court refusing to exercise its discretion to refer to the ECJ an important question of law the resolution of which is necessary for deciding the case.[87]

The question of which party is to bear the costs of a reference to the ECJ will be determined by the domestic court or tribunal which made the reference after the ECJ has given its decision on the question of law sent to it and after the case has returned to the domestic court or tribunal. A reference to the ECJ is treated as a stage in the domestic proceedings for the purposes of costs.[88]

V

It can thus be seen that sex discrimination law in the United Kingdom vitally depends on the content and the application of European Community law. The Sex Discrimination Act 1975 and the Equal Pay Act 1970, read on their own, are not exhaustive of the rights of complainants or of the obligations of defendants in this context.

[87] *ApS Samex* above, n. 84 at 1055–6. Bingham J. there explained 'Sitting as a judge in a national court asked to decide questions of Community law, I am very conscious of the advantages enjoyed by the Court of Justice. It has a panoramic view of the Community and its institutions, a detailed knowledge of the treaties and of much subordinate legislation made under them, and an intimate familiarity with the functioning of the Community market which no national judge denied the collective experience of the Court of Justice could hope to achieve. Where questions of administrative intention and practice arise the Court of Justice can receive submissions from the Community institutions, as also where relations between the Community and non-member states are in issue. Where the interests of member states are affected they can intervene to make their views known. That is a material consideration in this case since there is some slight evidence that the practice of different member states is divergent. Where comparison falls to be made between Community texts in different languages, all texts being equally authentic, the multinational Court of Justice is equipped to carry out the task in a way which no national judge, whatever his linguistic skills, could rival. The interpretation of Community instruments involves very often not the process familiar to common lawyers of laboriously extracting the meaning from words used but the more creative process of supplying flesh to a spare and loosely constructed skeleton. The choice between alternative submissions may turn not on purely legal considerations, but on a broader view of what the orderly development of the Community requires. These are matters which the Court of Justice is very much better placed to assess and determine than a national court.'

[88] *Macarthys* above, n. 4 at 693 (Court of Appeal). See also *Burton* v. *British Railways Board* [1983] ICR 544, where the EAT suggested that because it has very limited jurisdiction to award costs, it may, in future cases, consider it right, on referring a matter to the ECJ, to require an undertaking from the parties as to the payment of costs (that is, the costs of the reference will be paid by the unsuccessful party).

6

SEX DISCRIMINATION AND PREGNANCY:
ANATOMY IS NOT DESTINY

I

It is one of the many paradoxes of sex discrimination law that while women have been systematically denied employment and other opportunities because they are, or might become, pregnant, industrial tribunals and the Employment Appeal Tribunal have yet to accept that adverse treatment on grounds connected with pregnancy can constitute a violation of the Sex Discrimination Act 1975.

Irrespective of the impact of the 1975 Act, the pregnant woman is guaranteed some statutory employment rights.[1] But the limited scope of the protection against unfair dismissal, the right to maternity pay and the other rights protected by employment legislation (rights which are dependent on having been in continuous employment for a stated minimum period) ensures the importance to working women of the broader protection of the 1975 Act.[2] The rights of women not to be denied opportunities for

---

[1] See the Employment Protection (Consolidation) Act 1978: s. 60(1) (unfair dismissal); s. 31A, inserted by s. 13 of the Employment Act 1980 (paid time off work for antenatal care); ss. 33–6, as amended by s. 11 of the Employment Act 1980 (maternity pay); ss. 45–8 and 56, as modified by ss. 11–12 of the Employment Act 1980 (right to return to work after confinement). See also Robert Upex and Anne Morris, 'Maternity Rights—Illusion or Reality?' 10 *Industrial Law Journal* 218 (1981). In *Lavery* v. *Plessey Telecommunications Ltd* [1982] ICR 373, 379, Browne-Wilkinson J. for the EAT said that these statutory provisions 'are of inordinate complexity exceeding the worst excesses of a taxing statute; we find that especially regrettable bearing in mind that they are regulating the everyday rights of ordinary employers and employees'. The Court of Appeal agreed with these comments: [1983] ICR 534, 543. See similarly *Secretary of State for Employment* v. *Cox* [1984] ICR 867 (EAT).

[2] The 1975 Act contains a considerable overlap with the rights guaranteed by general employment law. It prohibits sex discrimination in decisions to dismiss an employee, for example, even though the female complainant may have other statutory protection. The existence of other statutory rights for women is no ground for narrowly defining the rights accorded by the 1975 Act. See *Laffey* v. *Northwest Airlines Inc* 567 F 2d 429, 445 (1976: US Court of Appeals) cert. denied 434 US 1086 (1978: US Supreme Court).

reasons connected with pregnancy will often be established under the 1975 Act or not at all. Can an employer dismiss, for becoming pregnant, a woman who has worked for it for only three months and who therefore has no protection against unfair dismissal? May it deny female employees of child-bearing age access to training programmes? May it require an employee to take mandatory maternity leave once she is aware that she is pregnant? Is it lawful for an employer to refuse to take on or to decline to promote a woman because she is pregnant? Can it in cases not covered by employment legislation,[3] deny an employee accrued seniority rights because she has been temporarily absent to have a baby?

The question of whether adverse treatment of a woman for reasons connected with pregnancy can constitute sex discrimination may arise in each of the contexts covered by the 1975 Act. This chapter concentrates on the question of principle in the context of employment. The conclusions are as valid in the contexts of education and the provision of goods, facilities, services, and premises.

II

The issue of discrimination for reasons connected with pregnancy was considered by an industrial tribunal in *Reaney* v. *Kanda Jean Products Ltd*[4] and by the EAT in *Turley* v. *Allders Department Stores Ltd*.[5] These decisions on the scope of the 1975 Act reveal fundamental errors with regard to the concept of direct discrimination.

[3] In those cases where a woman has the right to return to work after an absence due to pregnancy or confinement s. 45 of the Employment Protection (Consolidation) Act 1978 provides that the right is to return 'on terms and conditions not less favourable than those which would have been applicable to her if she had not been so absent'.

[4] [1978] IRLR 427.

[5] [1980] ICR 66. The decision of the EAT was followed by a Newcastle upon Tyne industrial tribunal in the unreported case of *Grilly* v. *Durham Area Health Authority* (1981). In *Hayes* v. *Malleable Working Men's Club and Institute* (1983, unreported), an industrial tribunal in Middlesborough held that the complainant had been dismissed from employment because she was pregnant, but that this was not sex discrimination because the tribunal was bound by the judgment in *Turley* 'even though it finds the dissenting opinion in that case to be very convincing'. A similar decision was reached by an industrial tribunal in London in *Maughan* v. *North-East London Magistrates' Courts Committee* (1984, unreported). In March 1985, the EAT heard appeals in *Hayes* and *Maughan* and was asked to overrule *Turley*. It has now done so: *The Times* 19 June 1985.

In each of the two cases a woman complained that she had been dismissed by her employer because she was pregnant. She was, in each case, unable to claim unfair dismissal because she had not been employed for the requisite number of weeks. In each case she was held, as a matter of law, to have no claim of direct discrimination under the 1975 Act.

It was argued for the employer in *Turley* that: 'It is not on the ground of her sex that you are treating her less favourably than you would treat a man, but on the ground that she is no longer simply a woman but is a woman carrying a child.'[6] The EAT did not decide against the applicant on this point, but was prepared to assume that 'to dismiss her for pregnancy is to dismiss her on the ground of her sex'.[7] The EAT was wrong to imply that the dismissal needs to be on the ground of her sex. Section 1(1)(a) requires the complainant to prove not that the constitutive act of the employer was on that ground, but that the less favourable treatment was on that ground. Dismissal may be due to many factors—misconduct, incompetence, redundancy, for example—that are not, *ex facie*, based on sex. Nevertheless, the case may be one of direct sex discrimination if a male employee whose relevant facts are the same or not materially different is not dismissed. The question, then, is whether the disparity (if any) between the treatment of the woman and the treatment of the male (or hypothetical male) is on the ground of her sex.

The EAT was, however, correct to assume that the less favourable treatment (if any) of the pregnant woman was on the ground of her sex. Because only women can become pregnant, the complainant who is dismissed because she is pregnant can argue that she would not have been less favourably treated but for her sex. It requires a very narrow construction of the statute to exclude less favourable treatment on the ground of a characteristic unique to one sex. It is quite true that not all women are (or become) pregnant. But it is important to note that direct discrimination exists not merely where the defendant applies a criterion that less favourably treats all women. It also exists where special, less favourable, treatment is accorded to a class consisting only of women, albeit not all women. Suppose an employer announces that it will employ any man with stated qualifications but only a

---

[6] [1980] ICR 66, 69.   [7] Ibid., 70.

woman who has those qualifications and who is over six feet tall. Albeit not all women are excluded, the employer has directly discriminated against women because it has imposed a criterion which less favourably treats a class composed entirely of women. That such treatment must constitute direct discrimination is emphasized by the fact that it would not give rise to a claim of indirect discrimination: the employer has not applied a condition or requirement equally to members of both sexes. There can be no doubt that Parliament intended to proscribe such conduct.

Less favourable treatment by reference to a criterion which affects only women, albeit not all women, has been considered by the US Federal courts in applying Title VII of the Civil Rights Act 1964. Section 703(a) of Title VII makes it unlawful for an employer 'to fail or refuse to hire or to discharge any individual or otherwise to discriminate against any individual with respect to his compensation, terms, conditions or privileges of employment, because of such individual's . . . sex . . .'. The US courts have held that 'sex-plus' criteria, those less favourably treating only women, but not all women, violate Title VII. In *Sprogis* v. *United Air Lines*,[8] the US Court of Appeals found that the defendants had breached Title VII by requiring female flight attendants to be unmarried. The court held that:

The scope of [the statute] is not confined to explicit discrimination based 'solely' on sex. In forbidding employers to discriminate against individuals because of their sex, Congress intended to strike at the entire spectrum of disparate treatment of men and women resulting from sex stereotypes. . . . The effect of the statute is not to be diluted because discrimination adversely affects only a portion of the protected class. Discrimination is not to be tolerated under the guise of physical properties possessed by one sex . . .[9]

A defendant violates Title VII 'by applying one standard for men and one for women'.[10] In *Phillips* v. *Martin Marietta Corp*,[11] the

---

[8] 444 F 2d 1194 (1971), cert. denied 404 US 991 (1971), cited with approval by the US Supreme Court in *City of Los Angeles Department of Water and Power v. Manhart* 435 US 702, 707 (1978).

[9] Ibid. 1198.   [10] Ibid.

[11] 400 US 542 (1971). On the impermissibility of sex-plus criteria see also Note 'Developments in the Law—Employment Discrimination and Title VII of the Civil Rights Act of 1964' 84 *Harvard Law Review* 1109, 1171–2 (1971) and see *Phillips* v. *Martin Marietta Corp* 416 F 2d 1257, 1260 (1969) per Chief Judge Brown dissenting from the refusal of the Court of Appeals to grant a rehearing. The US courts have

US Supreme Court found that a company's refusal to employ women with young children breached Title VII.

No English tribunal or court has yet analysed the question of sex-plus criteria. However, in *Hurley* v. *Mustoe*,[12] the EAT had no doubt that an employer who refused to employ women with young children was directly discriminating on the ground of sex contrary to the 1975 Act. Similarly in *Page* v. *Freight Hire (Tank Haulage) Ltd*[13] the EAT held that it was direct discrimination contrary to section 1(1)(a) for an employer to refuse to allow a woman of child-bearing age to drive a vehicle containing chemicals dangerous to such women. In that case, the conduct was validated by a specific exemption in the 1975 Act.[14] Still, the decision is clear authority for the proposition that an employment practice which is less favourable to a class consisting wholly of women, albeit not all women, is directly discriminatory on the ground of sex and is unlawful unless a specific provision of the 1975 Act validates it.

It is true that in *Hurley* and *Page* the less favourable treatment was expressly pointed at *women* who had stated attributes. The employer who dismisses an employee because she is pregnant does not expressly direct his policy at women. But the distinction is meaningless in this context. In *Page*, the less favourable treatment would not cease to be 'on the ground of her sex' if the employer refused to allow any person, male or female, who could give birth to a child to drive the vehicle containing the harmful chemical. Whether the less favourable treatment is 'on the ground of her sex' must depend on whether it can, in practice, affect only women, and not on how the employer labels the disadvantaged class. Because only women can become pregnant, the employer who dismisses a woman for reasons connected with pregnancy has treated her on the ground of a characteristic unique to her sex. It has applied special treatment to a class consisting only of women,

held that not all sex-plus criteria are in breach of Title VII: only those which are based on an immutable characteristic, interfere with a fundamental right (such as the right to marry) or have a significant impact on equal employment opportunity. See, for example, *Willingham* v. *Macon Telegraph Publishing Co* 507 F 2d 1084, 1091 (1975: US Court of Appeals). Pregnancy classifications satisfy each of these three tests.

[12] [1981] ICR 490.   [13] [1981] ICR 299.

[14] S. 51 of the 1975 Act validates acts done under statutory authority. The employer's actions were held to be necessary to comply with the provisions of the Health and Safety at Work etc Act 1974.

albeit that class does not consist of all women. The less favourable treatment (if any) is therefore 'on the ground of her sex'.

The decisions in *Turley* and *Reaney* concentrated on the second aspect of a claim for direct discrimination. Assuming that the treatment was on the ground of her sex, was it less favourable treatment than the treatment which was, or would have been, accorded to a comparable man?

In *Reaney*, the industrial tribunal concluded that:

> It is impossible for a man to become pregnant (at all events in the present state of scientific knowledge!). His situation therefore cannot be compared with that of a woman. The concept of discrimination involves by definition an act or treatment which in the case of a woman is less favourable than that which is or may be accorded to a man . . . [W]e can only make comparison of the cases of persons of different sex (under section 1(1)) where the relevant circumstances in the one case are the same or not materially different than those in the other. In so far as the applicant complains that she is the victim of discrimination by comparison with the case of any other (hypothetical) man, the respective circumstances in each case are very materially different for obvious reasons . . . [I]t is physically impossible for a man in the instant case to receive preferential treatment for the reason that his case and that of the applicant is incomparable.[15]

The majority judgment of the EAT in *Turley* adopted a similar approach: 'In order to see if she has been treated less favourably than a man the sense of the section is that you must compare like with like, and you cannot [because] there is no masculine equivalent [of pregnancy].'[16]

In *Turley*, the EAT made no reference at all to section 5(3) of the 1975 Act. Had it done so, and had the tribunal in *Reaney* properly construed that subsection, it would have been appreciated that section 5(3) required the judicial body to determine what were the 'relevant circumstances' and whether they could be 'the same, or not materially different' in the case of a man. Rather than consider these questions of fact, the tribunals treated the issue as a preliminary matter of law.

Had the questions of fact been investigated it would undoubtedly have been held that the case of a male employee cannot be 'the same' as that of a female employee who becomes pregnant: no man can become pregnant. However, the relevant circumstances

---

[15] Above, n. 4 at 428.   [16] Above, n. 5 at 70.

of the case of a male, or a hypothetical male, can be 'not materially different' from those of the female who is dismissed because she is pregnant. If the employer does not dismiss, or would not dismiss, a male employee who suffers from an incapacitating condition which necessitates or makes it desirable to take as much time off work as the pregnant employee requires, then the comparison between the treatment of the female and the treatment of the male employee is one based on 'relevant circumstances' which are 'not materially different'.[17] To reject such a comparison would be to ignore the wise advice of the EAT in *Peake* v. *Automotive Products Ltd* that 'in deciding whether the circumstances of the two cases are the same, or not materially different, one must put out of the picture any circumstances which necessarily follow from the fact that one is comparing the case of a man and of a woman'.[18]

There may be cases where the comparison with the treatment of other incapacitating conditions makes inevitable the conclusion that the employer has directly discriminated contrary to the 1975 Act. If it does not dismiss the male employee who takes several months off work to recover from a medical condition affecting the male sexual organs or to undergo voluntary or cosmetic surgery— for example, to have a hair transplant, dental treatment, a circumcision, or a vasectomy—but dismisses only for reasons related to pregnancy, direct discrimination will be established.

That less favourable treatment on grounds connected with pregnancy can constitute direct discrimination under the 1975 Act is implied by the EAT decision in *Page* v. *Freight Hire (Tank Haulage) Ltd*.[19] The decision suggests that an employer may not (unless it can, as in that case, rely upon a specific exemption in the

---

[17] This was the approach adopted by the dissenting member of the EAT in *Turley*, above n. 5 at 71 per Ms P. Smith: 'A man is in similar circumstances who is employed by the same employer and who in the course of the year will require time off for a hernia operation, to have his tonsils removed, or for other medical reasons.' See also the decision of an industrial tribunal in *Coyne* v. *Exports Credits Guarantee Department* [1981] IRLR 51 on the analogous problem under the Equal Pay Act 1970. And see *Southern Health Board* v. *Cronin*, Equality Officer's Recommendation No. EE 10/84 (6 June 1984) under the Irish Employment Equality Act 1977.

[18] [1977] ICR 480, 488. The decision was reversed by the Court of Appeal on other grounds: [1977] ICR 968. The Court of Appeal decision in *Peake* was itself disapproved by the Court of Appeal in *Ministry of Defence* v. *Jeremiah* [1980] ICR 13.

[19] Above, n. 13.

Act) refuse to employ women of child-bearing age. There is no hint in the judgment that such a practice ceases to be direct sex discrimination because the relevant circumstances of men, who can never bear children, are not the same or similar.[20] Indeed, the EAT decision in *Turley* proves far too much. If an employer may dismiss a woman because she is pregnant without any risk of breaching section 1(1)(a) of the 1975 Act, why should it not be similarly consistent with section 1(1)(a) for an employer to announce that it will employ and train any qualified applicant for a job, except those who might become pregnant? Such a practice would not less favourably treat all women, but it would clearly have a disastrous impact on job opportunities for a substantial proportion of women. The concept of indirect discrimination under the 1975 Act might well be an inadequate weapon against such a potential loophole.[21]

The correctness of the conclusion that less favourable treatment of a woman on grounds connected with pregnancy violates section 1(1)(a) is emphasized by reference to section 2(2) of the 1975 Act. Section 2 concerns sex discrimination against men. Section 2(1) provides that section 1 of the Act, which defines discrimination, is to be read as applying equally to the treatment of men. Section 2(2) provides that 'In the application of subsection (1) no account shall be taken of special treatment afforded to women in connection with pregnancy or childbirth'. The presence of section 2(2) strongly suggests that, but for its existence, a man would be able to claim that he had been less favourably treated on the ground of his sex when special benefits were provided to pregnant women. Yet, if the EAT judgment in *Turley* were correct, special benefits for pregnant women would not directly discriminate against men because no man can become pregnant and so no comparison could ever be made for the purpose of direct discrimination. Section 2(2) indicates that Parliament did not believe that pregnancy excludes the possibility of a comparison

---

[20] The EAT judgment in *Turley* was cited to the EAT in *Page*.

[21] On indirect discrimination in this context see below s. V. Note also that the argument of direct sex discrimination in this context gains support from cases stating that employers must not act on sex-based stereotyped assumptions: see ch. 2 nn. 39–46. Hence an employer must not act on the assumption that a woman will have children or interrupt her career for a lengthy period to rear children (without consideration of the circumstances of the individual woman).

between the treatment of men and women for the purposes of the 1975 Act.[22]

It is also helpful to have regard to the EAT decision in *Schmidt* v. *Austicks Bookshops Ltd.* There was held to be no direct discrimination contrary to the 1975 Act when female employees were forbidden to wear trousers when working in the sight of the public. The EAT said it was true that 'there was no comparable restriction which could be applied to the men [employees], equivalent to that applied to the women preventing them from wearing trousers, which could make it possible to lead to the conclusion that the women were being treated less favourably than the men'.[23] However, the EAT stated that the preferable basis for this decision was that male employees also had restrictions placed on their dress and appearance 'although obviously, women and men being different, the rules in the two cases were not the same'.[24] The EAT concluded that to examine whether both sexes were restricted in their choice of clothing and thereby treated alike 'is a better approach and more likely to lead to a sensible result than an approach which examines the situation point by point and garment by garment'. In *Turley*, unfortunately, the EAT retreated

---

[22] See similarly s. 17(2)(b) allowing the 'special treatment' of women police officers 'in connection with pregnancy or childbirth'. It is arguable that s. 2(2) is reconcilable with *Turley* because s. 2(2) is necessary to prevent men from succeeding in claims of indirect discrimination. But if Parliament believed that s. 2(2) served only this limited purpose no doubt it would have said so. The scope and purpose of s. 2(2) is to prevent men from bringing sex discrimination claims by reason of 'special treatment afforded to women', i.e. special beneficial treatment in connection with pregnancy and childbirth. Section 2(2) is not concerned with *adverse* treatment of women in connection with pregnancy and childbirth. It is part of a section of the Act dealing with 'sex discrimination against men'. The anti-discrimination statutes of other nations have provisions similar to s. 2(2): see the Sex Discrimination Act 1975 (South Australia) s. 16(4), the Human Rights Commission Act 1977 (New Zealand) s. 30, the Employment Equality Act 1977 (Ireland) s. 16, Sex Discrimination Act 1984 (Australia) s. 31. See also the EEC Directive on Equal Treatment, below n. 69. See also *Coyne* above, n. 17 at 53 where the industrial tribunal construed s. 6(1)(b) of the Equal Pay Act 1970, which permits employers to afford 'special treatment to women in connection with pregnancy or childbirth', to mean specially favourable treatment. The tribunal indicated that, in its view, s. 2(2) of the 1975 Act has a similar meaning. Cf. *California Federal Savings and Loan Association* v. *Guerra* 34 FEP Cases 562 (1984: US District Court): Title VII of the US Civil Rights Act requires that female employees are not more favourably treated than employees disabled by non-pregnancy related conditions.

[23] [1978] ICR 85, 87. On sex discrimination in grooming codes see ch. 7 s. III.

[24] [1978] ICR 85, 88.

from this earlier comprehension that differences between men and women do not prevent a comparison of the treatment accorded to one sex and that accorded to the other sex. If an employer dismisses for no incapacitation except pregnancy, the approach in *Schmidt* suggests that, taken as a whole, women are treated less favourably than men and direct discrimination on the ground of sex is established.

III

The undistinguished Parliamentary debates on the Sex Discrimination Bill 1975 do contain a few references which suggest that some speakers believed that section 1(1)(a) did not extend to less favourable treatment on grounds connected with pregnancy.[25] But such references are oblique and they provide no explanation of how such a view could be reconciled with the words of the legislation.[26]

It is also the case that the US Supreme Court has interpreted Title VII of the Civil Rights Act in a manner very restrictive of the rights of pregnant women. In *General Electric Co* v. *Gilbert*,[27] the Court held that there was no violation of Title VII when a company provided a disability plan for employees which paid them non-occupational sickness and accident benefits but excluded from coverage any disability arising from pregnancy. Rehnquist J., for the majority of the Court, stated that 'an exclusion of pregnancy from a disability-benefits plan providing general coverage is not a gender-based discrimination at all'.[28] He cited, with approval, the judgment of the Court in *Geduldig* v. *Aiello* where it had dismissed

---

[25] See Dr Shirley Summerskill, Under-Secretary of State for the Home Department, Standing Committee B, Second Sitting (24 Apr. 1975), Report at col. 92; Michael Alison, ibid. at col. 91; Baroness Summerskill, Second Reading Debate in the House of Lords (1 July 1975) 362 HL 129.

[26] Cf. Maureen Colquhoun, Standing Committee B, First Sitting (22 Apr. 1975), Report at col. 11, emphasizing the lack of clarity in the language of the Bill and the danger that inadequate drafting may sanctify the continuance of discrimination against women: 'The phrase "on the ground of her sex" could lead to unnecessary arguments about the precise grounds on which discrimination is being practised. This might result in the suggestion that a woman was discriminated against not on grounds of her sex, but on the grounds of her proneness to monthly off-days, physical weaknesses, tendencies to be emotional, or any of the other rationalisations that are constantly and consistently being used in our society to excuse unfairness to women.'

[27] 429 US 125 (1976).   [28] Ibid. 136.

a similar claim under the equal protection clause of the fourteenth amendment to the Constitution and had stated that:

The lack of identity between the excluded disability and gender as such under this insurance programme becomes clear upon the most cursory analysis. The programme divides potential recipients into two groups— pregnant women and non-pregnant persons. While the first group is exclusively female, the second includes members of both sexes.[29]

The defects in the Court's judgment in *General Electric* were obvious. The Court relied on 'what seems to us to be the "plain meaning" of the language used by Congress'[30] without seeking to explain how such a meaning could be reconciled with earlier cases on sex-plus criteria. More fundamentally, Rehnquist J. was prepared to acknowledge that where 'the exclusion of pregnancy disability benefits . . . is a simple pretext for discriminating against women' it would violate Title VII.[31] Yet his application of 'pretext' was, to say the least, perverse. He held that:

[W]e have here no question of excluding a disease or disability comparable in all other respects to covered diseases or disabilities and yet confined to the members of one race or sex. Pregnancy is, of course, confined to women, but it is in other ways significantly different from the typical covered disease or disability . . . [I]t is not a 'disease' at all, and is often a voluntarily undertaken and desired condition.[32]

The dissenting judgment of Justice Brennan (joined by Justice Marshall) answered each of these points. Brennan J. emphasized that many pregnancies are accidental.[33] Even if pregnancy usually flows from a *voluntary* act of sexual intercourse, still that does not distinguish it from other 'voluntary' disabilities which the employer's plan covered: 'sport injuries, attempted suicides, venereal disease, disabilities incurred in the commission of a crime or

---

[29] 417 US 484, 496–7n (1974). The Court did not explain how this dictum could be reconciled with its finding in *Cleveland Board of Education* v. *La Fleur* 414 US 632 (1974) that school board rules requiring pregnant school teachers to take mandatory maternity leave at least four months prior to the expected birth and making them ineligible to return to work until the child was three months old were a violation of constitutional rights.

[30] Above, n. 27 at 145.   [31] Ibid. 136.

[32] Ibid. Similarly *Newmon* v. *Delta Air Lines Inc* 374 F Supp 238, 246 (1973) where a district court, in rejecting a sex discrimination claim based on a pregnancy classification, held that pregnancy is not an illness and that 'the fact of its existence demonstrates that a woman is quite healthy and normal . . .'.

[33] Above, n. 27 at 151 n.

during a fight, and elective cosmetic surgery'.[34] The impugned plan therefore covered 'desired conditions' other than pregnancy. Moreover, it insured 'risks such as prostatectomies, vasectomies, and circumcisions that are specific to the reproductive system of men and for which there exist no female counterparts covered by the plan. Again, pregnancy affords the only disability, sex-specific or otherwise, that is excluded from coverage.'[35]

Brennan J. added that another reason why the label 'disease' or 'disability' could not be conclusive was that the impugned plan excluded the 10 per cent of pregnancies that end in debilitating miscarriages, the 10 per cent of cases where pregnancies are complicated by what we would all call diseases and cases where women recovering from childbirth are stricken by severe diseases unrelated to pregnancy.[36]

Whatever the description applied to pregnancy, there is no doubt that it has the same impact on an employer and an employee as any other disabling condition: it incapacitates the employee, causing her to take time off work and to suffer a temporary loss of remuneration (unless she is entitled to maternity pay).

The decision of the US Supreme Court in *General Electric*,[37] that less favourable treatment of pregnancy than of other incapacitating disabilities cannot constitute disparate treatment (i.e. direct discrimination) on the ground of sex,[38] is of little assistance to an English court faced with a similar issue. This is for several reasons. First, because of the stated defects in the

---

[34] Ibid., 151. In *Coyne* above, n. 17 at 53 the industrial tribunal held that the argument that sickness due to pregnancy or confinement was self-induced 'might carry weight if men were in any circumstances required to show that their illness was not self-induced (e.g. that a broken leg was not caused by rugby) . . .'.

[35] Ibid. at 152 per Brennan J. dissenting. He referred, at 152 n., to the 'shallowness' of the majority opinion: 'Had General Electric assembled a catalogue of all ailments that befall humanity, and then systematically proceeded to exclude from coverage *every* disability that is female-specific or predominantly afflicts women, the Court could still reason as here that the plan operates equally: Women, like men, would be entitled to draw disability payments for their circumcisions and prostatectomies, and neither sex could claim payment for pregnancies, breast cancer, and the other excluded female dominated disabilities.'

[36] Ibid. 151.

[37] It was followed by the US Supreme Court in *Nashville Gas Co* v. *Satty* 434 US 136 (1977).

[38] See below, s. V for a discussion of how pregnancy classifications can constitute disparate impact (i.e. indirect discrimination) contrary to Title VII of the US Civil Rights Act.

judgment.[39] Secondly, because the decision was contrary to the conclusion reached by all the Federal courts of appeals that had previously addressed the issue.[40] It was also contrary to the decisions of State courts that had earlier considered analogous issues.[41] It has been rejected by influential State courts which have since considered analogous questions.[42] Thirdly, the decision in

[39] For critical comments on the judgments in *Geduldig* and *General Electric* see Katharine T. Bartlett, 'Pregnancy and the Constitution: The Uniqueness Trap' 62 *California Law Review* 1532 (1974), Diane L. Zimmerman, 'Pregnancy Classifications and the Definition of Sex Discrimination' 75 *Columbia Law Review* 441 (1975), Joanne L. Levine, 'Pregnancy and Sex-Based Discrimination in Employment' 44 *University of Cincinnati Law Review* 57 (1975), Barbara Ungar Royston, 'Pregnancy Disability Benefits Denied: Narrowing the Scope of Title VII' 32 *University of Miami Law Review* 173 (1977), David L. Kirp and Dorothy Robyn, 'Pregnancy, Justice and the Justices' 57 *Texas Law Review* 947 (1979).

[40] *Wetzel* v. *Liberty Mutual Insurance Co* 511 F 2d 199 (1975), *Communications Workers* v. *American Tel & Tel Co* 513 F 2d 1024 (1975), *Holthaus* v. *Compton & Sons Inc* 514 F 2d 651 (1975), *Tyler* v. *Vickery* 517 F 2d 1089 (1975), *Gilbert* v. *General Electric Co* 519 F 2d 661 (1975), *Hutchison* v. *Lake Oswego School District* 519 F 2d 961 (1975), *Satty* v. *Nashville Gas Co* 522 F 2d 850 (1975). Cf. *Cohen* v. *Chesterfield County School Board* 474 F 2d 395, 397 (1973) (reversed sub nom *Cleveland Board of Education* v. *La Fleur* above, n. 29) where Chief Judge Haynsworth (whom President Nixon had nominated for appointment to the Supreme Court in 1969 but whom the Senate had refused to confirm) for the majority of the Court of Appeals said that 'The fact that only women experience pregnancy and motherhood removes all possibility of competition between the sexes in this area. No man-made law or regulation excludes males from those experiences, and no such laws or regulations can relieve females from all of the burdens which naturally accompany the joys and blessings of motherhood. . . .'

[41] *Cerra* v. *East Stroudsburg Area School District* 299 A 2d 277 (1973) (Supreme Court of Pennsylvania: the State Human Relations Act), *Board of Education of Union Free School District No. 2* v. *New York State Division of Human Rights* 319 NE 2d 202 (1974) (Court of Appeals of New York: the State Human Rights Law).

[42] *Massachusetts Electric Co* v. *Massachusetts Commission Against Discrimination* 375 NE 2d 1192 (1978) (Supreme Judicial Court of Massachusetts: State Anti-Discrimination Law), *Brooklyn Union Gas Co* v. *New York State Human Rights Appeal Board* 359 NE 2d 393 (1976) (Court of Appeals of New York: the State Human Rights Law), *Anderson* v. *Upper Bucks County Area Vocational Technical School* 373 A 2d 126 (1977) (Commonwealth Court of Pennsylvania: the State Human Relations Act), *Castellano* v. *Linden Board of Education* 386 A 2d 396 (1978) (Superior Court of New Jersey, Appellate Division: State Law Against Discrimination), *Quaker Oats Co* v. *Cedar Rapids Human Rights Commission* 268 NW 2d 862 (1978) (Supreme Court of Iowa: City Ordinance), *Goodyear Tire and Rubber Co* v. *Dept of Industry* 273 NW 2d 786 (1978) (Court of Appeals of Wisconsin: State Fair Employment Act), *Minnesota Mining and Manufacturing Co* v. *Minnesota* 289 NW 2d 396 (1979) (appeal dismissed 444 US 1041 (1980)) (Supreme Court of Minnesota: State Human Rights Act). The approach of the US Supreme Court in *General Electric* was, however, followed by the Supreme Court of Rhode Island in applying the State Fair Employment Practices Act in *Narragansett Electric Co* v. *Rhode Island Commission for Human Rights* 374 A 2d

General Electric is unhelpful to an English court because of subsequent uncertainty about the scope of the Supreme Court's ruling. One of the judges who concurred in *General Electric*, Justice Blackmun, stated in a concurring judgment in 1978 that *General Electric*'s existence as a precedent had become 'somewhat questionable. I do not say that this is necessarily bad.'[43] A US court of appeals has confined the holding in *General Electric* to the context of employers' disability benefits plans, concluding that the decision 'can hardly be regarded as precedent for excluding pregnancy from protection against *invidious* employment termination'.[44] Hence the dismissal of a woman employee because she was unmarried and pregnant was found to violate Title VII.[45] Fourthly, the persuasive value of *General Electric* is weakened by the fact that the decision was so unsatisfactory that in 1978 Congress amended Title VII to emphasize that discrimination on grounds connected with pregnancy is unlawful.[46] In amending

---

1022 (1977) and by the Supreme Court of Kansas in *Harder* v. *Kansas Commission on Civil Rights* 592 P 2d 456 (1979) in applying State anti-discrimination law. See similarly *Richards* v. *Omaha Public Schools* 232 NW 2d 29 (1975) (Supreme Court of Nebraska: State Fair Employment Practices Act) and *Illinois Bell Telephone Co* v. *FEPC* 407 NE 2d 539 (1980) (Illinois Supreme Court: State Fair Employment Practices Act).

[43] *City of Los Angeles Department of Water and Power* v. *Manhart* above, n. 8 at 725.

[44] *Jacobs* v. *Martin Sweets Co Inc* 550 F 2d 364, 370 n (1977), cert. denied 431 US 917 (1977: US Supreme Court).

[45] Ibid. The Court of Appeals explained, at 370, that 'To exclude such a basic civil right [i.e. pregnancy] against invidious employment termination would be contrary to the policy to which Title VII is directed, namely: that race, religion, nationality and sex are irrelevant factors in employment opportunity.' Other courts of appeals have taken a broader approach to the holding in *General Electric*. See *Condit* v. *United Air Lines* 631 F 2d 1136 (1980), *Abraham* v. *Graphic Arts International Union* 26 FEP Cases 818, 822–3 (1981), *Schwabenbauer* v. *Board of Education, Olean* 667 F 2d 305 (1981).

[46] The 1978 Amendment states: 'The terms "because of sex" or "on the basis of sex" include, but are not limited to, because of or on the basis of pregnancy, childbirth or related medical conditions; and women affected by pregnancy, childbirth or related medical conditions shall be treated the same for all employment-related purposes . . . as other persons not so affected but similar in their ability or inability to work . . .' See Andrew Weissmann, 'Sexual Equality Under the Pregnancy Discrimination Act' 83 *Columbia Law Review* 690 (1983). In *Newport News Shipbuilding and Dry Dock Co.* v. *EEOC* 103 S Ct 2622 (1983) the US Supreme Court held that it is a breach of Title VII, as so amended, for an employer to provide disability coverage for dependents of employees but to exclude from that coverage the pregnancy-related expenses of spouses of male employees.

Title VII, Congress announced that the decision in *General Electric* had been contrary to its intention in passing the legislation.[47] One should further note that the Supreme Court of India has stated that it is 'inclined to accept the dissenting opinion [of Brennan J. in *General Electric*] which seems to take a more reasonable and rational view'.[48]

Also of limited assistance in construing section 1(1)(a) of the 1975 Act is the decision of the Canadian Supreme Court in *Bliss* v. *Attorney-General of Canada*.[49] Ritchie J., for the Court, rejected a challenge to the Unemployment Insurance Act (which provides a code dealing, in part, with the entitlement of women to unemployment insurance benefits during a specified part of the period of pregnancy and childbirth) made by reference to the Canadian Bill of Rights. Section 1(b) of the Bill of Rights guaranteed 'the right of the individual to equality before the law and the protection of the law'. Ritchie J., approving the reasoning of the court below, held that if the code 'treats unemployed pregnant women differently from other unemployed persons, be they male or female, it is, it seems to me, because they are pregnant and not because they are women'. He suggested that 'Any inequality between the sexes in this area is not created by legislation but by nature. . . . Assuming the respondent to have been "discriminated against", it would not have been by reason of her sex . . . '.[50] This decision ignores the

[47] See Lea Brilmayer, Richard W. Hekeler, Douglas Laycock, and Teresa A. Sullivan, 'Sex Discrimination in Employer-Sponsored Insurance Plans: A Legal and Demographic Analysis' 47 *University of Chicago Law Review* 505, 521 n (1980), *Abraham* v. *Graphic Arts International Union* above, n. 45 at 822–3n.

[48] *Air India* v. *Nergesh Meerza* AIR 1981 SC 1829, 1851. The Court held that for a corporation controlled by the State to require air hostesses to resign if they become pregnant violated Article 14 of the Constitution, which guarantees equality before the law and the equal protection of the laws. The Court said, at 1850, that the rule 'is a most unreasonable and arbitrary provision which shocks the conscience of the court. . . . We are . . . unable to understand the argument of the Corporation that a woman after bearing children becomes weak in physique or in her constitution. There is neither any legal nor medical authority for this bald proposition.' Although the Court described the rule as 'not only a callous and cruel act but an open insult to Indian womanhood—the most sacrosanct and cherished institution—[which] . . . exhibits naked despotism', still the Court indicated, at 1855, that it would be lawful to require air hostesses to leave their jobs on their third pregnancy 'in the larger interest of the health of the Air Hostess concerned as also for the good upbringing of the children . . . [and by reason of] the problem of population explosion . . .'.

[49] 92 DLR (3d) 417 (1978).

[50] Ibid. at 422. Cf. *Wardley* v. *Ansett Transport Industries (Operations) Pty (Ltd)*, where the Equal Opportunity Board of Victoria held, in a decision of 6 June

relevance of sex-plus criteria in analysing sex discrimination, and it makes no effort to assess whether pregnant women were treated less favourably than men with disabilities similar in the degree and length of incapacitation they produce.

Albeit the US Supreme Court and the Canadian Supreme Court have not understood the complexities of sex discrimination by pregnancy classifications (i.e. adverse treatment for reasons connected with pregnancy), the interpretation of section 1(1)(a) of the 1975 Act to exclude the possibility of direct discrimination by less favourable treatment for reasons connected with pregnancy seems unjustified by reference to the language of the Act and the aspirations it embodies.[51] Pregnancy classifications emphasize that 'the difficult cases for sex discrimination law . . . arise when a practice that promotes women's inequality as a sex is predicated upon an actual difference between the sexes'.[52] It has been suggested that the conceptual problem of discrimination by reference to pregnancy

in its essence is an irreconcilable theoretical conflict between those who believe that the gender equality principle can only be applied where men and women are treated differently with respect to a shared characteristic (which pregnancy obviously is not) and those who believe that discrimination on the basis of physical characteristics inextricably linked to one sex must be sex discrimination.[53]

1979 applying the Equal Opportunity Act 1977 (now repealed and replaced by the Equal Opportunity Act 1984), that 'the child-bearing potential of women should not be used as an excuse to limit women's role in society'. Other aspects of this dispute were later considered by the High Court of Australia: 54 ALJR 210 (1979).

[51] See the *Equal Opportunities Commission Annual Report 1980* at 12: the EAT decision in *Turley* 'appears to run contrary to the intention of the legislation'. The dissenting member of the EAT in *Turley* argued that the judgment of the majority of the tribunal 'seems to me to contradict both the spirit and the letter of the statute': above, n. 5 at 70.

[52] Catharine A. MacKinnon, *Sexual Harassment of Working Women* (1979), 104.

[53] Babcock, Freedman, Norton, Ross, *Sex Discrimination and the Law: Causes and Remedies* (1978 Supplement) 67–8. Similarly Brennan J. dissenting in *General Electric* above, n. 27 at 147–8: 'This case is unusual in that it presents a question the resolution of which at first glance turns largely upon the conceptual framework chosen to identify and describe the operational features of the challenged disability programme. By directing their focus upon the risks excluded from the otherwise comprehensive programme, and upon the purported justifications for such exclusions, the Equal Employment Opportunity Commission, the women plaintiffs, and the lower courts reason that the pregnancy exclusion constitutes a prima facie violation of Title VII . . . . The Court's framework is diametrically different. It

Counsel for the applicant in *Turley* appears to have adopted the second approach.[54] Neither of the suggested approaches is, however, correct. A third, preferable, solution is that classification by reference to a characteristic unique to one sex (whether or not all members of that sex possess the characteristic) is treatment on the ground of sex. Whether it is less favourable treatment than that accorded to members of the other sex is a question of fact dependent on how the other sex is treated in 'not materially different' circumstances. The essential defect in the EAT judgment in *Turley* (and the industrial tribunal decision in *Reaney*) is the failure to consider the facts of the case and the insistence that the issue of pregnancy classification can be treated as a question of law. The EAT should avoid the simplistic, erroneous approach to sex discrimination law exemplified by the judgment of one US district court, that the dismissal of a woman because she is pregnant cannot be discrimination on the ground of sex 'simply because only women become pregnant and only men grow beards'.[55]

IV

It is relatively easy to reject the reasoning in *Turley* that a pregnancy classification can never constitute direct discrimination contrary to the 1975 Act. It is much more difficult to state principles to guide courts and tribunals with regard to the circumstances in which such classifications do violate section 1(1)(a) of the Act. When are the relevant circumstances of men 'not materially different' to those of pregnant women? The less favourable treatment on the ground of sex can most easily be proved where pregnancy is the only temporary disability or incapacitating condition to which an employer attaches adverse consequences or upon the occurrence of which the employer denies benefits that are consequent upon other such conditions. More difficult is the case where the employer imposes a detriment

views General Electric's plan as representing a gender-free assignment of risks in accordance with normal actuarial techniques.'

[54] Above, n. 5 at 69: 'Mrs Cox, on the applicant's behalf, submits that to dismiss a woman because she is pregnant is so obvious a case of the employer treating her on the ground of her sex less favourably than he would treat a man as to be really beyond argument.'

[55] *Rafford* v. *Randle Eastern Ambulance Service Inc* 348 F Supp 316, 320 (1972).

(or denies a benefit) in a number of circumstances, one of which concerns pregnancy. The question of fact for the tribunal will then be to assess whether, by reason of the structure of the employer's system for providing benefits or imposing detriments, a female employee is treated less favourably than a male employee. Does the system, as a whole, offer the woman the same total prospective benefits and no greater total prospective detriments? If not, and if the reason why the total scheme adversely affects women is because pregnancy is one condition among others given exceptional treatment, then the woman can persuasively contend that she has been treated less favourably on the ground of her sex. Applying such a test, it may well be contrary to section 1(1)(a) of the 1975 Act for an employer to dismiss for reasons connected with pregnancy even if it also dismisses employees for reasons associated with temporary disabilities unique to men. Such a conclusion would be justified by the argument that pregnancy is the disability unique to one sex which has the most social impact in the employment context. For an employer to classify pregnancy with circumcision, for example, as the only causes of temporary incapacitation for which he dismisses an employee creates no more than an illusion of equality between male and female in the workplace.

However, there may be cases where it is difficult to compare the treatment of a pregnant woman with the treatment accorded to a man because no male comparable exists. Suppose an employer dismisses an unmarried woman (or a teachers' training college expels an unmarried female student, or a landlord refuses to rent property to an unmarried woman) because she is pregnant and he morally disapproves of that status. Sex discrimination cannot be established by comparing the defendant's treatment of the pregnant woman with his treatment of a man with an incapacitating condition.[56] Perhaps one could compare the treatment she receives with that he accords to a man with venereal disease or to a man responsible for an unmarried woman being pregnant. Moreover, in such cases one can seek to apply the judgment of the

---

[56] The issues are hinted at in the judgment of the US District Court in *Harvey* v. *YWCA* 27 FEP Cases 1724 (1982) where it was held not to be a breach of Title VII of the US Civil Rights Act for an employer to dismiss a pregnant, unmarried employee because she intended to present herself to the young women and girls in her charge as a model of a lifestyle alternative to that promulgated by the YWCA.

Court of Appeal in *Skyrail Oceanic Ltd* v. *Coleman*[57] that it is direct discrimination contrary to the 1975 Act to impose a detriment on a woman by applying a sex-based assumption without ascertaining whether the assumption is correct in the circumstances of the individual case. In the present case, the sex-based assumption is that an unmarried woman who is pregnant is necessarily deserving of moral disapproval. The real need in cases of this type—where the adverse treatment of a pregnant woman is for moral reasons relating to her marital status—is to strengthen section 3 of the 1975 Act. At present, it prohibits discrimination against a married person on the ground of his or her marital status in the field of employment. It should be amended to make it unlawful to discriminate against a person (whether single or married) on the ground of his or her marital status in all the contexts covered by the 1975 Act.

V

As an alternative to a claim of direct discrimination contrary to the 1975 Act, a woman who is subjected to a detriment or denied a benefit for reasons connected with pregnancy may bring a claim of indirect discrimination under that Act. In *Turley*, the EAT was unable to consider this alternative claim because the industrial tribunal had not made relevant findings of fact.[58]

The elements of a claim of indirect discrimination under section 1(1)(b) of the 1975 Act may well be established by a pregnancy classification imposed by an employer. An employer dismisses those employees who become pregnant, or refuses to appoint or to promote or to give access to training programmes to persons who are or who might become pregnant, or requires an employee to

---

[57] [1981] ICR 864. See above, n. 21.

[58] The EAT said, above, n. 5 at 68, that the applicant 'was unable to present before us her further argument under s. 1(1)(b) of the Act because the only assumption the industrial tribunal, and this appeal tribunal, could make was that the applicant was dismissed because she was pregnant, an insufficient infrastructure for argument of a submission under s. 1(1)(b).' It is unclear why the EAT did not then remit the case to the tribunal to find the facts relevant to a claim of indirect discrimination. In *Deignan* v. *Lambeth, Southwark and Lewisham Area Health Authority (Teaching)* (1979, unreported), an industrial tribunal considered a requirement that all prospective employees take a chest X-ray. It held that although pregnant women might be reluctant to undertake the X-ray, the requirement was justifiable and so not indirectly discriminatory under the 1975 Act.

take mandatory leave as soon as she realizes she is pregnant, or denies seniority rights to an employee who returns to work after maternity leave. The employer denies that this is direct sex discrimination because it would apply the same rules to a male employee who was, had been or might become pregnant. The employer is, therefore, applying a condition or requirement to a female employee which it applies *or would apply* to a man. This brings the employer within the scope of the indirect discrimination provisions of the 1975 Act.

The employer may argue that it has not breached the 1975 Act as no man can become pregnant and as section 37 of the Act (which allows the Equal Opportunities Commission to commence proceedings in respect of a 'discriminatory practice') suggests that there is no act of unlawful indirect discrimination where the persons to whom the impugned requirement or condition is applied are 'all of one sex'. Such an argument misunderstands the content and the purpose of section 37.[59] It does not contemplate a case where the impugned requirement or condition is applicable to a pool of male and female workers but, by reason of the content of the requirement or condition, it imposes a detriment only upon employees of one sex. That is clear from the wording of section 37, which is concerned with to whom the requirement or condition is 'applied', in contrast to section 1(1)(b) which defines indirect discrimination to cover a requirement or condition which 'would apply equally to a man' in addition to a requirement or condition which the employer actually 'applies' to a man. What section 37 does contemplate is a case where there is no act of discrimination under section 1(1)(b) because the impugned requirement or condition is 'applied' only to persons of one sex: suppose an employer imposes a requirement or condition which has a disproportionate adverse impact on persons of one sex, for example that he will employ only persons who are over six feet tall, but the requirement or condition is not 'applied' to persons of the disadvantaged sex (female) because no women are interested in applying for the job or all those women interested in applying for the job *are* over six feet tall. In such a case there would be no

[59] S. 37(1) provides that '"discriminatory practice" means the application of a requirement or condition which results in an act of discrimination which is unlawful by virtue of . . . s. 1(1)(b) . . . or which would be likely to result in such an act of discrimination if the persons to whom it is applied were not all of one sex'.

indirectly discriminatory act contrary to section 1(1)(b) of the 1975 Act as there is no female complainant to whom the requirement or condition is applicable and upon whom it imposes a detriment. Because the requirement or condition nevertheless constitutes a discriminatory practice, section 37 gives the Equal Opportunities Commission power to bring proceedings.

Our concern, in discussing pregnancy classifications, is not with a condition or requirement which has a potential indirectly discriminatory impact if only a member of the disadvantaged female sex were within the pool of persons to whom the requirement or condition is applied. Our concern is with a condition or requirement which is applied to members of the disadvantaged class (women who are employed by the defendant) and would indeed apply equally to a male employee if he became pregnant.

This interpretation of section 37 of the 1975 Act is consistent with the purpose of the indirect discrimination provisions of the Act: to render unlawful in the contexts covered by the Act those criteria which, while not overtly sex-based, have a disproportionate adverse impact on one sex and cannot be justified by the defendant. Clearly, pregnancy classifications have such a disproportionate adverse impact. Such impact is not diminished, but is, rather, strengthened, by the fact that no man is adversely affected by a criterion imposing detriments or denying benefits for reasons connected with pregnancy. The indirect discrimination provisions of the 1975 Act[60] were introduced as a response to the decision of the US Supreme Court in *Griggs* v. *Duke Power Co*[61] which created the concept of disparate impact or indirect discrimination and read it into Title VII of the US Civil Rights Act 1964. The US Supreme Court has held that pregnancy classifications may be indirectly discriminatory contrary to Title VII.[62]

Because no man can become pregnant, it is likely to be the case

---

[60] See ch. 2 ss. III and IV.   [61] 401 US 424 (1971).

[62] *Nashville Gas Co* v. *Satty* above n. 37. See also the decisions of US Courts of Appeals: *In Re Southwestern Bell Telephone Co Maternity Benefits Litigation* 602 F 2d 845 (1979), *Burwell* v. *Eastern Airlines* 633 F 2d 361 (1980), *Harriss* v. *Pan Am World Airways* 649 F 2d 670 (1980), *Clanton* v. *Orleans Parish School Board* 26 FEP Cases 740 (1981), *Abraham* v. *Graphic Arts International Union* above n. 45, *Levin* v. *Delta Air Lines* 730 F 2d 994 (1984). See also *An Foras Forbartha* v. *A Worker*, 30 Apr. 1982, a decision of the Irish Labour Court under the Employment Equality Act 1977.

that, pursuant to section 1(1)(b) of the 1975 Act, 'the proportion of women who can comply' with a condition or requirement which imposes a pregnancy classification 'is considerably smaller than the proportion of men who can comply with it'. It is not open to an employer to argue that all women *can* comply with the condition or requirement as they can all avoid pregnancy (by abstaining from sexual intercourse or by the use of contraceptives). The EAT established in *Price* v. *Civil Service Commission* that:

It should not be said that a person 'can' do something merely because it is theoretically possible for him to do so: it is necessary to see whether he can do so in practice. Applying this approach to the circumstances of this case, it is relevant in determining whether women can comply with the condition to take into account the current usual behaviour of women in this respect, as observed in practice, putting on one side behaviour and responses which are unusual or extreme.[63]

Undoubtedly a requirement or condition which imposes a pregnancy classification is to the detriment of a female complainant who cannot comply with it. The crucial issue under section 1(1)(b) of the 1975 Act will be whether the employer can show the impugned requirement or condition to be 'justifiable irrespective of the sex of the person to whom it is applied.[64] Two decisions of US courts of appeal concerning air hostesses show the possible width or narrowness of a justification defence to a charge of disparate impact by a pregnancy classification. In *Harriss* v. *Pan Am World Airways* the Court held that the airline had proved that the possible impairment of job performance during pregnancy justified the rule that a flight attendant must take maternity leave immediately on learning that she is pregnant. Circuit Judge Schroeder, in a powerful dissenting opinion, argued that:

Pregnancy is the only physical condition which prompts such restrictions. Persons with any other physical condition which might interfere with performance of duties are permitted to fly if, upon a visual inspection prior to takeoff, they do not appear to be incapacitated. The employee making the visual inspection has no medical training. Pan American does not even require an annual physical examination of its flight attendants. . . . If, for example, persons suffering from ulcers, hernias, colitis, high blood pressure or heart disease are less likely to become incapacitated during flight than women in the early months of pregnancy, there is nothing in

---

[63] [1978] ICR 27, 31.   [64] See ch. 2 s. IV for the criteria of justifiability.

this record to prove it. . . . If Pan American desires its claimed safety precautions to withstand attack, it should design procedures, reviews and tests which measure the ability of all flight attendants who have medical conditions which might affect their performance in an emergency situation.[65]

In *Burwell* v. *Eastern Airlines* the Court of Appeals held that a requirement that flight attendants take mandatory leave as soon as they learn they are pregnant was in breach of Title VII as indirectly discriminatory so far as it applied to the first trimester of pregnancy (because there was insufficient evidence to show that passenger safety might be adversely affected) but that the requirement was justified by business necessity with regard to the second and third trimesters of pregnancy (when the evidence suggested that passenger safety might be adversely affected). Four judges out of nine dissented from the conclusions concerning the second and third trimesters. Judge Butzner's persuasive dissenting opinion emphasized that the airline's own medical expert agreed that:

[H]e permits his pregnant patients, depending on their individual capacities and experience, to continue to work, ride horses, ski and water ski. . . . There is no dispute that Eastern's rules dealing with pregnancy differ from its regulations for other physical conditions. Apart from its pregnancy policy, the airline has no written guidelines governing fitness of its flight attendants; nor does it routinely examine them. Eastern's medical director testified that the airline's normal method of handling physical and mental disabilities, other than pregnancy, is to rely upon self-monitoring. . . . Eastern permits stewardesses with controlled diabetes and controlled epilepsy to fly under supervision of the medical department, even though medical experts testified that these conditions are more likely to be disabling than pregnancy.[66]

The burden of proof is on the employer to establish that a requirement or condition which has a disproportionate adverse impact on women is justifiable. The English courts may well follow

[65] Above, n. 62 at 679–80.

[66] Above, n. 62 at 375–6. On the circumstances in which pregnancy discrimination may be justifiable because of potential danger to the foetus arising from the nature of the employment see *Harper* v. *Thiokol Chemical Corporation* 619 F 2d 489 (1980), *Zuniga* v. *Kleberg County Hospital* 692 F 2d 986 (1982), *Wright* v. *Olin Corporation* 697 F 2d 1172 (1982) and *Hayes* v. *Shelby Memorial Hospital* 34 FEP Cases 444 (1984), all decisions of US Courts of Appeals.

the approach of the dissenting judges in the US courts of appeals that a concern for safety cannot justify an impugned pregnancy classification if the employer adopts no similar safety measures with respect to other medical conditions which have a potentially disabling effect (save for the exceptional case where the nature of the employment poses particular health risks to the pregnant woman or to the foetus). Courts may be prepared to hold that pregnancy discrimination is unjustifiable even if other incapacitating conditions are similarly treated: given the prevalence of pregnancy, unnecessary conditions or requirements imposed by employers in relation to pregnancy are a major barrier to equality at work for men and women. Whatever approach the English courts adopt to this issue, the availability of a justification defence ensures that any woman who suffers from a pregnancy classification at work will want to plead her claim under the 1975 Act as one of direct discrimination and indirect discrimination in the alternative.

Such a female complainant may, if married, also claim that the imposition of a detriment or the denial of a benefit for reasons connected with pregnancy is indirectly discriminatory contrary to section 3(1)(b) of the 1975 Act. That subsection provides that it is unlawful for an employer to impose on a married person of either sex a condition or requirement which he applies or would apply equally to an unmarried person, but which is such that the proportion of married persons who can comply with it is considerably smaller than the proportion of unmarried persons of the same sex who can comply with it (a criterion satisfied by a pregnancy classification), which is to the complainant's detriment because she cannot comply with it, and which the employer cannot show to be justifiable irrespective of the marital status of the person to whom it is applied. The criterion of justifiability under section 3(1)(b) is unlikely to impose a different test on employers than that imposed by section 1(1)(b) in the context of pregnancy classifications.[67]

VI

It is important that courts and tribunals take a more constructive approach to questions of sex discrimination by the imposition of

---

[67] See *Hurley* v. *Mustoe* above, n. 12.

pregnancy classifications. The decision in *Turley* shows significant errors of principle. It implies the existence of troubling loopholes in the 1975 Act. It treats as a question of law an issue that can only satisfactorily be resolved by analysis of the relevant facts.

The 1975 Act offers some protection to women disadvantaged by pregnancy classifications. To establish direct discrimination, a female complainant will need to prove that she suffered less favourable treatment than that accorded (or which would be accorded) by the employer to a male employee with a similarly incapacitating condition. To establish indirect discrimination, the facts relevant to justifiability (on which issue the burden of proof is on the employer) will be decisive. It is because employers tend to place pregnancy in a class by itself, and to impose upon pregnant women detriments to which other employees (whether or not afflicted with a similarly incapacitating condition) are not subjected (or to deny pregnant women benefits awarded to other employees), that the treatment of a pregnant woman may well, on the facts of the individual case, breach the 1975 Act.

Should future cases reveal judicial reluctance broadly to construe the 1975 Act denying the degree of protection that pregnant women deserve, then three routes forward deserve consideration.

First, the 1975 Act could be amended to emphasize the intention to combat pregnancy classifications that impose detriments on women. The anti-discrimination law of Australia provides two possible models. Section 7 of the Sex Discrimination Act 1984 (Australia) provides that it is unlawful by reason of pregnancy, or a characteristic that appertains generally (or is generally imputed) to persons who are pregnant, to treat a person less favourably than, in circumstances that are the same or are not materially different, one treats or would treat a person who is not pregnant, if the less favourable treatment is not reasonable in all the circumstances. Section 24(1) of the Anti-Discrimination Act 1977 of New South Wales provides that one of the circumstances in which a person discriminates against another on the ground of her sex is where the less favourable treatment is on the basis of 'a characteristic that appertains generally' to persons of that sex or on the basis of 'a characteristic that is generally imputed to persons' of that sex. The Anti-Discrimination (Amendment) Act 1981 of New South Wales provides that for the purposes of section 24 of the 1977 Act, 'the fact that a woman is or may become pregnant is a characteristic that appertains generally to women'. It adds that 'the circumstances in which a person treats or would treat another person of the opposite sex are not materially different by reason of the fact that the persons between whom the discrimination occurs . . . are a woman who is pregnant and a man. . . .'.[68]

Secondly, one could seek to rely upon the EEC Equal Treatment Directive,[69] which states 'the principle of equal treatment for men and women as regards access to employment, including promotion, and to vocational training and as regards working conditions . . .'. It states that 'the principle of equal treatment shall mean that there shall be no discrimination whatsoever on grounds of sex either directly or indirectly by reference in particular to marital or family status'. Pregnancy is, arguably, a 'family status'.

Thirdly, it may be necessary to enact legislation specifically, and more comprehensively, to guarantee the rights of working women who wish to combine a career with family responsibilities. Positive measures, such as the mandatory provision of day-care centres for children of employees and guaranteed family-care leave of absence, deserve consideration.

This chapter concentrates on the 1975 Act which is, in many contexts, the only protection a working woman can rely upon against adverse treatment for reasons related to pregnancy. For the judiciary to continue to take a narrow view of the application of the 1975 Act to pregnancy classifications would be unmerited as

[68] Schedule 5, para. 8 of the Anti-Discrimination (Amendment) Act 1981 of New South Wales. Schedule 5 para. 9 of the 1981 Act creates two exceptions to the new principle. The Act does not protect a woman from less favourable treatment by reason of pregnancy 'if, at the date on which the woman applied to the employer for employment or, where the employer interviewed the woman in relation to her application for employment, at the date of the interview, the woman is pregnant'. Similarly, the Act does not protect a pregnant woman against dismissal by reason of pregnancy 'if, at the date on which the woman applied to the employer for employment or, where the employer interviewed the woman in relation to her application for employment, at the date of the interview, the woman was pregnant, unless, at that date, the woman did not know and could not reasonably be expected to have known that she was pregnant'.

[69] 76/207 EEC (9 Feb. 1976). Art. 2(3) of the Directive, like s. 2(2) of the 1975 Act (on which see n. 22 above) provides that the Directive 'shall be without prejudice to provisions concerning the protection of women, particularly as regards pregnancy and maternity'. See ch. 5 n. 33 on *Hofmann* v. *Barmer Ersatzkasse The Times* 24 July 1984—where the European Court of Justice held that art. 2(3) applies to maternity leave.

a matter of law and most regrettable as a matter of social policy. The inevitable consequence would be the perpetuation of stereotypes that have impeded the employment prospects of all women. It would be one more paradox that legislation designed to compel the similar treatment of persons who are biologically distinct should be held not to apply when the excuse for dissimilar treatment is that men and women are indeed physiologically different.

In *General Electric*, Stevens J. dissented from the judgment of the US Supreme Court because 'it is the capacity to become pregnant which primarily differentiates the female from the male'.[70] Industrial tribunals and the EAT have yet to understand that it was Parliament's purpose in enacting the Sex Discrimination Act 1975 to eradicate reliance on the theory of Sigmund Freud that 'anatomy is destiny'.[71]

---

[70] Above, n. 27 at 162. Stevens J. made similar observations in *Michael M.* v. *Superior Court of Sonoma County* 450 US 464, 498 (1981).

[71] For a perceptive account of how the physical characteristics of men are treated as assets while the physical characteristics of women are treated as defects see Gloria Steinem, 'If Men Could Menstruate' *Outrageous Acts and Everyday Rebellions* (1984), 337–40. The EAT has now accepted many of the arguments in this chapter and held that to treat a woman adversely by reason of her pregnancy can amount to direct sex discrimination. See *Hayes* and *Maughan* above, n. 5: *The Times* 19 June 1985.

7

SEXUAL HARASSMENT AT WORK, GROOMING CODES, AND INSURANCE

I

This chapter considers three areas in which sex discrimination law raises particularly difficult problems: sexual harassment at work, grooming codes, and insurance.

II

As various studies have shown, sexual harassment at work is a feature of society which has long troubled female victims.[1] In the USA, courts have acknowledged that such conduct may give rise to a cause of action for unlawful sex discrimination contrary to Title VII of the Civil Rights Act 1964. It is strongly arguable that the Sex Discrimination Act 1975 gives similar protection to that guaranteed to women in the USA.[2] This has been accepted in part by the EAT in Scotland.[3]

---

[1] See, for example, Bryan Gould and Linda McDougall, 'Keeping Women Down' *New Statesman* 23 Oct. 1981; Alfred Marks Bureau Survey *Daily Telegraph* 23 Apr. 1982; Marplan Poll *The Guardian* 23 June 1982; EEC Poll *The Times* 11 Feb. 1983; *Sexual Harassment at Work* (1983: TUC).

[2] That conclusion has been reached by various commentators, not only this one: David Pannick, 'Sexual Harassment and the Sex Discrimination Act' (1982) *Public Law* 42. See also Linda Clarke, 'Sexual Harassment and the Sex Discrimination Act 1975' (132) *New Law Journal* 1116 (1982); Michael Rubenstein, 'The Law of Sexual Harassment at Work' 12 *Industrial Law Journal* 1 (1983).

[3] *Porcelli* v. *Strathclyde Regional Council* [1984] IRLR 467, 469: 'We do not find it necessary to define the expression "sexual harassment" in precise terms. Unwelcome acts which involve physical contact of a sexual nature are obviously included . . . We consider that there can also be conduct falling short of such physical acts which can fairly be described as sexual harassment . . . An employer who dismisses a female employee because she has resisted or ceased to be interested in his advances would . . . be in breach of s. 6(2)(b) and s. 1(1) of the 1975 Act for reasons arising from sexual harassment. Similarly if, for the same reason, he takes other disciplinary action against her short of dismissal he would also be in breach.' See also nn. 29 and 35. In 1983 a female employee who was dismissed after refusing to succumb to the sexual advances of the employer's

In November 1980, the United States Equal Employment Opportunities Commission issued a set of guide-lines which concisely and helpfully define sexual harassment. The evil consists of unwelcome sexual advances, requests for sexual favours, and other verbal or physical conduct of a sexual nature in three situations. First, where submission to such conduct is expressly or impliedly made a term or condition of employment. Secondly, where submission to or rejection of such conduct is used as the basis for employment decisions affecting an individual, for example decisions on promotion or pay or dismissal. Thirdly, when such conduct has the effect or the purpose of unreasonably interfering with an individual's work performance by creating an intimidating, hostile, or offensive work environment. When sexual harassment takes one of these forms, it is, far from being a joke, an important contributory factor to the stereotype of a woman's role at work.

Lord Justice Lawton recognized, in the Court of Appeal, that '[p]ersistent and unwanted amorous advances by an employer to a female member of his staff would . . . clearly be . . . conduct' by the employer amounting to constructive dismissal of the employee, enabling her to sue for unfair dismissal if she can no longer tolerate such treatment.[4] Broader protection is offered by the Sex Discrimination Act 1975. It covers all aspects of work, from appointment, through promotion and working conditions, to dismissal. If, at any stage, a woman can show that she has been less favourably treated on the ground of her sex, she has a legal remedy.

In one of the early cases brought before a United States District Court, the claim of sex discrimination by sexual harassment was ridiculed. The Court asserted that if such a claim were to succeed, there 'would be a potential federal lawsuit every time any employee made amorous or sexually oriented advances toward another. The only sure way an employer could avoid such charges

---

accountant was awarded compensation of £2,255 by an industrial tribunal under the Sex Discrimination Act 1975: *The Times* 9 Sept. 1983.

[4] *Western Excavating (ECC) Ltd* v. *Sharp* [1978] QB 761, 772. See also *Wood* v. *Freeloader Ltd* [1977] IRLR 455, where an industrial tribunal held that the complainant was entitled to terminate her contract of employment and claim constructive dismissal because, by entering into a lesbian relationship with her, the company secretary had brought about an intolerable situation in which confidence between the two of them could not be maintained.

would be to have employees who were asexual.'[5] American courts have, since then, moved on to an understanding of the misery caused to working women by persistent and unwelcome sexual demands made of them at work and have recognized the unlawful nature of such conduct under sex discrimination law. Indeed, so far has the American jurisprudence developed that a US District Court has been prepared to issue an injunction to restrain male employees from making the lives of female co-workers intolerable by harassing them with comments such as 'Did you get any over the weekend?'.[6] The US courts have developed a sophisticated set of legal principles to answer three basic questions under Title VII of the Civil Rights Act 1964: Is sexual harassment discrimination on the ground of sex? What acts of harassment are prohibited? And when is an employer liable for the harassment which occurs in the workplace?[7] The answers given in the US courts deserve the attention of any British court which is asked to consider these issues.

In *Barnes* v. *Costle*, the US Court of Appeals held that for an employer to discharge a female employee because she refused to submit to sexual advances amounted to sex discrimination. This was because '[b]ut for her womanhood . . . her participation in sexual activity would never have been solicited' and because 'no male employee was susceptible to such an approach . . .'.[8] It is not the employer's demands for sexual activity that establish the violation of sex discrimination law. Rather it is that such demands are made only of women. Hence, a female employer will act unlawfully by harassing male employees.[9] A homosexual employer

---

[5] *Corne* v. *Bausch and Lomb* 390 F Supp 161, 163–4 (1975), vacated and remanded on other grounds 562 F 2d 55 (1977: US Court of Appeals). See similarly *Tomkins* v. *Public Service Electric & Gas Co.* 422 F Supp 553, 557 (1976: US District Court): the judge was concerned that 'an invitation to dinner could become an invitation to a federal lawsuit if a once harmonious relationship turned sour at some later time'. An appeal was there allowed and the case remanded for a further hearing: 568 F 2d 1044 (1977: US Court of Appeals).

[6] *Morgan* v. *Hertz Corp.* 542 F Supp 123, 128 (1981).

[7] See, generally, on the issues Catharine A. MacKinnon, *Sexual Harassment of Working Women* (1979); *Sexual Harassment and Labour Relations* (1981: the Bureau of National Affairs, Washington DC); Note 'Sexual Harassment and Title VII' 51 *New York University Law Review* 148 (1976); Note 'Legal Remedies for Employment-Related Sexual Harassment' 64 *Minnesota Law Review* 151 (1979).

[8] 561 F 2d 983, 990 (1977).

[9] Ibid. at 990 n.

acts unlawfully by harassing employees of the same sex.[10] But '[i]n the case of the bisexual superior, the insistence upon sexual favours would not constitute gender discrimination because it would apply to male and female employees alike'.[11]

It will, no doubt, be argued by UK employers, as it was, unsuccessfully, by American employers, that the sexual harassment of women employees is not sex discrimination because it is not on the ground of their sex, but on the ground of their attractiveness, that they are propositioned. The answer is that, but for their sex, the women would not have suffered this treatment. No man is so treated. Sex is the 'activating cause' of the treatment, or a 'substantial reason' for it.[12] As Catharine MacKinnon has explained, '[t]o say that a woman is fired not because she is a woman but because she refuses to have sex with her male superiors is like saying that a black man was fired not because he was black, but because he refused to shuffle for his white superiors'.[13] In each case, the employee refuses to conform to the demeaning stereotype imposed by the employer on persons of one sex or race.[14]

That the employer has not subjected all women to harassment, only those he finds attractive, is no defence to a claim of sex discrimination. US courts have called this the question of 'sex-plus' criteria: the detriment is imposed only on women, but not on all women. If sex-plus criteria are not directly discriminatory contrary to the 1975 Act, vast gaps would appear in that legislation, contrary to Parliament's intentions. Suppose an employer says it will employ any man with stated skills, but only those women who have the skills and are under 25 years old (or have no children or are over six feet tall). The concept of indirect discrimination does not capture such a case since the criteria are not applied equally to men and women. So the practice is either directly discriminatory or it is lawful. The US Supreme Court has held that sex-plus criteria are directly discriminatory.[15] The EAT

---

[10] Ibid. See *Wright* v. *Methodist Youth Services Inc.* 511 F Supp 307 (1981) and *Joyner* v. *AAA Cooper Transportation* 36 FEP Cases 1644 (1983) (decisions of the US District Court).

[11] Ibid.

[12] See ch. 2 nn. 8 and 36 for these criteria of direct discrimination.

[13] Above, n. 7 at 189.

[14] See ch. 2 nn. 39–46 on direct discrimination by acting on sexual stereotypes.

[15] *Phillips* v. *Martin Marietta Corporation* 400 US 542 (1971). See also Note 'Developments in the Law—Employment Discrimination and Title VII of the Civil Rights Act of 1964' 84 *Harvard Law Review* 1109, 1171–2 (1971).

implied a similar conclusion in *Hurley* v. *Mustoe* where it was held that an employer who refused to employ women with young children was directly discriminating on the ground of sex.[16] This must be correct: the employer is applying different criteria to men and to women. In *Barnes* v. *Castle*, the US Court of Appeals applied this reasoning and concluded that it is enough that 'while some but not all employees of one sex were subjected to the condition, no employee of the opposite sex was affected . . .'.[17] Nor can the employer successfully argue that sexual harassment is not sex discrimination because section 5(3) of the 1975 Act requires one to compare the 'relevant circumstances' of the female and male employees. The employer may argue that the circumstances cannot be the same or similar for any male employee because he necessarily lacks the qualities which inspire the employer's lusts. The answer is that an employer cannot make 'relevant' to the comparison under section 5(3) sexual characteristics which are otherwise irrelevant to the job. The EAT has stated that 'one must put out of the picture any circumstances which necessarily follow from the fact that one is comparing the case of a man and of a woman'.[18] Section 7 of the 1975 Act carefully defines the circumstances in which sex is a genuine occupational qualification for a job.[19]

If sexual harassment can amount to sex discrimination, the second issue concerns the types of acts which may be unlawful. The easiest cases are those where the complainant fails to be appointed or promoted or to obtain a pay increase, or is dismissed, because she refuses to comply with an employer's sexual demands. Similarly unlawful are the cases where the employer persuades the female complainant to comply with such demands as a condition of securing appointment, promotion, a pay rise, or retention of the job. Such conduct is unlawful whether or not the employer keeps his side of the bargain. Also unlawful is the case where the female complainant proves that the employer decided not to promote her (or to give her another benefit) but rather to promote another woman because that other woman complied with the employer's sexual demands where the employer would not have taken this

[16] [1981] ICR 490. On sex-plus criteria, see ch. 6 at nn. 8–14.

[17] Above, n. 8 at 991.

[18] *Peake* v. *Automotive Products Ltd* [1977] ICR 480, 488 (reversed on other grounds by the Court of Appeal: [1977] ICR 968).

[19] See ch. 9.

into account if the complainant were male.[20] All these cases would breach section 6 of the 1975 Act, which prohibits sex discrimination in employment.

US courts have emphasized that sex discrimination law does not prohibit 'an attempt to establish personal relationships', even if this occurs within the work-place. So a 'cause of action does not arise from an isolated incident or a mere flirtation'.[21] The difficulty is to draw the line between genuine and permissible 'sexual advances of an individual or personal nature'[22] and behaviour which breaches the law. Sexual advances are unlawful sexual harassment when they are backed by the express or implied threat or promise of employment detriments or benefits. This is known by US Courts of Appeals as 'quid pro quo' harassment, and is contrasted with harassment that creates an offensive work environment, or 'condition of work' harassment.[23] Both types are unlawful.

In *Bundy* v. *Jackson*,[24] an employee alleged that two supervisors had sexually harassed her by requests for sexual favours. When she had complained to a more senior manager, he told her that 'any man in his right mind would want to rape you'. He too propositioned her. The Court found this to be 'standard operating procedure' in the firm. The US Court of Appeals held that, although Title VII requires sex discrimination to be related to the 'terms, conditions or privileges of employment' before it can be unlawful, that phrase covered the psychological and emotional work environment. The Court accepted that 'the sexually stereotyped insults and demeaning propositions to which she was indisputably subjected and which caused her anxiety and debilitation . . . illegally poisoned that environment.'[25] Therefore she had been unlawfully discriminated against even though she had suffered no economic loss. As another US Court of Appeals explained in *Henson* v. *City of Dundee*,

---

[20] *Toscano* v. *Nimmo* 32 FEP Cases 1401 (1983: US District Court).

[21] *Heelan* v. *Johns-Manville Corp.* 451 F Supp 1382, 1388 (1978: US District Court).

[22] *Tomkins* above, n. 5: 568 F 2d 1044, 1048 (1977). Women 'must surely accept, and not be offended by, ordinary expressions of sexual interest': Mary Midgley and Judith Hughes *Women's Choices* (1983), 149.

[23] *Henson* v. *City of Dundee* 682 F 2d 897, 908n (1982); *Katz* v. *Dole* 709 F 2d 251, 254 (1983) citing a distinction drawn by MacKinnon above, n. 7 at 32–47.

[24] 641 F 2d 934 (1981).   [25] Ibid. at 944.

[s]exual harassment which creates a hostile or offensive environment for members of one sex is every bit the arbitrary barrier to sexual equality at the workplace that racial harassment is to racial equality. Surely a requirement that a man or woman runs a gauntlet of sexual abuse in return for the privilege of being allowed to work and make a living can be as demeaning and disconcerting as the harshest of racial epithets.[26]

For this reason, sexual harassment will state a claim under sex discrimination law if it is 'sufficiently pervasive so as to alter the conditions of employment and create an abusive working environment'.[27] This depends on the nature, frequency, and context of what is said and done.[28]

The 1975 Act admits of a similarly wide interpretation of the types of harassment which may be unlawful. It certainly prohibits sex discrimination by making employment decisions on appointment, promotion, and dismissal dependent on compliance with sexual demands. Section 6 of the 1975 Act further makes it unlawful for the employer to discriminate in the way it affords employees access to the benefits of employment or by subjecting them to any other detriment. An undoubted benefit of employment (the absence of which is a detriment) is a work environment free from sexual harassment by words or deeds that significantly reduce the quality of working conditions for women. Persistent and unwelcome sexual taunts, demands, or abuse will therefore be in breach of the 1975 Act if directed only at women.[29]

The third main legal issue raised by sexual harassment in the work-place is caused by the fact that the impugned conduct will often be the behaviour of male co-workers, not the behaviour of the employer. Title VII and the 1975 Act make *employers* liable for sex discrimination.[30] The US Court of Appeals has recognized that once the complainant

---

[26] Above, n. 23 at 902.

[27] Ibid. at 904. See Note 'Sexual Harassment Claims of Abusive Work Environment under Title VII' 97 *Harvard Law Review* 1449 (1984).

[28] In *Morgan* v. *Hertz Corp.* above, n. 6, therefore, the US District Court accepted that the 'addressing of sexually indecent comments to female employees is a form of sexual harassment and discrimination prohibited by Title VII . . .'. See also *Continental Can Co. Inc.* v. *State* 297 NW 2d 241 (1980), where the Supreme Court of Minnesota applied the prohibition of sex discrimination in the State Human Rights Act to sexual harassment creating an abusive working environment.

[29] In *Porcelli* above, n. 3, the EAT did not consider whether sexual harassment which adversely affected working conditions could amount to a sufficient detriment for this purpose.

[30] Under s. 42(2) of the 1975 Act an employee for whose act an employer is

proves that harassment took place, the most difficult legal question typically will concern the responsibility of the employer for that harassment. Except in situations where a proprietor, partner or corporate officer participates personally in the harassing behaviour, the plaintiff will have the additional responsibility of demonstrating the propriety of holding the employer liable . . .'[31]

US Courts of Appeals have held that the usual principles of tort law apply: an employer is liable for the acts of its employee done in the course of employment.[32] The US courts have distinguished between 'quid pro quo' and 'condition of work' cases. In the former case, employers have been held strictly liable for the conduct of supervisors because such persons rely upon their actual or ostensible authority 'to extort sexual consideration from an employee'; by contrast, in the condition of work case, the employer is not liable unless higher management knew or ought to have known of the sexual harassment and took no adequate remedial action.[33] To avoid liability in such condition of work cases, the employer needs to inform all employees that sexual harassment is prohibited; the employer should establish and publicize a scheme under which harassed employees may complain to management immediately and confidentially; and the employer must take all necessary steps to investigate all claims of harassment and to remedy by appropriate disciplinary sanctions all wrongs that are proved.[34]

Under section 41 of the 1975 Act, an employer is liable for anything done by an employee in the course of employment 'whether or not it was done with the employer's knowledge or approval'. However the employer has a defence on proving that it 'took such steps as were reasonably practicable to prevent the employee from doing that act, or from doing in the course of his employment acts of that description'. British courts will, no doubt,

---

vicariously liable under s. 41 of the Act is deemed to aid the doing of the unlawful act by the employer and so the employee can be liable under s. 42(1) of the Act. But this is all dependent on establishing that the employer is vicariously liable under s. 41 of the Act. On ss. 41 and 42 see ch. 3 nn. 104–7.

[31] *Katz* v. *Dole* above, n. 23 at 255.

[32] *Miller* v. *Bank of America* 600 F 2d 211 (1979); *Vinson* v. *Taylor* 36 FEP Cases 1423 (1985).

[33] *Henson* v. *City of Dundee* above, n. 23 at 910; similarly *Katz* v. *Dole* above, n. 23 at 255.

[34] *Bundy* v. *Jackson* above, n. 24 at 947.

develop similar tests to those stated by US courts to determine what 'reasonably practicable' steps are open to employers in these circumstances.[35]

Sexual harassment at work may sometimes be unlawful for reasons other than sex discrimination law. It may amount to the tort or crime of assault or battery.[36] These legal approaches, although worthy of consideration in extreme cases,[37] are unlikely to give greater relief to working women than the relatively speedy and cheap industrial tribunal procedures.

Even in the informal setting of an industrial tribunal deciding a claim of sexual harassment under sex discrimination law, a woman complainant will need to be brave. Her case will undoubtedly attract large publicity, much of it prurient. Lawyers representing her employer will possibly seek to suggest that, for various reasons, she welcomed the sexual advances of which she now complains. Some of the dangers of bringing this type of claim were demonstrated in an industrial tribunal claim of sex discrimination brought against the Metropolitan Police in December 1983. The tribunal held that a woman police constable had been unlawfully discriminated against on the ground of her sex because the police authorities had separated her working partnership with a married male officer, thereby damaging her career prospects. The police had so acted because they feared—totally without justification—that the working partners might develop a sexual relationship. The Chief Superintendent who made the decision to separate the partnership said in his evidence that one factor which influenced him was that he had heard that the woman police officer had previously had a relationship with a married male police officer. Under cross-examination, the Chief Superintendent agreed that he had never asked the woman about this, he accepted that in fact there was no basis for the allegation that she had acted improperly,

[35] The EAT has held that an employer unlawfully discriminates if it treats a complainant less favourably in order to resolve a problem caused by the racial prejudice of other employees: *Din* v. *Carrington Viyella* [1982] ICR 256. On s. 41 see ch. 3 nn. 105–7. In *Porcelli* above, n. 3 at 468–9, the EAT noted that the employers accepted legal responsibility for the sexual harassment carried out by male employees, but that the 'wide issue' of whether what was done was 'in the course of their employment . . . remains open for decision in a future case should one arise'.

[36] See *Rogers* v. *Loews L'Enfant Plaza Hotel* 526 F Supp 523 (1981: US District Court).

[37] See Catharine A. MacKinnon above, n. 7 at 158–74.

and he agreed that this all showed the danger of relying on unsubstantiated gossip. The next morning, the report of the case in the *Sun* newspaper was headlined '"Temptress" PC Wendy had live-in Cop Lover'.[38]

In *Priest* v. *Rotary,* a US District Court held that an employer being sued by a former employee under Title VII for alleged sexual harassment was not entitled to compel her to answer questions about her private sexual behaviour. The Court wisely concluded that '[w]ithout such protection from the courts, employees whose intimate lives are unjustifiably and offensively intruded upon in the work-place might face the "Catch 22" of invoking their statutory remedy only at the risk of enduring further intrusions into irrelevant details of their personal lives . . .'.[39] It is far from certain that British courts and tribunals would reach a similar conclusion. Indeed, it was the failure of the law to provide such basic protection for victims in rape cases that led to special legislative provisions in the Sexual Offences (Amendment) Act 1976.

To give herself the strongest prospects of succeeding in her sexual harassment claim, a woman complainant should protest in writing to her employer and, if the harassment is by fellow-workers, ask the employer to take all necessary steps to stop the harassment. She should keep a written record of all offensive incidents. She should report the matter to her trade union and discuss the problem with other female employees so as more widely to document the issues. If a woman does succeed in establishing that sexual harassment at work is unlawful sex discrimination, the publicity given to her case will ensure that employers (and others) will be made aware of their legal obligations and other female victims will be encouraged to assert their legal rights.[40]

---

[38] *Sun* 21 Dec. 1983. See ch. 3 n. 35. Cf. *C. Thorrez Industries* v. *Michigan Dept. of Civil Rights* 278 NW 2d 725 (1979) where the Michigan Court of Appeals held that it was not sex discrimination contrary to the State Fair Employment Practices Act for an employer to dismiss a semi-skilled woman in order to retain a skilled male worker who was about to leave his job at the insistence of his wife who was concerned that he had had a sexual relationship with the woman worker and who did not want the husband and the woman working under the same roof.

[39] 32 FEP Cases 1064, 1069 (1983).

[40] In Canada, the Ontario Human Rights Code 1981 protects employees from sexual harassment in the work-place by the employer, its agents, or by other

Sexual harassment at work is only one manifestation of a more pervasive problem. It is the consequence of a widely held set of prejudices which treat women workers as subservient to men. So long as women tend to be employed (if at all) in inferior jobs with low pay, so they will continue to be harassed by employers and by other employees who treat women as admitted into the work-place under sufferance. The power to make employment decisions tends to be retained by men. While occupational segregation persists, the boss will see nothing wrong in preferring an attractive female secretary who is willing to select birthday presents for the boss's wife. Stronger laws to promote equal employment opportunity will reduce the causes of sexual harassment at work. Meanwhile, sex discrimination law has an important role to play in deterring and remedying some of the more offensive manifestations of male employment superiority seen in sexual harassment. Proudhon, although believing that 'property is theft', offered the female a choice which is far less radical in its implications: 'housewife or harlot'.[41] Those women who reject both options, and who resent the attempts of employers or of co-workers to impose one or other of those alternatives upon them should look to their legal rights.

In extreme cases, whether sexual harassment is unlawful may depend on the nature of the job. For example, 'a topless dancer might be expected, without considering herself discriminated against, to tolerate more catcalls, insults, and even some sexual advances from customers than women in most other occupations'.[42] The sexual harassment of a female employee may result from customer reaction to the wearing of a uniform in circumstances where it is not reasonable to expect the employee to tolerate such treatment. In *EEOC* v. *Sage Realty Corp.*,[43] a US District Court held that the employer's requirement that a female employee wear a revealing, provocative uniform which the employers knew would

employees: s. 6(2). The Code also prohibits sexual harassment in the context of providing accommodation: s. 6(1). On Canadian law see Constance Backhouse, 'Canada's First Sexual Harassment Decision' 19 *University of Western Ontario Law Review* 141 (1981). Ss. 28–9 of the Sex Discrimination Act 1984 (Australia) make sexual harassment unlawful in employment and education. See similarly ss. 19–20 of the Equal Opportunity Act 1984 (Victoria) on sexual harassment in the contexts of employment and the provision of goods, services, and accommodation.

[41] Cited in Simone de Beauvoir, *The Second Sex* (Penguin ed. 1972), 143.
[42] Catharine A. MacKinnon above, n. 7 at 209.
[43] 507 F Supp 599 (1981). See similarly *Marentette* v. *Michigan Host Inc* 506 F Supp 909 (1980: US District Court).

lead to her sexual harassment by customers was unlawful sex discrimination: no male employee would have been required to wear such a uniform and there was no justification in the nature of the job (lobby attendant in an office building) for requiring her to wear such a uniform. Sexual harassment, then, may result from the grooming code imposed by an employer. The circumstances in which discriminatory grooming codes may be unlawful, whether or not there is sexual harassment, is the next topic in this chapter.

III

Part of the difficulty in achieving equal treatment for the sexes is to overcome traditional attitudes which are built on differences in gender beween men and women.[44] One of the more pervasive and important types of gender distinction is that concerned with the dress of men and women. Ideas of what it is appropriate for each sex to wear are by no means constant. In the eighteenth century, men wore wigs, stockings, and make-up; pirates (at least in fiction) wear ear-rings and scarves around their heads; Scotsmen wear kilts. Nevertheless, in each society there are standards for male dress and different standards for female dress. How does the law of sex discrimination deal with these social distinctions?

In *Schmidt* v. *Austicks Bookshops Ltd*, the EAT considered the question of employee grooming codes. The employer there required women employees working in contact with the public to wear skirts, not trousers, and to wear overalls. The woman complainant had refused to comply with the rule forbidding the wearing of trousers and so was dismissed. Male employees were not required to wear overalls and they were, of course, allowed to wear trousers. The EAT held that there was no sex discrimination because

if one considers the situation of the men and the situation of the women there was no comparable restriction which could be applied to the men, equivalent to that applied to the women preventing them from wearing trousers, which could make it possible to lead to the conclusion that the women were being treated less favourably than the men.

The EAT added that, in any event, men 'would not have been

---

[44] See ch. 1 n. 49.

allowed to wear, had they sought to do so, any out-of-the-way clothing'. The EAT suggested that when dealing with cases of this type, whether they concern skirts, ear-rings, or hair length, the way to formulate the issue

is to say that there were in force rules restricting wearing apparel and governing appearance which applied to men and also applied to women, although obviously, women and men being different, the rules in the two cases were not the same . . . [This is] a better approach and more likely to lead to a sensible result than an approach which examines the situation point by point and garment by garment.[45]

The approach of the EAT in *Schmidt* closely resembles that of US courts in dealing with similar problems under Title VII of the Civil Rights Act 1964. US courts have rejected claims of sex discrimination in employment based on different hair-length rules for men and women,[46] a requirement that women should not wear trousers to work[47] and a requirement that men should wear a tie to work.[48] The Federal Court of Australia has indicated a similar attitude to sex discrimination challenges to grooming codes enforced by employers.[49]

---

[45] [1978] ICR 85, 87–8.

[46] See decisions of US Courts of Appeals: *Fagan* v. *National Cash Register Co.* 481 F 2d 1115 (1973); *Dodge* v. *Giant Food Inc* 488 F 2d 1333 (1973); *Baker* v. *California Land Title Co.* 507 F 2d 895 (1974), cert. denied 422 US 1046 (1975); *Willingham* v. *Macon Telegraph Publishing Co.* 507 F 2d 1084 (1975); *Knott* v. *Missouri Pacific Railroad Co.* 527 F 2d 1249 (1975); *Earwood* v. *Continental Southeastern Lines Inc.* 539 F 2d 1349 (1976); *Longo* v. *Carlisle DeCoppet & Co.* 537 F 2d 685 (1976); *Barker* v. *Taft Broadcasting Co.* 549 F 2d 400 (1977). In early cases, some US District Courts did hold that grooming codes which imposed different hair-length rules for men and women amounted to unlawful sex discrimination: *Roberts* v. *General Mills Inc.* 337 F Supp 1055 (1971); *Donohue* v. *Shoe Corporation of America Inc* 337 F Supp 1357 (1972); *Rafford* v. *Randle Eastern Ambulance Service* 348 F Supp 316 (1972); *Aros* v. *McDonnell Douglas Corp.* 348 F Supp 661 (1972).

[47] *La Von Lanigan* v. *Bartlett and Company Grain* 466 F Supp. 1388 (1979: US District Court). See also *Blowers* v. *Lawyers Cooperative Publishing Co.* 25 FEP Cases 1425 (1981) where a US District Court held that it did not breach Title VII for an employer to impose a rule that women wearing trousers to work must wear a matching tunic or jacket, when there was no such requirement for male employees.

[48] *Fountain* v. *Safety Stores Inc.* 555 F 2d 753 (1977: US Court of Appeals).

[49] In *Australian Telecommunications Commission* v. *Hart* 43 ALR 165 (1982) the Federal Court of Australia held that an employer may lawfully require a male employee not to wear a caftan (an oriental garment consisting of a long under-tunic tied at the waist with a girdle) to work. Fox J. (with whom Sheppard J. agreed) held at 173–4 that this was not sex discrimination contrary to Convention No. III of the International Labour Conference of 1958. He noted that the employer's officers

There are certain aspects to the reasoning in *Schmidt* and in the US authorities which can immediately be rejected as unpersuasive. In this category falls the suggestion that 'an employer is entitled to a large measure of discretion in controlling the image of his establishment, including the appearance of staff, and especially so when, as a result of their duties, they come into contact with the public'.[50] Certainly, in an unfair dismissal case an employer has a margin of discretion in applying grooming codes which it believes are reasonably necessary in the interests of the business.[51] But employers have a statutory obligation not to discriminate on the ground of sex. Since the decision in *Schmidt* it has been established that it is no defence to a claim of sex discrimination that the employer acted for a good motive or in the interests of business administration.[52]

Nor can one accept the reasoning in the US Court of Appeals' decision in *Willingham* that sex discrimination law prohibits only those acts which affect fundamental rights or immutable characteristics.[53] The issue is whether the complainant has, on the ground of her sex, lost an employment opportunity or benefit or been subjected to a detriment.[54] In any event, the 1975 Act, unlike Title VII, states the exceptions to its principles, and the courts cannot

had said that 'if the garment had been worn by a woman there would probably have been no objection . . . This is in my view a long way from saying that a distinction was made by the employer on the basis of sex.'

[50] *Schmidt* above, n. 45 at 88. Similarly *Willingham* (an 11–4 majority decision) above, n. 46 at 1091 emphasizing that a policy concerned with 'grooming codes or length of hair is related more closely to the employer's choice of how to run his business than to equality of employment opportunity'. See also Peter F. Ziegler, 'Employer Dress and Appearance Codes and Title VII of the Civil Rights Act of 1964' 46 *Southern California Law Review* 965 (1973).

[51] See, for example, *Boychuk* v. *H. J. Symons Holdings Ltd* [1977] IRLR 395 where the EAT declined to interfere with the decision of an industrial tribunal that it was not unfair dismissal to dismiss a worker for refusing to remove a badge stating 'Lesbians Ignite'. Cf. industrial tribunal decisions in *Talbot* v. *Hugh M. Fulton Ltd* [1975] IRLR 52 and *Greenslade* v. *Hoveringham Gravels Ltd* [1975] IRLR 114.

[52] *Grieg* v. *Community Industry* [1979] ICR 356, 360 (EAT). In *Schmidt*, the EAT relied heavily on the Court of Appeal decision in *Peake* v. *Automotive Products Ltd* above, n. 18, but that case was disapproved by a subsequent Court of Appeal in *Ministry of Defence* v. *Jeremiah* [1980] ICR 13.

[53] Above, n. 46 at 1091.

[54] In *Earwood* above, n. 46 at 1352 Circuit Judge Winter dissented on the ground that the *Willingham* test 'imports *constitutional* notions of immutability and fundamentality into the process of *statutory* interpretation'. See similarly McCree J. dissenting in *Barker* v. *Taft Broadcasting Co.* above, n. 46 at 402–6.

imply other exceptions into its structure.[55] Moreover, there is an indication in the 1975 Act that it does cover sex discrimination in grooming codes. The Act expressly provides that it is not unlawful sex discrimination to treat men and women police officers differently with regard to requirements as to uniform.[56] The mention of uniforms in this respect strongly suggests that Parliament believed that the general principles stated in the Act would otherwise cover sex discrimination in dress codes for male and female employees.

An employer's policy can only amount to unlawful sex discrimination if women (or men) are treated less favourably on the ground of their sex. Separate treatment is not necessarily less favourable treatment.[57] All depends on the circumstances. So, in certain grooming code cases, US courts have found sex discrimination by the imposition of different, less favourable standards for women than for men: for example, where an airline allowed male cabin attendants, but not female cabin attendants, to wear spectacles and had a maximum weight requirement for those female employees but not for male employees;[58] or where an employer required female employees, but not male employees, to wear a uniform.[59] Grooming codes cannot be said to be excluded from the scope of the 1975 Act: they cover so many different

[55] *Grieg* above, n. 52.

[56] Ss. 17(2)(a) and 17(3).

[57] See ch. 2 n. 10.

[58] *Laffey* v. *Northwest Airlines Inc.* 366 F Supp 763 (1973) and 374 F Supp 1382 (1974: US District Court). There was no appeal on these aspects of the case: 567 F 2d 429 (1976: US Court of Appeals), cert. denied 434 US 1086 (1978). See also *Gerdom* v. *Continental Airlines* 692 F 2d 602 (1982) where a US Court of Appeals held that an airline breached Title VII by requiring female air hostesses, but not men doing like work, to comply with a maximum weight requirement.

[59] *Carroll* v. *Talman Federal Savings and Loan Association of Chicago* 604 F 2d 1028 (1979: US Court of Appeals). The Court held at 1032–3 that the 'disparate treatment is demeaning to women. While there is nothing offensive about uniforms *per se*, when some employees are uniformed and others not there is a natural tendency to assume that the uniformed women have a lesser professional status than their male colleagues attired in normal business clothes.' Judge Pell dissented, complaining, at 1033–4, that by this decision 'Big Brother—or perhaps in this case, Big Sister—has encroached . . . farther than the Congress intended or authorised into the domain of private enterprise . . . simply to respond to the emotional complaint of one disgruntled employee . . .'. In *EEOC* v. *Clayton Federal Savings and Loan Association* 25 FEP Cases 841 (1981) the US District Court held that an employer's policy of requiring female (but not male) employees to contribute to the purchase of, and to wear, uniforms could amount to sex discrimination contrary to Title VII.

policies, many of which, by overtly distinguishing between men and women, may limit job opportunities for women.

Is an employer's policy of refusing to allow women to wear trousers to work sex discrimination under the 1975 Act? The EAT decision in *Schmidt*, validating such a policy if analogous, albeit different, restrictions are imposed on men, is not convincing. That an employer is requiring men to do what they normally do—wear trousers—and asking women to do what they normally do—wear skirts—cannot, of itself, amount to a non-discriminatory policy. Otherwise employers would always have a defence if their practices mirrored social behaviour. This would clearly conflict with a major objective of the 1975 Act, which was introduced precisely because aspects of social behaviour were unfair to women.

In deciding whether a woman who is prevented from wearing trousers to work is being less favourably treated on the ground of her sex than a comparable man, courts and tribunals should be wary of arguments which seek to balance the fact that a woman is denied opportunity X with the fact that men are denied opportunity Y. This is especially so when the channelling of men and women into these different opportunities is based upon stereotypes of acceptable male and female behaviour.

The woman employee who genuinely wishes to wear trousers to work, and who is prevented from doing so, is being denied an opportunity which she would have were she a man. Because her preference is frustrated, she has suffered less favourable treatment than if she were a man. The concept of direct sex discrimination is concerned with the treatment of individual complainants; unlike the concept of indirect discrimination, it is not concerned with group rights, with whether men and women, in general, have received equal treatment. Hence, in *Grieg* v. *Community Industry*, the EAT held that it was unlawful sex discrimination to deny employment to a woman on the ground that she would have been the only woman on a team of six employees. It was no defence that a man would have been refused employment if he were applying for a vacancy on a team all the other members of which were female. The EAT stressed that tribunals should consider the particular opportunity which the complainant was denied, not some other, hypothetical opportunity.[60] This may mean that a

---

[60] Above, n. 52 at 360–1.

grooming code discriminates against a woman who wants to wear trousers to work, and against a man who wants to wear a skirt to work. As Brightman LJ said in the Court of Appeal in *Ministry of Defence* v. *Jeremiah*, 'both a male worker and a female worker might complain about the same discrimination and . . . both might be right. I see no anomaly in such a result.'[61]

Even if one is prepared to accept the reasoning that it is not sex discrimination to deny opportunity X to women, provided one denies a different opportunity Y to men, there may still be a strong claim of sex discrimination brought by a woman who wants to wear trousers to work. The treatment of men and women is not equal. The woman is denied the chance to pursue perfectly normal social behaviour. By contrast, the grooming code imposes on men a restriction (no wearing of skirts) which is far less onerous in its impact since very few, if any, men would in any event want to wear a skirt to work. This approach was adopted in *ASTMS* v. *Norwich Union Insurance Group*[62] where it was alleged that the employer had discriminated against a woman contrary to the Irish Employment Equality Act 1977 by refusing to allow her to wear trousers to work. The employer's grooming code required that men wear a suit or casual trousers (but not denim) to work and that women wear a dress or a skirt. The Equality Officer accepted the argument that this policy was sexually discriminatory because women were prevented from wearing part of the standard dress of females, whereas no such restriction was imposed on men. Therefore, it was held, women were less favourably treated on the ground of their sex. The Equality Officer recommended that as denim trousers were excluded from the range of acceptable clothes for men, the same restriction should apply to women.

Similar principles should be applied to assess whether other aspects of a grooming policy discriminate against men or women on the ground of their sex. If an employer prohibits long hair, lipstick, or eyeshadow for men, but allows it for women, and the employer refuses to employ or dismisses a male employee who will not comply with this policy, the employer will have difficulty defending a sex discrimination claim. The four judges who dissented from the decision of the US Court of Appeals in *Willingham* that Title VII does not apply to a grooming policy did

---

[61] Above, n. 52 at 31.
[62] Equality Officer Recommendation no. EE 19/1981 of 10 Dec. 1981.

so on the ground that the anti-discrimination law 'extends to all differences in the treatment of men and women resulting from sex stereotypes' and that the law 'does not permit one standard for men and another for women, where both are similarly situated'.[63] The stereotypes of acceptable male and female behaviour which many grooming codes adopt are inconsistent with a statute which requires employment decisions to be made without reference to the sex of employees.[64] Grooming codes which act on such stereotypes are part of the mischief at which the 1975 Act aimed. They define the treatment of individuals according to social expectations of what is appropriate for each sex. They adopt and they reinforce custom and prejudice based on gender and not on any characteristic inherent in men or in women.

IV

Sex discrimination is a common feature of insurance policies. Because of a belief that women are more prone to illness than men, women tend to be charged higher premiums than men in order to receive the same benefits in permanent health insurance and in many other forms of cover. Because women tend to live longer than men, they often pay lower premiums than men for life assurance and receive lower annuity rates.

[63] Above, n. 46 at 1093 referring to the reasons given at the original hearing: 482 F 2d 535, 537–8 (1973).

[64] One difficult problem hinted at by grooming codes is that raised by the characteristics of one sex which are, biologically, not shared by the other sex. US courts have held that it cannot amount to sex discrimination if an employer forbids male employees to wear beards or moustaches: *Rafford* v. *Randle Eastern Ambulance Service* above, n. 46; *Thomas* v. *Firestone Tire & Rubber Co.* 392 F Supp 373 (1975); *Kearney* v. *Safeway Stores* 14 FEP Cases 55 (1975); *Bertulli* v. *First National Stores Inc.* 20 FEP Cases 1527 (1979) (all decisions of US District Courts). See also *Indiana Civil Rights Commission* v. *Sutherland Lumber* 394 NE 2d 949 (1979: Indiana Court of Appeals). On the analysis of a rule or policy which applies only to one sex by reason of the fact that the relevant characteristic is uniquely male (or uniquely female) for biological reasons see ch. 6. On the importance of clothes as symbols of social status see Virginia Woolf, *Three Guineas* (1938), ch. 1: 'Not only are whole bodies of men dressed alike summer and winter—a strange characteristic to a sex which changes its clothes according to the season, and for reasons of private taste and comfort—but every button, rosette and stripe seems to have some symbolic meaning . . . [D]ress in its immense elaboration has obviously another function. It not only covers nakedness, gratifies vanity, and creates pleasure for the eye, but it serves to advertise the social, professional, or intellectual standing of the wearer.'

The 1975 Act allows some sex discrimination in insurance policies. Section 45 states that it is not unlawful to practise sex discrimination in relation to an annuity, life assurance policy, accident insurance policy, or similar matter involving the assessment of risk where two factors are shown to exist. First, the treatment must be effected by reference to actuarial or other data from a source on which it was reasonable to rely. Secondly, the treatment must be reasonable having regard to the data and to any other relevant factors. The 1975 Act is by no means alone among sex discrimination statutes in recognizing an exception in the context of insurance. Similar provisions are contained in section 34 of the South Australia Sex Discrimination Act 1975, section 37 of the New South Wales Anti-Discrimination Act 1977, section 24(6) of the New Zealand Human Rights Commission Act 1977, section 21 of the Ontario Human Rights Code 1981, and section 41(4) of the Sex Discrimination Act 1984 of Australia.

No cases have yet been decided under section 45 of the 1975 Act, although some claims brought against insurance companies have been settled on terms favourable to the complainant, with the insurance company agreeing to amend its policy to remove the sex discrimination.[65] It is strongly arguable that, as a matter of principle, the 1975 Act should not exempt insurance policies. The criterion of sex is an unreliable, unnecessary, and unfair one to use in the assessment of risk in insurance policies. In any event, it is doubtful whether many of the insurance policies which currently discriminate on the ground of sex would satisfy the criteria of section 45.

The practice of charging women more for equal benefits, or giving women lesser benefits for the same premium, is justified by insurance companies on the basis that statistics show that women, as a group, are more frequently ill than men, as a group, and that women tend to live longer than men. Sex discrimination in insurance cannot be defended unless this statistical basis is a reliable one. The problem for insurance companies is that '[i]nsurance rates are calculated from mortality tables based on persons already dead, and charged to persons who will live far into the future. Thus there is no reason to expect sex differences among

---

[65] *Turner* v. *Prudential Corporation The Times* 9 Jan. 1982 (County Court). See also *Almeida* v. *Legal and General Assurance Society The Times* 23 Feb. 1982 (Industrial Tribunal).

current insureds to match those reflected in the tables.'[66] Insurance companies use old, sometimes antiquated, statistics which are based on the behaviour of previous generations of men and women whose occupational and social experiences were vitally different from those of the current generation of insured persons. Because sex differences in the statistics are largely due to behavioural rather than genetic factors, the relevance of the statistics will critically depend on whether women (and men) have similar occupational and social patterns today. Changes in such patterns since the time to which the statistics relate will obviously have an impact on sickness and death rates for men and women. Often, the statistics will tell us little or nothing about sickness and mortality rates today because of important changes in society since the period to which the statistics relate. Furthermore, the sickness statistics may merely reflect occupational segregation between men and women: since women tend to do less responsible work, they are likely to take more time off work.

Even if the statistical information relied on by an insurance company shows that there are differences between the sickness and mortality rates which can be predicted for men and women working today, it may be unnecessary for insurers to discriminate between men and women in this way. Other factors, such as a person's age, class, occupation, family medical history, and whether the person smokes, may be far better predictors of illness and death than sex. In *Los Angeles Department of Water and Power* v. *Manhart*, the US Supreme Court held that it was unlawful sex discrimination contrary to Title VII of the Civil Rights Act 1964 for an employer to require female employees to make larger contributions than male employees to a pension fund in order to receive the same benefit. The employers argued that their practice was valid because women tend to live longer than men and so the average woman will tend to receive more out of the fund than the average man. One reason for the decision of the Court to reject this argument was that '[s]eparate mortality tables are easily interpreted as reflecting innate differences between the sexes; but a significant part of the longevity differential may be explained by the social fact that men are heavier smokers than

[66] Lea Brilmayer, Richard W. Hekeler, Douglas Laycock, and Teresa A. Sullivan, 'Sex Discrimination in Employer-Sponsored Insurance Plans: A Legal and Demographic Analysis' 47 *University of Chicago Law Review* 505, 531 (1980).

women'.[67] Often, insurance companies give no weight, or inadequate weight, to these other statistically valid factors; they merely charge one premium (or allow one payment) for women and a different premium (or payment) for men. Such policies take insufficient note of the fact that '[w]hile actuarial tables may be relatively accurate in predicting the average longevity of men and women respectively, quite a substantial deviation occurs within either sex',[68] for many non-sex based reasons.

A third reason for questioning sex discrimination in insurance is that it is unfair to individual men and women. Assume that sex-based differentials in health insurance or pension plans are statistically valid: that they are based on valid material and ignore no other relevant classifications, so that an insurance company can accurately predict significantly different risks for relevant men and for relevant women. In such circumstances, it may well be that the scheme treats men (as a group) equally with women (as a group), allocating roughly equal amounts of benefits to, and taking approximately equal contributions from, each sex when there are equal numbers of men and women who participate in the scheme. All women who belong to the scheme will be charged a higher premium for health insurance or for a pension than all men because of an assumption that, by reason of their sex, they will tend to become ill more frequently than, and to die later than, comparable men. This is irrespective of the characteristics of an individual woman, who may in fact be a good health risk or may die much sooner than a man of her age doing a similar job. The question is whether it is fair to impose this detriment on any woman because she is a woman, irrespective of her own individual attributes.

It is a general principle of anti-discrimination law that people should not be treated by reference to a stereotyped assumption based on their race or sex. They are entitled to treatment by reference to their individual characteristics irrespective of their race or sex.[69] Two arguments are used to defend the use of stereotyped assumptions in the context of insurance. First, that

---

[67] 435 US 702, 709–10 (1978). See also Brilmayer *et al.* above, n. 66 at 512–13 and 533–4, and Merton C. Bernstein and Lois G. Williams 'Title VII and the Problem of Sex Classifications in Pension Programmes' 74 *Columbia Law Review* 1203, 1208 (1974).

[68] Merton C. Bernstein and Lois G. Williams above, n. 67 at 1221.

[69] See ch. 2 nn. 39–46.

here the assumption is a true one: women do live longer than men. Secondly, that insurance is concerned with the assessment of risk and so it is here permissible to treat people by reference to the risk associated with persons of their sex.

In *Manhart*, the US Supreme Court recognized that the case before it did not 'involve a fictional difference between men and women. It involves a generalisation that the parties accept as unquestionably true: women, as a class, do live longer than men.'[70] But, said the Court, it is improper to act on a stereotyped assumption unless it is true of all women so treated. It may well be true that women tend to be less able than men to lift heavy weights. Still it would be unlawful sex discrimination for an employer to reject a woman for a job involving the lifting of such weights simply because she is a woman: she is entitled to be considered on her individual ability to do the job, not to be rejected because of an assumption true of most women. The concept of direct discrimination under the 1975 Act is concerned with the individual. Like Title VII of the US Civil Rights Act, it 'precludes treatment of individuals as simply components of a . . . sexual . . . class . . . Even a true generalisation about the class is an insufficient reason for disqualifying an individual to whom the generalisation does not apply.'[71] Those women who do not live as long as the average man will pay higher contributions to the pension fund while working, yet they will receive no compensating advantage when they retire. The fact that the erroneous assumption made about them was true of some other women—that those others would live longer than the average man—does not alter the fact that they have been classified according to their sex and that this has resulted in them suffering a disadvantage compared with similar men. Such treatment is particularly unfair because it penalizes a person for a factor outside her control and offers her no opportunity to decrease the relevant risk. Conversely, there will be many men who live longer than the average woman. They will pay lower pension premiums during their working lives, yet will receive considerable benefits during their prolonged retirement. They will receive these benefits, by comparison with comparable women, not because of their individual characteristics, but simply because of their sex. Since anti-discrimination law is

[70] Above, n. 67 at 707.   [71] Ibid. at 708.

primarily designed to entitle individuals to be treated by reference to their individual characteristics, it is as discriminatory to treat people by reference to a stereotyped assumption true of most women (or men) as it is to treat them according to an assumption true of few women (or men).

Nor is it a convincing defence of sex-based insurance policies that insurance is fundamentally concerned with the assessment of risk for people defined by reference to class characteristics. As the US Supreme Court emphasized in *Manhart*, '[i]t is true that insurance is concerned with events that are individually unpredictable, but that is characteristic of many employment decisions'.[72] When deciding whether to appoint, promote, or dismiss a worker, employers need to weigh risks and to assess future potential. But employers are prohibited from doing this by reference to stereotyped assumptions. No doubt it is more expensive for employers to undertake an individual assessment of whether a woman applicant is capable of lifting the heavy weights, which is part of the job, rather than merely refusing the application of all women because most women could not lift such weights. Why should different principles apply to insurance practices? Indeed,

when insurance risks are grouped, the better risks always subsidise the poorer risks. Healthy persons subsidise medical benefits for the less healthy; unmarried workers subsidise the pensions of married workers; persons who eat, drink or smoke to excess may subsidise pension benefits for persons whose habits are more temperate. Treating different classes of risk as though they were the same for purposes of group insurance is a common practice that has never been considered inherently unfair. To insure the flabby and the fit as though they were equivalent risks may be more common than treating men and women alike; but nothing more than habit makes one 'subsidy' seem less fair than the other.[73]

One further factor suggests that insurance companies are

---

[72] Ibid. at 710.

[73] Ibid. See also Janet Sydlaske, 'Comment: Gender Classifications in the Insurance Industry' 75 *Columbia Law Review* 1381 (1975): 'The insurance industry is predicated on the need to group individuals into risk categories and thereby spread the cost of the risk more equitably. While some form of group classification is thus essential to the industry, insurance is also a means of pooling risks among insureds. There is a necessary tension between these two goals—the former leads to utilizing an increasing number of narrow classifications and, ultimately, to the assignment of risk on an individual basis, while the latter leads toward the abolition of group distinctions and the treatment of all insureds on an equal basis.'

capable of avoiding discriminatory policies even when those policies could be justified statistically. The US Supreme Court noted in *Manhart* that '[a]ctuarial studies could unquestionably identify differences in life expectancy based on race or national origin, as well as sex'.[74] Insurers did, at one time, use race-segregated insurance tables.[75] Yet the Race Relations Act 1976 does not allow insurance companies to treat persons of different races in a disparate manner by reference to actuarial data on which it is reasonable to rely. As the US Supreme Court said in *Arizona Governing Committee* v. *Norris* (applying the *Manhart* principle of equality between the sexes so as to find it unlawful sex discrimination for an employer to pay out lower monthly annuity payments to women than to men who had made equal contributions prior to retirement), it is impossible to see any difference of principle between race classifications and sex classifications in this context.[76]

The objective of securing equal treatment for men and women, irrespective of sex, requires the avoidance of different insurance terms for each sex. A woman may be charged a higher premium than a man because of her individual characteristics, but not because she is a woman and he is a man. In insurance, as elsewhere, '[p]ractices that classify [persons] in terms of . . . sex tend to preserve traditional assumptions about groups rather than thoughtful scrutiny of individuals'.[77] To impose higher premiums on persons, or to give them lower benefits, because of their sex and because of assumptions based on sexual stereotypes is to use unreliable, unnecessary, and unfair criteria.

Section 45 of the 1975 Act, by including references to whether it is 'reasonable' to rely on the actuarial data in all the relevant circumstances, no doubt offers courts the opportunity to limit the amount of sex discrimination which may lawfully be practised by insurance companies. But even the references to reasonableness cannot excuse section 45 and its approval of some such sex discrimination. The existence of section 45 owes much to the lobbying powers of the insurance industry in 1975. It is time for section 45 to be repealed.

For similar reasons, there is no justification for maintaining a different State pension age for men (65) and women (60), or for giving different occupational pension benefits to persons according

---

[74] Ibid. at 709.
[75] See Brilmayer *et al.* above, n. 66 at 538.
[76] 103 S Ct 3492, 3498 (1983).
[77] *Manhart* above, n. 67 at 709.

to their sex. When State pensions were introduced in 1908, the retirement age was fixed at 70 for men and for women. This was reduced to 65 in 1925. The lower pension age for women dates from 1940. The major objections today to providing equal treatment for the sexes are the cost to the State and the frustration of the expectations of women who expect to retire at 60. A unified State retiring age of 63 would be a significant contribution to equality of the sexes. It would be unlikely to impose extra costs on the State. If working women are thought to have a valid expectation of retiring at 60, the change could be phased in.[78]

The Sex Discrimination Act 1975 and the Equal Pay Act 1970 each exclude provision in relation to death or retirement from their scope.[79] The different treatment of men and women in the terms of occupational pension schemes, which is very common, therefore cannot be challenged under domestic law. During the Report Stage of the Equal Pay (No. 2) Bill 1970, Mrs Barbara Castle, the Secretary of State for Employment, explained that there were too many 'complexities' to include pensions in the legislation. Mr Robert Carr, for the Conservative Opposition, was justifiably 'nervous that if we let this Bill get on the statute book it may be a long time before we make a beginning on the subject again. This is the trouble with a difficult problem, particularly one which is enshrined in custom, convention and practice and there is a considerable amount of inertia to overcome before one can get down to a solution.'[80] Sex discrimination in occupational pension schemes will sometimes be contrary to EEC law, and therefore open to legal challenge in United Kingdom courts.[81] Parliament should attempt to overcome the inertia and bring pensions within the Equal Pay Act 1970 before the European Court of Justice compels it to do so.

[78] See generally Equal Opportunities Commission, *Equalising the Pension Age* (1978).

[79] S. 6(4) Sex Discrimination Act 1975; s. 6(1A) Equal Pay Act 1970. See ch. 3 n. 19 and ch. 4 n. 112. See similarly s. 11(4) of the 1975 Act (on partnerships) and s. 12(4) of the Act (on trade unions and other bodies). Cf. *Bartmess* v. *Drewrys USA Inc.* 444 F 2d 1186 (1971), cert. denied 404 US 939 (1971): the US Court of Appeals held that it was a breach of Title VII of the US Civil Rights Act 1964 for an employer to adopt and apply a retirement plan under which female employees retired at 62 and male employees retired at 65. See similarly *Rosen* v. *Public Service Electric and Gas Company* 477 F 2d 90 (1973: US Court of Appeals).

[80] 800 HC 739–746 (23 Apr. 1970).

[81] See ch. 5 nn. 13–18 on Community law.

8

HOMOSEXUALS, TRANSSEXUALS, AND THE SEX DISCRIMINATION ACT

I

In *Corbett* v. *Corbett*,[1] Ormrod J. decided that an individual who was born a male but had had 'a so-called "sex-change operation"'[2] prior to a ceremony of marriage with a man was not a woman who could validly marry a man. In deciding 'this unusual case'[3] the judge suggested that 'legal relations can be classified into those in which the sex of the individuals concerned is either irrelevant, relevant or an essential determinant of the nature of the relationship. Over a very large area the law is indifferent to sex.'[4] The Sex Discrimination Act 1975 is manifestly not indifferent to sex.

Section 5(2) and section 82(1) both state that for the purposes of the 1975 Act, '"man" includes a male of any age' and '"woman" includes a female of any age.' These definitions rather beg the question of who else could possibly be a 'man' and who could be included within the class of 'women' other than females of any age. The 1975 Act gives no other guidance on the proper application of the fundamental concepts of sex upon which the legislation is based. Two important issues of sexual status and treatment are posed by the 1975 Act. First, what protection, if any, does the legislation offer to homosexuals who suffer adverse treatment by reason of their sexual preferences? Secondly, how does the law determine the sex of transsexuals (and others whose sexual identity is equivocal) and what protection, if any, does it offer such individuals against adverse treatment by reason of their sexual status?

II

Section 1 of the Sexual Offences Act 1967 established that a homosexual act committed in private between two consenting

---

[1] [1971] P 83.   [2] Ibid. at 90.   [3] Ibid. at 92.   [4] Ibid. at 105.

adults was not a criminal offence. Nevertheless, the law continues to treat homosexuals less favourably than heterosexuals in a number of important respects.[5] The age of consent for homosexual acts is 21, not 16 as it is for heterosexual acts; such acts remain criminal if committed in the armed forces, the merchant navy, Jersey, or the Isle of Man;[6] the law of conspiracy to corrupt public morals hinders social and sexual intercourse between homosexuals; and an employee dismissed from his job by reason of his sexual preferences is unlikely to succeed in a claim for unfair dismissal even if there is no evidence that those preferences adversely affected his ability to do the job.[7] As well as facing general harassment, homosexuals suffer particular disadvantages in housing, inheritance, family and tax law because society declines to accord to permanent homosexual relationships the same treatment which it accords to such heterosexual relationships.

In these, and other contexts,[8] the only explanation for the adverse treatment of homosexuals is prejudice and personal aversion for a private life-style different from that of the majority. English law here mirrors the constitutional jurisprudence of the United States Supreme Court which has yet to recognize the homosexual community as one of the 'discrete and insular minorities'[9] protected by judicial strict scrutiny (under the equal

---

[5] For a more detailed analysis, see Tony Honoré, *Sex Law* (1978), ch. 4 and Paul Crane, *Gays and the Law* (1982).

[6] The Homosexual Offences (Northern Ireland) Order 1982 amended the law following the decision of the European Court of Human Rights in *Dudgeon* v. *United Kingdom* 4 EHRR 149 (1982) that the UK was violating the guarantee of respect for private life in Art. 8 of the European Convention on Human Rights by retaining criminal penalties for homosexual acts committed between consenting adults in private in Northern Ireland. Guernsey has similarly now amended its laws against homosexuality: *The Guardian*, 31 Mar. 1983.

[7] *Saunders* v. *Scottish National Camps Association Ltd* [1980] IRLR 174 (EAT), [1981] IRLR 277 (Court of Session); *Wiseman* v. *Salford City Council* [1981] IRLR 202 (EAT); *Nottinghamshire County Council* v. *Bowly* [1978] IRLR 252 (EAT).

[8] See, e.g. Re D. [1977] AC 602: the House of Lords upheld the decision of a county court judge that a homosexual father had unreasonably withheld his consent to the claim of the mother (and stepfather) of their child to adopt the child (of whom the mother had custody), one reason for the mother and stepfather wishing to adopt the child being their concern about the possible effect on the child of learning that his father was homosexual.

[9] *US* v. *Carolene Products Co.* 304 US 144, 152–3 n. (1938), per Stone J.

protection clause of the fourteenth amendment to the Constitution) of classifications which directly burden it.[10]

To establish direct discrimination under the 1975 Act, it is necessary for complainants to prove that on the ground of their sex they have been less favourably treated than a person of the opposite sex. The 1975 Act, like Title VII of the US Civil Rights Act 1964 (which prohibits an employer from discriminating against an individual, *inter alia*, 'because of such individual's . . . sex'), therefore cannot be said to make unlawful *per se* the less favourable treatment of a person by reason of his sexual preferences.[11] However, it would be wrong to conclude, as did a US District Court, that Title VII (or the 1975 Act) is not concerned with 'situations involving . . . homosexuals'.[12] In Canada, the Saskatchewan Queen's Bench made a similar error in analysing the scope of section 3 of the province's Fair Employment Practices Act (which makes it unlawful for an employer to 'discriminate against any person in regard to employment . . . because of his . . . sex'). Johnson J. held that the prohibition of sex

[10] See *Doe* v. *Commonwealth's Attorney* 403 F Supp 1199 (1975: US District Court), aff'd. 425 US 901 (1976). Laurence H. Tribe points out that *Doe*, and more recent cases, 'stand for little except that the issue of homosexual rights is being left for another day, when public sentiment is clearer and legal theory more fully developed. Meanwhile, the Supreme Court has not rushed to commit the nation to an inflexible position': *American Constitutional Law* (1979 Supplement), 87. See also Note 'The Constitutionality of Laws Forbidding Private Homosexual Conduct' 72 *Michigan Law Review* 1613 (1974). In *Carey* v. *Population Services International* 431 US 678, 688 n. and 694 n. (1977), the US Supreme Court acknowledged that it 'has not definitively answered the difficult question whether and to what extent the Constitution prohibits State statutes regulating [private consensual sexual] behaviour among adults'. Note also *Morrison* v. *State Board of Education* 461 P 2d 375, 385 n. (1969) where the Supreme Court of California held that a homosexual teacher was not subject to disciplinary action under a statute penalizing immoral conduct in the absence of any evidence that his behaviour indicated an unfitness to teach. The Court explained that a 'particular sexual orientation might be dangerous in one profession and irrelevant to another. Necrophilism and necrosadism might be objectionable in a funeral director or embalmer, urolagnia in a laboratory technician, zooerastism in a veterinarian or trainer of guide-dogs, prolagnia in a fireman, undinism in a sailor, or dendrophilia in an arborist, yet none of these unusual tastes would seem to warrant disciplinary action against a geologist or shorthand reporter.'

[11] *Smith* v. *Liberty Mutual Insurance Co.* 569 F 2d 325 (1978); *DeSantis* v. *Pacific Telephone and Telegraph Co. Inc.* 608 F 2d 327 (1979); *Blum* v. *Gulf Oil Corpn.* 597 F 2d 936 (1979) (all decisions of US Courts of Appeals); EEOC Dec. no. 76–75 (1975), 19 FEP Cases 1823 (1975).

[12] *Voyles* v. *Davies Medical Centre* 403 F Supp 456 (1975); aff'd. without opinion 570 F 2d 354 (1978).

discrimination concerns decisions taken by reference to 'whether or not [the complainant] was a man or woman, not on his sexual orientation, his sexual proclivity or sexual activity'. And he drew from this premiss the conclusions that 'If the Legislature had intended the word "sex" . . . to cover homosexuality or lesbianism, it ought to have said so in express language, and its failure to do so confirms my view that it did not so intend' and that the Saskatchewan Human Rights Commission had no power to enquire into the legality of the employer's adverse treatment of a male homosexual because of his sexual preferences.[13]

Adverse treatment of an individual by reason of his or her sexual preferences may constitute sex discrimination notwithstanding that sex discrimination can only be established by comparing the treatment of the complainant with the treatment of a person of the opposite sex. The relevant facts concerning sexual preferences are merely the context within which one may be able to establish the elements of a sex discrimination claim. It is the less favourable treatment, not the constitutive act complained of (for example, dismissal from a job), which the complainant must show was on the ground of sex. Hence, although the dismissal may have been by reason of the complainant's sexual preferences, he may be able to show that he has suffered less favourable treatment than a comparable woman has, or would, suffer, and that the less favourable treatment is on the ground of sex.

The simplest case is where the employer refuses to employ male homosexuals but is willing to employ lesbians. A male homosexual who is refused employment by reason of his sexual preferences can establish direct discrimination contrary to the 1975 Act: he has been less favourably treated by reason of his sex than a woman whose 'relevant circumstances . . . are the same, or not materially different', the comparison required by section 5(3). The Employment Appeal Tribunal has emphasized that 'in deciding whether the circumstances of the two cases are the same, or not materially different, one must put out of the picture any circumstances which necessarily follow from the fact that one is comparing the case of a man and of a woman'.[14] It would therefore be difficult for a

---

[13] *Board of Governors of the University of Saskatchewan* v. *Saskatchewan Human Rights Commission* (1976) 3 WWR 385, 389. See also *Gay Alliance Toward Equality* v. *The Vancouver Sun* (1979) 2 SCR 435 (Supreme Court of Canada).

[14] *Peake* v. *Automotive Products Ltd* [1977] ICR 480, 488, reversed on other grounds by the Court of Appeal [1977] ICR 968.

defendant to challenge the male homosexual's comparison of his treatment with that accorded to a lesbian. There is very little judicial authority on this aspect of discrimination law. In *Macauley* v. *Massachusetts Commission Against Discrimination*,[15] the Supreme Judicial Court of Massachusetts held that the State Fair Employment Practices Act (which prohibits discrimination 'because of the . . . sex . . . of any individual') does not prohibit discrimination on the ground of sexual preference but prohibits only discrimination between men and women. But the Court emphasized that it did not decide, as the issue was not before it, whether the Act prohibits an employer from treating a male homosexual less favourably than a lesbian. In *Valdes* v. *Lumbermen's Mutual Casualty Co.*,[16] a US District Court indicated that a woman stated a claim under Title VII of the Civil Rights Act when she alleged that her employer refused to promote lesbians but was willing to promote homosexual males.

A claim of direct sex discrimination can also be formulated if the defendant adversely treats homosexuals of each sex because of their sexual preferences. The less favourable treatment of the complainant on the ground of his or her sex compared with a person of the other sex might, again, be established. Suppose the employer dismisses a male homosexual from employment because he has a rule that he will employ neither men nor women who have sexual preferences for persons of their own sex. The complainant can argue that this is sex discrimination because if two employees —one male, and one female—are romantically or sexually attached to the same actual or hypothetical male non-employee, the employer treats the male employee less favourably on the ground of his sex than he treats the female employee. In *Macauley*, the Massachusetts Supreme Judicial Court said it would not determine the strength of this argument as the issue was not before it. However, the California Supreme Court, in deciding a case under the State Fair Employment Practices Act (which prohibits discrimination on the ground of 'sex') rejected a similar analysis. While recognizing that 'as a semantic argument, the contention may have some appeal', the Court concluded that the legislation did not contemplate discrimination against homosexuals.[17]

[15] 397 NE 2d 670 (1979).   [16] 507 F Supp 10 (1980).
[17] *Gay Law Students Association* v. *Pacific Telephone and Telegraph Co.* 595 P 2d 592, 612 (1979).

In *DeSantis* v. *Pacific Telephone and Telegraph Co. Inc.*, the US Court of Appeals considered the argument that discrimination against homosexuals breached Title VII because 'if a male employee prefers males as sexual partners, he will be treated differently from a female who prefers male partners . . . [T]he employer thus uses different employment criteria for men and women.' The Court firmly rejected the 'appellants' efforts to "bootstrap" Title VII protection for homosexuals . . . [W]e note that whether dealing with men or women the employer is using the same criterion: it will not hire or promote a person who prefers sexual partners of the same sex. Thus this policy does not involve different decisional criteria for the sexes.'[18]

The judgment of the US Court of Appeals in *DeSantis* emphasizes that one's conclusion on the validity of this claim of sex discrimination depends on the classification of the problem and the precise comparison one adopts with regard to the treatment of a man and a woman. Should one conclude that if a male employee is adversely treated for his sexual relationship with a third party X (a male) when a female employee is not so treated for her sexual relationship with the same X, such a disparity in treatment is by reason of the sex of the employee? Or should one conclude that the comparison is false as one of the employees is a homosexual and the other is not. This difficult issue will be determined by an English court or tribunal pursuant to section 5(3) of the 1975 Act. In making the comparison between the treatment of the male employee and the female employee, are we dealing with cases which are 'such that the relevant circumstances in the one case are the same, or not materially different, in the other'? The problem is that the 1975 Act provides no criteria of 'relevance'. The Employment Appeal Tribunal held in *Grieg* v. *Community Industry* that section 5(3) is 'principally although not exclusively talking about . . . the personal qualifications of the person involved as compared with some other person'.[19] It is arguable that, on this criterion, the private sexual preferences of the complainant are not 'relevant circumstances' unless the employer can establish that the sexual preferences of his staff are material to their ability to perform the job. This argument is strengthened by the fact that section 5(3) applies an objective test and does not

---

[18] Above, n. 11 at 331.   [19] [1979] ICR 356, 361.

provide for the comparison to be made by reference to those circumstances that the employer deems relevant.

The homosexual who suffers a detriment by reason of his sexual orientation can, by comparing his treatment with the more favourable treatment of the person of the sex opposite to his, show that he has been less favourably treated on the ground of his sex. In *Seide* v. *Gillette Industries Ltd*,[20] a case under the Race Relations Act 1976, the EAT said that to prove discrimination on racial grounds it is not sufficient to show that the complainant's race 'is any part of the background, or is . . . a *causa sine qua non* of what happens'. The issue is 'whether the activating cause of what happens is that the employer has treated a person less favourably than others on racial grounds'. In the case of sexual preferences, the sex of the complainant (and the sexual stereotypes which the employer associates with that sex) is very much in the foreground as the activating cause of the less favourable treatment of which complaint is made. The employer who has said that a sexual relationship with Mr X is conduct permissible in a female employee but conduct impermissible in a male employee has clearly differentiated in treatment of male and female employees. The differentiation is on the ground of sex: women may have relationships with Mr X and retain their jobs; if men have such relationships they will be sacked. The employer may well believe that he has good reason for differentiating between men and women in this respect. But, subject to the express exceptions contained in the 1975 Act, it is no defence for the employer to say that 'what was done was done with good motives or was done, even objectively, in the best interests of the person concerned or in the best interests of the business with which the case is concerned'.[21] That the employer has an ulterior motive for differentiating in his treatment of men and women cannot abrogate the conclusion that such differentiation is on the ground of sex.

This issue of whether the different treatment of men and women is sex discrimination raises a problem seen in other contexts. In seeking to provide equal treatment for men and women, to what extent should we take into account the fact that there are biological and cultural differences between the sexes? Is it sex

---

[20] [1980] IRLR 427, 431.   [21] Above, n. 19 at 360.

discrimination to dismiss a worker for becoming pregnant when workers are dismissed for no other temporary incapacitating condition? Is it sex discrimination to dismiss a female employee for refusing to comply with a grooming code that requires women to wear skirts when men are allowed to wear trousers? The EAT has held, in *Turley* v. *Allders Department Stores Ltd.*[22] and in *Schmidt* v. *Austicks Bookshops Ltd*,[23] that neither circumstance constitutes unlawful sex discrimination. In *Schmidt*, the EAT said that there was no sex discrimination because the employers applied a grooming code to men and women, albeit with differences in the demands made of each sex. The EAT said that 'obviously, men and women being different, the rules in the two cases were not the same'.[24] The judgments in *Turley* and *Schmidt*, while far from convincing, suggest a theory of sex discrimination law that would deny legal success to the male employee sacked for having a relationship with Mr X when a female employee is permitted to have such a relationship. The theory would be that the 1975 Act must take into account the biological and social differences between men and women; it must accept as non-discriminatory less favourable treatment of a man than the treatment accorded to a woman (and vice versa) when the treatment is by reference to those differences; and that here, as in *Schmidt*, the employer imposes restrictions on men and on women—male employees are sacked for sleeping with men and female employees are sacked for sleeping with women. The problem with such a theory is that the 1975 Act was introduced precisely to prevent reliance on real or perceived biological or cultural differences between the sexes, except where Parliament expressly provided an exception to the anti-discrimination principle. It is no defence to a charge of sex discrimination in one's treatment of men that one has discriminated against women in another respect. The 1975 Act requires equal treatment of the sexes. It cannot permit employers, and others, to impose detriment X on men, and to justify it by the fact that they impose detriment Y on women, and by reference to what they believe to be relevant differences between the sexes.

A man adversely treated by reason of his sexual preferences may also have a claim of indirect discrimination under the 1975 Act. The basis of the claim would be that an employer's policy of

---

[22] [1980] ICR 66. See ch. 6.
[23] [1978] ICR 85. See ch. 7 s. III.   [24] Ibid. at 88.

refusing to employ male or female homosexuals has a disproportionate adverse impact on men because the incidence of homosexuality is greater among males than among females and because male homosexuality is less easily concealed from the employer than is female homosexuality,[25] and that such a policy cannot be justified by the employer. In *DeSantis*, the US Court of Appeals rejected such a claim under Title VII. Although Title VII prohibits an employment policy which has such a disproportionate adverse impact and which cannot be justified by business necessity,[26] the Court of Appeals held that '[a]doption of this bootstrap device' to provide 'protection for homosexuals under the guise of protecting men generally' would 'frustrate Congressional objectives . . . .'.[27]

Even assuming that an employer is unable to justify a policy of refusing to employ homosexuals,[28] a claim of indirect discrimination is unlikely to succeed under the 1975 Act. Unless the proportion of male homosexuals in any pool of employees or prospective employees is large, it will be difficult to establish that the proportion of men who can comply with a condition or requirement that one should not be homosexual is considerably smaller than the proportion of women who can comply with it.

The 1975 Act offers some protection, at least, to the individual adversely treated by reason of his or her sexual preferences. The extent of that protection will depend upon the spirit in which the legislation is construed. Courts and tribunals should, in performing that role, bear in mind the recommendation passed by the Parliamentary Assembly of the Council of Europe on discrimination against homosexuals. The recommendation, adopted on 1 October 1981, calls on Member States to guarantee equality of treatment for homosexuals with regard to employment, pay, and job security, particularly in the public sector.[29]

Should the 1975 Act be held not to provide a cause of action for

[25] See Gary R. Siniscalco, 'Homosexual Discrimination in Employment' (1976) 16 *Santa Clara Law Review* 495; Joel Wm. Friedman. 'Constitutional and Statutory Challenges to Discrimination in Employment Based on Sexual Orientation' (1979) 64 *Iowa Law Review* 527, 566–8.

[26] *Griggs* v. *Duke Power Co.* 401 US 424 (1971); *Dothard* v. *Rawlinson* 433 US 321 (1977) (decisions of the US Supreme Court).

[27] Above, n. 11 at 330.

[28] For the criteria of 'justifiability' in an indirect discrimination claim see ch. 2 s. IV.

[29] Recommendation 924 (1981). See also Resolution 756 (1981) of the Parliamentary Assembly of the Council of Europe on discrimination against

those persons adversely treated by reason of their sexual preferences, amending legislation should be considered. The Human
Rights Act 1977 of the District of Columbia USA, provides a
possible model, prohibiting discrimination by reason of, *inter alia*,
'sexual orientation'.[30] Homosexuality is akin to colour, race,
nationality, ethnic or national origin, and sex (prohibited grounds
for action in the contexts covered by the Race Relations Act 1976
and the Sex Discrimination Act 1975) in that it is an immutable
characteristic which is generally irrelevant to the provision of

homosexuals (1 Oct. 1981) and the Resolution of the European Parliament on
Sexual Discrimination at the Work-place adopted on 13 Mar. 1984: OJ no. C
104/46, 16 Apr. 1984.

[30] See also the Pennsylvania Executive Order 1975–5, as amended on 19 Sept.
1978, prohibiting discrimination in public employment and in the provision of other
benefits by the state by reason of an individual's 'sexual or affectional orientation'.
Similarly, a Californian Executive Order B–54–79 of 4 Apr. 1979, prohibits
discrimination in state employment on the ground of an individual's 'sexual
preference'. The Wisconsin Fair Employment Act, as amended in Mar. 1982, makes
employment discrimination on the ground of a person's 'sexual orientation'
unlawful, and defines sexual orientation to mean 'having a preference for
heterosexuality, homosexuality, bisexuality, having a history of such a preference,
or being identified with such a preference'. One of the grounds on which
discrimination in various contexts is made unlawful by s. 12 of the Quebec Charter
of Human Rights and Freedoms 1975 is that of 'sexual orientation'. See
L'Association ADGQ v. *Catholic School Commission of Montreal* (1979) 112 DLR
(3d) 230, where the Quebec Superior Court held that a Catholic School Board
which offered to rent out buildings to the general public violated s. 12 of the
Charter by refusing to rent to a homosexual association. S. 119 of the Anti-
Discrimination Act 1977 of New South Wales provides that for the purpose of
eliminating discrimination and promoting equality and equal treatment for all
human beings, the Anti-Discrimination Board may carry out investigations,
research, and inquiries relating, *inter alia*, to discrimination against a person on the
grounds of homosexuality, a characteristic that appertains generally to homosexuals,
or a characteristic that is generally imputed to homosexuals. The New South Wales
Anti-Discrimination Board has published a report recommending that homosexuals
should be given equal rights in all legal matters, and that laws should be enacted to
prohibit discrimination against homosexuals 9 *Commonwealth Law Bulletin* 301
(1983). The New Zealand Human Rights Commission, on the other hand, has
recommended that discrimination on the ground of a person's 'sexual orientation'
should not be made unlawful. The Commission argued that such discrimination is
not analogous to race or sex discrimination 7 *Commonwealth Law Bulletin* 1136
(1981). In Mar. 1983, the Equal Opportunities Commission for Northern Ireland
published proposals for the amendment of the Sex Discrimination (Northern
Ireland) Order 1976 (which is closely analogous to the 1975 Act). They stated that
the legal protection of homosexuals against discrimination on grounds of sexual
orientation 'would be consonant with the purpose of the Sex Discrimination Order
that people should be treated as individuals rather than as sexual categories', and
they recommended that 'the Sex Discrimination Order be amended to outlaw
discrimination on the grounds of sexual orientation'.

employment and other benefits but which has been and continues to be the subject of adverse action for reasons of prejudice to the disadvantage of a powerless section of the community. Where sexual preferences generally (or particular types of sexual orientation) do constitute a genuine qualification or criterion for the provision of benefits, legislation can provide (as it does in the 1975 and 1976 Acts) for exceptions to the general principle that it is impermissible to give persons less favourable treatment by reference to the protected characteristic.

An anti-discrimination law prohibiting discrimination against persons on the ground of their sexual preferences in certain contexts and with defined exceptions, coupled with a repeal of the barriers to homosexual equality contained in existing legislation and common law, would be an important statement of the values of tolerance of a civilised society. Nor would such an anti-discrimination law be premature while specific examples of differential treatment of homosexuals remain on the statute book. The Sex Discrimination Act 1975 is not without value because health and safety legislation allows women to be less favourably treated on the ground of their sex in certain contexts. Nor does the Race Relations Act 1976 lack importance by reason of the fact that immigration and nationality law permits less favourable treatment of persons by reference to their nationality or race.

III

A transsexual is an individual anatomically of one sex but who believes that he or she belongs to the other sex. This belief is so strong that transscxuals want their bodily appearance and social status altered to conform to what they perceive to be their true sex. Transsexualism is neither a sexual preference nor a mode of sexual conduct. The transsexual is distinct from the transvestite (who obtains gratification from dressing in the clothes of the opposite sex) and from the homosexual (who enjoys sexual relationships with persons of the same sex).[31] In addition to the

[31] See Jan Morris, *Conundrum* (1974). For an interesting, but unsympathetic, feminist perspective, see Janice G. Raymond, *The Transsexual Empire* (1980). See also John Archer and Barbara Lloyd, *Sex and Gender* (1982). Sex changes are not confined to human beings. Those who condemn such behaviour as unnatural will be interested to note that scientists have discovered that some fish and reptiles spontaneously change their sex. 'One of the discoveries was a particular type of reef

'difficulties under which these people inevitably live',[32] the availability in recent years of sex-change operations has added to the wide range of legal problems for transsexuals.[33] A remarkably large number of cases under Title VII of the US Civil Rights Act 1964, and one action under the Sex Discrimination Act 1975, indicate that one context in which the problems of transsexuals need to be considered is that of sex discrimination law.[34]

In *Grossman* v. *Bernards Township Board of Education*,[35] a US District Court held that an employee dismissed because she had had a sex-change operation to become a woman had no claim under Title VII. It found it

unnecessary and, indeed, has no desire, to engage in the resolution of a dispute as to the plaintiff's present sex. Rather we assume for the purpose of this action that the plaintiff is a member of the female gender . . . [S]he was discharged by the defendant school board *not* because of her status as a female, but rather because of her *change* in sex from the male to the female gender.[36]

The Court said that in the absence of any legislative history indicating a Congressional intent to include transsexuals within the language of Title VII, it was 'reluctant to ascribe any import to the

fish which has only a single male in each school. When the male is lost the largest female begins acting like a male within a few hours, producing sperm within ten days . . . Yet the process by which the sex change takes place remains a mystery . . . [T]he sex of a maturing lizard may be determined by environmental temperature, while a school of trout can be made entirely male by adding a certain hormone to the water': 'Science Report: Mystery of Fish that change Sex', *The Times* 14 Dec. 1984.

[32] *Corbett* v. *Corbett*, above, n. 1 at 98.

[33] Douglas K. Smith, 'Transsexualism, Sex Reassignment Surgery and the Law' (1971) 56 *Cornell Law Review*, 963; Note, 'Transsexuals in Limbo: The Search for a Legal Definition of Sex' (1971) 31 *Maryland Law Review*, 236; Edward S. David, 'The Law and Transsexualism: A Faltering Response to a Conceptual Dilemma' (1975) 7 *Connecticut Law Review* 288. See also S. A. Strauss. 'The Sex-Change Operation: Two Interesting Decisions' (1967) 84 *South African Law Journal* 214.

[34] During the Standing Committee debates on the Sex Discrimination Bill 1975, Mr David Lane asked whether the Government were sure that the proposed legislation 'adequately and clearly covers the cases of sex change, which we read about occasionally and which we should hate to be overlooked in such a comprehensive Bill?' Dr Shirley Summerskill, Under-Secretary of State for the Home Department, replied: 'We considered this. Clearly people who have legally changed sex will be covered by the Bill, under whatever sex they have legally changed to' (Standing Committee B, Second Sitting, 24 Apr. 1975, cols. 102–3).

[35] 11 FEP Cases 1196 (1975); aff'd. 538 F 2d 319 (1976); cert. denied 429 US 897 (1976).

[36] Ibid. at 1198.

term "sex" other than its plain meaning.' Similar decisions have been reached by other District Courts.[37] Three decisions of the US Court of Appeals have approved of the reasoning in these cases. In *Holloway* v. *Arthur Andersen & Co.*,[38] the Court held that an employee may be dismissed, consistently with Title VII, for commencing sex-change treatment to become a female since 'Congress had only the traditional notions of "sex" in mind' in enacting Title VII. In *Ulane* v. *Eastern Airlines*[39] the court held that 'a prohibition against discrimination based on an individual's sex is not synonymous with a prohibition against discrimination based on an individual's sexual identity disorder or discontent with the sex into which they were born', and that therefore it was not a breach of Title VII for an employer to dismiss an employee by reason of her transsexual status. In *Sommers* v. *Budget Marketing Inc.*,[40] the Court dismissed the claim under Title VII of a plaintiff with the anatomical body of a man but who claimed to be a female (but had not had a sex-change operation) and who was dismissed for misrepresenting himself as a female when taken on in the job. The Court said that 'the plain meaning' should be ascribed to the term 'sex' in Title VII and that 'the legislative history does not show any intention to include transsexualism in Title VII'. The Court was worried by the threats of the employer's other female employees that they would leave if the plaintiff was permitted to use the women's lavatory. The Court confessed that it was uncertain what an employer should do in such a case. 'Should Budget allow Sommers to use the female restroom, the male restroom, or one for Sommers' own use? Perhaps', it urged, 'some reasonable accommodation could be worked out between the parties.'

[37] *Voyles* v. *Davies Medical Centre* above, n. 12 (where an employee was dismissed on telling the employer of her intention to have a sex-change operation); *Powell* v. *Read's Inc.* 436 F Supp 369 (1977) (where a male employee living as a female prior to having a sex-change operation was dismissed when the employer found out that the employee was a man); *Terry* v. *EEOC* 35 FEP Cases 1395 (1980) (where an employer refused to hire a man as an employee because that man intended to have a sex-change operation).

[38] 566 F 2d 659 (1977).

[39] 35 FEP Cases 1348 (1984). The Court of Appeals allowed the employer's appeal from the decision of the District Court judge that the dismissal of an employee because of her transsexual status amounted to dismissal because of her sex and so breached Title VII: 35 FEP Cases 1332 (1984).

[40] 667 F 2d 748 (1982).

The facts of *Sommers* are closely analogous to those of the only reported English case to raise the issue of transsexualism in the context of sex discrimination law. In *E. A. White* v. *British Sugar Corporation*,[41] the complainant was anatomically a female who wanted to be treated as a male. She completed an application form for a job with the respondents in her male name (under which she was registered with the DHSS); at an interview she dressed as a man and gave no indication that she was other than a man; the employer offered her a job in the belief that she was male and dismissed her when he discovered the truth. An industrial tribunal, considering her claim under the 1975 Act, described it as 'a most unusual case', but despite 'sympathy with the applicant in her personal and personality predicament', it held that, for the purposes of the 1975 Act, she was a woman and had no cause of action. The tribunal said that the question was whether the employer had treated

the applicant on the ground of her sex less favourably than they would have treated a man? If the applicant had been a man and had he held himself out to the respondents as a female and been employed as such and used the female toilet facilities and the like and it had then been discovered that he was a man, the Tribunal had no hesitation in deciding that in the circumstances the respondents would have dismissed him. Accordingly in the present case there was no discrimination on the ground of the applicant's sex.[42]

Even these decisions acknowledge that transsexuals do have some protection under Title VII and under the 1975 Act. The US Court of Appeals emphasized in *Holloway* that

consistent with the determination of this court, transsexuals claiming discrimination because of their sex, male or female, would clearly state a cause of action under Title VII. Holloway has not claimed to have [been] treated discriminatorily because she is male or female, but rather because she is a transsexual who chose to change her sex.[43]

A transsexual who is less favourably treated on the ground of his or her sex will have the same protection under anti-discrimination law as other persons of that sex. Hence, if an employer refuses to employ women for a certain job, a transsexual woman rejected for the job because she is a woman has a cause of action. Furthermore,

---

[41] [1977] IRLR 121.   [42] Ibid. at 123.
[43] Above, n. 38 at 664. See similarly *Ulane*, above, n. 39 at 1353.

as the industrial tribunal recognized in *E. A. White*, where an employer applies a less favourable test to those who have changed their sex from male to female than the test he applies to those who have changed their sex from female to male (or vice versa), sex discrimination exists.[44] As in cases concerning homosexuals, the sexual status of the complainant is merely the context in which the comparison of persons of different sex is made in order to prove less favourable treatment on the ground of sex. Before considering whether the courts are correct in their conclusion that adverse treatment for reasons connected with transsexualism gives no cause of action in sex discrimination law, unless the defendant distinguishes between male–female change and female–male change, it is important to note one consequence of the undoubted relevance of sex discrimination law to cases involving transsexuals. Because in such cases it will be the task of the court or tribunal to compare the treatment of the transsexual complainant with the treatment accorded to a person of the opposite sex (and not the treatment accorded to a person of the sex opposite to the sex which the complainant believes himself or herself to possess, and not the treatment accorded to a person of the sex opposite to that which the defendant believes the complainant to possess), it will be necessary for the court or tribunal to determine the sex of the complainant for the purposes of sex discrimination law.

The matters relevant to the determining of a person's sex are chromosomal constitution, gonadal factors (i.e. the presence or absence of testes or ovaries), internal sex organs other than gonads (e.g. uterus, sperm ducts), external genitalia, sex hormone pattern, secondary sexual characteristics (e.g. facial hair, breast development), and psychological factors (such as the sex of rearing and the assumed sex role). For the overwhelming majority of individuals, all these indicators point in the same direction. It is when the factors do not produce a unanimous conclusion that problems of sexual identity arise. No one factor is necessary and sufficient to establish membership of the male or female sex.[45] The courts are faced with the difficulty of developing criteria to resolve cases where the evidence of sexual identity is conflicting.

In *E. A. White*, the industrial tribunal concluded:

[44] See also EEOC Dec. No. 75–030 (1974), 12 FEP Cases 1355 (1974).
[45] See Douglas K. Smith, above, n. 33 at 965–8; Edward S. David, above, n. 33 at 290–1.

The current edition of *The Shorter Oxford English Dictionary* defines male as of or belonging to the sex which begets offspring or performs the fecundating function. The same dictionary defines female as belonging to the sex which bears offspring. On her own evidence the applicant, whatever her physiological [psychological?] make up may be, does not have male reproductive organs and there was no evidence that she could not bear children. Accordingly . . . the Tribunal decided that for the purposes of the [1975] Act the applicant was a woman.[46]

Of course, many women cannot (for a variety of reasons) bear children. Many men have atypical reproductive organs and, whether or not for that reason, many men are unable to beget offspring. The tribunal's decision does not state whether the applicant had undergone hormonal treatment but it does disclose that she 'had the physical attributes and sexual organs of a female. She had a soft voice and did not grow facial hair.' She had been advised that a sex-change operation would not be successful. It appears that the only indicators of masculinity in this case were the psychological and social factors (including the fact that the applicant's unemployment benefit card, registration with the DHSS, driving licence, and certificate of motor insurance were in her male name). Such factors will not outweigh the clear physiological evidence in assigning a person's sex for the purposes of the 1975 Act. The legislation is concerned with 'sex' not with gender.

Slightly more difficult, but probably leading to the same conclusion, are cases of pre-operative transsexuals who have had hormone treatment with consequent changes in secondary sexual characteristics. Much more difficult to assign are the cases of post-operative transsexuals. When, if at all, does the sex assigned at birth (assuming it not to have been erroneously recorded) change by reason of medical treatment? Sex is not rigidly bipolar, but a continuum with each individual placed at a different point along the scale.[47] Yet, in attempting to state principles to determine the sexual assignment of persons near the middle of the continuum, 'the laws of this country and the [1975] Act in particular envisage

---

[46] Above, n. 41 at 123.
[47] See Catharine A. MacKinnon, *Sexual Harassment of Working Women* (1979), at 150–6; Jan Morris, above, n. 31 at 52. See also the 1974 White Paper, *Equality for Women* (Cmnd. 5724), para. 16: 'The differences within each sex far outweigh the differences between the sexes.'

only two sexes, namely male and female'.[48] It is, to say the least, a considerable irony of legislation that seeks to abrogate reliance on stereotyped notions of sexual roles that it embodies and perpetuates a rigid and false dichotomy of *all* individuals into the categories of male or female, despite the absence of necessary and sufficient conditions for belonging to either sex. As Catharine A. MacKinnon has observed: 'There is a real question whether it makes sense of the evidence to conceptualise the reality of sex in terms of differences at all, except in the socially constructed sense—which social construction is what the [sex discrimination] law is attempting to address as the *problem*.'[49]

In *Corbett* v. *Corbett*, Ormrod J. considered the sex of a post-operative transsexual for the purposes of the law of marriage. Prior to the operation, the respondent had male external genitalia. After treatment with female hormones, the respondent had a sex-change operation which involved the removal of the male genitalia and their replacement by 'a so-called "artificial vagina"'.[50] After the operation, the respondent lived as a woman (although Ormrod J. gave his opinion that her 'voice, manner, gestures and attitudes became increasingly reminiscent of the accomplished female impersonator')[51] and was issued with a woman's insurance card by the Ministry of National Insurance. A chromosome test after the operation showed that the cells examined were male. The petitioner, a man, married the respondent after the operation and in full knowledge of her history. Ormrod J. granted the petitioner's application for a declaration that the marriage was null and void because, at the time of the wedding ceremony, the respondent was a man and the law recognizes a marriage only if it is between a man and a woman.

Ormrod J. stated the possible criteria for determining the sex of an individual and concluded:

Having regard to the essentially heterosexual character of the relationship which is called marriage, the criteria must, in my judgment, be biological, for even the most extreme degree of transsexualism in a male or the most severe hormonal imbalance which can exist in a person with male

---

[48] *E. A. White* v. *British Sugar Corporation*, above, n. 41 at 123.
[49] Above, n. 47 at 155.
[50] Above, n. 1 at 90. On *Corbett*, see Ian McColl Kennedy, 'Transsexualism and Single Sex Marriage' 2 *Anglo-American Law Review* 112 (1973).
[51] Ibid. at 104.

chromosomes, male gonads and male genitalia cannot reproduce a person who is naturally capable of performing the essential role of a woman in marriage. In other words, the law should adopt in the first place, the first three of the doctors' criteria, i.e. the chromosomal, gonadal and genital tests, and if all three are congruent, determine the sex for the purpose of marriage accordingly, and ignore any operative intervention. The real difficulties, of course, will occur if these three criteria are not congruent. This question does not arise in the present case and I must not anticipate, but it would seem to me to follow from what I have said that the greater weight would probably be given to the genital criteria than to the other two. This problem and, in particular, the question of the effect of surgical operations in such cases of physical inter-sex, must be left until it comes for decision. My conclusion, therefore, is that the respondent is not a woman for the purposes of marriage but is a biological male and has been so since birth.[52]

This passage poses several problems. First, what did the judge mean by 'the essential role of a woman in marriage'? A woman cannot be defined by the capacity to bear children, as many women cannot do so, for a variety of reasons. If Ormrod J. meant, rather, to refer to a capacity 'for natural heterosexual intercourse',[53] then the issue is whether a person whose natural female genitalia are unsuitable for such intercourse but who has had artificial female genitalia provided which serve that function is, for that reason, not a woman for the purposes of the law of marriage. In *S. Y.* v. *S. Y.*, Willmer LJ for the Court of Appeal, in a judgment difficult to reconcile with the reasoning of Ormrod J., held that, if a woman had abnormal sexual organs that prevented intercourse, then 'the creation out of nothing of an artificial vagina, sufficient in size to enable full penetration to be achieved . . . located precisely in the position where a natural vagina would be', would allow a natural act of intercourse sufficient to consummate a marriage between a woman and her husband (even though the woman could not give birth to a child).[54]

A second difficulty with the judgment of Ormrod J. presents itself. If the thesis of the 'essential role of a woman in marriage' provides no guidance, why should sex assignment in difficult cases depend upon those criteria stated by Ormrod J. rather than upon the absence, at the date of marriage, of external male genitalia and the existence at that time of secondary female sex characteristics,

---

[52] Ibid. at 106.   [53] Ibid. at 105.   [54] [1963] P 37, 58–60.

female sex hormones, and a social and psychological female role? Thirdly, the judgment of Ormrod J. adopts the reasoning of the medical witnesses that 'the biological sexual constitution of an individual is fixed at birth (at the latest) and cannot be changed, either by the natural development of organs of the opposite sex or by medical or surgical means'.[55] Such a premiss is far from self-evident. Ormrod J. gave no reason for adopting it as a legal test of biological sex. Without such a premiss, the genital test of sex, which Ormrod J. stated to be the most important of the three main criteria, would surely take into account the removal of the respondent's male genitalia, the substitution of (artificial) female external genitalia, and the fact that many women lack, for a variety of reasons, the internal female organs which the sex-change operation did not provide for the respondent.

In *R. v. Tan and others*,[56] the Court of Appeal held that a person who was born male and had undergone sex-change surgery 'consisting essentially of the removal of the external male organs and the creation of an artificial vaginal pocket' remained legally male for the purposes of a conviction for living on the earnings of prostitution contrary to section 30 of the Sexual Offences Act 1956 (an offence which only a man can commit) and for the purposes of a conviction of the transsexual's 'husband' for living on the earnings of male prostitution by the transsexual contrary to section 5 of the Sexual Offences Act 1967. Parker J., for the Court, approved the judgment in *Corbett*. He rejected the contention that 'if the person had become philosophically or psychologically or socially female that person should be held not to be a man'. He asserted that 'both common sense and the desirability of certainty and consistency' demanded this result. It is far from clear that common sense requires one to insist that once male, always male, irrespective of social, psychological, and medical change, especially in the context of prostitution where the transsexual is providing sexual services as a female. Nor should certainty and consistency be overriding values justifying an inaccurate or misleading label that may conflict with an individual's fundamental right to determine his or her own private life.

Also unsatisfactory is the decision of Nestadt J. in the

---

[55] Above, n. 1 at 104.

[56] [1983] 1 QB 1053, 1063-4. See P. J. Pace, 'Sexual Identity and the Criminal Law' (1983) *Criminal Law Review* 317.

Witwatersrand Local Division of the Supreme Court of South Africa in *W*. v. *W*. The Court held null and void a marriage between a wife, who had been born male and had had a sex-change operation prior to the wedding ceremony, and a husband who was aware of the wife's history at that time. The judge found that the wife was male at the time of the wedding ceremony. The evidence, he said,

does not show that the operation converted her into a female. What it did was to artificially supply her with certain of the attributes of a woman, namely breasts and a vagina-like cavity . . . The issue is not whether, after the operation, the plaintiff was an effective male, nor whether she looked like a female (which she does), nor whether society has accepted her as a female, nor whether she is capable of having sex with a male; the issue is whether the plaintiff at the time of the marriage was a woman.[57]

In holding that '[i]mitation cannot be equated with actual transformation',[58] Nestadt J. gave no indication of precisely what the wife lacked that was necessary to make her a female in the eyes of the law for the purposes of marriage.

Ormrod J. emphasized in *Corbett* that he was 'not concerned to determine the "legal sex" of the respondent at large', and that marriage, for the purposes of which he was assigning a sex to the respondent, has 'differences [which] are obviously fundamental'[59] when compared with other social and legal relationships. It would therefore be wrong to treat the decision of Ormrod J. as necessarily binding authority on the assignment of sex for the purposes of sex discrimination law.[60] In any event, the reasoning

[57] (1976) 2 SALR 308, 313–14.
[58] Ibid. at 314.
[59] Above, n. 1 at 106–7.
[60] The only other authority of a British court on the sexual identity of a transsexual appears to be *Re X* 1957 SLT (Sh. Ct.) 61, where the Sheriff Court of Perth and Angus refused to authorize the Registrar of Births, Deaths and Marriages to amend the recorded particulars of a transsexual's sex from male to female. The individual had been born male but claimed he was a woman. The Court held that it had power to direct an entry to be corrected only when the information recorded was erroneous at the date it was entered, and that, in any event, 'skin and blood tests still show X's basic [?] sex to be male and . . . the changes have not yet reached the deepest level of sex determination'. US courts have, in some cases, similarly refused to direct the provision of new birth certificates for transsexuals after a sex-change operation: *Anonymous* v. *Wiener* 270 NYS 2d 319 (1966); *Hartin* v. *Director of Bureau of Records and Statistics* 347 NYS 2d 515 (1973); and *Anonymous* v. *Mellon* 398 NYS 2d 99 (1977) (all decisions

of certain American courts on the determination of an individual's sex is more persuasive than that of Ormrod J. (or Nestadt J. or Parker J.) and is to be preferred.

In *M. T.* v. *J. T.* the Superior Court of New Jersey, Appellate Division decided not to follow *Corbett* in another case where a husband claimed his marriage to a transsexual wife was void. The wife had been born a male and had had a sex-change operation, paid for by the husband, prior to the wedding ceremony. The court said that it was

> impelled to the conclusion that for marital purposes if the anatomical or genital features of a genuine transsexual are made to conform to the person's gender, psyche or psychological sex, then identity by sex must be governed by the congruence of these standards . . . If . . . sex reassignment surgery is successful . . . we perceive no legal barrier, cognizable social taboo, or reason grounded in public policy to prevent that person's identification at least for purposes of marriage to the sex finally indicated . . . Such recognition will promote the individual's quest for inner peace and personal happiness, while in no way disserving any social interest, principle of public order or precept of morality.[61]

The marriage was therefore held to be valid.

Similarly, in *Re Anonymous*, the Civil Court of the City of New York granted an order requested by a transsexual permitting her to change her name from male to female. The Court held that:

> Where there is disharmony between the psychological sex and the anatomical sex, the social sex or gender of the individual will be determined by the anatomical sex. Where, however, with or without medical intervention, the psychological sex and the anatomical sex are harmonised, then the social sex or gender of the individual should be made to conform to the harmonised status of the individual. . . .[62]

---

of the New York Supreme Court). Note also that an industrial tribunal in Birmingham has held that an employee was unfairly dismissed for seeking to change his sex: *The Times*, 22 Apr. 1982.

[61] 355 A 2d 204, 209–11 (1976); cert. denied: 364 A 2d 1076 (1976) (New Jersey Supreme Court).

[62] 293 NYS 2d 834, 837 (1968). See also *Richards* v. *U.S. Tennis Association* 400 NYS 2d 267 (1977) where the New York Supreme Court held that the insistence of the defendants that Dr Renee Richards (who had undergone a sex-change operation to become a woman after being a ranked male tennis player in the men's aged 35 and over group) should take and pass a chromosome test before being permitted to enter the ladies' singles competition in the US Open was 'grossly unfair, discriminatory and inequitable and violative of her rights'. The Court

Also of value in determining legal problems posed by the sexual identity of transsexuals is the case law under the European Convention of Human Rights. In *Van Oosterwijck* v. *Belgium*,[63] the European Court of Human Rights held that the claim of a transsexual (born female but who had had a sex-change operation to become male) concerning the failure of the State to give official recognition to his new sex could not be determined on its merits because the applicant had failed to exhaust domestic remedies. However, the European Commission of Human Rights (which has power to refer cases to the Court) did rule upon the merits of the claim. With respect to the contention that the State's attitude constituted a violation of Article 8 of the Convention, which guarantees the right to respect for private and family life, the Commission observed:

It would appear scarcely compatible with the obligation to respect private life to force a person who on the recommendation of his doctor and by undergoing a lawful treatment has taken on the appearance, and, to a large extent, the characteristics of the sex opposite that which appears on his birth certificate to carry identity documents which are manifestly incompatible with his appearance. In such a case he would in fact be exposed to having to reveal to anyone information relating to his private life and subsequently to being excluded from certain employments, activities and relationships on account of the explanations about his position which he had improperly been required to give.[64]

In deciding, unanimously, that the State had breached Article 8, the Commission found that the State:

concluded that previously the defendants had relied on observation of primary and secondary sex characteristics to determine the sex of potential competitors; that the defendants had instituted the test (which Dr Richards would have failed) for the sole purpose of excluding her; and that she 'is now female' as her external organs, her appearance, and her psychological and social status were that of a woman and her internal sexual structure was anatomically similar to that of a person born female who had suffered a total hysterectomy and ovariectomy. Dr Richards was beaten 6–1, 6–4 by Virginia Wade (Wimbledon ladies' champion in 1977) in the first round of the ladies' singles in the US Open in 1977. The Wimbledon Lawn Tennis Association refused Dr Richards's application to compete in 1977 without asking her to take a sex test and without giving a reason. The referee in charge of the Wimbledon championships announced that 'Wimbledon have a rule which says we do not have to give any reason why any player's entry is refused': *The Times*, 14 June 1977.

[63] 3 EHRR 557 (1981).
[64] App. no. 7654/76, Report of the Commission, 3 EHRR 582, para. 46.

has refused to recognise an essential element of his personality: his sexual identity resulting from his changed physical form, his psychical make-up and his social role. In doing so, it treats him as an ambiguous being, an 'appearance,' disregarding in particular the effects of a lawful medical treatment aimed at bringing the physical sex and the psychical sex into accord with each other. As regards institutionalised society, . . . [the State] restricts the applicant to a sex which can now scarcely be considered his own.[65]

A majority of the Commission also found that the applicant had proved a violation of Article 12 of the Convention, which guarantees the right to marry and to found a family. The Commission noted that because the State did not recognize that the applicant was a man, and because, for him, marriage to a man 'is inconceivable for psychological, physical and social reasons',[66] he is denied the right to marry. It held that:

the applicant now possesses the external physical forms of the masculine sex, he behaves as a man and is socially accepted as such . . . He stresses that the phalloplasty enables him to have sexual relations . . . [T]here is nothing to support the conclusion that the capacity to procreate is an essential condition of marriage or even that procreation is an essential purpose of marriage.[67]

Unlike Ormrod J. the Commission was well 'aware that transsexualism raises relatively new and complex questions to which States must find solutions compatible with the respect for fundamental rights'.[68]

It is to be hoped that, if and when an English court needs to determine the sexual status of a transsexual for the purposes of the

---

[65] Ibid. at 584, para. 52. [66] Ibid. at 585, para. 54.

[67] Ibid. at 586, paras. 58–9.

[68] Ibid. at para. 60. See also *X* v. *Federal Republic of Germany*, where the European Commission of Human Rights declared admissible a complaint that the State's refusal to give official recognition to the new sex of a transsexual and the resulting adverse consequences to the complainant amounted to degrading treatment contrary to art. 3 of the European Convention and seriously hindered the complainant's private life contrary to art. 8 of the European Convention: (1977) 11 D. & R. 16. The Commission thereafter adopted a report stating the terms of a friendly settlement of the case, that, pursuant to a decision of a German national court, the record of the transsexual's sex had been altered in the birth register and an *ex gratia* payment had been made to the complainant: (1979) 17 D. & R. 21. In Mar. 1984, the Commission declared admissible *Application No. 9532/81* v. *UK* in which a post-operative male transsexual (born female) complained of a breach of his fundamental rights by the refusal of English law to allow him to marry a woman and to have his birth certificate altered to show his present sex.

Sex Discrimination Act 1975 (or for any other purpose), the reasoning and the principles stated in these American cases[69] and by the European Commission, and not the reasoning in *Corbett*, will be adopted.

Similar principles should be applied to resolve the problem of assigning a sex for legal purposes to a hermaphrodite—a person born with the primary sexual characteristics of both sexes. The Family Court of Australia considered the problem in the case of *In the Marriage of C and D*.[70] A woman was granted a nullity decree after a marriage ceremony with a person who had a female chromosome pattern and, prior to surgery, possessed male and female gonads (one ovary and one testis), a short penis, a tiny uterus, a rudimentary vagina, and well-formed breasts. Surgery prior to the marriage ceremony had removed the female organs and allowed the respondent to continue to play the male social role he had adopted since birth. The nullity decree was granted, *inter alia*, on the ground that marriage is the voluntary union of one man and one woman, but that in this case 'the husband was neither man nor woman but was a combination of both . . .'. Rather than depriving the respondent of the legal capacity to marry, the Court should have decided that surgery had brought the anatomical

---

[69] There are some less happy decisions of US courts on transsexualism. In *B*. v. *B*. 355 NYS 2d 712 (1974), the Supreme Court of New York held void a marriage between a woman and a transsexual born female but who had had a sex-change operation prior to the marriage ceremony: 'Apparently, hormone treatments and surgery have not succeeded in supplying the necessary apparatus to enable defendant to function as a man for the purposes of procreation. In the same way surgery has not reached that point that can provide a man with something resembling a normal female sexual organ, transplanting ovaries or a womb. Those are still beyond reach.'

[70] 28 ALR 524 (1979). The case is discussed by Rebecca J. Bailey (1979) 53 *Australian Law Journal* 659 and by H. A. Finlay, 'Sex Identity and the Law of Nullity' (1980) 54 *Australian Law Journal* 115. See also G. W. Bartholomew, '"Hermaphrodites" and the Law' (1960) 2 *University of Malaya Law Review* 83. Cf. Bracton's thirteenth-century treatise, *On the Laws and Customs of England* (1968, trans. Samuel E. Thorne), ii. 31–2: 'Mankind may also be classified in another way: male, female or hermaphrodite. . . . A hermaphrodite is classed with male or female according to the predominance of the sexual organs.' In Plato's *The Symposium* (1951, trans. Walter Hamilton), p. 59, it is suggested by Aristophanes that 'originally . . . there were three sexes, not, as with us, two, male and female; the third partook of the nature of both the others and has vanished, though its name survives. The hermaphrodite was a distinct sex in form as well as in name, with the characteristics of both male and female, but now the name alone remains, and that solely as a term of abuse.'

indicators of sex into line with the psychological indicators, thereby rendering the respondent a male for legal purposes.

IV

Having determined that there are undoubtedly circumstances in which a transsexual may claim the protection of the 1975 Act, and having stated the principles relevant to the assignment of sex to a transsexual for the purposes of sex discrimination law, it remains to be considered whether the decisions of the American courts and the decision of the industrial tribunal in *E. A. White* are correct in concluding that adverse treatment for reasons connected with transsexualism does not give a cause of action in sex discrimination law (unless the defendant distinguishes between a male–female change and a female–male change).

Suppose a person born male but who has had a sex-change operation to become a female is dismissed (or refused appointment to a job) because of that operation. If she brings a claim under the 1975 Act, she will need to show that she has been less favourably treated on the ground of her sex than a person of the other sex is or would be treated. Because her sex is female, she needs to compare her treatment with that accorded (or which would be accorded) to a man. She should make the comparison with the person most closely resembling her in qualifications for the job and being distinct from her only in being of the male sex: that is herself prior to the operation. Since the employer would have appointed the complainant or kept her on in the job had she remained male, the less favourable treatment is arguably on the ground of her sex. As in the case of less favourable treatment for reasons connected with sexual preferences, the attitude taken by an industrial tribunal or a court to such a claim will depend upon the interpretation of section 5(3) of the 1975 Act. In comparing the treatment of the post-operative transsexual woman and the treatment she would have received had she remained male, is the fact that the former has had a sex-change operation and the latter has not a 'relevant circumstance' for the purposes of the Act? It is arguable that the fact of the sex-change operation is not *per se* relevant in comparing the treatment of the two sexes, and that therefore the less favourable treatment of the woman is on the ground of her sex in that she would not have been so treated had she remained male. For the sex-change operation to be 'relevant' in distinguishing the cases of the man and the woman, the employer must point to a consequence of the operation which makes it more difficult for an employee who has changed sex to perform the job or otherwise affects the efficiency of the place of work.

Section 5(3) is similarly crucial in deciding the claim of an applicant who has not had a sex-change operation but who is adversely treated for adopting the social role associated with the other sex. The complainant in *E. A. White*, for example, alleged that if she were a man she would not have been dismissed. The success of her action under the 1975 Act depends on whether the deception she practised to obtain the job or the embarrassment her condition caused to other workers is a 'relevant circumstance' in distinguishing the treatment she would have received had she been male. Clearly, it is strongly arguable that the element of deception is 'relevant', since it goes to the trustworthiness of the employee, and so must be the reaction of other workers if it has a serious impact on the efficiency of the place of work. But the employer cannot make 'relevant' to a comparison of the treatment of the complainant and the treatment she would have received if she were a man those psychological problems from which the complainant suffers unless they have an impact of this sort or a connection with her ability to do the job. Hence, a male employee dismissed for being overtly effeminate may have a sex discrimination claim[71] on the basis that if he were a woman he would not have been dismissed and, in making the comparison between the treatment he received and that which he would have received were he a woman, it is not a 'relevant circumstance' that distinguishes his case from that of the female comparison that he adopts social characteristics associated with the sex opposite to his whereas the female comparison adopts social characteristics connected with her own sex. That is not a 'relevant circumstance' because it has no impact on the complainant's ability to perform the job in question.

Section 5(3) leaves the analysis of the criteria of relevance to judicial determination. The conclusions reached on the application of the 1975 Act to cases of pre-operative and post-operative transsexuals, where a comparison is made with how the complainant

---

[71] Cf. *Smith* v. *Liberty Mutual Assurance Co.*, above, n. 11, where the US Court of Appeals held that no Title VII claim exists in such a case.

would have been treated if of the opposite sex, will depend on how courts and tribunals perform the task of developing criteria of relevance. It is evident that, under section 5(3), the different sexes of the complainant and the person with whom he or she seeks to be compared cannot be a 'relevant circumstance' distinguishing the treatment of the complainant and that accorded to the other person. Otherwise no claim of direct sex discrimination could ever be established. The issue to be decided in cases involving transsexuals who are adversely treated by reason of their sexual status and identity is the extent to which factors connected with sex are similarly irrelevant for the purposes of section 5(3) of the 1975 Act.[72]

V

The degree of protection offered by the 1975 Act to persons adversely treated by reason of their sexual preferences or sexual identity depends, to a large extent, on judicial construction of the opaque language of the legislation. It is for courts and tribunals to decide to what extent, if any, sex discrimination law neutralizes such factors in the contexts covered by the Act or whether the law 'was designed only to change . . . the stereotypes that abound concerning the capabilities of each sex . . . [and] was not designed to change other views that society holds about sexuality'.[73]

A plausible argument can be presented to support the proposition that the 1975 Act makes it unlawful in certain circumstances for defendants to treat homosexuals and transsexuals adversely by reason of their sexual orientation or status or identity. This is far from saying that courts and tribunals will find such an argument to be convincing. Still, the manner in which such claims are determined will tell us much about judicial interpretation of the concepts contained in the 1975 Act. It will indicate, in cases concerning homosexuals, how willing our courts are to protect weak, oppressed minorities. It will demonstrate, in cases involving transsexuals, how equipped our judiciary is to resolve social

[72] See also Stuart A. Wein and Cynthia Lark Remmers, 'Employment Protection and Gender Dysphoria: Legal Definitions of Unequal Treatment on the Basis of Sex and Disability' (1979) 30 *Hastings Law Journal* 1075.

[73] Note, 'Developments in the Law-Employment Discrimination and Title VII of the Civil Rights Act of 1964' (1971) 84 *Harvard Law Review* 1109, 1184.

problems that arise from the development of new medical techniques.

Our treatment of homosexuals and transsexuals under the 1975 Act will show how tolerant we are of persons who diverge from the norm. The legal treatment of such persons hitherto shows legal intolerance at its worst. The 1975 Act offers the opportunity for a new approach. It would be one more paradox of a statute designed to eradicate reliance on stereotyped notions of what men and women can do and how they should behave,[74] if it offered little or no protection to those homosexual and transsexual individuals who suffer less favourable treatment precisely because they decline to behave in the manner expected of a person of a particular sex.

[74] See ch. 2 at nn. 39–46.

9

WHEN IS SEX A GENUINE OCCUPATIONAL QUALIFICATION?

I

The Sex Discrimination Act 1975 requires that men and women receive equal treatment irrespective of their sex in defined contexts. One of the more difficult problems posed by such a principle is to decide in what circumstances physical and social differences between men and women are relevant in determining whether equal treatment has been accorded. Section 7 of the 1975 Act defines when being a man, or being a woman, is a 'genuine occupational qualification' (or 'GOQ') making sex discrimination lawful in the context of employment. The manner in which Parliament recognized sex differences in section 7, and the way in which courts and tribunals have applied section 7, tell us a great deal about the extent of our commitment to equality for men and women.

The White Paper which preceded the 1975 legislation, *Equality for Women*, recognized that

all exceptions weaken the principle of non-discrimination. The aim must be, therefore, to limit exceptions to the necessary minimum. These must include provisions to ensure that the legislation does not apply to personal and intimate relationships and that the application of the principle of non-discrimination does not produce manifest anomalies or absurdities.[1]

Very similar general sentiments were expressed by Government spokesmen during the Parliamentary debates on the Sex Discrimination Bill 1975.[2]

---

[1] Cmnd. 5724 (1974), para. 39.
[2] See, for example, Dr David Owen (Minister of State, Department of Health and Social Security) 893 HC 1543 (18 June 1975, Report Stage); Lord Jacques (Government Whip in the House of Lords) 362 HL 1066 (14 July 1975, Committee Stage); Lord Crowther-Hunt (Minister of State, Department of Education and Science) ibid. 1086.

The GOQ exception[3] attempts to lay down the criteria of jobs with regard to which physical or cultural differences between men and women excuse sex discrimination by the employer. Where sex is a GOQ for a job, it is not unlawful for an employer to discriminate in the arrangements it makes for determining who

---

[3] S. 7(1) states that in relation to sex discrimination it is not unlawful for an employer to discriminate in the arrangements made for the purpose of determining who should be offered employment or by refusing or deliberately omitting to offer employment 'where being a man is a genuine occupational qualification for the job' and it is not unlawful to discriminate in affording employees access to opportunities for promotion or transfer to, or training for, such employment. S. 7(2) provides:

Being a man is a genuine occupational qualification for a job only where—
- (a) the essential nature of the job calls for a man for reasons of physiology (excluding physical strength or stamina) or, in dramatic performances or other entertainment, for reasons of authenticity, so that the essential nature of the job would be materially different if carried out by a woman; or
- (b) the job needs to be held by a man to preserve decency or privacy because—
    - (i) it is likely to involve physical contact with men in circumstances where they might reasonably object to its being carried out by a woman, or
    - (ii) the holder of the job is likely to do his work in circumstances where men might reasonably object to the presence of a woman because they are in a state of undress or are using sanitary facilities; or
- (c) the nature or location of the establishment makes it impracticable for the holder of the job to live elsewhere than in premises provided by the employer, and—
    - (i) the only such premises which are available for persons holding that kind of job are lived in, or normally lived in, by men and are not equipped with separate sleeping accommodation for women and sanitary facilities which could be used by women in privacy from men, and
    - (ii) it is not reasonable to expect the employer either to equip those premises with such accommodation and facilities or to provide other premises for women; or
- (d) the nature of the establishment, or of the part of it within which the work is done, requires the job to be held by a man because—
    - (i) it is, or is part of, a hospital, prison or other establishment for persons requiring special care, supervision or attention, and
    - (ii) those persons are all men (disregarding any woman whose presence is exceptional), and
    - (iii) it is reasonable, having regard to the essential character of the establishment or that part, that the job should not be held by a woman; or
- (e) the holder of the job provides individuals with personal services promoting their welfare or education, or similar personal services, and those services can most effectively be provided by a man; or
- (f) the job needs to be held by a man because of restrictions imposed by the laws regulating the employment of women; or
- (g) the job needs to be held by a man because it is likely to involve the performance of duties outside the United Kingdom in a country whose laws or customs are such that the duties could not, or could not effectively, be performed by a woman; or
- (h) the job is one of two to be held by a married couple.

should be offered the employment, or by refusing or deliberately omitting to offer that employment to a person, or in the way it affords access to opportunities for promotion or transfer to, or training for, such employment. The section 7 exception does not validate discrimination in the terms on which employment is offered or in dismissing an employee or subjecting her to any other detriment (presumably because the sex of the employee cannot be relevant to these issues even if sex is a GOQ for the job). Nor does the exception apply to marital discrimination or to victimization. However, it is clearly an important potential defence for an employer charged with sex discrimination.[4] Section 7(2) defines precisely when sex is a GOQ. Although it is phrased in terms of when 'being a man' is a GOQ, section 2(1) requires one to read the provision as applying equally to the treatment of women, with appropriate modifications.

II

During the second reading of the Sex Discrimination Bill, the Home Secretary, Roy Jenkins, explained that to set out the criteria for judging when sex is a GOQ 'is inevitably a difficult drafting job'. However, he had no doubt that 'it is much better to start with a general provision against discrimination and to exempt where necessary rather than to start the other way round . . .'.[5] This principle is recognized in section 7. Sex is made a GOQ under section 7(2) 'only' where the job satisfies the criteria there stated. During the Committee Stage of the Bill, the Conservative Opposition suggested an amendment (described by its proposer, Ian Gilmour, as 'just a safety-net amendment') to provide that sex should be a GOQ where 'the tribunal is so satisfied having regard to equity and the substantial merits of the case'. This was defeated on the ground that it was so vague that the principle of no sex discrimination in employment would be threatened.[6] Hence exceptions to that principle 'are permitted only to the extent that they are specifically spelled out in the defined categories where

---

[4] S. 9 (discrimination by a principal against contract workers) and s. 11 (discrimination by a partnership) incorporate the GOQ defence in ss. 9(3) and 11(3).

[5] 889 HC 517 (26 Mar. 1975).

[6] Standing Committee B, Fourth Sitting (1 May 1975), cols. 177–80.

being a man (or woman) is to be admitted as "a genuine occupational qualification for a job"'.[7] If an employer is shown to have discriminated against a person it is therefore 'no answer to say that what was done was done with good motives or was done, even objectively, in the best interests of the person concerned or in the best interests of the business with which the case is involved'.[8] An employer must consider the individual's ability to do the job, irrespective of sex and irrespective of stereotyped assumptions about the general ability of women (or men).[9] Section 7 does not provide a defence to an employer who refuses to employ or promote a woman by reason of such stereotyped assumptions or because it thinks it will cost it more to employ women or because customers would prefer to be served by men, unless the case falls within one of the specific criteria defined in section 7(2).[10]

Title VII of the US Civil Rights Act 1964 similarly prohibits discrimination in employment on the ground (*inter alia*) of sex. It too validates discrimination when sex is a 'bona fide occupational qualification [BFOQ] reasonably necessary to the normal operation of that particular business or enterprise'. The US Supreme Court has emphasized that whatever the precise formulation of the BFOQ exception, 'it is impermissible under Title VII to refuse to hire an individual woman or man on the basis of stereotyped characterisations of the sexes . . .'.[11] In construing section 7

---

[7] *Shields* v. *E. Coomes (Holdings) Ltd* [1978] ICR 1159, 1178 per Bridge LJ (in the Court of Appeal). See also *Grieg* v. *Community Industry* [1979] ICR 356, 362 (EAT). Cf. s. 30(2)(h) of the Sex Discrimination Act 1984 (Australia): the relevant authorities have power to declare, by regulations, that sex is a GOQ for any specified job.

[8] *Grieg* ibid., 360. See ch. 2 n. 7.   [9] See ch. 2 nn. 39–46.

[10] See *Equality for Women* above, n. 1 para. 48. Conservative Party proposals in 1973 for an anti-discrimination law would have made it unlawful to discriminate in employment except 'where it could be shown that for performance of personal services strong preferences among customers or clients make the employment of a man (or a woman) essential to the business'.

[11] *Dothard* v. *Rawlinson* 433 US 321, 333 (1977). See similarly Equal Employment Opportunity Commission (EEOC) Guidelines on BFOQ applied by the US Court of Appeals in *Rosenfeld* v. *Southern Pacific Co* 444 F 2d 1219, 1224 (1971): sex is not a BFOQ where the refusal to hire an individual is 'based on stereotyped characterisations of the sexes. Such stereotypes include, for example, that men are less capable of assembling intricate equipment; that women are less capable of aggressive salesmanship. The principle of non-discrimination requires that individuals be considered on the basis of individual capacities and not on the basis of any characteristics generally attributed to the group.' See also 'Developments in the Law—Employment Discrimination and Title VII of the Civil Rights Act of 1964' 84 *Harvard Law Review* 1109, 1178 (1971).

English courts and tribunals should adopt the approach of the US Court of Appeals that 'it would be totally anomalous' to adopt a statutory construction 'that would, in effect, permit the exception to swallow the rule'.[12] It would not seem that much turns on the fact that the 1975 Act validates discrimination where sex is a 'genuine' occupational qualification, whereas Title VII recognizes an exception in 'bona fide' cases. The language of section 7 is, however, preferable in avoiding any inference that the defence depends on the state of mind of the employer rather than the objective nature of the job in question.[13]

The US Supreme Court has stated that 'the BFOQ exception was in fact meant to be an extremely narrow exception to the general prohibition of discrimination on the basis of sex'.[14] Although one has no doubt that the same is true of section 7, it is unfortunate that there is no express statement in the 1975 Act that the burden of proving the GOQ defence lies upon the employer defendant. The White Paper,[15] the Home Office Guide to the Act,[16] and judgments of the Employment Appeal Tribunal (EAT)[17] all suggest that the burden of proof is on the employer to bring itself within section 7. Because the facts relevant to a section 7 defence will tend to be within the control of the employer, and because section 7 provides for a narrow exception, the onus of proof should be on the employer. There is no need for the employer to rely upon a section 7 defence unless an act of sex discrimination is first proved against it. (Non-employers may also seek to rely upon section 7, for example if they are accused of aiding an employer to discriminate unlawfully.)

In construing section 7 it should also be borne in mind that we are concerned with the specific job in question, and not with jobs

---

[12] *Diaz* v. *Pan American World Airways Inc* 442 F 2d 385, 387 (1971); cert denied 404 US 950 (1971).

[13] See the Special Report of the Select Committee of the House of Commons on the Anti-Discrimination (no. 2) Bill 1973, 27. D. J. Walker, *Sex Discrimination* (1975) suggests at 33, perhaps not altogether seriously, that 'the word "genuine" . . . was apparently included to cover the case of Danny La Rue [a female impersonator]'.

[14] Above, n. 11 at 334.

[15] Above, n. 1 at 46.

[16] *Sex Discrimination—A Guide to the Sex Discrimination Act 1975*, para. 3.11.

[17] *Timex Corporation* v. *Hodgson* [1982] ICR 63, 65; *Secretary of State for Scotland* v. *Henley* (EAT, Scotland: 19 May 1983, unreported, transcript p. 2). See also ch. 3 at n. 108.

of this type generally or elsewhere in industry.[18] One further point of general importance in construing section 7 is that, so far as possible, the 1975 Act is to be interpreted consistently with European Community law.[19] EEC Council Directive 76/207/EEC of 9 February 1976 requires equal treatment of men and women as regards access to employment, including promotion, and to vocational training, and as regards working conditions. Article 2(2) of this Directive provides, however, that the principle of equal treatment 'shall be without prejudice to the right of Member States to exclude from its field of application those occupational activities and, where appropriate, the training leading thereto, for which, by reason of their nature or the context in which they are carried out, the sex of the worker constitutes a determining factor'. Article 9(2) of the Directive requires Member States periodically to 'assess the occupational activities referred to in Article 2(2) in order to decide, in the light of social developments, whether there is justification for maintaining the exclusions'.[20] Section 7 should be construed consistently with the power to exclude the general principle of no discrimination only if sex is 'a determining factor' and if the exclusion of men (or women) from the job is 'justified'.

Section 7(3) and section 7(4) give further guidance on when the sex of the worker is such 'a determining factor'. During the Parliamentary debates on the 1975 Bill in the House of Lords, Baroness Seear proposed an amendment to omit section 7(3).[21] She was concerned that it 'positively invites the situation in which an employer who wishes to exclude women will put certain matters

---

[18] *Badley* v. *Home Office* (an unreported decision of an industrial tribunal sitting at Ashford, Kent on 10 May 1984).

[19] *Garland* v. *British Rail Engineering Ltd* [1982] ICR 420, 437–9 (House of Lords).

[20] In *Commission of the European Communities* v. *United Kingdom* [1984] ICR 192, the European Court of Justice considered whether the provisions of the Sex Discrimination Act 1975 on employment in a private household and employment of midwives complied with the Equal Treatment Directive. The Court said that 'the principle of respect for private life' and the 'personal sensitivities' of patients are relevant to the application of Article 2(2) of the Directive. The Advocate General said, at 199, that 'since art. 2(2) of the Directive provides for an exception it must be strictly construed . . . [I]t is for the Member States to prove that a particular occupational activity may be excluded from the field of application of the Directive'. See ch. 5 on Community Law.

[21] S. 7(3) provides: 'Subsection (2) applies where some only of the duties of the job fall within paragraphs (*a*) to (*g*) as well as where all of them do.'

into the job, construct the job in such a way, so that he will then be able . . . to ensure that only a man is employed'. Lord Jacques successfully resisted the amendment on behalf of the Government, confidently predicting that 'it will not be possible for an employer to evade the spirit of the Bill by attaching a tiny, unnecessary percentage of genuine occupational qualification work to each job in his employ'.[22] Certainly the reference to 'duties' in section 7(3) and the references in various parts of section 7(2) to 'the essential nature of the job' and what the job 'needs' or 'requires' suggest an objective test of the character of the job and the responsibilities that go with it. Such an approach is approved by the judgment of the EAT in *Timex Corporation* v. *Hodgson*. The EAT considered whether certain job duties were 'genuinely introduced' or 'introduced as a pretext for dismissing' an employee in deciding the application of section 7.[23]

Section 7(4)[24] is an important provision which, as Lord Jacques emphasized on behalf of the Government in 1975, 'will ensure that even if genuine occupational qualification duties are attached to a job, the employer will need to demonstrate that they cannot reasonably be reallocated'.[25] Section 7(4) applies to all the examples of a GOQ mentioned in section 7(2) with the exception of section 7(2)(h). Section 7(4) applies 'in relation to the filling of a vacancy', and this should be construed to cover promotion, transfer, and training cases as well as cases of appointments.

---

[22] 362 HL 1062–3 (14 July 1975, Committee Stage).

[23] Above, n. 17, 67–8.

[24] S. 7(4) provides:

Paragraph (*a*), (*b*), (*c*), (*d*), (*e*), (*f*) or (*g*) of subsection (2) does not apply in relation to the filling of a vacancy at a time when the employer already has male employees—

(*a*) who are capable of carrying out the duties falling within that paragraph, and
(*b*) whom it would be reasonable to employ on those duties, and
(*c*) whose numbers are sufficient to meet the employer's likely requirements in respect of those duties without undue inconvenience.

There is an intimate link between s. 7(3) and s. 7(4) because 'the smaller the proportion of duties of a particular job which are covered by the GOQ defence, the easier it will be to argue that the duties could reasonably have been performed by another employee': Richard Townshend-Smith, 'Note' 11 *Industrial Journal* 130, 132 (1982).

[25] Above, n. 22, 1063. The US federal courts have implied into Title VII of the Civil Rights Act a principle similar to that stated in s. 7(4): see, for example, *Hardin* v. *Stynchcomb* 691 F 2d 1364 (1982: US Court of Appeals). Similarly, the Maine Supreme Judicial Court in *Percy* v. *Allen* 449 A 2d 337, 343–5 (1982) on when sex is a BFOQ under State law.

It is unfortunate that in the first EAT case on section 7, the attention of the EAT was not drawn to section 7(4). In *Timex Corporation* v. *Hodgson*[26] the male complainant had been employed as one of three supervisors in a department. His department, along with others, was reorganized because of a decline in orders. Only one supervisor was now required. Both of the other supervisors had shorter service than the complainant. So if 'last in, first out' was applied, he would not have been made redundant. However a female supervisor, Mrs L, was selected to remain rather than the complainant. The employers so acted because all other female supervisors at the factory were leaving and because they felt it necessary to retain a female supervisor to deal with the personal and private problems of the female staff. She could have responsibility for first aid for such employees, keeping machines in the ladies' lavatory stocked with items, and taking urine samples from females in areas of work involving toxic materials if the woman from the personnel department whose task this was should be ill or otherwise unavailable. There was no doubt that if the complainant had been a woman, he would not have been dismissed by reason of redundancy, since he had longer relevant service than Mrs L. The issue was whether the employer could rely on a section 7 defence.

There were three problems. First, did the discrimination concern dismissal (in which case section 7 did not cover it)? Secondly, was sex a GOQ for the job within section 7(2)? Thirdly, what was the effect of section 7(4)?

As explained above, section 7(1) provides that sex cannot be a GOQ as a defence to an act of sex discrimination in dismissing an employee[27] (or subjecting her to any other detriment). *Timex* suggests that the careful demarcation in section 7(1) of the circumstances in which the GOQ principle applies is unworkably artificial and that the EAT will apply section 7 sensibly in this respect. The EAT held that the discrimination here was with regard to selection to do the revised job, not with regard to dismissal, and so it fell within section 7(1). The alternative would

---

[26] Above, n. 17.

[27] Above, p. 227. See *Gallagher* v. *Home Office* (unreported decision of a Newcastle industrial tribunal, 1985): once a woman is appointed as a prison officer in a male prison, the GOQ defence does not apply and cannot make lawful the refusal of the Home Office to allow her to do overtime discipline duties.

mean that an employer could not genuinely alter a job description at a time of redundancy and so prefer an existing female (or male) employee for the revised job even though the case otherwise satisfied the criteria of section 7(2); but if the employer dismissed the employees it could then prefer a man (or a woman) on the ground of their sex in filling the vacancy for the new job.

On whether the facts of the *Timex* case fell within section 7(2), making sex a GOQ for the job, the industrial tribunal rejected the employers' claim that the additional duties needed to be performed by a woman to preserve decency or privacy under section 7(2)(b). However, the industrial tribunal reasoned that this was partly because the duties could have been given to other senior female employees. The EAT held that the industrial tribunal 'cannot tell the employers how to manage their business and that they need not have included the additional duties in the revised job'. Therefore the case was remitted to the industrial tribunal to decide whether the additional duties did fall within section 7(2)(b). The EAT did not decide whether sex was a GOQ in the circumstances of the case.

The EAT did not consider (because it was not drawn to their attention) the impact of section 7(4). It would appear that the industrial tribunal were reaching conclusions relevant to a finding under section 7(4) that the employers already had female employees capable of carrying out the additional duties, whom it would be reasonable to employ on those duties and whose numbers were sufficient to meet the employer's likely requirements in respect of those duties without undue inconvenience. Therefore the complaint of unlawful sex discrimination should have been upheld on the ground that, by reason of section 7(4), there was no GOQ defence.

III

In order properly to construe and apply section 7 of the 1975 Act, it is necessary to understand its rationale. A law prohibiting sex discrimination and requiring equal treatment for men and women faces difficult analytical and practical problems in contexts where there are physical or cultural differences between the sexes.

Section 7 attempts to deal with a range of differences, biological and social, between the sexes which may justify differential treatment of men and women in employment. It covers cases where by reason of his (or her) bodily structure no man (or no woman) can perform the essential nature of the job. There are very few jobs the essential nature of which only one sex can perform. Examples are rather artificial, and removed from everyday experience. Employment as a sperm donor or as a wet nurse are the examples most commonly given. Employment as a sperm donor demands characteristics found in most men but in no women. Employment as a wet nurse requires attributes possessed by most women but no men. Of course, it is, in any event, difficult to envisage a woman complaining that she has been excluded from consideration for a job as a sperm donor, if only because no woman has the relevant qualifications to be appointed to the job. The first half of section 7(2)(a), which covers such cases, is, however, necessary to permit employers to make arrangements to employ only men for such a job. Section 7(2)(a) does not only cover cases where no man (or no woman) can do the job by reason of biological factors. It also covers cases where either sex could physically perform the job duties, but where the essential nature of the job requires that it is performed by a person with a female bodily structure: for example, a model, escort, strip-tease artiste.

The second half of section 7(2)(a), dealing with dramatic performances or entertainment, similarly concerns cases where a woman can perform the job, but not as effectively as a man. It thus moves away from biological differences between the sexes to sociological differences. Similarly, section 7(2)(d) and section 7(2)(e) are based on the premiss that, in certain circumstances (particular jobs in establishments for persons requiring special care, supervision or attention, or jobs where the employee provides individuals with personal services promoting their welfare or education) social differences between men and women mean that men are necessarily less proficient at performing certain tasks than women. Section 7(2)(f) and section 7(2)(g) are based on social differences between the sexes which have their origin in legal restrictions (domestic or foreign) or foreign customary restrictions on the employment of women. Section 7(2)(h) concerns the particular case of sex discrimination where the job is one of two to be held by a married couple.

In addition to validating sex discrimination in employment where women cannot perform the job at all, or cannot perform it as effectively as men, section 7 also covers cases where a woman cannot do the job because of problems of privacy or decency. Section 7(2)(b) and section 7(2)(c) deal with these social differences which result from the biological distinctions between men and women.

Part of the difficulty with section 7 is that it attempts to deal with three separate types of cases, those of physical, functional, and social differences between the sexes. The physical differences concern cases where, by reason of his or her sex, a person is simply unable to perform the job. The functional differences concern cases where Parliament has recognized that, by reason of her sex, a person is less able effectively to perform the job. Such cases are hard to reconcile with the fundamental premiss of the 1975 Act that one should consider persons as individuals irrespective of the qualities commonly possessed by or associated with their sex.[28] Section 7(2)(d) and section 7(2)(e) also seem inconsistent with the principle that sex is not a GOQ merely because of customer preference.[29] The social differences between men and women recognized by section 7 include those concerned with privacy and decency. Clearly it is a matter of social policy to what extent privacy and decency should limit the employment opportunities of one sex. Different societies adopt different values relating to the sharing of sleeping accommodation by men and women at work or relating to states of undress at work. Because the values of our society may well change over time, it is of particular importance in this context to note the power of the Secretary of State for Home Affairs conferred by section 80(1) of the 1975 Act to lay before Parliament a draft order to amend certain sections of the Act, including section 7, after consultation with the Equal Opportunities Commission.[30]

[28] Above, nn. 10–11.

[29] Above, n. 10. See also the EEOC Guidelines on sex as a BFOQ: the refusal to hire an individual because of the preferences of co-workers, the employer, clients or customers does not make sex a BFOQ except in cases of authenticity or genuineness, such as that of actors and actresses. In a 1971 case, the EEOC refused to recognize sex as a BFOQ where an employer declined to promote a female employee to the position of branch manager because the job involved taking male customers to football games, dinners and hunting trips and it was argued that customers would not go with female managers 'unless they were "built like Racquel Welch"' (a sex-symbol of the 1970s), cited in Michael L. Sirota 'Sex Discrimination: Title VII and the Bona Fide Occupational Qualification' 55 *Texas Law Review* 1025, 1055–6 (1977).

[30] See ch. 3 s. VIII.

The scope and application of each part of section 7(2) defining when sex is a GOQ will be analysed in the remaining parts of this chapter. The task is to assess whether section 7 furthers the legislative aim of limiting exceptions to 'the necessary minimum'[31] where 'the sex of the worker constitutes a determining factor'.[32]

In analysing each part of section 7(2), together with the problems it poses for the general principle of no sex discrimination in employment, two further matters should be borne in mind. First, the Race Relations Act 1976 recognizes, by section 5, that being of a particular racial group may be a GOQ. This is in contrast to Title VII of the US Civil Rights Act 1964 under which race (unlike sex) cannot be a BFOQ excusing employment discrimination. The terms of section 5 can, in certain respects, be profitably contrasted with the terms of section 7 of the 1975 Act. Secondly, the 1975 Act and the US Civil Rights Act are not the only anti-discrimination statutes to acknowledge that sex may sometimes be a GOQ thereby validating sex discrimination in some employment cases. It is useful to compare and contrast section 7 with the provisions of the Sex Discrimination Act 1975 (South Australia), the Anti-Discrimination Act 1977 (New South Wales), the New Zealand Human Rights Commission Act 1977, the Canadian Human Rights Act 1977, the Employment Equality Act 1977 (Ireland), the Ontario Human Rights Code 1981, the Equal Opportunity Act 1984 (Victoria), and the Sex Discrimination Act 1984 (Australia). Some of these statutes are similar to section 7 in their detailed definition of the circumstances in which sex is a GOQ.[33]

Each part of section 7(2) purports to specify when it is

[31] Above, n. 1.

[32] EEC Directive 76/207 art. 2(2). The narrowest approach to this is that taken by a US lawyer, Flo Kennedy: 'the only men's jobs and women's jobs are those which can't be done without a penis or a vagina' (quoted in Rosalind Miles, *Danger! Men at Work* (1983), 341).

[33] S. 18(5) of the South Australia statute, s. 14 of the Canadian statute, and s. 23(b) of the Ontario Code recognize the GOQ defence but without specifying its scope in detail. See also *Muthamma* v. *Union of India* AIR 1979 SC 1868 where Krishna Iyer J. for the Indian Supreme Court held unlawful the rule of Government employment that a female may be required to resign after marriage if the Government were satisfied that her family and domestic commitments were likely to impede her efficient discharge of her work duties. The Court held that 'If a married man has a right, a married woman, other things being equal, stands on no worse footing'. However, the Court recognized that exceptions would occur: 'We do not mean to universalise or dogmatise that men and women are equal in all

permissible for an employer to adopt and apply stereotypes of the abilities of men and women and to refuse to consider a woman for a job simply because she is a woman. This is because Parliament has decided that in these circumstances no woman could perform the job adequately or at all. Hence considering female candidates would serve no purpose. The sex of the candidate is relevant in such cases to the ability to satisfy the job criteria. As we shall see, Parliament was not justified in reaching this conclusion with regard to all the cases within section 7(2).

IV

During the Standing Committee debates in the House of Commons on the 1975 Bill, the Under-Secretary of State for the Home Department, Dr Shirley Summerskill, said that 'of all the complex sections of a complicated Bill [clause 7(2)(a)] has proved perhaps the most difficult to draft in a wholly satisfactory form'.[34] The final drafting of section 7(2)(a),[35] while not 'wholly satisfactory', is undoubtedly a distinct improvement on the text in the original Bill. This suggested that sex should be a GOQ where 'the essential nature of the job calls for authentic male characteristics, so that it would be wholly different if carried out by a woman'. Such a provision would have given the courts the unenviable task of deciding what are 'authentic male characteristics'.

The first part of section 7(2)(a) concerns cases where for 'reasons of physiology (excluding physical strength or stamina)' the essential nature of the job calls for a woman (or a man) to perform it. Section 31(2)(a) of the Anti-Discrimination Act 1977 of New South Wales contained an identical provision. However, it has been amended[36] to substitute 'physiognomy or physique' for 'physiology'. The term 'physiology', being 'the study and description of natural objects; natural science' or 'the science of the normal functions and phenomena of living things', does not seem

occupations and all situations and do not exclude the need to pragmatise where the requirements of particular employment, the sensitivities of sex or the peculiarities of societal sectors or the handicaps of either sex may compel selectivity.'

[34] Standing Committee B, Third Sitting (29 Apr. 1975), col. 146. See similarly Lord Jacques, 362 HL 1024 (14 July 1975, Committee Stage).

[35] Above, n. 3.

[36] Anti-Discrimination (Amendment) Act 1981, sched. 5, para. 13.

quite appropriate in this context.[37] 'Physiognomy' being 'the art of judging character and disposition from the features of the face or the form and lineaments of the body generally', and 'physique', being 'the physical or bodily structure, organization and development; the characteristic appearance or physical powers (of an individual or a race)',[38] seem more accurately to capture Parliament's intention here to cover (in addition to the artificial cases of wet nurse and sperm donor) jobs like that of the model, escort, or strip-tease artiste.[39]

In these cases, the sex of the employee is 'an essential ingredient of the job',[40] either because no man (or no woman) can do the job, or because no man (or no woman) can perform the job duties effectively. Once one moves away from the obvious examples of cases where the essential nature of the job calls for a person of a particular sex for reasons of 'physiology', difficult questions are raised of what is 'the essential nature' of a job and when is its performance 'materially different' because carried out by a man (or a woman)? Suppose a company which manufactures motor cars wishes to advertise its product by hiring attractive models to be photographed in a state of undress lying on the bonnet. Although it wants to employ women, and not men, for reasons of physiology, it is unclear whether the essential nature of the job would be materially different if performed by a male model. Even if the company is correct in assuming that it will sell more cars by employing *female* models, this is insufficient to make sex a GOQ for the job. There is a thin, but important, line between sex as a GOQ where the essential nature of the job requires a woman, and the case where the job can more effectively be performed by a woman because of customer reaction. A publican cannot refuse to employ men behind the bar because he believes (rightly or

---

[37] S. 17(2)(a) of the Irish Employment Equality Act 1977 is very similar to s. 7(2)(a) of the 1975 Act in referring to sex as an occupational qualification 'on grounds of physiology (excluding physical strength or stamina)'. See also s. 30(2)(a) Sex Discrimination Act 1984 (Australia): sex is a GOQ where 'the duties of the position can be performed only by a person having particular physical attributes (other than attributes of strength or stamina) that are not possessed by persons of the opposite sex . . .'

[38] These definitions are from the *Shorter Oxford English Dictionary*.

[39] See Michael Beloff, *Sex Discrimination: The New Law* (1976), 32. See also *Equality for Women* above, n. 1 para. 47(a) and the Home Office Guide above, n. 16 para. 3.12.

[40] 'Developments in the Law' above, n. 11 at 1183.

wrongly) that a barmaid attracts more custom. The essential nature of the job, that is serving alcohol, would not be materially different if performed by a man. The reference in section 7(2)(a) to 'the essential nature of the job' and to whether it would be 'materially different' if carried out by a man requires the court to look objectively at the job in its context. If a men's club employs topless waitresses, sex may be a GOQ even though in other circumstances the essential nature of the job (serving customers) is not materially different when performed by a man. The court is required to look at the essence of the job and to reject an employer's attempt to add sex appeal to the job definition unless that is part of the essential nature of the job.[41]

In *Wilson* v. *Southwest Airlines Co*,[42] a US District Court held that an airline acted contrary to Title VII in employing only stewardesses, and not stewards, when it adopted the public image of the 'love airline', using sex appeal to attract male customers. Sex was, said the Court, not a BFOQ in this context. The Court emphasized that the company was not in the business of providing primarily sex-oriented services, and 'sex does not become a BFOQ merely because an employer chooses to exploit female sexuality as a marketing tool, or to better ensure profitability'. The Court distinguished the case before it from jobs where 'sex or vicarious sexual recreation is the primary service provided, e.g. a social escort or topless dancer'. In such cases, the job automatically calls exclusively for one sex; the sex of the employee and the service provided are inseparable. The Court cited with approval decisions of the New York State Human Rights Appeal Board that being female is a BFOQ for the job of a Playboy Bunny. This was because female sexuality was, in such circumstances, 'reasonably necessary to perform the dominant purpose of the job which is forthrightly to titillate and entice male customers'.[43]

---

[41] Section 7(2)(a) requires a more rigorous analysis of the nature of the job than s. 5(2)(a) of the Race Relations Act 1976 which makes membership of a particular racial group a GOQ where the job 'involves' certain activities.

[42] 517 F Supp 292 (1981).

[43] Michael L. Sirota above, n. 29 at 1067–8 sensibly suggests that in this context 'the law must recognise the existence of sex appeal as a fact of life'. He cites the decision of the New York State Human Rights Appeal Board in *St Cross* v. *Playboy Club* (1971) where it was held that 'the restriction to females only of eligibility for employment as a Bunny constitutes a BFOQ . . .'. The Board said that while 'a business such as Respondent's which is based upon the commercial exploitation of

In recognizing that sex may be a GOQ for reasons of physiology, section 7(2)(a) expressly excludes 'physical strength or stamina'. It is doubtful whether the attributes of strength or stamina can properly be described as physiological matters. Moreover it is difficult to conceive of circumstances in which the essential nature of the job would be materially different if done by a woman (or a man) for reasons of strength or stamina. Such attributes are not characteristic of one sex. It may be the case that most men have greater strength and stamina than most women. But many women do have more strength and stamina than many men. Hence, where strength and stamina are relevant to the job, there is no reason for employers to do other than apply the basic principle of considering individuals, irrespective of their sex, by reference to whether or not they can perform the job duties. The express exclusion of physical strength and stamina in section 7(2)(a) should be understood as emphasizing this basic principle even though there is little doubt that, even in the absence of the express exclusion, physical strength or stamina could not be relied upon as reasons of physiology creating a GOQ defence to an act of employment discrimination.

The second part of section 7(2)(a) concerns sex discrimination 'for reasons of authenticity' in dramatic performances or other entertainment. One should note the restricted scope of this GOQ compared with that permitted by section 5 of the Race Relations Act 1976. Membership of a racial group is a GOQ not merely where the job involves participation in dramatic performances or other entertainment, but also in two other contexts concerned with 'authenticity': where the job involves working in a place where food or drink is provided to and consumed by members of the public or a section of the public in a particular setting for which, in that job, a person of that racial group is required for reasons of authenticity; or where the job involves participation as an artist's or photographic model in the production of a work of art, visual image, or sequence of visual images for which a person of that racial group is required for reasons of authenticity. Nor is section 7(2)(a) as wide as the guide-lines on Title VII of the US Civil Rights Act published by the Equal Employment Opportunity

sex appeal and deliberately seeks so to titillate and entice has little to recommend its establishment or perpetuation, its existence is not in violation of the [State] Human Rights Law'.

Commission (EEOC). The guide-lines consider sex to be a BFOQ 'where it is necessary for the purposes of authenticity or genuineness', giving as an example the case of an actor or actress.[44] That 'authenticity or genuineness' may have wide application is illustrated by the decision of the Supreme Court of New York in *Button* v. *Rockefeller*: sex was held to be a BFOQ under State law, for reasons of authenticity, in offering some jobs in the police force because 'undercover assignments to investigate episodes of purse snatching and unlawful abortion are just two examples of situations that would probably require a female undercover agent'.[45]

In considering whether authenticity requires particular acting, singing, or dancing roles to be performed by a man (or a woman), we should not ignore the fact that, as was pointed out by Lord Maybray-King during the Parliamentary debates on the 1975 Bill, Sarah Bernhardt played Hamlet with great success. Baroness Wootton confessed that she too was 'rather puzzled about the word "authenticity" in this context. We must remember that in Shakespearean plays women's parts were originally very frequently played by boys, and those were accepted as authentic performances.'[46] In pantomimes, the principal boy is very often played by a female and the dame is usually played by a male. The context in which the dramatic performance or entertainment is given will, therefore, be crucial in determining whether the essential nature of the job would be materially different if performed by a man.

---

[44] See similarly s. 15(3)(a) of the New Zealand Human Rights Commission Act 1977: 'For reasons of authenticity, as in theatrical performances, posing for artists, or being a model for the display of clothes, sex is a bona fide occupational qualification for the position or employment.' See also s. 30(2)(b) of the Sex Discrimination Act 1984 (Australia): sex is a GOQ where 'the duties of the position involve performing in a dramatic performance or other entertainment in a role that, for reasons of authenticity, aesthetics or tradition, is required to be performed by a person of the relevant sex'. See similarly s. 21(4)(b) of the Equal Opportunity Act 1984 (Victoria).

[45] 351 NYS 2d 488, 492 (1973).

[46] 362 HL 1026 (14 July 1975, Committee Stage). Samuel Pepys, a regular theatregoer, recorded in his diary for 3 Jan, 1661 that it was 'the first time that ever I saw women come upon the stage': Robert Latham and William Matthews, eds. *The Diary of Samuel Pepys* (1970), ii. 5.

V

The 'decency or privacy' GOQ in section 7(2)(b)[47] was included in the 1975 Act because the Government did 'not want the legislation to fall into disrepute'.[48] It is defined by reference to physical contact, states of undress or the use of sanitary facilities and whether a man 'might reasonably object' to a woman doing the job.

Section 7(2)(b)(i) on physical contact is much broader than the equivalent provision in the Anti-Discrimination Act 1977 of New South Wales which merely specifies that sex is a GOQ in two contexts relating to physical contact: where the job involves the fitting of clothes or the searching of individuals.[49] Certainly these are jobs potentially within the broader scope of section 7(2)(b)(i). During the Parliamentary debates on the 1975 Bill, Mr John Fraser, Under-Secretary of State for Employment, gave the example of the assistant who attends ladies trying on corsets in a private changing-room in a shop as the sort of job covered by the provision. He explained that 'we really are not fighting to have men inside women's changing-rooms'.[50]

On the subject of physical contact in changing-rooms, Mr Fraser ventured a rare joke during the Standing Committee debates. He remarked on 'the man who was measured for a suit by a lady tailor. When she had measured him for the trousers she said "What about the jacket?" and he said "No, I will have another pair

[47]   Above, n. 3.

[48]   John Fraser, Under-Secretary of State for Employment, Standing Committee B, Third Sitting (29 Apr. 1975) col. 150. The White Paper, above, n. 1, para. 47(d) originally defined the privacy and decency exception, and the communal accommodation exception in s. 7(2)(c), in the following terms: sex is a GOQ 'where the nature of the job, or the essential surrounding circumstances, are such that the employment of a woman (or man) would be unsuitable on grounds of propriety and privacy (e.g. some lavatory attendants, or employment on some small ships where there needs to be communal sleeping or sanitary accommodation)'.

[49]   S. 31(2)(b) and (d). See also s. 15(3)(b) of the New Zealand Human Rights Commission Act 1977 which provides a defence for sex discrimination where '[i]n the case of a position such as that of attendant in a public lavatory or as a person responsible for the fitting of clothes to customers or others, the position needs to be held by one sex to preserve reasonable standards of privacy . . .'. Decency is not there mentioned.

[50]   Above, n. 48 at 150–1. Prisons and similar institutions pose special problems here as an inmate may 'be searched only by an officer of the same sex' as the inmate: Prison Rules 1964 SI no. 388, rule 39(4); Detention Centre Rules 1983 SI No. 569, rule 43(4); Youth Custody Centre Rules 1983 SI No. 570, rule 43(4). See below, n. 66.

of trousers."' In *Wylie* v. *Dee & Co (Menswear) Ltd*,[51] an industrial tribunal was asked to decide the application of section 7(2)(b)(i) to a menswear shop which refused to employ a woman as an assistant on the ground that the job would require her to take inside-leg measurements for men. The tribunal held that the subsection gave no defence here because when it was necessary for the inside-leg measurement to be taken (and this was itself rare: many men know their measurement and the measurement can be accurately assessed by an experienced person such as the complainant by taking the outside-leg measurement) and when a man was reluctant to allow a woman to perform that task, one of the seven male assistants could do the job. The tribunal appears, therefore, to have decided the case by reference to the fact that because physical contact would be rare, section 7(4) on the reallocation of duties would apply. The more rare the physical contact, obviously the easier it is for the employer to reallocate the relevant duties. In *Kingscote* v. *Mann* (an unreported decision in 1981), an industrial tribunal held that sex was a GOQ under section 7(2)(b)(i) for the job of selling women's dresses in a shop. The tribunal were satisfied that 'it is certainly likely that there would be [physical] contact in the course of trying on and fitting dresses'. The tribunal also accepted that women might reasonably object to a man doing the job.

In *Sisley* v. *Britannia Security Systems Ltd* (an unreported decision in 1982), an industrial tribunal held that 'physical contact' in section 7(2)(b)(i) means actual touching and mere close physical proximity is not sufficient. Not surprisingly, this aspect of the decision was not challenged when *Sisley* was appealed to the EAT on the proper construction of section 7(2)(b)(ii) and section 7(2)(c).

The industrial tribunal in *Wylie* does not appear to have decided whether men 'might reasonably object' to a woman carrying out the physical contact. The tribunal would have been entitled to conclude that as the degree of contact diminishes, it becomes less reasonable for a man to object to the job being carried out by a woman. It is not necessary, however, for the employer to prove that men do or would so object, only that they 'might'. The relevant men for the purpose of determining whether there might

51 [1978] IRLR 103.

be such an objection appear to those with whom the woman would have the physical contact if employed in the job.[52] But, given that different men have very different views on the acceptability of physical contact with women in different circumstances, how are we to decide whether those men might 'reasonably' object to the job being performed by a woman? It is not enough that the men do or might object. It must be a 'reasonable' objection. In assessing the criteria of reasonableness we should bear in mind that section 7(2)(b) exists 'to preserve decency or privacy'. So it is not enough to bring the case within section 7(2)(b)(i) that the men might object to the woman carrying out the job by reason of paternalism or prejudice; it must be an objection reasonable from the perspective of decency or privacy. It is to be hoped that courts and tribunals interpret the criterion of reasonableness with due regard for the context of a liberalizing statute designed to ensure equal opportunity for men and women.

The interpretation of the criterion of reasonableness becomes of crucial importance when one considers other jobs to which section 7(2)(b)(i) has potential application. During the Standing Committee debates, Ms Jo Richardson asked how the provision would apply 'in the case of men being treated by women doctors, nurses, physiotherapists, radiographers, or a wide range of medical workers who could, legitimately under this clause, be objected to by the man in terms of the work that they are carrying out'.[53] One assumes, as did Mr John Fraser in replying to the question on behalf of the Government, that men do not nowadays object to women in such jobs. But it is unfortunate that the protection of

[52] In *City of Philadelphia* v. *Pennsylvania Human Relations Commission* 300 A 2d 97, 102–103 (1973) the Commonwealth Court of Pennsylvania held that sex is a BFOQ under State law for the post of supervisor at a youth study centre for resident children aged 7–16. This was partly for reasons of privacy and decency analogous to those stated in s. 7(2)(b). But it was not here suggested that the views of the children were relevant: 'To subject a girl in this age group to a thorough search of her body [to search for contraband] by a male supervisor could cause not only a temporary traumatic condition but also permanent irreparable harm to her psyche. It is no different where females supervise male juveniles. To have a woman supervisor observe daily showers of the boys at a time in life when sex is a mysterious and often troubling force is to risk a permanent emotional impairment under the guise of equality.'

[53] Above, n. 48 at 149. See *Drummond* v. *Hillingdon Health Authority*: an industrial tribunal held in Nov. 1983 that being a woman was not a GOQ for the job of airport medical officer which involved the medical examination of immigrant women.

such women from employment discrimination depends on judicial assessment of whether any such objection is 'reasonable'. John Fraser acknowledged that '[t]here may be some problems with people of the Moslem religion or something like that . . .'.[54] How is a court to determine whether religious objections to a woman treating a man (or vice versa) are 'reasonable', making sex a GOQ for employment in areas with a large immigrant population?

Similarly, being a woman may well be a GOQ for certain nursing tasks. In *Backus* v. *Baptist Medical Centre*,[55] a US District Court held that being a female was a BFOQ under Title VII of the Civil Rights Act for the job of labour or delivery nurse in the obstetrics and gynaecology department of a hospital, partly by reason of the privacy rights of the female patients. This was because 'there are few duties which a registered nurse can perform in relation to an obstetrical patient which are not sensitive or intimate'. Similarly, in *EEOC* v. *Mercy Health Centre*,[56] another US District Court held that being a woman was a BFOQ for the job of staff nurse in the hospital's labour and delivery area. This was because of objections raised by doctors and patients to the employment of male nurses, the sensitive and intimate duties performed by nurses and the danger that the employment of men would create medically undesirable tension. If the GOQ defence were to be relied upon in such circumstances under the 1975 Act, a court or tribunal would need to ask whether the objection to a male nurse was reasonable given that male doctors (or, in emergencies, ambulancemen) deliver babies and perform the sensitive and intimate duties. The amendment of section 20 of the 1975 Act[57]—which provided an exception to the principle of non-discrimination in the employment of midwives—does not directly answer the issues under section 7(2)(b)(i). However, it strongly suggests that Parliament does not intend sex to be a GOQ for such jobs. (Sex is also potentially a GOQ for hospital jobs under section 7(2)(d) and (e), considered below.)

In the unreported 1980 decision of *Stubbs* v. *Hughesdon*, an industrial tribunal held that section 7(2)(b)(i) makes sex a GOQ

---

[54] Ibid. 152.
[55] 510 F Supp 1191 (1981); vacated on other grounds 671 F 2d 1100 (1982).
[56] 29 FEP Cases 159 (1982).
[57] Sex Discrimination Act 1975 (Amendment of Section 20) Order 1983 SI no. 1202. See ch. 3 n. 26.

for the post of nurse at a home for the elderly where all of the residents were female. The tribunal found that the duties involved intimate physical contact with the patients, that female residents might well object to the employment of a male nurse for these purposes, and that the duties therefore needed to be carried out by a woman to ensure privacy and decency.

In *Sisley* v. *Britannia Security Systems Ltd*,[58] the EAT suggested that section 7(2)(b)(ii)[59] does not cover cases where someone other than the holder of the job is in a state of undress. This conclusion, not necessary to the decision in the case, is contrary to the language of the provision and to the legislative aim. If section 7(2)(b)(ii) were to apply only where the holder of the job is in a state of undress (or using sanitary facilities) it would read: 'the holder of the job is likely to do his work in circumstances where men might reasonably object to the presence of a woman because *the holder of the job is* in a state of undress or is using sanitary facilities'. Parliament used wider language. It specified cases where 'men' might object to the presence of women because 'they' are in a state of undress or are using sanitary facilities. If it was only the state of undress of the holder of the job which mattered, Parliament would surely have provided that the objection to the presence of women should come from the holder of the job himself, not from 'men' generally. The 'men' who might object because 'they' are in a state of undress or are using sanitary facilities are not limited to 'the holder of the job'. The 'men' may be employees or customers. This is further emphasized by the fact that it is difficult to think of jobs where the employee's occupational duties involve him in using sanitary facilities. Parliament, by referring to sanitary facilities, had in mind the case of customer use of such facilities, making sex a potential GOQ for the job of lavatory attendant. The pre-legislative materials, as well as the language of section 7(2)(b)(ii), show that Parliament intended to cover the case of customer (as well as employee) states of undress or use of sanitary facilities. The White Paper, *Equality for Women*,[60] and the Under-Secretary of State for Employment,[61] gave the example of the lavatory attendant as falling within section

[58] [1983] ICR 628, 635–6.
[59] Above, n. 3.
[60] Above, n. 1 at para. 47(d).
[61] Standing Committee B, Third Sitting (29 Apr. 1975), col. 150.

7(2)(b)(ii).[62] Furthermore, the purpose of section 7(2)(b)—to preserve decency or privacy—is contradicted by the EAT approach in *Sisley*.

Under section 7(2)(b)(ii), as under section 7(2)(b)(i), the problem arises of how to assess whether men might 'reasonably object' to the presence of a woman in the job. It is particularly obvious in this context that the requirements of decency and privacy are dependent on the mores of a particular society at a given time. A different society, or the same society at a different time, would give another answer to the same question concerning the requirements of decency and privacy.[63] During the Standing Committee debates on the GOQ provisions of the 1975 Bill, Mrs Millie Miller pointed out that the French have public toilets for men wherein women are employed as attendants. Mr John Fraser, for the Government, accepted that 'standards of decency and privacy will probably change over the years'.[64]

Courts and tribunals are given the important task under section 7(2)(b) of ensuring that the legislative aim of equal treatment for the sexes in employment is not frustrated by antediluvian concepts of what can reasonably be required by privacy and decency. The context in which the objections to the employment of a man (or a woman) are made may well be decisive of whether sex is a GOQ for privacy and decency reasons. A prisoner's right to privacy may well be less protected by the criterion of reasonableness than the

---

[62] Furthermore this aspect of *Sisley* is inconsistent with the judgment of the EAT in *Henley* above, n. 17 where sex would have been a GOQ for the job of assistant governor in a male prison because of the state of undress of the prisoners but for the experimental policy of appointing women to such posts. S. 31(2) of the Anti-Discrimination Act 1977 (New South Wales) specifically makes sex a GOQ where '(c) the job requires the holder of the job to enter a lavatory ordinarily used by men while it is used by men [or] . . . (e) the job requires the holder of the job to enter areas ordinarily used by men while men are in a state of undress or are bathing or showering'. See similarly s. 30(2)(e) of the Sex Discrimination Act 1984 (Australia). S. 30(2)(c) makes sex a GOQ in cases where the job involves the fitting of clothing and so affects privacy or decency. S. 30(2)(d) makes it a GOQ where the job duties include the conduct of searches of the clothing or bodies of people. S. 30(2)(g) makes sex a GOQ where the job-holder is required to enter areas ordinarily used only by persons in a state of undress.

[63] In the seventeenth century bedrooms at inns were often shared by men and women who had previously been strangers to each other: see *The Diary of Samuel Pepys* above, n. 46, i. 150. See also Barbara A. Brown and others 'The Equal Rights Amendment: A Constitutional Basis for Equal Rights for Women' 80 *Yale Law Journal* 871, 902 (1971).

[64] Above, n. 61, col. 152–3.

right of a customer in a shop or a member of the public in a lavatory. In *Henley* v. *Secretary of State for Scotland* (an unreported decision in 1982), an industrial tribunal held that being male was not a GOQ under section 7(2)(b)(ii) for the post of assistant governor at a male prison in Edinburgh. The tribunal accepted that 'there are likely to be some social difficulties for male prisoners and staff in relation to the presence of a woman assistant governor in the area of toilet facilities'. However, the tribunal said that it was significant that there had been no express objection by prisoners during the previous three years when another woman had been doing a similar job. The EAT,[65] rejecting an appeal against this decision, said that the prisoners 'may feel that it is not in their interests to object . . . Reasonable objections may still be made, notwithstanding that none have so far.' The EAT thus suggested that 'might' in section 7(2)(b)(ii) requires consideration of the likelihood of such objections being made.

US courts have, on occasions, held that being a man is a BFOQ for a job in a prison because of privacy and decency considerations or because of the need for employees to carry out intimate body searches of prisoners.[66] In *Griffin* v. *Michigan Department of Corrections*,[67] on the other hand, a US District Court held that sex

[65] Above, n. 17.

[66] For example, *Owens* v. *Rush* 24 FEP Cases 1543 (1979) (US District Court), aff'd in part 636 F 2d 283 (1980) (US Court of Appeals); *Carey* v. *New York State Human Rights Appeal Board* 402 NYS 2d 207 (1978) (New York Supreme Court, Appellate Division); aff'd by Court of Appeals, New York 390 NE 2d 301 (1979); appeal dismissed 444 US 891 (1979) (US Supreme Court). See similarly, *Equal Opportunities Commission* v. *Prison Officers' Association*: an industrial tribunal held in Dec. 1983 that being a man was a GOQ under s. 7(2)(b)(i) for the job of a catering officer in a male detention centre. This was because one of the job duties was to search male inmates, which could only be done by a man, above, n. 50, and staff shortages meant it was not reasonable to reallocate the search duties to male officers under s. 7(4) (on which see above, n. 24).

[67] 30 FEP Cases 638 (1982). In this case, and in the case concerning deputy sheriffs in a jail, *Hardin* v. *Stynchcomb* above, n. 25, it was held that in any event the prison authorities could rearrange job schedules to ensure that female staff would not have to perform duties impinging on the privacy rights of inmates. Similarly, *Gunther* v. *Iowa State Men's Reformatory* 612 F 2d 1079, 1085–7 (1980) (US Court of Appeals), cert. denied 446 US 966 (1980) (US Supreme Court). Cf. s. 7(4) of the 1975 Act, above, n. 24. See also *Hand* v. *Briggs* 360 F Supp 484 (1973) where a male prisoner at San Quentin Penitentiary complained about the employment of female guards. One basis of his claim was that a female guard, Snyder, 'bears a strong physical resemblance to his wife, with whom he had a normal marital relationship prior to his imprisonment, and that Snyder's presence

was not a BFOQ under the Civil Rights Act so as to justify the refusal to allow women to work in prisoner-contact positions in a male prison. The Court rejected 'the notion that the viewing of a nude or defecating inmate by a correctional officer of the opposite sex is intrinsically more odious [to the prisoner] than a viewing by a correctional officer of the same sex'. The court further rejected arguments from prisoner privacy as resting 'on assumptions and stereotypical sexual characteristics which have been expressly prohibited by Title VII'.

Two other points on section 7(2)(b) emphasize the limits of its application. First, it does not make sex a GOQ merely because the holder of the job is likely to do the work in circumstances where women might reasonably object to the presence of a man on the ground that it would cause serious embarrassment. Section 7(2)(b) can be contrasted in this respect with section 35(1)(c)(i) of the 1975 Act. The latter provision states an exception to liability for sex discrimination in the supply of facilities and services to the public or a section of the public where they are to be used by two or more persons at the same time and are such that 'male users are likely to suffer serious embarrassment at the presence of a woman'. So sex is not a GOQ for the job of selling female or male items of a personal or medical nature.[68] Secondly, as section 7(3) of the 1975 Act indicates, sex is only a GOQ in the circumstances stated in section 7(2)(b) where the physical contact, state of undress or use of sanitary facilities is closely associated with 'the duties of the job'. Sex cannot be a GOQ merely because there is gratuitous physical contact, states of undress, or use of sanitary facilities unconnected with the job duties.

In *Sisley*[69] the EAT held that section 7(2)(b)(ii) applies not only to a state of undress required by the job duties but also to a state of undress reasonably connected with those duties. Women employees working on lengthy shifts in a security control room were allowed

accordingly disturbs him by reminding him of his inability to continue his marital activities with his wife. As a result of these problems . . . he claims that he is being subjected to cruel and unusual punishment.' The US District Court dismissed the claim.

[68] John Fraser, Under-Secretary of State for Employment, acknowledged that s. 7(2)(b) 'does not allow discrimination in the employment of people who sell ladies' underwear. It does not allow discrimination in the employment of men to sell corsets': above n. 61 col. 151. On s. 35(1)(c)(i) of the 1975 Act see ch. 3 n. 91.

[69] Above, n. 58.

to rest on a bed when the pressure of work so permitted. The women were in the habit of taking off their uniforms before lying down on the bed in their underwear 'in order to prevent their uniforms being crumpled'. The employer refused to appoint men to the job for this reason. The EAT noted that the industrial tribunal found that it was necessary to have rest periods during the shift and that it was reasonably incidental to the rest period to remove the clothing. Therefore the EAT held that sex was a GOQ for the job under section 7(2)(b)(ii). It is, though, very doubtful whether a state of undress which is not required by the job duties should excuse sex discrimination against men (or women). Section 7(3) suggests that sex is a GOQ only where the job 'duties' so require. Section 7(2)(b)(ii) refers to the 'needs' of the job. The reference to 'sanitary facilities' in section 7(2)(b)(ii) does not, as the EAT suggested, show that the subsection extends further than job duties. When men might reasonably object to the presence of a woman because the men are using sanitary facilities, it is the job *duties* of the lavatory attendant which make sex a GOQ for the job. The attendant *needs*, by reason of the essence of the job, to be present where the sanitary facilities are being used.

Section 7(2) and the EEC Directive 76/207 demand a compelling justification before sex discrimination is validated in employment. *Sisley* does not appear to present such a justification since there was no need for women employees to take off their clothes; in any event, there was no reason why they should not change into leisure clothes in the lavatory area and rest on the bed in those clothes rather than in their underwear. If there is a clash between the desire of female employees not to crumple their uniforms and the desire of Mr Sisley to be considered for a job vacancy irrespective of his sex, the former must give way to the latter. The policy of the 1975 Act and the EEC Directive admits of no other solution.

Section 17(2)(d) of the Irish Employment Equality Act 1977 provided that sex was an occupational qualification 'where either the nature of or the duties attached to a post justify on grounds of privacy or decency the employment of persons of a particular sex'. After receiving an indication from the European Commission that this body considered section 17(2)(d) to be inconsistent with EEC Directive 76/207/EEC, the Irish Government repealed section 17(2)(d) by the European Communities (Employment Equality) Regulations 1982. This action, expressly carried out 'for the purpose of giving effect to Council Directive 76/207/EEC', strongly suggests that section 7(2)(b) of the 1975 Act should be given a narrow construction whenever possible so as to ensure consistency with the Directive. Section 7(2)(b), like the other parts of section 7(2) of the 1975 Act, should be held to make sex a GOQ for a job only where there is 'justification' for so doing under the EEC Directive.

VI

Section 7(2)(c)[70] was 'designed to cover, for example, jobs in ships, lighthouses and remote construction sites'.[71] Similar provisions appear in section 31(2)(f) of the Anti-Discrimination Act 1977 (New South Wales), section 15(3)(d) of the New Zealand Human Rights Commission Act 1977, section 17(2)(e) of the Employment Equality Act 1977 (Ireland), and section 30(2)(f) of the Sex Discrimination Act 1984 (Australia).

The exception stated in section 7(2)(c) applies only where the employees 'live' in premises provided by the employer. In *Sisley* v. *Britannia Security Systems Ltd*[72] the EAT held that employees 'live' in the premises only where they reside there permanently or temporarily. The EAT allowed an appeal on this point from the decision of an industrial tribunal which had held that 'to live' in the premises means 'to carry out the normal functions of being alive'. The industrial tribunal had therefore held that section 7(2)(c) was applicable to the case of workers who did a six- or twelve-hour shift in a security control room and who returned home after each shift. As the EAT said, if the industrial tribunal were correct in its approach, millions of workers would be brought within section 7(2)(c). The EAT suggested that the provision covered jobs in lighthouses and oil rigs and possibly cases where a worker does a twenty-four-hour shift. But, in the present case, the employees did not reside on the premises, albeit they were permitted to rest

[70] Above, n. 3. See also. s. 46 of the 1975 Act which provides that sex discrimination is not unlawful in the admission of persons to communal accommodation if that accommodation is managed in a way which, given the exigencies of the situation, comes as near as may be to fair and equitable treatment of men and women. See ch. 3 n. 112.

[71] John Fraser, Under-Secretary of State for Employment, 893 HC 1502 (18 June 1975, Report Stage).

[72] Above, n. 58.

during the shift when the pressure of work relaxed. Any other decision than that reached by the EAT would destroy the contrast clearly implied by section 7(2)(c) between employees who merely work on the premises and those who 'live' there.

If the employees do 'live' in the premises provided by the employer, the case may come within section 7(2)(c) whether it is the location of the establishment which makes it necessary for them to do so (for example, its remote siting, as in the case of an oil rig or lighthouse) or the 'nature' of the establishment (for example, its relationship to official secrets or the danger of health risks associated with the work). No doubt, courts and tribunals will take a sensible approach to what constitutes an 'establishment' for this purpose. The 1975 Act gives some guidance. Section 10(4) states that 'Where work is not done at an establishment it shall be treated for the relevant purposes as done at the establishment from which it is done or (where it is not done from any establishment) at the establishment with which it has the closest connection'. For example, a firm of decorators does not carry out its work 'at' its offices. However, those offices are treated as the 'establishment' because the work is done 'from' there or it is the establishment which has the closest connection with the work (perhaps because orders from customers are taken there). The reference in section 7(2)(c) to premises 'provided by the employer' also needs to be carefully construed to make sense of the subsection. The employer may provide premises merely by paying hotel expenses for employees if it is impracticable for the job to be done otherwise than by employees living in hotels permanently or temporarily.

The words 'for persons holding that kind of job' were added to section 7(2)(c)(i) because the Government were concerned to cover cases where there were separate blocks of accommodation for different kinds of jobs (or for different shifts), for example on a ship.[73] Without these words, it was feared that the provision would deal only with the totality of accommodation provided by the employer. However, if the employer does provide separate accommodation for other job-holders, it would be strongly arguable that it could reasonably be expected to make arrangements for separate accommodation for the sexes in respect of the

[73] 363 HL 975–6 (29 July 1975, Report Stage).

job in question, and that the employer would therefore fail to establish a GOQ because of section 7(2)(c)(ii). The words 'or normally lived in' were added to section 7(2)(c)(i), again at the request of the Government, to cover cases where no one is living in the ship (or other accommodation) when applications are made for the job.[74] However, it is unclear how ships (or other premises), if new, can be such that they '*are . . . normally lived in by men*'.

'Separate sleeping accommodation' for the sexes is provided, for the purposes of section 7(2)(c)(i), if men and women have individual bedrooms or if they have dormitories restricted to one sex. This was the conclusion of an industrial tribunal in an unreported 1982 decision: *Curran* v. *Scottish Episcopal Theological College*. However, in *Hermolle* v. *Government Communications HQ* (an unreported decision in 1979), another industrial tribunal held that a self-contained, lockable bedroom was not 'separate sleeping accommodation' because 'the bedrooms are all in one block without any division between men and women . . . There is no separate part of the block which is allocated or could be allocated for women only.' There is nothing in section 7(2)(c)(i) to suggest such an interpretation. Accommodation in separate bedrooms, similar to that provided in hotels (where single men and women are housed in the same block), must be 'separate sleeping accommodation'. The purpose of section 7(2)(c) is to ensure that men and women do not have to sleep in one another's presence. Section 7(2)(c) does not require that the separate accommodation for one sex be isolated from that provided for the other sex.[75]

Similarly, there are 'sanitary facilities which could be used by women in privacy from men' where individual lavatories and bathrooms open to men and women can be used in privacy by locking the door. In *Curran*, the industrial tribunal adopted this approach, noting that facilities of this kind are 'commonly

---

[74] 893 HC 1502–3 (18 June 1975, Report Stage).

[75] S. 17(2)(e) of the Irish Employment Equality Act 1977 makes sex an occupational qualification 'where because of the nature of the employment it is necessary to provide sleeping and sanitary accommodation for employees *on a communal basis* and it would be unreasonable to expect the provision of separate such accommodation or impracticable for an employer so to provide' (my emphasis). See the recommendation of the Equality Officer in *Galway Social Service Council* v. *Employment Equality Agency* (29 Apr. 1983): 17(2)(e) did not apply to make sex an occupational qualification for staff at a hostel for homeless men.

encountered in small hotels and boarding-houses for use by both sexes'. Again in *Hermolle* the industrial tribunal took an unjustifiably narrow approach. It held that a lavatory situated in a utility room in fairly regular use by men did not give privacy to women using that lavatory albeit that lavatory could be locked. Section 7(2)(c)(i) talks of 'privacy', not 'seclusion'. It does not require the sanitary facilities to be 'separate'. There is no reason to construe privacy in this context to require more than the common arrangements in trains or aeroplanes with regard to sanitary facilities.

In the unreported industrial tribunal decision in *West* v. *Johns* in 1983, it was held that sex was a GOQ under section 7(2)(c) for a post in a survey team visiting remote areas. The tribunal suggested that it was relevant to the application of section 7(2)(c) that the practice of the men hitherto doing the job had been to economize on their expenses by sharing a room in a boarding-house and that this could not be done if a woman was on the team. The economy benefited the men, not the employer. If the available premises had separate accommodation for women, it is quite irrelevant that other employees would prefer such accommodation not to be used, for extraneous reasons. The tribunal decision is unsatisfactory in another respect. It concluded that 'it is not realistic to assume that separate accommodation can always be obtained in [the remote areas visited] at all times of the year'. The tribunal did not state what evidence supported such a finding. In any event, it cannot be enough to satisfy section 7(2)(c) that occasionally there would not be separate accommodation available for women. The less frequent such occurrences, the stronger the argument for applying section 7(4) on the reallocation of duties and for concluding that sex is therefore not a GOQ for the post.

If the employee has to live in premises provided by the employer, and if separate sleeping accommodation or private sanitary facilities are not provided for the sexes, then the issue becomes whether it is 'reasonable' under section 7(2)(c)(ii) to expect the employer to provide such accommodation or facilities in these or other premises. The Government refused to accept an amendment to the 1975 Bill which would have explained that the employer's action must be 'reasonable on grounds of cost'. It was said that the clause had to cover 'the direct and indirect effects of making the necessary alterations' (for example, not merely the direct building costs on a ship if separate accommodation for women were to be provided, but also the lost revenue if cargo space were reduced and the cost of delay in sailing while the work was carried out). However, it was agreed that the employer could not claim to have acted reasonably in refusing to provide separate accommodation or sanitary facilities for women simply because it believed the job to be unsuitable for women.[76]

The vague criterion of reasonableness in section 7(2)(c)(ii) gives courts and tribunals the unenviable task of deciding how to balance a person's right not to be discriminated against on the ground of their sex and an employer's plea that it should not have to incur a financial burden in employing that person. In *Hermolle* the industrial tribunal held that the 1975 Act imposes a 'substantial burden' on employers in this respect. The tribunal had regard to the practice of comparable employers and held that the defendant employers had acted unreasonably.[77]

In deciding what is 'reasonable' under section 7(2)(c)(ii) it is unfortunately not relevant that, as Baroness Seear emphasized in Parliament, in other European countries 'it is far more common for men and women to share certain premises and conveniences' (for example, train couchettes).[78] The question under section 7(2)(c)(ii) is whether it is reasonable to expect the employer to provide separate sleeping accommodation and private sanitary facilities for each sex, not whether it is reasonable to refuse to employ women because there are no such facilities provided. Section 7(2)(c) adopts a very conservative approach to this question, allowing employers to refuse jobs to women even if women are prepared to share facilities with men, and even if those men are prepared to share the facilities with the women. It is not a precondition for the applicability of section 7(2)(c), as it is for the applicability of section 7(2)(b), that relevant men (or women) 'might reasonably object' to the employment of members of the

---

[76] 363 HL 977–9 (29 July 1975, Report Stage).
[77] See also *McLean* v. *State of Alaska* 583 P 2d 867 (1978): the Alaska Supreme Court held that ferry-owners breached the State anti-discrimination law by refusing to employ women. The employer's explanation, that there was no accommodation for women, was rejected on the ground that the problem could be solved by '[a] little creative imagination on the part of the ferry system, which may necessitate some shifting of crew members . . .'.
[78] 362 HL 1037 (14 July 1975, Committee Stage).

other sex. Section 7(2)(c) needs amendment to include such a precondition.

VII

Section 7(2)(d)[79] makes sex a GOQ for certain jobs in institutions such as prisons, hospitals, old people's homes, and children's homes,[80] where the institution (or part of the institution) is for men only (or for women only). The GOQ exists only where it is 'reasonable' having regard to the essential character of the institution (or the relevant part of it) that the job should not be held by a woman. The reference to reasonableness is partly intended to ensure that sex would be a GOQ only for jobs directly connected with the special care, supervision, or attention given to the people using the institution and not, for example, kitchen staff or clerical workers.[81]

The difficulty with section 7(2)(d) is to understand why it is necessary. Why should sex be a GOQ in jobs done in special establishments where the privacy and decency GOQ in section 7(2)(b) does not apply, when the communal accommodation GOQ of section 7(2)(c) does not apply, and where the personal services GOQ of section 7(2)(e) does not apply? If any of these other bases for a GOQ supply the rationale for section 7(2)(d), then section 7(2)(d) is otiose. If these other factors are not relevant, what is the rationale for section 7(2)(d)? No rationale different from those presented in section 7(2)(b) and section 7(2)(e) was suggested by the Government during the Parliamentary debates on the Bill. The argument that prisoners, or patients, or persons in other institutions need to be dealt with by a person of their own sex (even though this is neither to preserve decency or privacy nor because persons of that sex can most effectively provide personal services) badly smells of the offensive sex stereotyping that the 1975 Act aims to eradicate. Of course, many

---

[79] Above, n. 3. The White Paper, above, n. 1 para. 47(c), originally spoke of sex as a GOQ 'in predominantly single-sex institutions where the employment mainly of members of one sex is legitimately related to the character of the institution (e.g. prison officers)'.

[80] Other examples given by Lord Jacques on behalf of the Government during the Committee Stage of the Bill in the House of Lords were hostels for unmarried mothers or for prisoners on parole: 362 HL 1043 (14 July 1975).

[81] Ibid. 1044.

women do not have the qualifications to serve in a men's prison or in a hostel for male vagrants. But many men, similarly, are unqualified for such jobs. Some women may possess the required attributes; they are entitled to be considered for the vacancies, not rejected because of an assumption that women cannot do the job. The absence of section 7(2)(d) would not entitle a woman to be appointed to a job in a men's prison: rather it would mean she could claim to be considered for a vacancy on her merits.

The general principle of the 1975 Act that employers should not apply sex stereotypes can be (and should be) recognized by courts in deciding whether it is 'reasonable' that a job should be held by a woman, under section 7(2)(d)(iii). It is not enough to satisfy section 7(2)(d) that most women would be unable to perform the job. At the very least, employers should be required to present justifications for sex discrimination similar to those accepted by the US Supreme Court in *Dothard* v. *Rawlinson* where it was held that being male was a BFOQ for the job of prison officer in a male, maximum security prison. The majority of the Court held that

The likelihood that inmates would assault a woman because she was a woman would pose a real threat not only to the victim of the assault but also to the basic control of the penitentiary and protection of its inmates and the other security personnel. The employee's very womanhood would thus directly undermine her capacity to provide the security that is the essence of a correctional counsellor's responsibility.[82]

This does at least present an argument for making sex a GOQ in a particular institution. It is an argument only applicable to cases where the job directly relates to keeping extremely violent people in custody; so it cannot, in any event, justify the much broader scope of section 7(2)(d).[83] Even if one were so to restrict section 7(2)(d), *Dothard* still does not make such a GOQ necessary or desirable. First, the threat of assault in that case was the result of what Justices Marshall and Brennan in their dissenting judgment

[82] Above, n. 11 at 336. See similarly the decision of the Punjab and Haryana High Court in India in *Raghubans* v. *The State* AIR 1972 P & H 117 that it is not contrary to the constitutional guarantee of equality to make women ineligible for the post of warden in a men's gaol because a woman would find it 'awkward and hazardous' to maintain discipline.

[83] S. 7(2)(d) can be contrasted with the analogous provision in s. 31(2)(g) of the Anti-Discrimination Act 1977 of New South Wales: sex is a GOQ where 'the job requires the holder of the job to keep men in custody in a prison or other institution or in part of a prison or other institution'.

described as the unconstitutionally degrading conditions of the prisoners in the gaol. Secondly, the dissenting judges pointed out that there was no evidence that the threats of violence were due to the sex of the officer: violence was endemic in the institution.[84] Thirdly, even if one assumes that female employees would be special targets for attacks because of their sex in this institution or in any other, the task of government is to prevent or punish such incidents and not to make women 'pay the price in lost job opportunities'.[85] At root, section 7(2)(d) and the judgment in *Dothard* are unfortunate examples of sex stereotyping or unnecessary cases of paternalism. No woman is forced to work in a men's prison. Those who wish to do so, and who have the required qualities, should be considered on their merits. When certain jobs are thought to be too dangerous for women, special provision is made by Parliament and section 7(2)(f) makes sex a GOQ for the position. So not even paternalism can justify the existence of section 7(2)(d).[86]

Similar criticisms should be made of the judgment of the Court of Appeal of California in *Long* v. *California State Personnel Board*[87] that being a man was a BFOQ under Title VII of the Civil Rights Act for the post of chaplain at a residential training centre for the rehabilitation of delinquent males aged 18–23. The Court gave two main reasons for its decision. First, the alleged dangers of rape by the delinquents: 'to expect that no sexual assault will be committed by any of up to four hundred men of the average age of nineteen and a half years who are in effect imprisoned while undergoing a rehabilitative process is to expect too much. At best it is foolish to put temptation of this sort into the path of such wards when it can reasonably be avoided'. Secondly, the Court relied on the alleged danger of escape: 'it is indisputable that a male chaplain would generally better be able to prevent an escape (or attempt to escape) or control a quarrel or fight among wards

---

[84] Cf. *Gunther* v. *Iowa State Men's Reformatory* above, n. 67 at 1085–6: because the Iowa male reformatory was not the 'stygian spectre' which faced the Supreme Court in *Dothard*, the US Court of Appeals held that it was a breach of Title VII of the Civil Rights Act to exclude women from jobs as correctional officers.

[85] *Dothard* v. *Rawlinson* above, n. 11 at 345 per Marshall and Brennan JJ dissenting.

[86] There are a number of cases where US courts have considered whether sex is a BFOQ for jobs in male prisons for reasons of decency and privacy. See above, nn. 66–7.

[87] 116 Cal Rptr 562 (1974).

than a woman'. The judgment wrongly accepts unlawful violence by others (or the prospect of it) and stereotypes of women's ability as rationalizations for the denial of equal employment opportunity for women.

In *Secretary of State for Scotland* v. *Henley*[88] similar issues to those raised in *Dothard* were considered. A female assistant governor in the Scottish prison service was refused the opportunity to transfer to a post as assistant governor at Edinburgh prison, a closed training prison for men. The tribunal suggested that if the prison service had maintained a policy of refusing to appoint women to such posts 'there could have been a persuasive argument under section 7(2)(d)'. However, because another woman had been doing the relevant job in the Edinburgh prison for three years and because the prison service had operated an experimental policy of opening up such posts to women elsewhere, section 7(2)(d) could no longer apply. The EAT agreed that as long as the experiment continued it could not be reasonable to deny the job to a woman on the ground of her sex. The conclusion suggests, wrongly, that whether sex is a GOQ is a matter within the discretion of the prison service: if they adopt an experimental policy of allowing women to do the job, sex is no longer a GOQ; if they refuse to allow women to do the job, sex may be a GOQ. Whether sex is a GOQ must depend, rather, on an objective assessment of the facts.

The tribunal in *Henley* also suggested that although the GOQ defence could not be established while the experiment continued,

[t]he position might be different if circumstances changed. For example, if an incident of violence did occur in which a woman assistant governor proved to be more vulnerable to attack or being taken hostage, or if there was some failure in command or control due to her being a woman, then it might be open to the Service to reconsider the whole question of appointing women to posts as hall governors in male institutions . . .

The EAT correctly repudiated this reasoning: the vulnerability or lack of leadership qualities in an individual woman cannot make sex relevant to the ability to do the job without adopting the offensive sex stereotyping which the 1975 Act aims to eradicate.[89]

---

[88] Above, n. 17.

[89] That Parliament intended to remove such antiquated conceptions of the abilities of women in the context of the prison service is supported by reference to s. 18 of the 1975 Act. This provides that the employment provisions of the Act do

The EAT added that 'it may be open to argument that it is not reasonable on other grounds for a woman to hold the job of hall governor in an all male prison . . . [I]f section 7(2)(d) is to have any meaning at all Parliament must have envisaged that there are some jobs in male prisons which should not reasonably be held by women'. The EAT expressed the view that but for the fact that the Secretary of State had introduced the experimental employment of a woman as hall governor in an all male prison, 'it would not have been difficult to establish a genuine occupational qualification under both section 7(2)(b)(ii) and section 7(2)(d)'.

Section 17(2)(c) of the Irish Employment Equality Act 1977 was closely analogous to section 7(2)(d) of the 1975 Act.[90] It is of considerable interest to note that, following notification from the European Commission that this body was contemplating proceedings in the European Court of Justice against Ireland to establish that section 17(2)(c) was incompatible with the EEC Directive on Equal Treatment in employment, the Irish Government repealed section 17(2)(c) with effect from 30 September 1982. This was achieved by the European Communities (Employment Equality) Regulations 1982. They expressly stated that they were made for the purpose of giving effect to Directive 76/207/EEC.

VIII

Jobs potentially within the scope of section 7(2)(e)[91] as providing

not render unlawful any discrimination between male and female prison officers as to height requirements and it provides for the repeal of the words in the Prison Act 1952 that 'if women only are received in a prison the Governor shall be a woman'. S. 18 strongly suggests that, with the exception of the height requirement, the basic principles of anti-discrimination law apply in the prison service. It is another issue why height requirements are specifically exempted. The average man is taller than the average woman, but so what? A standard height requirement for men and women might have a disparate impact on women, but would be lawful if justified by the employers. See above, n. 50 on the requirement that an inmate be searched only by an officer of the same sex as the inmate.

[90] It provided that sex was an occupational qualification 'where an establishment or institution is confined (either wholly or partly) to persons of one sex requiring special care, supervision or treatment and the employment of persons of that sex is related to either the character of the establishment or institution or the type of care, supervision or treatment provided in it'.

[91] Above, n. 3. The White Paper, above, n. 1 para 47(b), originally spoke of sex as a GOQ 'in forms of social and personnel work with members of both sexes or in mixed educational establishments, where it is necessary to maintain a team including members of each sex (e.g. a team of probation officers)'.

individuals with 'personal services promoting their welfare or education, or similar personal services' would appear to be those of probation officer, personnel officer, social or welfare worker, and teacher.[92] The difficulty with section 7(2)(e)[93] is to determine when 'those services can most effectively be provided by a man'. The subsection may seem to imply a recognition of the sex stereotyping which it is a basic principle of the 1975 Act to reject.[94] But in referring to whether the services can most effectively be provided by a man, section 7(2)(e) is not validating sex discrimination where an employer decides that most women do not have the qualities necessary for the job and so refuses to consider women applicants by reference to their individual abilities. Rather, it is concerned with a case where a woman who has the relevant qualifications for the job still would be unable to provide the services as effectively as a man with similar qualifications because the potential recipient of the services will not react as favourably to the woman in the job. For example, the rape victim may react more favourably to a woman (any woman) than to a man (no matter how kind and understanding) investigating the complaint.

[92] See Standing Committee B, Fourth Sitting (1 May 1975), col. 172; 362 HL 1047–51 (14 July 1975, Committee Stage), where Lord Jacques on behalf of the Government gave the further example of a teacher of English to immigrant women who would only attend if taught by a woman; 363 HL 1000 (29 July 1975, Report Stage), where Lord Crowther-Hunt, Minister of State at the Department of Education and Science, said that Oxbridge Colleges could rely on s. 7(2)(e) in jobs which involved counselling or pastoral care of students.

[93] It is similar to s. 5(2)(d) of the Race Relations Act 1976 which makes membership of a particular racial group a GOQ where 'the holder of the job provides persons of that racial group with personal services promoting their welfare, and those services can most effectively be provided by a person of that racial group'. See also s. 21(4)(e) Equal Opportunity Act 1984 (Victoria) which gives a defence where the welfare services provided by the job 'can most effectively be provided by a person of the same sex . . .' See also the analogous s. 17(2)(b) of the Irish Employment Equality Act 1977 which makes sex an occupational qualification 'where the duties of a post involve personal services and it is necessary to have persons of both sexes engaged in such duties'. It is suggested by Michael Beloff above, n. 39 at 101 that s. 7(2)(e) refers to 'individuals' rather than 'persons' to exclude services given to corporations: see *Whitney* v. *Inland Revenue Commissioners* [1926] AC 37, 43.

[94] See *Button* v. *Rockefeller* above, n. 45 where the Supreme Court of New York rejected as 'stereotyped characteristics of the sexes' claims that 'female troopers would be more qualified by virtue of their sex to interview female complainants and witnesses in sex crimes or family complaints . . . While it obviously is true that interviewing and interrogating women in certain situations will often require great sensitivity and perhaps empathy, it cannot be said as a general proposition that these qualities are inherent in women and lacking in men.'

Similarly, immigrant women may be prepared to go to classes to learn English only if taught by a woman.

In other words, section 7(2)(e) recognizes that sex is a GOQ in particular cases of customer preference. There may be cases where a woman holder of the job cannot provide the services as effectively as a man for reasons other than customer preference, but it is difficult to think of examples not already covered by sections 7(2)(f) and (g). It is of interest to note that the equivalent provision to section 7(2)(e) in the Anti-Discrimination Act 1977 of New South Wales expressly limits the GOQ to cases of customer preference.[95]

In *M. Roadburg* v. *Lothian Regional Council*,[96] an industrial tribunal rejected the argument that sex was a GOQ under section 7(2)(e) for employment as a volunteer services officer because most clients were male and some visited the office in a drunken state, resorting to disorderly or threatening behaviour and because the clients better related to a male officer. The tribunal held that it had not been established that the services could most effectively be provided by a man. In *Goddard* v. *Helen Elizabeth Ltd*, another industrial tribunal (in an unreported 1981 decision) rejected a claim that being a woman was a GOQ for the job of assistant cashier because the duties included dealing with the other employees, most of whom were females, and because, it was argued, 'an assistant cashier would have to deal on some occasions with tears, on other occasions with anger at pay being docked and so on'.

Customer preference does not provide a general excuse for sex discrimination. It is no defence for an employer who refuses to employ a woman to drive his lorries to say that his customers will only do business with him if the goods are delivered by a man. It is true that when the employee's sex is 'an essential ingredient of the job' by reason of his or her physiology the 1975 Act recognizes customer preference (for example, in the jobs of model and escort) as excusing sex discrimination under section 7(2)(a). But why should customer preference validate sex discrimination in the

---

[95] S. 31(2)(h) of the New South Wales law provides that sex is a GOQ where 'the holder of the job provides men with personal services relating to their welfare or education, or similar personal services, and they or a substantial number of them might reasonably object to its being carried out by a woman'.

[96] [1976] IRLR 283.

circumstances covered by section 7(2)(e) where no such 'physiological' factors are involved?

In *Diaz* v. *Pan American World Airways Inc,* a US Court of Appeals held that an airline had discriminated contrary to Title VII of the Civil Rights Act by refusing to employ a man as a flight cabin steward. The airline's argument, that customers prefer female stewardesses, since women better cater for their psychological needs, was rejected. The Court stated that:

While we recognize that the public's expectation of finding one sex in a particular role may create some initial difficulty, it would be totally anomalous if we were to allow the preferences and prejudices of the customers to determine whether the sex discrimination was valid. Indeed, it was, to a large extent, these very prejudices the Act was meant to overcome. Thus, we feel that customer preference may be taken into account only when it is based on the company's inability to perform the primary function or service it offers.

In that case, it was held that 'the primary function of an airline is to transport passengers safely from one point to another . . . No one has suggested that having male stewards will so seriously affect the operation of an airline as to jeopardise or even minimise its ability to provide safe transportation from one point to another.' Sex is a BFOQ, the Court added, 'only when the *essence* of the business operation would be undermined by not hiring members of one sex exclusively'.[97]

Section 7(2)(e) has adopted the reasoning of *Diaz.* It has recognized that, in certain cases, the sex of the employee is vital to the ability to provide the service, and that not hiring a woman would undermine the essence of the business. The rape crisis centre and the classes to teach English to immigrant women may be areas of employment which satisfy these strict criteria.[98] Section 7(2)(e) should be interpreted according to these principles. It does

[97] Above, n. 12 at 388–9.

[98] See also the decision of the Commonwealth Court of Pennsylvania in *City of Philadelphia* above, n. 52 at 103. In finding that sex was a BFOQ for the job of supervisor at a youth study centre for resident children aged 7–16, the Court said that one should not 'expect the city to produce cold, empirical facts to show that girls and boys at this age relate better to supervisors of the same sex. It is common sense that a young girl with a sexual or emotional problem will usually approach someone of her own sex . . . seeking comfort and answers . . . A like situation prevails for the boys. To expect a female or a male supervisor to gain the confidence of troubled youths of the opposite sex in order to be able to alleviate

not validate sex discrimination by reason of stereotypes of male and female abilities; nor by reason of mere customer preference. It will only provide a defence where the essence of the services provided would be undermined by the failure to hire only men. If section 7(2)(e) receives a broader interpretation from the courts, it should be amended to specify that it makes sex a GOQ only where the job-holder provides individuals with personal services promoting their welfare or education or similar personal services and where the nature of the services is directly related to the sex of the person providing them.[99]

IX

Section 7(2)(f)[100] recognizes the large number of legal restrictions on the employment of women, for example the prohibition on women working night shifts in certain circumstances. These restrictions are summarized in the 1979 report of the Equal Opportunities Commission *Health and Safety Legislation: Should We Distinguish Between Men and Women?* As this report suggests, there are very few protective measures which should be confined specifically to women. In most cases the protective measures should either be abolished or made applicable to men and women, together with the enactment of measures to protect existing employees from being compelled to work night-shifts or otherwise to change their existing practices. There is a strong case for arguing, as did the Supreme Court of California in 1971, that 'protective' laws, if 'applied to racial or ethnic minorities would readily be recognized as invidious and impermissible. The pedestal upon which women have been placed has all too often, upon closer inspection, been revealed as a cage.'[101]

Sex is not a BFOQ under Title VII of the US Civil Rights Act 1964 merely by reason of employer compliance with State

emotional and sexual problems is to expect the impossible. This is clearly a situation in which the sexual characteristics of the employee are crucial to the successful performance of the job.'

[99] This is the substance of a Mar. 1983 recommendation of the Equal Opportunities Commission for Northern Ireland for a change in the analogous Article 10(2)(e) of the Sex Discrimination (Northern Ireland) Order 1976.

[100] Above, n. 3.

[101] *Sail'er Inn* v. *Kirby* 485 P 2d 529, 541 (1971).

protective legislation.[102] Nor is a GOQ provision required in UK law for this purpose. Section 51 of the 1975 Act already provides a defence when an act of sex discrimination is 'necessary . . . in order to comply with a requirement' of another statute or of an instrument made or approved by or under another statute.

Section 7(2)(f) only covers cases where the job 'needs' to be held by a man because of legal restrictions on the employment of women. It is not sufficient that the job could, for this reason, more effectively be held by a man. What if the employer could lawfully employ women if it obtained an exemption order under the Factories Act 1961? Assuming that no such order has been obtained, but that one could be obtained, does the job then 'need' to be held by a man? There are conflicting authorities.[103] As a matter of principle, it is difficult to see why sex should be a GOQ where an exemption order is easily obtainable. The more difficult it is to obtain an exemption order, speedily or at all, the stronger the case for saying that the job 'needs' to be held by a man and therefore section 7(2)(f) applies.[104]

It is very doubtful whether section 7(2)(f) is compatible with the Equal Treatment Directive. Article 2(3) of that Directive states that it is 'without prejudice to provisions concerning the protection of women, particularly as regards pregnancy and maternity'. But

---

[102] *Rosenfeld* above, n. 11 at 1226–7 and 'Developments in the Law' above, n. 11 at 1186–95. Indeed, Title VII has led to the virtual eradication of special protective legislation concerning the employment of women. The only question in the US is whether the protective laws should be abolished or extended to apply to men as well as to women: see Schlei and Grossman *Employment Discrimination Law* (2nd edn. Bureau of National Affairs, Washington, DC, 1983), 360–6. See ch. 6 n. 66 for US cases concerning the circumstances in which sex discrimination may be justifiable because of potential danger to the foetus.

[103] See *United Biscuits Ltd* v. *Young* [1978] IRLR 15 where the EAT implied, though the point was not directly considered, that the employer need not apply for an exemption. In *E. A. White* v. *British Sugar Corporation Ltd* [1977] IRLR 121 the industrial tribunal suggested that the employer would have been obliged to apply for an exemption order but for the fact that the job was temporary and the order could not have been obtained speedily. In *Green* v. *E. Cookson & Son Ltd Exhibition Bakery* (1982, unreported), the industrial tribunal held that the employer could not rely on s. 7(2)(f) because it had failed to apply for an exemption order which would undoubtedly have been granted.

[104] But see the EAT's interpretation of the job 'needs' under s. 7(2)(b) in *Sisley* above, n. 69. See also *Page* v. *Freight Hire (Tank Haulage) Ltd* [1981] ICR 299: in deciding whether it was 'necessary' for the employer to discriminate to comply with a requirement of another statute (in order to establish a defence under s. 51 of the 1975 Act), the employer must be allowed to carry out the only reasonably practicable way of complying with health and safety legislation (EAT).

'protection' must be based upon physical distinctions between men and women, not on stereotyped assumptions about ability or attitudes (for example, women's ability or willingness to do night-work). Article 3(2)(c) of the Directive explains that 'those laws, regulations and administrative provisions contrary to the principle of equal treatment when the concern for protection which originally inspired them is no longer well founded shall be revised . . .'.

X

Section 7(2)(g)[105] was added to the Sex Discrimination Bill during the House of Commons Standing Committee Stage. The Under-Secretary of State for Employment, John Fraser, said it was necessary 'to deal with what one might call the Middle East export salesman problem'.[106]

The provision against sex discrimination in employment contained in section 6 of the 1975 Act only covers employment where the work is done or to be done wholly or partly within Great Britain.[107] So the section 7(2)(g) exception is relevant only to jobs where incidental or partial or infrequent duties are carried out abroad. To take advantage of section 7(2)(g), an employer would have to show that it is the laws or the customs of a foreign country, and not merely the prejudices or inclinations of individuals or groups within that foreign country, which result in the woman being unable to perform the job duties effectively or at all. It was explained by Lord Jacques on behalf of the Government during the Parliamentary debates that the words 'or could not effectively' were required to cover a case where, for example, a job involved duties in Saudi Arabia, but the local staff or contractors would not obey the instructions of a woman because of her sex.[108]

Two objections were raised to section 7(2)(g) during those Parliamentary debates. Neither of them received a satisfactory answer. First, which countries have laws or customs which prevent the performance (or effective performance) of which jobs by

[105] Above, n. 3.
[106] Standing Committee B, Fourth Sitting (1 May 1975) col. 173. Similar provisions are contained in s. 17(2)(f) of the Irish Employment Equality Act 1977 and in s. 15(9) of the New Zealand Human Rights Commission Act 1977.
[107] See s. 10 of the 1975 Act. See also ch. 3 n. 2.
[108] 363 HL 984 (29 July 1975, Report Stage).

women (or men)? It is difficult to assess the propriety of an exception to the general anti-discrimination principle unless one knows precisely what one is validating. Lord Jacques would say only that the exception in section 7(2)(g) was added 'after considering representations made by the CBI and others that the Bill should allow employers to discriminate in respect of jobs involving work in overseas countries, mainly in the Middle East, where women are not acceptable in business life'. He argued that if there are, indeed, no jobs where foreign laws or customs require male employees, there is no cause for alarm or for opposition to the existence of the GOQ in section 7(2)(g).[109] The Home Office Guide to the 1975 Act[110] gave an example of a case potentially within section 7(2)(g): 'a job might involve driving a car, but it is to be performed in a country where women are forbidden to drive'. The Guide did not say in which countries (if any) this is the case. In *O'Connor* v. *Contiki Travel Ltd* (an unreported decision in 1976), an industrial tribunal held that being male was not a GOQ under section 7(2)(g) for driving a coach tour to Turkey: 'No evidence was tendered to show that female drivers are unacceptable in the parts of Turkey to which the applicant would have gone.' (However, in that case it was held that the work was done wholly outside Great Britain, and so there was, in any event, no unlawful discrimination contrary to section 6 of the 1975 Act.)

The second objection to the existence of section 7(2)(g) was that we should not 'enshrine in our legislation a concession to the prejudices of other countries . . .'.[111] It was emphasized by those unhappy about section 7(2)(g) that the 1975 Act would be a model for amended legislation prohibiting race discrimination: surely we would not allow employers to discriminate against blacks or Jews in filling jobs whose partial duties were performed in Great Britain, on the ground that some duties were to be performed in a less enlightened country where such individuals would, by reason of that country's laws or customs, be unable to perform the duties adequately or at all.[112] Indeed, the Race Relations Act 1976 does not make membership of a particular racial group a GOQ in

---

[109] 362 HL 1051–61 (14 July 1975, Committee Stage).
[110] Above, n. 16 at para. 3.12.
[111] Roderick MacFarquhar, Standing Committee B, Fourth Sitting (1 May 1975), col. 175.
[112] Ibid. col. 175–7.

circumstances similar to those defined in section 7(2)(g). In *American Jewish Congress* v. *Carter*,[113] Aramco, an oil company with interests in Saudi Arabia, were accused of acting contrary to the New York State Law against Discrimination by refusing to employ Jews for work which might involve travel to Saudi Arabia. They discriminated in this way because the King of Saudi Arabia not only prohibited the employment of Jews there but also 'strenuously objects to the employment of Jews in any part of Aramco's operation'. The judge in the Supreme Court of New York rejected the claim that being a non-Jew was a BFOQ for the job. He declared that:

This court does not pretend to assert that Saudi Arabia may not do as it pleases with regard to whom it will employ within the borders of Saudi Arabia . . . What this court does say is that Aramco cannot defy the declared public policy of New York State and violate its statute within New York State, no matter what the King of Saudi Arabia says. New York State is not a province of Saudi Arabia, nor is the constitution and statute of New York State to be cast aside to protect the oil profits of Aramco.

He said that if Aramco cannot employ Jews because of the orders of the King, 'the answer of New York State is simply—Go elsewhere to serve your Arab master—but not in New York State'.

Sex discrimination should not be permitted where race discrimination is prohibited. That section 7(2)(g) should be amended by the Home Secretary exercising his powers under section 80(1) of the 1975 Act is emphasized by reference to a decision of a US Court of Appeals under Title VII of the Civil Rights Act. In *Fernandez* v. *Wynn Oil Co*, a woman complained that a company had, on the ground of her sex, refused to promote her to be Director of International Operations. The Court accepted the company's evidence that other reasons explained the lack of promotion. The claim was therefore dismissed. However, the Court also ruled on the company's alternative defence: if there was sex discrimination, the company said, it was lawful as sex was a BFOQ for the job because the Latin American clients of the company would react negatively to a woman in this post. In addition to finding that there was no factual basis for such a

---

[113] 190 NYS 2d 218 (1959), affirmed on different grounds 199 NYS 2d 157 (1960) (Supreme Court of New York, Appellate Division) and 213 NYS 2d 60 (1961) (Court of Appeals of New York).

defence, the Court ruled that even if the facts were as alleged by the company, sex would not be a BFOQ: 'Though the United States cannot impose standards of non-discriminatory conduct on other nations through its legal system, the [company's argument] would allow other nations to dictate discrimination in this country. No foreign nation can compel the non-enforcement of Title VII here.'[114] We should adopt a similar approach under the 1975 Act. If employers cannot send women to perform particular tasks in certain nations, there is nothing to stop the employers using local agents or recruiting the necessary staff in those countries. But there is no reason why we should permit sex discrimination to occur when the recruitment takes place in our country and when the work is partly done in Great Britain. At the very least, the 1975 Act needs amendment so that only jobs involving duties outside the EEC can fall within section 7(2)(g). If all the duties are to be performed within the EEC the job will be covered by the EEC Directive and so there is no reason to make sex a GOQ because of a discriminatory law or custom in that EEC country. The employer should have to bring itself within one of the other cases of a GOQ specified in section 7(2) if it wishes to excuse its sex discrimination.

XI

Section 7(2)(h)[115] covers jobs, such as those in a public house, where an employer requires a husband and wife team. The exemption does not apply where there is a job for one person (male or female) and the employer requires the employee to live in the premises with his or her spouse: there must be two jobs, one for each spouse. Nor does the exemption apply if the jobs are to be held by an unmarried (heterosexual or homosexual) couple. However, the employer will be in breach of section 3 of the 1975 Act if it specifies that the couple must be unmarried. Section

[114] 653 F 2d 1273 (1981). Cf. 'Developments in the Law' above, n. 11 at 1186: 'Sex may also be a BFOQ for positions whose occupants face cultural bias outside the effective reach of the statute. For example, men only could be hired for a position that called primarily for business dealings with a foreign culture in which women are totally unacceptable in a business context'. On *Fernandez* see Debra A. Stegura 'The Biases of Customers in a Host Country as a BFOQ' 57 *Southern California Law Review* 335 (1984).

[115] Above, n. 3. S. 31(2)(i) of the Anti-Discrimination Act 1977 of New South Wales contains an identical provision and s. 15(5) of the New Zealand Human Rights Commission Act 1977 contains a similar provision.

7(2)(h) is the only case of a GOQ to which section 7(3) on some of the duties and section 7(4) on the reallocation of duties do not apply.

The rationale of section 7(2)(h) is difficult to comprehend. If by section 7(2)(h) Parliament merely wished to allow employers to continue to require a married couple to perform the two jobs, then the subsection is otiose. A single person applying for one of the jobs, or an unmarried couple applying for the jobs, would have no legal complaint. There would be no sex discrimination, and section 3 prohibits discrimination on the ground of marital status only when it is against married persons. Presumably, therefore, Parliament intended to allow an employer, taking on a married couple for two jobs, to specify which job should be done by which spouse. Why is it unlawful for an employer to require that, in its offices, its caretaker must be male or to require that its cleaner must be female, but lawful for the employer to require a married couple to act as caretaker and cleaner and to specify that the husband must be the caretaker and the wife must be the cleaner? One hopes that courts and tribunals would interpret section 7(2)(h) to prevent employers abusing this exemption by requiring a married couple as a pretext for sex discrimination.

Section 7(2)(h) serves no valid purpose. It is potentially open to abuse. The Home Secretary should exercise the powers under section 80(1) of the 1975 Act to repeal this exception to the principle of no sex discrimination in employment.

XII

Section 7 of the Sex Discrimination Act 1975 states the existence and the scope of the GOQ exception to the principle of no sex discrimination in employment. It 'evidences a judgment that certain functional differences, both physically and culturally defined, exist between the sexes, and that employers can legitimately accommodate such differences'[116] in certain employment decisions. Parliament's efforts were not completely successful in separating the circumstances in which a person's sex legitimately goes to the essence of the job from cases of sex stereotyping or mere prejudice or customer preference. Section 7 covers social

[116] 'Developments in the Law' above, n. 11 at 1176 on Title VII of the US Civil Rights Act 1964 and the BFOQ exception.

and functional, as well as physical, differences between men and women. These social and functional differences are based on gender, not sex, being the consequence of the way in which society reacts to the physical differences between men and women. Hence the scope of the GOQ defence is intimately connected with social standards in a context where one would hope that the 1975 Act has already had an impact in limiting the circumstances in which society sees sex differences as going to the essence of a job.

The late Sir Ronald Bell MP vigorously opposed the 1975 Bill in Parliament. However, he welcomed the clause which became section 7. He described it as 'a good, old clause about the authentic male characteristics. It is the lavatory clause—and all that. Nothing would help the Bill to make sense, but if we did not have Clause 7 the Bill would be such manifest nonsense that it would have been laughed out on Second Reading.'[117] Section 7 indeed more often furthers the objectives of those who opposed the 1975 Act than the objectives of those who supported the legislation. Because section 7 was drafted too widely and because standards have already changed since 1975, the time is ripe for the Home Secretary to exercise the powers under section 80(1) of the 1975 Act to recommend amendments to section 7 to reduce the circumstances in which sex is recognized as a GOQ. If the Home Secretary does not take such action, there is a strong prospect that section 7 will, in large part, be held by the European Court of Justice to contravene the guarantee of equal treatment of the sexes in employment stated in Directive 76/207/EEC.

[117] 893 HC 1504–5 (18 June 1975, Report Stage).

10

THE EQUAL OPPORTUNITIES
COMMISSION AND CLASS ACTIONS

I

The Sex Discrimination Act 1975 introduced a new model of enforcement of anti-discrimination law in the United Kingdom. Under the Race Relations Act 1965, individual victims could not bring proceedings in court. This function was conferred on the Attorney-General. The Race Relations Act 1968 transferred the function to the Race Relations Board but still denied individual victims access to the courts. The 1975 Act adopted what the Government described as 'a new and radical approach, combining the right of individual access to legal remedies with the positive and strategic functions of a powerful Equal Opportunities Commission, responsible for enforcing the law in the public interest on behalf of the community as a whole'.[1] This chapter examines the more prosaic reality of an EOC given inadequate powers to enforce the law.

II

The EOC are given three statutory duties:[2] to work towards the elimination of discrimination;[3] to promote equality of opportunity between men and women generally;[4] and to keep under review the working of the 1975 Act and the Equal Pay Act 1970 and, when the EOC are so required by the Secretary of State or otherwise

---

[1] *Equality for Women* (Cmnd. 5724: 1974), para. 81.

[2] S. 53(1) Sex Discrimination Act 1975.

[3] This means the elimination of sex discrimination made unlawful by the 1975 Act and by the Equal Pay Act 1970: see *Home Office* v. *CRE* [1982] QB 385, 395–6 on the analogous provision in the Race Relations Act 1976.

[4] Again this probably means in circumstances where sex discrimination would be unlawful: cf. *Home Office* v. *CRE* ibid. at 396–7.

think it necessary, to draw up and submit to the Secretary of State proposals for amending those Acts.[5]

In pursuance of these duties, the EOC are given various statutory powers. The first main power of the EOC is to give assistance, including advice and arranging for legal representation, to a complainant in relation to proceedings under the 1975 or 1970 Acts if the case raises a question of principle or it is unreasonable to expect the complainant to deal with the case unaided, for example because of the complexity of the matter.[6] Secondly, the EOC, but not individual victims, may bring proceedings in respect of unlawful discriminatory advertisements, instructions to discriminate, or pressure to discriminate.[7] Thirdly, the EOC may bring proceedings in an industrial tribunal alleging that a person has done an act contrary to the employment provisions of the 1975 Act or contrary to the 1970 Act.[8] There are three main limitations on the utility of these proceedings: such a case may only be brought 'with a view to making an application' for persistent or continuing sex discrimination;[9] the industrial tribunal cannot award compensation if it finds the application to be well founded; such an application can only be made in employment cases, not in education, goods, facilities, services, or premises cases.

The fourth power possessed by the EOC is to bring proceedings for persistent or continuing discrimination against a person who

---

[5] For a critical examination of the manner in which the EOC have performed their duties see Anna Coote and Beatrix Campbell, *Sweet Freedom: The Struggle for Women's Liberation* (1982), 123–9.

[6] S. 75 of the 1975 Act. In *Walsall MBC* v. *Sidhu* [1980] ICR 519, the EAT held that a successful complainant in a race discrimination case supported by the CRE, under its equivalent of the s. 75 powers, could not recover costs from the discriminator since the costs had been incurred by the CRE which was not a party to the claim. The CRE had there given assistance to the complainant 'on the terms that she would herself not incur any expenses': at 522. S. 75(3) of the 1975 Act, like s. 66(5) of the Race Relations Act 1976, shows that assistance by the EOC is not intended to preclude the obtaining of an order for costs against a discriminator which may then be recovered by the Commission. It is well established that a party is entitled to recover costs even though a third party—here the EOC—has indemnified him or her against costs, so long as there is no express agreement between the party and their solicitor that they will never be held liable to pay any part of the costs: see *Davies* v. *Taylor (no. 2)* [1974] AC 225; *R.* v. *Miller and Glennie* [1983] 1 WLR 1056.

[7] S. 72 of the 1975 Act gives the EOC exclusive power to bring such proceedings for acts contrary to ss. 38, 39, and 40. Compensation cannot be awarded in such proceedings: s. 72(2).

[8] S. 73(1) of the 1975 Act.   [9] See below, n. 10.

has already been found to have discriminated unlawfully, when it appears that, unless restrained, he or she is likely to commit another such act.[10] The fifth main power of the EOC is to issue Codes of Practice.[11] This power extends only to the field of employment. A draft Code has been issued. Sixth, the EOC may undertake or assist research or educational activities which appear necessary or expedient for the furtherance of the objectives of the EOC.[12]

Seventh, the EOC may conduct formal investigations, in the course of which they may issue a non-discrimination notice which may be enforced in persistent discrimination proceedings.[13] One of the matters which may lead to the issue of a non-discrimination notice is the existence of a discriminatory practice.[14]

The paucity of powers for the EOC to bring legal proceedings against alleged discriminators in their own name in the courts was intended to be balanced by the formal investigation and non-discrimination notice powers of the Commission. Although the EOC could not normally sue alleged discriminators, they were given powers to conduct their own investigations as a statutory agency with special expertise in this context. Fears were expressed about the width of these investigatory powers. During the Second Reading Debate on the Sex Discrimination Bill 1975, Ian Gilmour, for the Conservative Opposition, said he wanted carefully 'to examine all the powers of the Equal Opportunities Commission— a body which seems to be policewoman, prosecutor, judge, jury and even probation and after-care officer for those caught in this peculiar brand of sexual delinquency'.[15] In *Science Research Council* v. *Nassé*, Lord Denning in the Court of Appeal

---

[10] Under s. 71 or s. 72(4) of the 1975 Act. Although section 73(1) proceedings, above n. 8, can be taken 'with a view to making an application under section 71(1) . . .', the Parliamentary draftsman has, in error, failed to refer in s. 71(1) to a finding under s. 73(1) proceedings as a basis for persistent discrimination proceedings.

[11] S. 56A of the 1975 Act. The Code is not legally binding on employers, but an industrial tribunal may take it into account in determining any question to which it is relevant: s. 56A(10). The CRE has issued a Code of Practice pursuant to its analogous power under the Race Relations Act 1976. It was brought into force on 1 Apr. 1984 by the Race Relations Code of Practice Order, 1983 SI no. 1081.

[12] S. 54 of the 1975 Act.   [13] Ss. 57–61 and 67–71 of the 1975 Act.

[14] See ch. 3 at n. 98 on the concept of a discriminatory practice under s. 37 of the 1975 Act. Proceedings in respect of such a practice may only be brought by the EOC in accordance with ss. 67–71 of the 1975 Act.

[15] 889 HC 534 (26 Mar. 1975).

described the EOC as possessing 'inquisitorial powers of a kind never before known to the law . . . immense powers . . . [such that] [y]ou might think that we were back in the days of the Inquisition'.[16]

In reality, the formal investigation and non-discrimination notice powers have proved to be ineffective. The complexity of the legislation governing these powers ensures that formal investigations tend to be lengthy and costly battles full of legal minefields. They are often unsuitable methods for analysing and resolving issues of sex discrimination. Consequently, few formal investigations are started. Even less are completed.

III

In carrying out their duties, the EOC may (and, if required by the Secretary of State, must) conduct a formal investigation ('FI'). The EOC may nominate one or more Commissioners (with or without one or more additional Commissioners) to conduct an FI on behalf of the Commission and may delegate to those nominated people any of the EOC's functions in relation to the FI.[17]

Because unlawful discrimination 'may take a whole variety of subtle forms that are not easy to uncover . . . not the least important of the powers exercisable by the Commission is the power to conduct formal investigations . . .'.[18] There are three types of FI: one requested by the Secretary of State; a formal investigation of a general character; and a formal investigation into the conduct of a person named in terms of reference whom the EOC believe may have done or may be doing unlawful discriminatory acts contrary to the 1975 or 1970 statutes.

The EOC must draw up terms of reference for a general investigation or a named person investigation. If the Commission are required by the Secretary of State to conduct the FI, the terms of reference are drawn up by the Secretary of State after consulting the Commission.[19] The terms of reference of an FI may be revised

---

[16] [1978] ICR 1124, 1136, 1138–9. The Court of Appeal decision in *Nassé* was upheld by the House of Lords on other grounds [1980] AC 1028.

[17] S. 57 of the 1975 Act.

[18] *R. v. CRE ex parte Hillingdon LBC* [1982] AC 779, 784 per Lord Diplock for the House of Lords on the similar provisions of the Race Relations Act 1976 giving the CRE power to commence a formal investigation.

[19] S. 58(2) of the 1975 Act.

at a later stage.[20] For an investigation into the activities of named persons, 'the Commission should have formed the belief, and should so state in the terms of reference, that the named persons may have done or may be doing discriminatory acts made unlawful by the Act of a kind specified in the terms of reference'.[21] At the start of the FI, the EOC must have 'at any rate *some* grounds for so suspecting, albeit that the grounds upon which any such suspicion was based might, at that stage, be no more than tenuous because they had not yet been tested'.[22] Furthermore, the terms of reference must make '[r]eference to each kind of unlawful acts as to which the [EOC] propose to investigate whether or not the named person has done them . . .'.[23] Because of the wide scope of the 1975 Act, 'fairness requires that the statement in the terms of reference as to the kind of acts which the Commission believe the persons named may have done or may be doing should not be expressed in any wider language than is justified by the genuine extent of the Commission's belief'.[24] It is the terms of reference that determine the scope of an FI, not the content of any press notice or the intentions of the EOC.[25] By contrast with such an 'accusatory' FI into the conduct of named persons, a general FI is 'exploratory', for example into the practices of particular industries.[26] The EOC must give general notice of the holding of a general investigation. Where the FI is confined to the activities of named persons, the EOC must give notice to such persons before starting such an FI or before amending the terms of reference of an FI which has already started.[27]

Section 58(3A) of the 1975 Act describes the notice to be given

---

[20] S. 58(4) of the 1975 Act. See *CRE* v. *Prestige Group PLC* [1984] ICR 473, 482 per Lord Diplock for the House of Lords on the analogous provision of the Race Relations Act 1976: 'This enables them to enlarge the terms of reference if, after embarking on the formal investigation, further information reaches them, whether as a result of the formal investigation or not, which in their opinion makes such enlargement desirable in order to enable them to perform their statutory duties effectively.'

[21] *Hillingdon* above, n. 18 at 786.

[22] *Prestige* above, n. 20 at 481.   [23] Ibid. at 485.

[24] *Hillingdon* above, n. 18 at 786.   [25] Ibid. at 792.

[26] *Prestige* above, n. 20 at 483. The House of Lords there decided that a named person investigation can only be accusatory.

[27] S. 58(3) and (4). In *Prestige* above, n. 20 at 486–7, the House of Lords held that where the Commission form the belief during an investigation that unlawful acts of discrimination have been committed, notice must then be given to that person.

by the EOC when they are minded to conduct an FI into a named person's suspected unlawful activities (or before they are minded to amend the terms of reference of such an FI once it has started). When the EOC are contemplating such a course, 'there are not yet in existence "terms of reference" in the strict sense of that term'.[28] The EOC must inform the person of the belief that it has done unlawful acts and of the proposal to investigate the acts. The EOC must offer the named person the opportunity of making oral and written representations. If the named person wishes to make oral representations, it may be represented by a barrister or a solicitor (or by some other suitable person).

The 1975 Act 'lays down no detailed rules for the conduct of the preliminary inquiry . . . It is not an occasion for adducing evidence to the Commission . . .'.[29] The purpose of the preliminary inquiry is, rather, to give to any named person against whom the EOC are minded to commence an accusatory investigation

notice of what are the unlawful acts which are to form the subject of a formal investigation as to whether or not he has done them, and to give to him the opportunity to make representations to the [EOC] with a view to persuading them either not to embark upon the proposed named-person investigation at all, or before issuing definitive terms of reference (which at the stage of the preliminary inquiry will be in draft form only), to amend them so as to exclude from the matters proposed to be investigated questions whether or not the employer [or other person being investigated] has done particular kinds of unlawful acts which he denies that he has ever committed.[30]

The right of a person to be heard in support of an objection to a proposal to embark on an FI in respect of its activities 'cannot be exercised effectively unless that person is informed with reasonable specificity what are the kinds of acts to which the proposed investigation is to be directed and confined. The Commission cannot "throw the book at him" . . .'.[31]

To entitle the EOC to embark upon an FI, having heard and considered the representations (if any) of the named person,

it is enough that there should be material before the Commission

---

[28] *Prestige* above, n. 20 at 485.   [29] *Hillingdon* above, n. 18 at 787.

[30] *Prestige* above, n. 20 at 485. See similarly *Hillingdon* above n. 18 at 786: the requirement at this preliminary stage is to inform the named person of 'any act which the Commission propose to investigate' and it covers 'every such act'.

[31] *Hillingdon* above, n. 18 at 787–8.

sufficient to raise in the minds of reasonable men, possessed of the experience of covert [sex] discrimination that has been acquired by the Commission, a suspicion that there may have been acts by the person named of [sex] discrimination of the kind which it is proposed to investigate.

The Commission, at the stage of embarking upon an FI, do not need to show reason to believe that it is more likely than not that there may have been an act of unlawful discrimination.[32] Nor do the terms of reference need to be confined to the same acts as the material on which the EOC decide to commence an FI. If the Commission draw the inference from the material before them that there is a suspicion that the named person may be following a more general policy of sex discrimination, then 'the Commission are entitled to draw up terms of reference wide enough to enable them to ascertain whether such inference is justified or not'.[33]

After the preliminary inquiry, and the EOC's decision to proceed on stated terms of reference, the FI begins. The 1975 Act gives very little guidance on the procedure to be followed. In a named person investigation, or if the Secretary of State gives his authorization, the EOC have power to obtain information from any person, whether by disclosure of documents or by written or oral communication.[34] It is peculiar that although a named person has an express right to an oral hearing before the EOC commence an FI, such a person has no such express right once the FI has started and before the EOC reach their conclusions. Indeed, it is unclear what purpose is served by a hearing prior to the commencement of an FI, given the narrow issues which need to be determined by the Commission at that early stage. Such a hearing can only cause unnecessary delay in most cases. Parliament had, in fact, intended to give a right to a hearing once the FI had started. However, it appears that due to defective drafting in the Race Relations Act 1976—Schedule 4 of which amended the Sex Discrimination Act provisions on FIs—Parliament erroneously enacted a right to a hearing at the preliminary stage in both sex discrimination and race discrimination formal investigations.[35]

---

[32] Ibid. at 791.   [33] Ibid.

[34] S. 59 of the 1975 Act. S. 61 imposes restrictions on the disclosure of information given to the EOC by any person in connection with an FI.

[35] See *R.* v. *CRE ex parte Hillingdon LBC* [1982] QB 276, 285–6 per Lord Denning in the Court of Appeal. Griffiths LJ concluded at 296 that it is implicit in

Undoubtedly the EOC have a duty to comply with the rules of natural justice. The Commission must act fairly in all the circumstances.[36] So the substance of all allegations must be put to the named person, who must have an opportunity to respond. However, this does not connote 'any right . . . to be able to cross-examine witnesses whom the Commission have seen and from whom they have taken statements'.[37] The EOC are not bound by the technical rules of evidence. They must base their decision upon material which is of probative value. The weight of that material is a matter for the EOC, not for the courts, provided, of course, that the Commission do not act in bad faith or in an arbitrary manner.[38] The EOC (or the investigating Commissioners to whom functions have been delegated) may rely upon the staff of the Commission to collect information. But it must be the EOC (or the investigating Commissioners) who make the relevant decisions on the information obtained.[39]

The EOC prepare a report of their findings in the FI. The report is published, or made available for inspection by the public. In the light of the findings made in an FI, the EOC may make recommendations to any persons for changes in their policies or procedures or as to other matters with a view to promoting equality of opportunity between men and women. The Commission may also make recommendations to the Secretary of State, for example as to changes in the law, as a result of the findings in an FI.[40]

If, in the course of an FI, the EOC become satisfied that a person is committing, or has committed, an unlawful discriminatory act contrary to the 1975 Act or contrary to the Equal Pay Act 1970,

---

the legislation that a named person has a right to make oral representations during the course of an FI.

[36] See R. v. *CRE ex parte Cottrell and Rothon* [1980] 1 WLR 1580, 1586 (Divisional Court on the Race Relations Act 1976); and see *Hillingdon* above, n. 35 per Lord Denning at 286.

[37] *Cottrell* ibid. at 1587. Similarly *CRE* v. *Amari Plastics Ltd* [1982] ICR 304, 312 per Lord Denning in the Court of Appeal on the powers and duties of the CRE in an FI carried out under the analogous provisions of the Race Relations Act 1976.

[38] *Cottrell* above, n. 36 at 1588.

[39] Ibid. See also R. v. *Race Relations Board ex parte Selvarajan* [1975] 1 WLR 1686, 1694 (Lord Denning) and 1698 (Lawton LJ) on the exercise of functions under the Race Relations Act 1968 (Court of Appeal).

[40] S. 60 of the 1975 Act.

the EOC may serve on that person a non-discrimination notice.[41] This must be in the prescribed form.[42] The non-discrimination notice will require the person not to commit any such unlawful acts. Where this requires changes in that person's practices or other arrangements the notice may require that person to inform the EOC of changes introduced and to notify other persons of these changes. The notice may also require the person on whom it is served to give the EOC information to enable them to check that the notice has been complied with.

Before serving a non-discrimination notice, the EOC must first give the person to be named in it notice that the EOC are minded to issue the notice, specifying the grounds and, secondly, must give that person an opportunity of making oral and written representations.[43] If, after considering any such representations, the EOC decide to issue such a non-discrimination notice, the person on whom it is served has six weeks in which to appeal against any requirement of the notice. If the requirement in the notice relates to unlawful acts within the jurisdiction of an industrial tribunal (that is in employment matters), the appeal is to the industrial tribunal. Requirements relating to unlawful acts in the contexts of education, goods, facilities, services, and premises may be challenged in the county court (or, in Scotland, the sheriff court). Where the tribunal or court hearing such an appeal against a requirement of a non-discrimination notice considers the requirement 'to be unreasonable because it is based on an incorrect finding of fact or for any other reason', the tribunal or court will quash the requirement. It may then direct that the non-discrimination notice shall be treated as containing a different requirement.[44]

The nature of such an appeal against the requirements of a non-discrimination notice was considered by the Court of Appeal in the Race Relations Act 1976 case of *CRE* v. *Amari Plastics Ltd*. As Griffiths LJ noted,

before a non-discrimination notice is served, the Commission have carried out a searching inquisitorial inquiry to satisfy themselves of the truth of the facts upon which the notice is based and have given at least two and

[41] S. 67 of the 1975 Act. The Commission does not have this power in certain education cases which can only be referred to the Secretary of State: s. 67(6).

[42] The Sex Discrimination (Formal Investigations) (Amendment) Regulations 1977 SI no. 843.

[43] S. 67(5) of the 1975 Act.   [44] S. 68 of the 1975 Act.

probably three opportunities to the person to put his case, either orally or in writing . . . This is necessarily an expensive and a time-consuming process.[45]

Therefore, it was argued before the Court of Appeal, the appeal against the requirements of the non-discrimination notice cannot reopen the findings of fact upon which the Commission based their conclusions in the FI. Surely, it was argued, Parliament has given the Commission the task of fact-finding for the purpose of a non-discrimination notice (subject only to the safeguard that judicial review will lie if the Commission do not act fairly or reasonably). Griffiths LJ said that but for the plain wording of the statute he

should be most sympathetic to the Commission's argument. If Parliament empowers a body to carry out a formal investigation and hedges the procedure with safeguards to ensure that the person investigated shall have every opportunity to state his case and then requires that body to publish its findings, one might be forgiven for thinking that Parliament intended that that would be the end of the matter.

However, he said, it is 'clear from the language of this statute that such is not the case'.[46]

A person who is served with a non-discrimination notice may appeal against all relevant findings of fact by the EOC. Such questions of fact then need to be decided anew by the tribunal or court hearing the appeal. The procedure is divided into two stages. First, the EOC should state the facts upon which they relied as the basis of the requirement in the non-discrimination notice. Secondly, the person served with the notice should say which of the findings of fact they dispute. These exchanges would be in the nature of written pleadings.[47] At the hearing the burden will be on the person served with the notice to show that the true facts are different from those set out by the Commission so as to render unreasonable the requirements in the non-discrimination notice.[48]

The nature of the appeal against a non-discrimination notice

---

[45] Above, n. 37 at 314.   [46] Ibid. at 315.

[47] Ibid. at 312–13 per Lord Denning and at 317 per Griffiths LJ. Sir Sebag Shaw, at 317, agreed with both judgments.

[48] *CRE* v. *Amari Plastics Ltd* [1981] ICR 767, 776 (EAT) approved by the Court of Appeal: [1982] ICR 304, 312 per Lord Denning and at 317 per Griffiths LJ. The High Court can grant judicial review of a non-discrimination notice where there is no dispute on the relevant facts: *R.* v. *CRE ex parte Westminster City Council* [1984] ICR 770, 774 (Divisional Court).

poses a problem for the EOC with regard to the report of the FI which it is obliged to publish or make available for inspection by the public. The EOC will be reluctant to publish (or make available for inspection) a report with findings adverse to a person when the factual basis for those findings is being assessed in a tribunal or court hearing all the evidence. In these circumstances, the EOC do not act unlawfully in delaying publication of the report.[49] But to hold up the publication of the report until after the appeal is decided will mean that 'the whole affair is likely to be years old and stale and to have ceased to be of any interest to anyone'.[50]

The EOC are required to maintain a register of non-discrimination notices.[51] A non-discrimination notice 'does not of itself impose any punishment for past unlawful discrimination, but it does provide the foundation to prevent further unlawful acts'.[52] Within five years of a non-discrimination notice served on a person becoming final[53] the EOC may, if it appears that such a person is likely to commit further unlawful acts contrary to the 1975 or 1970 statutes, apply to a county court (or in Scotland a sheriff court) for an injunction to restrain that person from acting in that manner.[54] Such an order must be carefully worded so as to tell the person concerned precisely what they may or may not do.[55]

IV

In *CRE* v. *Amari Plastics Ltd* Lord Denning said that he was 'very sorry for the Commission, but they have been caught up in a spider's web spun by Parliament from which there is little hope of their escaping'. The machinery established by Parliament for an FI is 'so elaborate and so cumbersome that it is in danger of grinding to a halt'.[56] The provisions relating to a non-discrimination notice

---

[49] *Amari Plastics* above, n. 37 at 313 per Lord Denning.
[50] Ibid. at 314–15 per Griffiths LJ.   [51] S. 70 of the 1975 Act.
[52] *Amari Plastics* above n. 37 at 314 per Griffiths LJ.
[53] See s. 82(4) of the 1975 Act for the meaning of 'final'.
[54] S. 71(1) of the 1975 Act. S. 69 of the Act also allows for an FI to determine whether the requirements of a non-discrimination notice have been observed.
[55] *Hillingdon* above, n. 35 at 287 per Lord Denning. See also *CRE* v. *Genture Restaurants Ltd*, an unreported Court of Appeal decision of 15 Apr. 1981.
[56] Above, n. 37 at 313. Lord Denning said, at 310, that the 'machinery set up under the Act is exceedingly complicated. So complicated that I will not attempt to explain it'.

establish a 'cumbrous and unsatisfactory procedure'.[57] FIs are lengthy, complex, and expensive. Even if the EOC jump over all the procedural barriers built by Parliament, the availability of an appeal against a non-discrimination notice opening up all of the findings of fact made by the EOC destroys much of the value an FI might otherwise have. There is, in any event, no power in the EOC to secure compensation for victims of what are found, in the FI, to be unlawful practices. This is no power in the EOC to order changes in such practices. The EOC can only make recommendations.

Parliament could have entrusted the EOC as the fact-finding body in this area of the law, with regulatory powers, leaving the EOC to develop their own procedures in accordance with natural justice, and making the EOC subject to judicial review only if they acted unfairly or arbitrarily. Parliament has chosen a different approach. Because of the stigma attached to a finding of sex discrimination, and the potential controversy of such a finding, Parliament has decided that the powers, procedures, and conclusions of the EOC in an FI need to be rigidly controlled to ensure that the ordinary tribunals and courts are, in the final analysis, judges of the correctness of the findings of fact made by the EOC in an FI. Parliament may well be justified in denying the EOC broad powers to make conclusive findings of fact out of court. But the inevitable consequence of such an approach is to deny much of the value of an FI. If the EOC are not to replace court functions in this context, it is difficult to argue against giving the EOC a further role in court and tribunal proceedings. Under the Race Relations Act 1968 the statutory body, but not individual victims of unlawful discrimination, could bring cases to court. Under the 1975 Act, by contrast, the individual victim, but not the statutory body, can bring cases to court.[58] There is room for a compromise: the EOC, like individual victims, should have power to commence legal proceedings against persons they suspect of unlawful discrimination. The original

---

[57] *Hillingdon* above, n. 18 at 788. It is for these reasons that the EOC have started few FIs, and completed even less. The difficulties are unfairly minimized in an article very critical of the EOC's performance in this area: George Applebey and Evelyn Ellis, 'Formal Investigations: The Commission for Racial Equality and the Equal Opportunities Commission as Law Enforcement Agencies' (1984) *Public Law* 236.

[58] The exceptional cases in which the EOC can bring legal proceedings in their own name are explained above, nn. 7–10.

reason for depriving the EOC of such a power—that they could, instead, commence an FI—has been shown to be a bad reason because of the lack of effective powers in an FI. Giving the EOC power to commence legal proceedings in their own name would be a more effective method of enforcing anti-discrimination law than leaving such action solely to individual victims. It would also provide a means of bringing before courts and tribunals complex and pervasive discriminatory practices without adopting the problematic procedural device of the class action.

V

A fundamental problem of discrimination law is the extent to which it gives rights to individuals to be treated irrespective of their race or sex, and the extent to which rights arise and are proved by reference to and by reason of membership of a racial or sexual group. Plainly it is a basic premiss of the Sex Discrimination Act 1975 that an individual has a right to be treated on his or her merits, irrespective of the general characteristics of persons of his or her sex.[59] Yet in proving a claim that an applicant has been denied an employment opportunity by reason of sex, it is relevant to show that the employer has few persons of that sex on the staff.[60] Indirect discrimination proceeds on a theory of group entitlements: the complainant is entitled to relief if it can be shown that he or she is a victim of a practice which, although apparently neutral, has a disproportionate adverse impact on his or her sex and which the employer cannot show to be justifiable. The principle of positive discrimination, whether by the reservation of jobs for women, or by the recognition that women require special training or encouragement, similarly proceeds on a theory of group entitlements. It was the belief of the US Supreme Court as recently as 1977 that 'it is ordinarily to be expected that nondiscriminatory hiring practices will in time result in a work force more or less representative of the racial and ethnic composition of the population in the community from which employees are hired . . .'.[61] As courts and observers begin to recognize that there exist more basic impediments to occupational and social integration, and as they realize that the present law is simply not producing a larger

[59] See ch. 2 nn. 39–46.   [60] See ch. 3 n. 148.
[61] *International Brotherhood of Teamsters* v. *US* 431 US 324, 340 n (1977).

share of benefits for hitherto disadvantaged racial groups, or for women, there is little doubt that the individualistic theory of discrimination, valuable though it is, will be seen less and less as a solution to certain problems of society. Mr Justice Marshall, joined by Brennan J., dissented in part in that same 1977 decision. He emphasized (quoting a Senate Report) that when the Civil Rights Act 1964 was enacted

employment discrimination tended to be viewed as a series of isolated and distinguishable events, for the most part due to ill-will on the part of some identifiable individual or organisation . . . Experience has shown this view to be false . . . Employment discrimination as viewed today is a far more complex and pervasive phenomenon. Experts familiar with the subject now generally describe the problem in terms of 'systems' and 'effects' rather than simply intentional wrongs . . .'[62]

Just as collective rights are the necessary foundation of trade union strength, so collective rights and remedies may be necessary if civil rights legislation is effectively to overcome such systematic discrimination. The class action is a collective remedy that deserves consideration in this context.

The enforcement of the substantive goals of the law is inefficiently furthered by an individual action for discrimination, in which the plaintiff has the burden of proof. At best, he or she can hope to be awarded a remedy confined to the facts of the case. The defendant may offer, and the complainant may, understandably, accept, a generous settlement of the individual case to avoid a judgment of discrimination that may encourage other potential complainants to come forward, may result in adverse publicity and may necessitate the amendment of impugned practices.

The class action is a possible solution to the defects of a discrimination law based on an individualistic theory of rights and remedies. As developed by American jurisprudence, the class action involves the litigation and determination in one action of a common question of law or fact between each member of the class and the defendant.[63] It is an exception to the general rule of civil procedure that only parties to the case are bound by the judgment of the court. The plaintiff begins a legal action on behalf of the

---

[62] Ibid. at 383 n, 391 n.

[63] The defendant may also represent a class, but for the purposes of this chapter I shall concentrate on the case of the plaintiff representing a class.

class, the other members of which play no active part in the litigation but are bound by the result and are equally liable for the costs.

The general advantages of the class action are simply stated:

1. It enables individuals, each of whom has suffered a common wrong at the hand of the defendant but none of whom has suffered damage large enough to make separate litigation desirable or practical, to join together to fight the impugned practice and to enforce the substantive goals of the law.
2. It offers wide scope for discovery of documents and other information relevant to the dispute.
3. It helps to eradicate inequality of bargaining power in litigation.
4. It provides the plaintiff with the supportive solidarity consequent upon the knowledge that he or she is acting on behalf of a class. This may disincline a plaintiff to accept an offer of settlement.
5. It facilitates 'prompt, efficient judicial administration'[64] by bringing before the court for a binding determination in one case all disputes on a common question of law or fact.
6. It furthers the goal of producing judicial decisions and remedies that are appropriate to resolve the grievance at issue by notifying the court of the potential impact of any judgment the court may be minded to make.[65]

---

[64] *Eisen* v. *Carlisle and Jacquelin* 417 US 156, 185 (1974) per Douglas J. dissenting in part (in the US Supreme Court). See also the US Court of Appeals in the same case: 'Class actions serve an important function in our judicial system. By establishing a technique whereby the claims of many individuals can be resolved at the same time, the class suit both eliminates the possibility of repetitious litigation and provides small claimants with a method of obtaining redress for claims which would otherwise be too small to warrant individual litigation': 391 F 2d 555, 560 (1968). See also Abram Chayes, 'The Role of the Judge in Public Law Litigation' 89 *Harvard Law Review* 1281, 1291 (1976): 'The class action is a reflection of our growing awareness that a host of important public and private interactions . . . are conducted on a routine or bureaucratized basis and can no longer be visualized as bilateral transactions between private individuals.'

[65] See 'Developments in the Law—Class Actions' 89 *Harvard Law Review* 1318, 1353 (1976). In the equal pay case of *Electrolux Ltd* v. *Hutchinson* [1977] ICR 252, 258–9, the EAT was troubled by the thought that 'in a complicated situation, such as that confronting the employers, where there are hundreds of claims and the circumstances of the applicants are not identical, a process of litigation under the Equal Pay Act 1970 can never produce a satisfactory result. Although the litigation in each individual case may produce a theoretically correct answer in accordance with the terms of the Equal Pay Act 1970 it is unlikely that the individual answers

The English rules of civil procedure know nothing of the class action. The closest analogy is the representative action,[66] which is inferior to the class action in a number of important respects. Courts have strictly construed the requirement that a party suing in a representative capacity must have the same interest as the persons he or she seeks to represent.[67] Although judges have, on occasions, indicated that the rules relating to representative proceedings should be flexibly applied in the interests of justice,[68] it is clear that only in very rare circumstances can a plaintiff recover damages on behalf of the represented class.[69] The judgment in a representative action does bind those who are represented, but it may not be enforced against them without the leave of the court, which may be refused on the ground that there are facts and matters peculiar to the individual case. Represented persons are not liable for costs,[70] nor are they subject to the ordinary liabilities of litigants in respect of discovery of documents.

It is possible to find hidden in the history of the English law of unincorporated associations procedural devices akin to the class

---

put together can produce a coherent wage structure capable of general application in other cases.' Phillips J., for the EAT, suggested that the desired goal could only be reached 'by negotiation, applying the current views, and statutory prescriptions, on equal pay and equal opportunities. It may be that the Equal Opportunities Commission could be of assistance in such an exercise. Certainly it lies beyond our competence and jurisdiction.' The class action could provide the EAT with the necessary information to resolve a dispute of which the individual action presents merely a portion. Similarly in *Steel* v. *Union of Post Office Workers* [1978] ICR 181, 189, where Phillips, J. for the EAT noted that 'there are many other cases pending before industrial tribunals, to which the Post Office are party, raising matters similar to that in issue in the present appeal. Assuming that the issues in the various cases, or some of them, are the same, it seems desirable that at least one of them—perhaps this one—should be decided on the basis of full evidence and full legal argument. It may be, we cannot of course say for certain, that the evidence will be voluminous as the Post Office may wish to explain the extent of the problem, the workings of the seniority system and so on, and the claimant may wish to explain the extent of the discrimination if the practice complained of is allowed to persist.'

[66] Order 15 Rule 12 of the Rules of the Supreme Court; Order 5 Rule 5 of the County Court Rules. See Robin Widdison, 'Class Actions: A Survey' 133 New Law Journal 778 (1983) for other procedural devices similar to class actions.

[67] See, for example, *Smith* v. *Cardiff Corporation* [1954] 1 QB 210.

[68] See, for example, *John* v. *Rees* [1970] Ch. 345, 370.

[69] *Markt & Co. Ltd* v. *Knight Steamship Co. Ltd* [1910] 2 KB 1021; *Prudential Assurance Co. Ltd* v. *Newman Industries Ltd* [1980] 2 WLR 339; *EMI Records Ltd* v. *Riley* [1981] 1 WLR 923.

[70] *Markt & Co. Ltd* ibid. at 1039.

action.[71] Moreover, in Commonwealth jurisdictions there are indications that the representative action is not so strictly confined as it is here.[72] Notwithstanding these developments, one must agree with one commentator that it is 'beyond the bounds of possibility'[73] for a class action on the American model to develop from within the present rules governing representative actions. In any event, the Industrial Tribunal Rules do not provide for representative applicants. The Employment Appeal Tribunal Rules permit joinder of parties but make no mention of representative proceedings.[74]

Because of the defects of the representative action, and because of the potential advantages of the class action, various commentators and bodies have given thought to the merits and demerits of introducing the class action into common law procedure outside the US courts.[75] In 1977, the Law Reform Committee of South Australia recommended the introduction of a class action, as did a discussion paper in 1979 by the Australian Law Reform Commission.[76] Much of the debate has focused on the advantages of a *consumer* class action. In that context, the case for an improved procedure was well stated by the Court of Appeal of Ontario in *Naken* v. *General Motors of Canada Ltd*. The plaintiff sued on behalf of himself and as representative of other purchasers of a car which allegedly contained a design fault. The defendants sought to strike out the representative action as there were issues of fact—such as whether each purchaser had relied on warranties and what damages each purchaser had suffered—which were not common to those represented. The Court of Appeal of Ontario acknowledged the deficiencies in the concept of the representative

---

[71] 'Developments in the Law—Class Actions' above, n. 65 at 1332 ff.

[72] *Shaw* v. *Real Estate Board of Greater Vancouver* 36 DLR (3d) 250 (1973: British Columbia Court of Appeal); *Northdown Drywall & Construction Ltd* v. *Austin Co. Ltd* 6 OR (2d) 223 (1974: Ontario High Court). But see *Shields* v. *Mayor* (1953) 1 DLR 776 (Ontario Court of Appeal).

[73] J. A. Jolowicz, 'Representative Actions, Class Actions and Damages—A Compromise Solution?' 39 *Cambridge Law Journal* 237, 238 (1980).

[74] See the Industrial Tribunals (Rules of Procedure) Regulations 1985 SI no. 16, Rule 14; and the Employment Appeal Tribunal Rules 1980 SI no. 2035, Rule 14.

[75] See Gerry Bates, 'A Case for the Introduction of Class Actions into English Law' 130 *New Law Journal* 560 (1980); Bruce M. Debelle, 'Class Actions for Australia? Do they already Exist?' 54 *Australian Law Journal* 508 (1980); Neil J. Williams, 'Class Actions—The Canadian Experience' 53 *Law Institute Journal* 721 (1979).

[76] *Access to the Courts II: Class Actions* (Discussion Paper no. 11: June 1979).

action, but allowed the case to continue so long as it was confined to purchasers who had actually seen the defendants' advertisement and had relied on it to purchase the car. The court added:

In these days of mass merchandising of consumer goods, accompanied as it often is by widespread or national advertising, large numbers of persons are almost inevitably going to find themselves in approximately the same situation if the article in question has a defect that turns up when the article is put to use. In many instances, the pecuniary damages suffered by any one purchaser may be small, even if the article is useless. It is not practical for any one purchaser to sue a huge manufacturer for his individual damages but the sum of the damages suffered by each individual purchaser may be very large indeed.

In such cases it would clearly be both convenient and in the public interest if some mechanism or procedure existed whereby the purchasers could sue as a class with appropriate safeguards for defendants, who ought not to be subjected to expensive law suits by class action plaintiffs who cannot pay costs if they lose.[77]

It was for reasons of this type that Justice Douglas of the US Supreme Court described the class action as 'one of the few legal remedies the small claimant has against those who command the status quo'.[78] The case for the class action is most powerfully presented in the consumer context; but, as US federal courts have recognized, 'suits alleging racial or ethnic [or sex] discrimination are often by their very nature class suits, involving classwide wrongs'[79] because 'the evil sought to be ended is discrimination on

[77] 21 OR (2d) 780, 784–5 (1979). The Supreme Court of Canada allowed an appeal against the decision of the Court of Appeal, finding that the case could not proceed as a class action, in part because of the substantial practical difficulties such a procedure would create: [1983] 1 SCR 72. See below, n. 99 for some of those difficulties. See also Larry M. Fox, '*Naken* v. *General Motors of Canada Ltd*: Class Actions Deferred' 6 *Supreme Court Law Review* 335 (1984).

[78] *Eisen* v. *Carlisle and Jacquelin* above, n. 64 at 185–6. He explained that '[i]n our society that is growing in complexity there are bound to be innumerable people in common disasters, calamities or ventures who would go begging for justice without the class action but who could with all regard to due process be protected by it. Some of these are consumers whose claims may seem *de minimis* but who alone have no practical recourse for either remuneration or injunctive relief. Some may be environmentalists who . . . suffer perceptibly by smoke, noxious gases or radiation. Or the unnamed individual may be only a ratepayer being excessively charged by a utility or a homeowner whose assessment is slowly rising beyond his ability to pay.'

[79] *East Texas Motor Freight System Inc.* v. *Rodriguez* 431 US 395, 405 (1977: US Supreme Court).

the basis of a class characteristic'.[80] If the defendant has discriminated against the complainant on the ground of sex it is most likely that the defendant has similarly treated other persons of that sex. Whether in the context of consumer actions or of discrimination claims, the advantages and the disadvantages of the class action deserve close attention. As Patrick Devlin has explained:

the obligation on a State to provide justice is not discharged by devising a single and inflexible mode of trial whose cost is beyond the reach of the individual citizen. Its obligation is to provide as many modes of trial as are necessary to cover the variety of disputes that may commonly arise so that for each type there may be selected a mode that will offer a reasonable standard of justice at a reasonable cost. To neglect this obligation in pursuit of a single mode which is considered to be the best is bound to end in a denial of justice to many.[81]

Only some of the potential advantages of the class action are relevant to discrimination law in the United Kingdom. The powers of the Equal Opportunities Commission to provide assistance to persons suffering from an alleged act of discrimination[82] limit the number of cases where unlawful acts of discrimination go unlitigated because a complainant lacks financial resources. The EOC further provide, to some extent, the supportive solidarity and the expertise to reduce a complainant's feeling of isolation and to remove inequality of bargaining power. Certainly the class action offers in discrimination law, as elsewhere, other potential advantages: wide scope for discovery of documents, more efficient judicial administration, and decisions based on an appreciation of the width and impact of the issues raised. To determine whether these potential advantages justify the introduction of the class action we need to look carefully at the problems posed by the concept of the class action and at other potential means of achieving necessary reforms of discrimination law.

One can best appreciate the potential difficulties posed by the introduction of the class action by referring to Rule 23 of the US Federal Rules of Civil Procedure. This Rule, as amended in 1966, states the current criteria for commencing a class action in the US. One or more members of a class may sue or be sued as

---

[80] *Bowe* v. *Colgate-Palmolive* 416 F 2d 711, 719 (1969: US Court of Appeals).
[81] *The Judge* (1979), 69.   [82] Above, n. 6.

representative parties on behalf of the members of a class if two tests are satisfied. First, it must be shown that the class is so numerous that joinder of all the members is not practical, that questions of fact or law are common to members of the class, that the claims (or defences) of the representative parties are typical of the class, and that the representative parties will fairly and adequately protect the interests of the class. Secondly, the case must satisfy at least one of the three rationales for the class action:

1. that the prosecution of separate actions by or against individual members of the class would create the risk of inconsistent or varying adjudications with respect to individual members of the class, creating incompatible standards of conduct for the party opposing the class or impeding the interests of other members of the class not parties to the adjudication;
2. that the party opposing the class has acted or refused to act on grounds generally applicable to the class, making it appropriate to award final injunctive relief with respect to the class as a whole; or
3. that questions of law or fact common to members of the class predominate over any questions affecting only individual members and that the class action is superior to other available methods of trial for the fair and efficient adjudication of the controversy.

These criteria hint at a range of procedural difficulties posed by the class action. The requirement that the class must consist of too many individuals for joinder to be a practical option 'has been a concept given content on a case-by-case basis; the numerosity requirement is simply not susceptible of doctrinal analysis'.[83] At the other extreme, the class must not be so large as to be unmanageable. A class action on behalf of 'all consumers of eggs in the United States' was struck out for this reason.[84] Further, one cannot define, with any element of precision, what constitutes a common question of law or fact. In discrimination cases, a common question only exists where one is challenging an alleged pattern or practice. Claims for the restructuring of policies on hiring, promotion, seniority, dismissal, pay, and working con-

[83] 'Developments in the Law—Class Actions' above, n. 65 at 1454.
[84] *United Egg Producers* v. *Bauer International Corp.* 312 F Supp 319 (1970: US District Court).

ditions are evidently most suited for adjudication on a classwide basis. Because of the eradication of most overt discrimination, such cases are likely nowadays to involve covert, indirect discrimination. The theory of indirect discrimination seems 'designed for classwide application. Evidence of disproportionate impact inevitably is evidence that an entire class has suffered from a violation'[85] of the law.

In indirect discrimination cases, classwide relief for the unlawful pattern or practice would be relatively unproblematic. Once the pattern or practice is shown to have a disproportionate adverse impact on members of the relevant sex and is assessed for its justifiability—the answers to which questions would be the same for each member of the class—it remains only to prove that the pattern or practice is to the detriment of each member of the class because he or she cannot comply with it. If this can be established, appropriate relief can be granted to each member of the class. Because damages for indirect discrimination contrary to the Sex Discrimination Act 1975 cannot be awarded if the respondent proves that the requirement or condition in question was not applied with the intention of treating the complainant unfavourably on sexual grounds,[86] it will rarely be necessary to assess individual damages for each member of the class.

When each member of the class is entitled to damages for an indirectly discriminatory practice, the court will face the problem of reconciling the defendant's wish only to pay damages to the extent of the loss proved by each individual with conflicting arguments derived from the purpose of the class action. To require each member of the class to prove his or her loss would be expensive and would deter them from doing so, thereby weakening the value of the class action. For this reason, in the US:

A range of techniques, including reference to masters, streamlined summary judgment procedures, shifts in burdens of proof, class-wide calculation of damages, administrative processing of individual claims, and the so-called fluid class recovery—in which damages are calculated in the aggregate and distributed through a proof-of-claim procedure with any residue being distributed for the benefit of class members—have been

---

[85] George Rutherglen, 'Title VII Class Actions' 47 *University of Chicago Law Review* 688, 713 (1980).

[86] Ss. 65(1)(b) and 66(3) of the 1975 Act. For a discussion of the concept of indirect discrimination see ch. 2 ss. III and IV.

proposed as means for making delivery of relief feasible in class actions involving individually non-recoverable or nonviable claims.[87]

The practice of splitting the trial into two stages, dealing first with legal liability and only later with assessment of damages, ensures that many defendants who are found to be liable for unlawful acts of discrimination will negotiate a settlement of the amount of damages they should pay.

In cases where the disputed practice or procedure of the defendant involves unlawful direct discrimination, the problems of relief to individuals within the class are compounded in the United States. Even though the defendant may have refused to employ women, it is not necessarily the case that each woman who applied but was rejected for a job vacancy with the defendant in the past was denied the employment opportunity on the ground of sex, or, indeed, that each member of the class has suffered identical damages. Some members of the class may have been rejected because they lacked relevant qualifications. Others, although qualified, may merely have lost the opportunity to be considered because a better qualified candidate was appointed. Only some of the members of the class would have been appointed but for the discriminatory practice.

The problems of proof of individual claims within the class cannot be ignored. The US Supreme Court has responded by ruling that, once a pattern or practice of discrimination is proved in a class action, there then exists a prima-facie case of discrimination in respect of each member of the class. The burden shifts to the defendant to rebut the charge in each individual case. As the court explained in *International Brotherhood of Teamsters* v. *US*:

Although the prima-facie case did not conclusively demonstrate that all of the employer's decisions were part of the proved discriminatory pattern and practice, it did create a greater likelihood that any single decision was a component of the overall pattern. Moreover, the finding of a pattern or practice changed the position of the employer to that of a proved wrongdoer. Finally, the employer was in the best position to show why any individual employee was denied an employment opportunity. Insofar as the reasons related to available vacancies or the employer's evaluation of the applicant's qualifications, the company's records were the most relevant items of proof. If the refusal to hire was based on other factors,

[87] 'Developments in the Law—Class Actions' above, n. 65 at 1517.

the employer and its agents knew best what those factors were and the extent to which they influenced the decision making process.[88]

Similar problems arise when one considers whether any particular individual ought to be recognized as a member of the class. The class of persons aggrieved by a policy of refusing to employ women does not consist only of those women who applied for jobs and were rejected. It consists also of those who would have applied for the vacancy but for the discriminatory policy. Those deterred from making an application because they knew it was futile are victims of the unlawful practice.[89] Each potential applicant will need to establish her membership of the class by proving that, but for the policy, an application would have been submitted.

Problems of relief for individual members of the class constitute one area in which due process of law must be reconciled with the class action. Similar difficulties arise by reason of the impact of the class action and the consequent need to protect members of the class. Because all members of the class are bound by the judgment in a class action, there are 'catastrophic consequences if the plaintiff loses and carries the class down with him, or proves only such limited facts that no practice or policy can be found, leaving him afloat but sinking the class.[90] It is therefore essential for there to be a pre-trial hearing to ascertain whether the plaintiff has interests antagonistic to those of the class and whether she and her lawyers are competent to represent the class. Although common questions of law or fact are often present in discrimination cases, 'the mere fact that a complaint alleges racial or ethnic [or sex] discrimination does not in itself ensure that the party who has brought the lawsuit will be an adequate representative of those who may have been the real victims of that discrimination'.[91]

---

[88] Above, n. 61 at 359–60 n. See also *Franks* v. *Bowman Transportation Co.* 424 US 747 (1976: US Supreme Court).

[89] Ibid. at 364–8. See also *Hugh-Jones* v. *St John's College, Cambridge* [1979] ICR 848, 851 (EAT).

[90] *Johnson* v. *Georgia Highway Express Inc.* 417 F 2d 1122, 1126 (1969) per Judge Godbold in the US Court of Appeals.

[91] *East Texas Motor Freight System Inc.* above, n. 79 at 405–6. See also *Eisen* v. *Carlisle and Jacquelin* 391 F 2d 555, 562 (1968) where the US Court of Appeals said that 'an essential concomitant of adequate representation is that the party's attorney be qualified, experienced and generally able to conduct the proposed litigation. Additionally, it is necessary to eliminate so far as possible the likelihood that the litigants are involved in a collusive suit or that the plaintiff has interests antagonistic to those of the remainder of the class.'

Similarly, a pre-trial hearing will be necessary for the court to satisfy itself that there are no differences of interest within the class. That task can be performed only once the content of the class is identified. American courts have adopted a test similar to that used by the English law to ascertain whether the beneficiaries of a discretionary trust are validly identified: so long as one can say, at any given moment, whether a particular individual is or is not a member of the class, sufficient certainty exists.[92] Differences of interest within the class can be resolved by redrawing the boundaries of the class. Because the discriminatory practices of an employer will benefit some members of trade unions and disadvantage others, it will rarely be appropriate for a trade union to act as the representative of a class in a discrimination action.

An especially problematic feature of a pre-trial hearing will be the question of whether the plaintiff should have to give notice of the action to all members of the class that he or she seeks to represent. Since members of the class are to be bound by the judgment in a class action, and since they are to be liable for a proportion of the costs of the action, elementary standards of due process of law compel the conclusion that notice should be given and that putative class members should be granted the option to exclude themselves from the class. The US Supreme Court reached this conclusion in an antitrust case under Rule 23. It rejected the petitioner's argument that 'the prohibitively high cost of providing individual notice to 2,250,000 class members would end this suit as a class action and effectively frustrate petitioner's attempt to vindicate the policies underlying the antitrust and securities laws.' The Court held that there was 'nothing in Rule 23 to suggest that the notice requirements can be tailored to fit the pocket-books of particular plaintiffs'.[93] Notice could, perhaps, be accomplished by advertising on television, radio or other media and not necessarily by individual letters. Still, the cost is likely to deter the use of class actions in cases other than those of a small class or a homogeneous class. A possible solution is to adopt an opt-in procedure: one is a member of the class only if one expressly requests admission to the class. The difficulty with this solution is that expensive advertising may be needed to inform potential class members of their option and that, while many

[92] See *McPhail* v. *Doulton* [1971] AC 424.
[93] *Eisen* v. *Carlisle and Jacquelin* above, n. 64 at 175–6.

potential members may be happy to be included in the class, a much smaller number will be prepared to take the positive step of writing to request admission.

Because they tend to embrace a wide spectrum of facts, class actions often involve the discovery of documents on a gigantic scale. The difficulty is to do justice to the defendant and to provide the court with adequate information about the size and the identity of the class, yet to avoid burdening class members with onerous requests that they disclose documents and answer interrogatories or requests for particulars of their claims. Since each class member is likely to have only a small financial interest in the proceedings—indeed, that is one reason why the class action is necessary—it will be contrary to their interests to hire lawyers to advise them on how to respond to requests for information. If they decide to remain passive partners in the class action, should the court remove them from the class? Clearly the court will need to steer a very fine line between furtherance of the goal of the class action and recognition that fairness to the defendant entails the provision of basic information concerning the individual claims of members of the class.

Because the class action binds all members of the class, it is essential to provide for judicial approval of any settlement of the dispute. The defendant's offer may split the class, as it may be in the interests of a sub-class to accept the offer. 'Even if offers are made to all class members, acceptance by only a fraction of the class might prevent the class suit from going forward, either because numerosity would be destroyed, or because the claim is no longer economically viable.'[94] Similar problems arise if the plaintiff decides to accept the defendant's offer or if the plaintiff's claim becomes moot. The US Supreme Court has ruled that a class action remains alive so long as the dispute continues between the defendant and the other members of the class.[95]

In deciding whether to amend English law and practice to introduce the class action one cannot ignore these procedural complexities. Moreover, the existence of contingent fees and the fact that costs do not follow the event are two features of US legal practice that have assisted the development of the class action. Their absence here—with the consequence that members of the

---

[94] 'Developments in the Law—Class Actions' above, n. 65 at 1547.
[95] *Franks* v. *Bowman Transportation Co.* above, n. 88.

class will be liable to pay their lawyers and the other party to the dispute if the case is lost—at the very least ensures that the American concept of the class action cannot simply be transplanted into English procedure. Indeed, unless our costs rules are amended or contingent fees permitted or legal aid extended, permitting class actions may well be an empty gesture since few could afford to litigate a class action.

Less troublesome, however, are the arguments which defendants would undoubtedly raise in opposition to the concept of the class action. Should scarce legal resources be used to litigate the complaint of a large group, each member of which has suffered minimal damage? Because the defendant faces the prospect of having to pay enormous sums of damages and costs if it loses a class action, it may have no alternative but to settle even frivolous claims at the earliest possible stage. Class actions, it will further be argued, can be abused: in 1972, for example, the Heart Disease Research Corporation sued General Motors Corporation on behalf of 125 million residents of metropolitan areas in America for air pollution damages. The amount claimed was $375 trillion, more than 300 times the gross national product of the US at the time.[96] For these reasons, it will be contended by defendants, the class action is an 'engine of destruction' and a 'form of legalised blackmail'.[97] One judge on the US Court of Appeals urged his colleagues in one case to 'put an end to this Frankenstein monster posing as a class action'.[98]

These arguments against the class action are far from persuasive. That corporate entities, who have prima facie breached the law, are to be faced by a collective force equal to their own, with similar bargaining power, is hardly likely to provoke sympathy. The ridiculously large class action will be struck out as unmanageable. The essential question will be whether the class action achieves its purpose of enforcing the substantive goals of the law. Defendants have, hitherto, escaped liability for their wrongdoing because of the absence of adequate procedural mechanisms. If it is possible to develop a class action that adequately protects the interests of class

[96] Gerry Bates above, n. 75 at 561.
[97] 'Developments in the Law—Class Actions' above, n. 65 at 1325 citing various critics of the class action.
[98] *Eisen* v. *Carlisle and Jacquelin* above, n. 91 at 572 per Lumbard CJ dissenting in the US Court of Appeals.

members, of society, and of defendants, the case for the class action is established.

It is the practical problems, not the arguments of principle, that pose most difficulty. Despite the very real need for the class action in English procedure, one cannot be optimistic that the practical complexities can be adequately resolved. Such issues as defining the class; ensuring that the class does not contain differences of interest; giving notice to members of the class; resolving issues of discovery and settlement; ascertaining when a common question of law or fact exists; computing the damages (if any) to be awarded to members of the class; assessing the bona fides and the capability of a plaintiff who seeks to represent the class; and ensuring that the class action is manageable and not concerned with too wide a class—all these need to be resolved by careful drafting of the relevant legislation, or by sympathetic judicial application of the principles of class actions.[99]

In the US, the lack of expertise of the private plaintiff has necessitated the assistance of public bodies to ensure that the interests of the members of the class (who are bound by the judgment) are protected.[100] If class actions are to be introduced in the United Kingdom, they are likely to be confined to actions brought by public bodies (such as the EOC) or private organizations with the necessary expertise, bona fides, and funds. It is difficult to envisage Parliament listing (or anyone wanting Parliament to list) non-statutory organizations approved for the purpose of commencing a class action; nor would one find it easy to draft criteria to define the bodies which ought to be permitted to commence class actions. It is, however, even more unlikely that Parliament would amend the law to allow individuals who have no necessary expertise or financial resources or bona fides to bring an action that would bind members of a class; nor is it likely that Parliament would present the judiciary with the task of assessing, at a pre-trial hearing, whether the relevant individual has the expertise, the financial resources, and the interests of the class at heart.

[99] See *Naken* v. *General Motors of Canada Ltd* above, n. 77 at 785: 'The subject [of class actions] raises complicated questions of great difficulty in the areas of the delineation of the class, identity of the causes of action of the class members, discovery and production from plaintiffs, proof of the breach of contract or tort that caused loss to the class, assessment of damages and allocation of proceeds.'

[100] 'Developments in the Law—Class Actions' above, n. 65 at 1643.

Given that the concept of the class action poses considerable procedural complexities, and given that it is, at most, likely to be introduced as a device which statutory bodies like the EOC (and possibly non-statutory bodies) could use, one next needs to ask whether the goals of the EOC of enforcing discrimination law would be best advanced by the introduction of the class action, or whether preferable alternatives exist. The better performance of their statutory functions by the EOC undoubtedly depends on the provision of greater access to the courts. Title VII of the US Civil Rights Act 1964 (which makes it unlawful for an employer to discriminate on the grounds of, *inter alia*, race and sex) originally provided that the role of the Equal Employment Opportunity Commission (EEOC) in eliminating unlawful employment practices was limited to informal methods of conference, conciliation, and persuasion. If the EEOC failed to secure voluntary compliance with the law, a civil action could be commenced by an aggrieved individual. By 1971, Congress had become convinced that the 'failure to grant the EEOC meaningful enforcement powers has proved to be a major flaw in the operation of Title VII'.[101] A brief consideration of the amendments to Title VII made in 1972 suggests that there are alternative means to the class action of enforcing more effectively the substantive goals of the 1975 and 1970 Acts.

The 1972 amendments to Title VII expanded the powers of the EEOC in two respects. First, they allowed the EEOC to bring a civil action against a defendant reasonably suspected of breaching Title VII. The EEOC may commence such proceedings on behalf of an aggrieved individual (or individuals) after one or more has filed charges with the organization. Secondly, the amendments transferred to the EEOC a power previously held by the Attorney-General to commence proceedings against a defendant whom it has reasonable cause to believe responsible for a 'pattern or practice' of unlawful discrimination. In *General Tel. Co. of the Northwest Inc.* v. *EEOC*, the US Supreme Court explained that, in so expanding the powers of the EEOC, 'Congress sought to implement the public interest as well as to bring about more effective enforcement of private rights.'[102]

[101] Senate Report no. 92–145, 92d Congress 1st Session 4 (1971) cited in *General Tel. Co. of the Northwest Inc.* v. *EEOC* 446 US 318, 325 (1980: US Supreme Court). [102] Ibid. at 326.

Private enforcement of Title VII, however, remains possible: the aggrieved individual may bring his or her own action at the expiry of a 180-day period of exclusive EEOC jurisdiction after the filing of a charge. The private action at the end of that period may be the consequence of the EEOC's failure to proceed with sufficient speed to satisfy the complainant, or of an EEOC decision not to sue or of the EEOC wanting a compromise or settlement with the defendant which the complainant finds unsatisfactory. But although 'Title VII does provide for two separate approaches to enforcement . . . it clearly favours the public mechanism of EEOC suits. Private enforcement is secondary, serving as a supplementary technique and designed in part as a check against Commission inaction or delay.'[103] In *General Tel. Co. of the Northwest Inc.* v. *EEOC*,[104] the US Supreme Court held that EEOC actions, whether pursuant to an individual complaint or in respect of an alleged pattern or practice of discrimination, are not class actions; the EEOC does not need to satisfy the criteria of Rule 23, nor is the judgment binding on those individuals who have brought the matter to the attention of the EEOC or who are adversely affected by the pattern or practice.

Widening the powers of the EOC to commence legal proceedings for discriminatory acts and practices would remedy many of the defects of the present law. It would reduce the reliance on individual complainants and litigants who are prepared to withstand the pressure of publicity (although even an action brought by the EOC would normally depend upon the evidence of complainants). It would ensure the more efficient adjudication of complex disputes and the presentation to the court of evidence and argument that enabled the judge to understand the pervasive impact of any decision he or she might make. Legal actions by the EOC could achieve much of what the class action is designed to achieve, particularly if the EOC were empowered to commence litigation without receiving a complaint from a victim and if the court were to be empowered to grant damages to a defined class of victims in addition to declaratory and injunctive relief. No doubt, an action by the EOC would pose similar procedural problems to those that afflict the class action. These problems are, however,

---

[103] Gary Ian Horowitz, 'The Binding Effect of EEOC-Initiated Actions' 80 *Columbia Law Review* 395, 417–18 (1980).
[104] Above, n. 101.

more readily soluble in the confined context of a discrimination action brought by statutory bodies with defined functions.

VI

There are three basic models of law which are available to remedy wrongs: civil law, criminal law, and regulatory law. Civil law, giving rights to victims of discrimination which they can enforce in courts, has limitations. Observance of the law depends upon individuals standing up for their rights. However, such victims may be ignorant of the protection provided by the law or unwilling to spend the time or money necessary to secure their rights, especially as the remedies available in sex discrimination cases are far from generous. Nor does civil law guarantee the eradication of discriminatory practices. Discriminators often settle cases against complainants without changing their unlawful practices. The prosecution of discriminators by the State, leading to the stigma of a criminal conviction, is not appropriate for this type of wrong. Empowering regulatory bodies to enforce the law by seeking remedies in non-criminal proceedings is a more recent, and often more effective, method of deterring and remedying wrongdoing.[105]

Parliament needs to empower the EOC to bring legal proceedings against those suspected of committing unlawful sex discrimination. Without such provisions, the law will not satisfy the 'essential' criterion identified by the White Paper which preceded the 1975 Act: it will not be 'capable of providing adequate redress'.[106] It is difficult to formulate the case against providing a law-enforcement body with the powers to enforce the law by taking to court persons reasonably suspected of breaking the law. It is similarly difficult to understand why the EOC should be given the important task of conducting formal investigations into alleged discriminatory practices (in particular on complex matters suitable for an administrative investigation),[107] if the findings of fact made by the Commission can be reopened in an industrial tribunal or

---

[105] See, for example, the powers of the Director General of Fair Trading under Part III of the Fair Trading Act 1973.

[106] Above, n. 1 at para. 81.

[107] See above, n. 65 for examples of issues that might be best resolved by an administrative body with adequate enforcement powers.

county court. The findings made by the Commission should be final, subject to the normal principles of judicial review of administrative action in the Divisional Court.[108]

---

[108] See *Council of Civil Service Unions* v. *Minister for the Civil Service* [1984] 3 WLR 1174, 1196 per Lord Diplock: 'one can conveniently classify under three heads the grounds upon which administrative action is subject to control by judicial review. The first ground I would call "illegality". the second "irrationality" and the third "procedural impropriety".'

11

CONCLUSIONS

I

The draftsman of the Sex Discrimination Act 1975 has explained the premiss from which he worked. He had the task of ensuring, as he saw it,

> that provocative language must as far as possible be avoided. The red-blooded terms of political controversy are toned down. The prose style is flat. This sometimes disappoints MP's who have campaigned for a controversial measure, and would like to see it finally enacted in ringing tones. (Such disappointment was expressed, for example, over the Sex Discrimination Act in 1975.) But it is safer so.[1]

The draftsman's success in achieving his objective with regard to the 1975 Act goes some way towards explaining the limited success of the 1975 Act in achieving its objectives. An Act which aims, in part, to educate public opinion and which needs sympathetic judicial application requires other than the flat prose style and the 'toned down' phrases usually adopted by the Parliamentary draftsman. It requires a style which can be communicated to and understood by those the legislation seeks to influence; it needs language which conveys the fundamental principles which underlie the law. To the extent that the Act has failed, part of that failure is the consequence of the adoption of the technique of the taxing statute.

Where the 1975 Act has undoubtedly succeeded is in eradicating most of the overt sex discrimination in employment and other contexts which was fairly widespread prior to 1975. It has done this by education and by deterrence. What the Act has failed to achieve is significantly to shift the structure of society to give women a much fairer share of jobs of influence or responsibility.

The basic statistics, taken from the Equal Opportunities

---

[1] Francis Bennion, *Statute Law* (2nd edn. 1983), 37. He adds at 24, that in the preparation of the 1975 Act there was 'an experiment in the use of a computer for legislative drafting . . . the first time a computer had been used in the drafting of British legislation . . .'.

Commission Annual Report for 1983, make depressing reading. Women make up 51.4 per cent of the population of Great Britain. The education, training, and employment of those women show that sex stereotypes persist to the disadvantage of women. Ninety-eight per cent of O-level passes in cookery but only 3 per cent of passes in technical drawing were achieved by females. At O-level and at A-level females are responsible for the vast majority of passes in English literature and in domestic subjects, but for few passes in physics, computer science, and mathematics. At university, women amount to 65 per cent of undergraduates studying education and 69 per cent studying language, literature, and related subjects. Yet only 9 per cent of students reading engineering and technology are women. Sixty per cent of the labour force is male, 40 per cent female. Today, a high proportion of women work for much of their adult lives. Childbirth and childrearing tend to be interruptions to a life of work, with women no longer choosing between marriage and employment. Yet these working women are largely concentrated in the less responsible positions in certain industries traditionally associated with women. Sixty per cent of all female manual workers are employed in catering, cleaning, hairdressing, or other personal services. In non-manual employment, 52 per cent of all female workers are in clerical and related occupations. In career structures for which statistics are readily available (for example the Civil Service and the teaching profession), it is clear that women tend to be concentrated in the lower grades. As one progresses further up the career ladder, fewer women hold the relevant posts. Partly because women are concentrated in these lower status jobs they receive lower pay than men. The general average gross hourly earnings (excluding the effect of overtime) of women are 74 per cent those of men. In 1970, the proportion was 63 per cent. In 1975, immediately prior to the implementation of the Equal Pay Act, the proportion was 72 per cent.

The evidence, then, shows that widespread job segregation persists. Some improvements have occurred since 1975. But the educational statistics suggest that we are unlikely to move towards job integration at a fast rate. In a case heard by the Court of Appeal in 1980, Lord Denning saw occupational segregation as 'a natural division which comes about because of the different physical qualities of the two sexes'.[2] An alternative explanation is that such segregation is the consequence of sex stereotyping at school and thereafter, of pervasive concepts of 'men's work' and 'women's work' and of institutional discrimination which the Sex Discrimination Act and the Equal Pay Act are not equipped to tackle.

II

There is a vicious circle afflicting this area of the law. Because few cases are brought, lawyers and tribunals have little expertise in dealing with the issues. This contributes to the low success rate which, in turn, deters potential complainants from coming forward. Because potential complainants do not litigate, lawyers and tribunals have little opportunity to develop the necessary expertise adequately to deal with cases in this field.[3]

The EOC Annual Report for 1983 shows that in 1976, there were 1,742 applications made under the Equal Pay Act 1970. About 40 per cent proceeded to a hearing, of which just under a third succeeded. By 1983, there were only 26 applications made under the 1970 Act. Only nine cases were heard by tribunals. Six claims succeeded. In 1976, there were 243 applications made under the Sex Discrimination Act 1975. Fifty per cent of the claims proceeded to a hearing, of which a fifth succeeded in establishing a breach of the law. In 1983, 256 applications were made under the 1975 Act; 114 cases were heard by tribunals; 61 claims were found to be established.

---

[2] *Noble* v. *David Gold & Son (Holdings) Ltd* [1980] ICR 543, 549. Lord Denning was commenting on the fact that 'in the Inns of Court the heavy work is done by outside porters. They do the lifting and carrying, and so forth. Inside, at the tables, the waiting and the serving of the meals is done by the women.' Little has changed with regard to occupational segregation since 1929 when Virginia Woolf observed in Chapter 2 of *A Room of One's Own* that '[t]he most transient visitor to this planet . . . could not fail to be aware . . . that England is under the rule of a patriarchy . . . His was the power and the money and the influence. He was the proprietor of the paper and its editor and sub-editor. He was the Foreign Secretary and the Judge. He was the cricketer; he owned the racehorses and the yachts. He was the director of the company that pays two hundred per cent to its shareholders. He left millions to charities and colleges that were ruled by himself . . .'.

[3] See B. A. Hepple, 'Judging Equal Rights' (1983) *Current Legal Problems* 71, 72–4.

During this period of 1976–83 there were only a handful of applications made to county courts under the 1975 Act in the contexts of education and the provision of goods, facilities, services, and premises. Of course, the legislation has an impact on conduct which does not manifest itself in legal proceedings. Furthermore, many applications are made but are settled prior to a formal hearing before a tribunal or a court, no doubt in some cases on terms advantageous to the complainant. Nevertheless, the statistics suggest that the legislation is rarely used, and, when used, that it lacks potency and effect. This is of particular concern in the light of the evidence that the problems of occupational segregation and lower pay for women persist.

III

To ensure equal opportunity for women in employment and other contexts, the law needs amendment in vital respects.[4] The complexity of the overlapping provisions of the Sex Discrimination Act 1975 and the Equal Pay Act 1970 would deter all but the most persistent litigant. The Equal Pay Act is an unsophisticated and unsatisfactory statute the inadequacies of which prevent it from achieving its objectives. It should be repealed. Sex discrimination in pay and in other contractual conditions of employment should be brought within the scope of the Sex Discrimination Act. The Race Relations Act 1976 covers pay as well as other aspects of employment discrimination. There is no good reason why the Sex Discrimination Act should not have a similar scope.[5]

The 1975 Act needs a radical overhaul. First, there are indefensible exceptions to its scope which should be removed. It should apply to the provision of death or retirement benefits by employers;[6] to insurance facilities;[7] to employment in a private household, small employers and mineworkers;[8] and to the

---

[4] My proposals for amendment of the substance of the law rely heavily on the consultative paper published by the Commission for Racial Equality, *The Race Relations Act 1976—Time for a Change?* (1983) and on the amendments to the Sex Discrimination Act 1975 and the Equal Pay Act 1970 proposed by the EOC in Appendix 5 to their 1980 *Annual Report.*

[5] See ch. 4 on the 1970 Act. S. 5(3) of the 1975 Act (on which see ch. 2 n. 6) would need to explain that a woman is entitled to compare her pay with that of a man doing like work or work of equal value in the same employment.

[6] See ch. 3 n. 19.

[7] See ch. 7 s. IV.

[8] See ch. 3 nn. 15, 17, 18, and 21.

provision of facilities by clubs which admit men and women to membership but discriminate in their treatment of those who are members.[9] The 'genuine occupational qualification' defence needs amendment.[10] The Act should clarify the fact that section 29, on the provision of facilities to the public, covers the exercise of statutory discretionary powers by local and national public authorities.[11]

The exemption of acts done under statutory authority (which covers a wide variety of instruments short of Acts of Parliament) is inconsistent with Article 5(2)(a) of the EEC Equal Treatment Directive which requires that Member States should take the necessary steps to ensure that any laws, regulations, and administrative provisions contrary to the principle of equal treatment for men and women should be abolished. Section 51 of the 1975 Act, which deals with acts done under statutory authority, validates sex discrimination carried out pursuant to a vague and open class of instruments.[12] If acts done under statutory authority are to be exempt from the provisions of the 1975 Act, that Act should include a Schedule of relevant provisions which excuse sex discrimination. With regard to future instruments, Parliament should adopt the language of section 46 of the Ontario Human Rights Code 1981. This provides that where a provision in an Act or regulation (enacted or made more than two years after the Code came into force) purports to require or to authorize conduct that is a contravention of the principles of non-discrimination stated in the Code, the Code 'applies and prevails unless the Act or regulation specifically provides that it is to apply notwithstanding this' Code. At the very least, the 1975 Act should be amended to ensure that it applies to taxation, social security, immigration, and nationality law. The Government can hardly expect others to take seriously the prohibition of sex discrimination when the Government itself exhibits such blatant discrimination in these areas.

Even more important than these substantive amendments are improvements to the scheme of remedies available under the 1975

[9] See ch. 3 n. 80.
[10] See ch. 9.
[11] See ch. 3 n. 59.
[12] On s. 51 see ch. 3 n. 113. On the Equal Treatment Directive see ch. 5 n. 26.

Act.[13] The willingness of complainants to commence and pursue proceedings and the readiness of respondents to amend discriminatory practices prior to and on being found liable by courts and tribunals depend, to a large degree, on the efficacy of the remedies provided by the law. There is no power to award an injunction against an employer who has discriminated (other than in the very limited cases where the EOC may bring proceedings).[14] Although tribunals can make recommendations to employers who have discriminated, the tribunal has no power to order the reinstatement of an employee (or the engagement of a prospective employee) who has been discriminated against. Such a power is possessed by tribunals in unfair dismissal cases (albeit further compensation is the only sanction if the employer fails to comply with the order). At present, tribunals make very limited use of their power to make recommendations. In employment cases and in cases brought in county courts, compensation orders are far from generous to the complainant and they are inadequate to deter respondents from discriminating. There is no power to award compensation in cases of indirect discrimination unless the respondent had a discriminatory motive. This reduces the deterrent effect of the provisions forbidding indirect discrimination. In all cases, an industrial tribunal has a discretion to deny compensation if it is 'just and equitable' to do so, albeit there has been sex discrimination and albeit the applicant has suffered loss as a result. A tougher scheme of remedies is required to concentrate the minds of potential discriminators on their legal obligations.

A complainant who establishes that she has been discriminated against and has suffered loss as a result (including injury to her feelings) should be entitled to compensation. The right to compensation should cover indirect as well as direct discrimination cases. Employers and others should not be immune from liability to pay compensation because they have closed their eyes to the existence of an unlawful practice. In employment cases, the tribunal should have the power to order reinstatement or engagement. Recommendations should be supplemented by the

[13] See ch. 3 s. VII. There is room for doubt whether the remedies for employment discrimination under the 1975 Act satisfy the criteria of Community law that they must ensure real and effective legal protection and must have a genuine deterrent effect on the employer: *Von Colson* and *Kamann The Times* 25 Apr. 1984. See ch. 5 n. 44.

[14] See ch. 10 n. 10.

power to make binding orders requiring the respondent to take, within a specified period, action to terminate unlawful practices or to obviate the consequences of such practices. The Employment Appeal Tribunal should have the power to award an injunction, if necessary, to enforce such an order. To deter potential wrong-doers, exemplary damages (that is damages exceeding the loss suffered by the complainant) should be awarded when a defendant has acted without due regard for the rights of the complainant and where such damages are appropriate in all the circumstances of the case. Tribunals should have the power to award interlocutory injunctions in appropriate cases. Too often, the victim of sex discrimination knows that by the time her claim is heard, it will be too late to secure her the remedy she needs: she wants to be protected from dismissal, for example. Where there appears a reasonable likelihood of eventual success in the claim, and where the balance of convenience would not be harmed, such injunctions should be available to maintain the status quo prior to a full hearing.

Other procedural reforms are necessary to secure the efficacy of anti-discrimination law. The burden of proof in direct discrimination cases[15] should be altered. Once the complainant has shown that she was less favourably treated than a comparable man, the onus should be on the defendant to show that this was not by reason of the complainant's sex. The relevant factual and other material is in the control of the defendant and it is appropriate that it should have to satisfy the court or tribunal that it acted for admissible reasons. The strict time limits applicable to an anti-discrimination claim[16] should be loosened. Many such claims become out of time without any prejudice to the defendant and in circumstances where the complexity of the issues prevents the claim being commenced in time. There is no good reason why the complainant should only be allowed to proceed with her claim if she can persuade a court or tribunal that it is 'just and equitable' to waive the time limits. The current time limits of three months in employment cases and six months in other cases should be doubled. The usual limitation period in county court actions for tort is three or six years. Sex discrimination is, under section 66(1) of the 1975 Act, treated as a statutory tort. The six-month time-limit is, therefore, indefensible.

[15] See ch. 3 s. VII.   [16] See ch. 3 nn. 121–6.

The EOC, as the body charged with the duty of working towards the elimination of sex discrimination and of promoting equality of opportunity between men and women generally, should be given much broader powers to commence proceedings in courts and tribunals for alleged discrimination on behalf of individuals or groups of individuals.[17] It is anomalous that certain claims of discrimination in the context of education cannot be brought unless the claimant has given notice to the Secretary of State.[18] The powers of the EOC in relation to formal investigations are cumbersome and require radical revision (in particular, to ensure that the findings made by the Commission cannot be reopened in an industrial tribunal or county court: the normal principles of judicial review of administrative action in the Divisional Court should apply).[19] The power of the EOC to issue Codes of Practice should not be confined to the field of employment.[20]

The litigation of sex discrimination claims already has a considerable importance for public policy as well as for private rights. The manner in which the 1975 Act is interpreted helps to determine the extent to which the objectives of the legislation can be fulfilled to the advantage of all women. To that extent, the private lawsuit between complainant and respondent is an inadequate vehicle. The issues of public policy will be decided by a court or tribunal which hears only the arguments addressed to it by two, opposed parties with particular private interests. Yet the decision reached will have a considerable impact on other persons, whether potential complainants, potential respondents, or persons more indirectly affected by the matter.[21] Many of the issues raised before industrial tribunals or county courts under the 1975 Act are of considerable factual and legal complexity. Where litigation under the 1975 Act amounts to a test case, or raises matters of considerable factual or legal complexity having wide social implications, it is desirable that there should be a procedure for transferring the case to give the EAT (in employment cases) or the High Court (in the other contexts covered by the 1975 Act) original jurisdiction to hear and decide the issues. At present there is no power to transfer a case from an industrial tribunal to the

---

[17] See ch. 10 nn. 58 and 106. [18] See ch. 3 nn. 120 and 122.
[19] See ch. 10 s. III and VI. [20] See ch. 10 n. 11.
[21] See Abram Chayes, 'The Role of the Judge in Public Law Litigation' 89 *Harvard Law Review* 1281 (1976).

EAT in this way. The EAT does already have jurisdiction to hear appeals on questions of fact and law from various decisions of the Certification Officer in matters concerning trade unions. It also has jurisdiction to determine applications for compensation for unreasonable expulsion or exclusion from a trade union. There is a general power in the county court to transfer cases to the High Court, but only where the High Court would itself have jurisdiction, which is not the case under the 1975 Act.[22]

If cases were transferred to the EAT or to the High Court because of the complexity or importance of the issues, the EOC should be invited to produce expert evidence and argument to assist the proper determination of the issues.[23] In the absence of such expert material, there is a danger that there may be a 'mismatch between the structure of the judicial process and the purposive social engineering it was asked to undertake . . .'.[24] Lawyers need to grapple with social facts in this context more than in most. The adjudication of indirect discrimination claims, which depend on a theory of group entitlements, raises the problem in a particularly acute form. It is the public law aspects of anti-discrimination litigation which make entirely inadequate the present remedies of limited compensation and recommendations. To achieve the social goal of reducing sex discrimination, British courts need to be equipped, like US courts, with the power to enforce positive remedies such as the mandatory injunction requiring specific action to change behaviour.[25]

In those sex discrimination cases which remain in industrial tribunals and in county courts, those who sit in judgment do need to make greater efforts to construe the legislation with greater sympathy for its objectives. More women on tribunals and more

[22] See s. 42 of the County Courts Act 1984. It is arguable that the power of the High Court itself to transfer a case to it from the county court under s. 41 of the 1984 Act applies to a case under the 1975 Act.

[23] The EOC has appeared as a type of amicus curiae in some important anti-discrimination law cases: see *Shields* v. *E. Coomes (Holdings) Ltd* [1978] ICR 1159 (Court of Appeal); *Science Research Council* v. *Nassé* [1980] AC 1028 (House of Lords); *Page* v. *Freight Hire (Tank Haulage) Ltd* [1981] ICR 299 (EAT).

[24] B. A. Hepple above, n. 3 at 75.

[25] See Roger Cotterrell, 'The Impact of Sex Discrimination Legislation' (1981) *Public Law* 469; see also B. A. Hepple above, n. 3 at 77. Particularly unhelpful in this respect is the reluctance of the EAT to state general principles and the preference for defining difficult issues as questions of fact for the discretion of the industrial tribunal: see ch. 2 n. 95.

women judges would help in this respect.[26] It is impossible for the
law to achieve equality of opportunity between men and women,
and to encourage the public to believe that such a goal is being
vigorously pursued, when law cases are decided by a judiciary
which consists overwhelmingly of males. Whether or not justice is
done, it is certainly not seen to be done. Special anti-discrimination
tribunals are not the solution, even if there were an adequate case
load to occupy such a body and even if we could agree on the
criteria by which persons should be appointed. What matters is the
quality of those who sit in judgment, not the name of the forum in
which they sit. Special training seminars in anti-discrimination law
would undoubtedly benefit those who adjudicate upon such
claims.

If the 1975 Act is to achieve its objectives 'to eliminate anti-
social practices; to provide remedies for the victim of unfair
discrimination; and indirectly to change the prejudiced attitudes
expressed as discrimination',[27] all these procedural reforms are
essential. The concept of discrimination contained in the 1975 Act
also needs amendment. The concept of direct discrimination[28]
should specify, by analogy with the Race Relations Act 1976, that
it covers less favourable treatment 'on the ground of sex', not
merely on the ground of the sex of the complainant. So, if a
barman is dismissed for serving a woman customer who his
employers, in pursuance of a policy of sex discrimination, ordered
him not to serve, he would have a remedy under the 1975 Act.[29]

---

[26] See the White Paper, *Equality for Women* (Cmnd. 5724, 1974), para. 83: 'The
number of women appointed to the tribunals is being increased. The aim is to have
sufficient women so that at least one person of each sex will normally be on a
tribunal which is hearing a sex discrimination or equal pay case.' In *Habib* v.
Elkington & Co. Ltd [1981] ICR 435, the EAT held that an undertaking given in
the House of Lords that the Government intended to ensure that at least one lay
member of a tribunal hearing a complaint under the Race Relations Act 1976 had
specific knowledge of race relations did not, if breached, affect the legal authority
of an industrial tribunal hearing the case. See also *Blank* v. *Sullivan and Cromwell*
418 F Supp 1 (1975) where a US District Court judge refused to accede to the
request of a defendant accused of sex discrimination that she should disqualify
herself on the ground of bias because she was of the same sex as the plaintiff and
had argued civil rights cases before her appointment to the Bench. See similarly
Commonwealth of Pennsylvania v. *Local Union* 542 388 F Supp. 155 (1974) (US
District Court in race discrimination case), aff'd 478 F 2d 1398 (1975), cert. denied
421 US 999 (1975). For examples of hostile judicial attitudes to women see Polly
Pattullo, *Judging Women* (1983).

[27] *Equality for Women*, ibid. at para. 20.

[28] See ch. 2 s. II.   [29] See ch. 2 n. 9.

Direct discrimination also needs amendment to provide, for the avoidance of doubt, that it covers a case where a defendant treats a woman less favourably by reason of pregnancy (or associated factors) than he treats or would treat a man affected by some other temporary incapacitating condition.[30]

The concept of indirect discrimination needs strengthening and simplification to explain that it concerns a policy or practice (whether or not it constitutes an 'absolute bar') which, in fact, has a serious disparate impact on women compared with men (or vice versa), which the defendant cannot show to be necessary irrespective of sex, and which is to the detriment of the complainant to whom it is or was applied.[31] To assist employers to understand the nature of indirect discrimination, large employers should be required to keep records of the sex of their employees and job applicants in each category of job.

Discrimination on the ground of marital status should cover education and the provision of goods, services, facilities, and premises as well as employment. It should also be widened to prohibit less favourable treatment on the ground of any marital or family status.[32] The provisions on victimization need strengthening to protect a person against any adverse action taken on the ground that they acted by or with reference to the 1975 Act.[33]

IV

Women are poorly represented in jobs of influence and responsibility. This is, in part, by reason of past discrimination and because of the burden of family responsibilities which society, and nature, impose on women. The virtual exclusion, in practice, of women from positions of responsibility and authority in politics, business, the law, education, and other areas of influence and control, is undesirable for society as well as for the individual women who would wish to take up such posts. A society makes inadequate use of its human resources if those in positions of leadership are derived almost exclusively from the male half of the population.

One partial remedy is affirmative action. This connotes the reservation for members of a class (defined by reference to sex, race, colour, etc.) of certain benefits, or the taking into account of

[30] See ch. 6.   [31] See ch. 2 ss. III and IV.
[32] Ibid. s. V.   [33] Ibid. s. VI.

the applicant's sex, race, colour etc. as one positive factor in deciding to whom to award particular benefits. The arguments for and against affirmative action have been well rehearsed in political debate in recent years in the context of race relations law.[34] Those who approve of such a policy point out that one does not remedy past discrimination by adopting a neutral attitude prohibiting such discrimination for the future. The continuing effects of past discrimination will ensure that the disadvantages suffered by the victims of earlier prejudice make them unable now to compete on genuinely equal terms for the resources and opportunities offered by society. Proponents of affirmative action stress that race and sex discrimination are offensive not because they adopt the criteria of race and sex in distributing benefits and detriments but because they assert hostility to persons by reason of their race or sex. Affirmative action implies no such hostility. Its motive, and its effect, are to assist those who are disadvantaged. It does this by temporary, beneficial measures which are aimed at helping persons of a particular race or sex where that group is, as a whole, disadvantaged compared with other groups. The advocates of affirmative action stress that the law against discrimination should seek to ensure equal treatment through equal achievement by different races and sexes.[35] Opponents of affirmative action emphasize the problem of deciding which groups are to benefit (and to what extent), the error of assuming that each member of the disadvantaged group will need or deserve assistance at all (or to a greater extent than the white male who would have received the relevant benefit but for the affirmative action), and the stigma involved in marking out a group, defined by race, colour, or sex, as requiring affirmative action in its favour to enable it to compete for resources on genuinely equal terms.

Because 'to discriminate' has a pejorative meaning, suggesting unfair or arbitrary differentiations,[36] I have avoided the use of the

---

[34] For discussion of the merits and the defects of affirmative action programmes see Cohen, Nagel, and Scanlon (eds.), *Equality and Preferential Treatment* (1977); Alan H. Goldman, *Justice and Reverse Discrimination* (1979); Ronald Dworkin *Taking Rights Seriously* (1977), ch. 9; Richard A. Wasserstrom, 'Racism, Sexism and Preferential Treatment: An Approach to the Topics' 24 *University of California at Los Angeles Law Review* 581 (1977).

[35] See Owen M. Fiss, 'A Theory of Fair Employment Laws' 38 *University of Chicago Law Review* 235, 237–8 (1971).

[36] See ch. 1 n. 62.

term 'positive discrimination' and have referred, instead, to affirmative action. The 1975 Act validates affirmative action in a very narrow range of circumstances. Section 2(2) permits special treatment of women (which means specially favourable treatment) in connection with pregnancy and childbirth.[37] Sections 47–9 allow some affirmative action in training women (or men) for work, by encouraging them to take up opportunities to do that work and in taking up seats on elective bodies in certain organizations.[38] Two essential points emerge from these provisions. First, there is no requirement under the Act to give specially favourable treatment to women in any circumstances. All the 1975 Act does is to make it lawful, in a limited number of cases, to give specially favourable treatment to women. Secondly, the affirmative action provisions in the 1975 Act (with the limited exception of section 2(2)) apply to training and to other minor matters: it remains unlawful for an employer to give specially favourable treatment to female employees or potential employees on the ground of their sex in deciding whom to appoint, promote, or dismiss or in deciding what benefits to provide. In these central decisions affirmative action is unlawful, even where an employer wishes to compensate women for past sex discrimination or is concerned about the paucity of

[37] See ch. 6 n. 22.
[38] S. 47 permits affirmative action by designated training bodies on behalf of women (or men) when it appears that at any time during the previous twelve months there were no persons of the sex to be benefited or a 'comparatively small' number of such persons doing particular work in Great Britain or in an area within Great Britain. In such circumstances the designated training body (that is an industrial training board, the Manpower Services Commission, or any other person designated for this purpose by the Secretary of State: see s. 47(4)) may afford only women (or only men) access to facilities for training which would help to fit them for the work in question, or may encourage only women (or only men) to take advantage of opportunities for doing that work. S. 47 also provides that in connection with affording persons access to facilities for training, a designated training body may give specially favourable treatment to women (or to men) who have been discharging family or domestic responsibilities (to the exclusion of regular full-time employment) and so are in special need of such training. S. 48(1) contains similar provisions empowering employers to take positive steps to train or encourage women to do certain work. S. 48(2) permits such action by organizations of workers or employers, or professional or trade organizations. S. 48(3) allows those organizations to encourage only women (or only men) to become members. S. 49 permits those organizations to take affirmative action in relation to representation on their elective bodies by reserving (or making available extra) seats for women (or men) so as to ensure a reasonable lower limit to the number of women (or men) serving on the body.

women doing such work and wishes to increase the number of women doing such work.

The limited legality of affirmative action under the 1975 Act (and under the Race Relations Act 1976, which contains very similar provisions) is unjustifiable. In employment decisions relating to hiring, firing, promoting, and determining job conditions men and women have to be treated the same irrespective of their sex. Yet by reason of past sex discrimination and by reason of current domestic or family responsibilities which are, in practice, borne by women rather than men, it is the case that women are too often unable to compete for employment and other opportunities with men on equal terms unless affirmative action is applied.

In determining the acceptability of affirmative action for women it is of value to note the recognition of this concept in other legal systems and in international law. The EEC Directive on the implementation of equal treatment for men and women as regards access to employment, vocational training, promotion, and working conditions[39] provides, by Article 2(4), that it is 'without prejudice to measures to promote equal opportunity for men and women, in particular by removing existing inequalities which affect women's opportunities . . .'. The US Supreme Court has held that Title VII of the Civil Rights Act 1964 (which makes it unlawful for an employer to discriminate on the grounds, *inter alia*, of race or sex) does not forbid employers and unions from agreeing upon bona fide affirmative action plans which act upon racial classifications by reserving for black employees 50 per cent of the openings in an in-plant craft-training programme. In *United Steelworkers of America* v. *Weber*, the Court held that the purposes of such a plan mirrored

---

[39] Council Directive 76/207/EEC of 9 Feb. 1976. A similar provision is applied by s. 13 of the Ontario Human Rights Code 1981. This provides that the right to non-discriminatory treatment 'is not infringed by the implementation of a special programme designed to relieve hardship or economic disadvantage or to assist disadvantaged persons or groups to achieve or attempt to achieve equal opportunity or that is likely to contribute to the elimination of the infringement of rights' under the Code. See also s. 28(1) of the New Zealand Human Rights Commission Act 1977. This states that the Commission may 'approve in writing any special plan or programme submitted to it by any person if it considers that (a) the plan or programme will assist or advance particular persons or groups of persons, being in each case persons of a particular sex . . . and (b) those persons or groups need or may reasonably be supposed to need assistance or advancement in order to achieve an equal place with other members of the community.' S. 15(1) of the Canadian Human Rights Act 1977 is to similar effect. See also s. 33 of the Sex Discrimination Act 1984 (Australia).

the objectives of Title VII itself: to break down old patterns of racial segregation and hierarchy. The Court concluded that the plan was a permissible form of affirmative action because it did not require the discharge of white workers or their replacement by blacks; it did not create an absolute bar to the advancement of white employees, since half of those trained in the programme would be white; moreover, the plan was a temporary measure which would end as soon as the percentage of black skilled craft workers in the plant reached the percentage level of blacks in the local labour force; and the plan was not intended to maintain a racial balance but to eliminate a manifest imbalance and injustice.[40]

The ruling in *Weber* has been applied by the US Court of Appeals to sex discrimination under Title VII. In *La Riviere* v. *EEOC*,[41] the Court held that, by analogy with *Weber*, Title VII does not prohibit 'voluntary affirmative action programmes designed to correct long-standing sexual imbalances in the work force'. Where, as in that case, the plan satisfied the criteria stated in *Weber* (being designed to break down old patterns of occupational segregation; not requiring the discharge of male workers and not prohibiting their employment; being a temporary measure intended to eliminate a sexual imbalance in the work force) the plan may be applied consistently with Title VII without giving rise to liability to male applicants who would have been selected for the relevant benefits had they been female.

A number of Constitutions authorise affirmative action in favour of disadvantaged groups. The US Supreme Court has held consistent with the equal protection clause of the fourteenth amendment to the Constitution classifications by sex which are designed to benefit women by compensating them for burdens which have a disparate impact on them compared with men.[42] Its decisions 'upholding the use of gender-based classifications rested upon the Court's perception of the laudatory purposes of those

---

[40] 443 US 193, 208–9 (1979). The dissenting opinion of Mr Justice Rehnquist, joined by Chief Justice Burger, angrily suggested that 'by a *tour de force* reminiscent not of jurists such as Hale, Holmes and Hughes, but of escape artists such as Houdini, the Court eludes clear statutory language, "uncontradicted" legislative history and uniform precedent in concluding that employers are, after all, permitted to consider race in making employment decisions': 222.

[41] 682 F 2d 1275, 1279 (1982).

[42] *Kahn* v. *Shevin* 416 US 351 (1974); *Schlesinger* v. *Ballard* 419 US 498 (1975); *Mississippi University for Women* v. *Hogan* 458 US 718 (1982).

318   *Conclusions*

laws as remedying disadvantageous conditions suffered by women
in economic and military life'.[43] However, the Court has made it
clear that 'the mere recitation of a benign, compensatory purpose
is not an automatic shield which protects against any enquiry into
the actual purposes underlying a statutory scheme'.[44] The Court
will not uphold against a challenge under the equal protection
clause a gender-based classification which 'rather than advantaging
women to compensate for past wrongs compounds those wrongs
by penalising women'.[45]

Article 15(4) of the Indian Constitution provides that the
guarantee of equality before the law and the equal protection of
the laws shall not prevent the States from 'making any special
provision for the advancement of any socially and educationally
backward classes of citizens or for the Scheduled Castes and the
Scheduled Tribes'.[46] The Indian Supreme Court has explained that
this is not an exception to the general principle of equality.
Rather, it is a manifestation of what equality requires in particular
circumstances.[47]

The international law of human rights similarly recognizes the
validity of affirmative action programmes where 'legal inequalities
tend only to correct factual inequalities'.[48] The UN Convention on
the Elimination of all Forms of Discrimination Against Women
1979 provides, by Article 4, that the adoption of 'temporary
special measures aimed at accelerating *de facto* equality between

---

[43] *Craig* v. *Boren* 429 US 190, 198 n (1976).

[44] *Weinberger* v. *Wiesenfeld* 420 US 636, 648 (1975).

[45] *Califano* v. *Goldfarb* 430 US 199, 209 n (1977). See also two decisions of the
US Supreme Court on the legality of affirmative action programmes for blacks
under the equal protection clause: *DeFunis* v. *Odegaard* 416 US 312 (1974) (where
the issue was held to be moot); *Regents of the University of California* v. *Bakke* 438
US 265 (1978) (where the Court held 5–4 that the university acted unlawfully by
reserving 16 out of 100 places solely for ethnic minorities, at least where there was
no finding of past discrimination against the university itself; but the Court also
held, 5–4, that race could be used as one criterion among others when the
university decided how to allocate places, if the purpose of having regard to race
was to create a diverse student body).

[46] Similarly art. 16(4). Art. 15(3) allows States to make 'any special provision for
women . . .'.

[47] See *M. R. Balaji* v. *State of Mysore* (1963) Supp 1 SCR 439; *State of Kerala* v.
N. M. Thomas (1976) 1 SCR 906.

[48] *Belgian Languages Case*, Judgment of the European Court of Human Rights
(Merits), 23 July 1968, para. 10, 24–5 on art. 14 of the European Convention on
Human Rights which guarantees equality in the enjoyment of the other rights
protected under the Convention. See below, n. 82 on art. 14.

men and women shall not be considered discrimination as defined in the present Convention, but shall in no way entail as a consequence the maintenance of unequal or separate standards; these measures shall be discontinued when the objectives of equality of opportunity and treatment have been achieved'.[49] Affirmative action is therefore consistent with international law when it satisfies criteria similar to those stated by the US Supreme Court in *Weber*: the plan must be designed to assist a particular group to overcome disadvantages and to remedy manifest imbalances in employment or other contexts; it must not be contrary to the wishes of that group; it must not deny employment or other opportunities to other groups; and it must be a temporary measure which will end as soon as the objective is fulfilled.

The concept of equality involves treating like with like and treating unlikes differently.[50] To the extent that groups defined by reference to their sex or colour or race are disadvantaged and suffering the present effects of past discrimination, they are not like other groups. Hence to treat them in the same way as other groups is to deny them equality, not to provide equality to them. To repudiate affirmative action, and to label it discrimination against men, or against whites, is to fail to understand that not every differentiation in treatment is discrimination. In the absence of affirmative action plans to assist women, it is most unlikely that the occupational segregation of the sexes will be rectified. Formal equality of treatment will never be translated into genuine equality of achievement by men and women. The experience of other legal systems which have considered the same problem, and the teaching of international law, further suggest that it should be lawful for employers to give preferential treatment to women on the ground of their sex in making employment decisions when the criteria stated in *Weber* are satisfied. Where employers see the

---

[49] See similarly art. 1(4) of the UN Convention on the Elimination of All Forms of Racial Discrimination 1966: 'Special measures taken for the sole purpose of securing adequate advancement of certain racial or ethnic groups or individuals requiring such protection as may be necessary in order to ensure such groups or individuals equal enjoyment or exercise of human rights and fundamental freedoms shall not be deemed racial discrimination, provided, however, that such measures do not, as a consequence, lead to the maintenance of separate rights for different racial groups and that they shall not be continued after the objectives for which they were taken have been achieved.'
[50] See ch. 1 s. IV.

force of the arguments for affirmative action it is wrong that the law should forbid them to act upon these considerations.

V

Affirmative action programmes and drafting amendments to the 1975 Act would not, of themselves, be sufficient to ensure that more women would be able to take jobs of importance and responsibility. The White Paper, *Equality for Women*, which preceded the 1975 Act recognized that an anti-discrimination law is relevant only to the extent that economic and social conditions enable people to compete for resources on equal terms. The law is of little assistance if social pressures cause women not to take advantage of opportunities for employment or higher education. Similarly, mothers will obtain minimum benefit 'if there is inadequate provision for part-time work or flexible working hours, or for day nurseries'.[51] In the absence of such measures, and in the light of the tendency of women rather than men to care for children, it becomes difficult for women to work and to build careers. At present, the requirements of a career worker are defined in a way that exclude many women because of family care responsibilities (causing breaks in their career or part-time working) the performance of which by women frees men to build their careers.

Equality for Women concluded that

[l]egislation is a necessary precondition for an effective equal opportunity policy but it is not a sufficient condition. A wide range of administrative and voluntary measures will be needed to translate the ideal of equal opportunity into practical reality. The responsibility for these wider measures does not rest with Government alone. It must be accepted by employers and trade unions, by commercial undertakings and the professions, by universities, colleges and schools, and by the community as a whole.[52]

Neither the community as a whole, nor these constituent parts of it, have fully accepted these responsibilities. With a few honourable exceptions, employers, trade unions, and educational establish-

---

[51] Above, n. 26 at para. 21.
[52] Ibid. See similarly Roy Jenkins (Home Secretary) 889 HC 524–5 (Second Reading Debate on the Sex Discrimination Bill 1975: 26 Mar. 1975).

ments have failed to provide day-care facilities for children, to recognize flexible working hours, paternity leave, time off work when children are ill, job-sharing, and seniority rules that do not unfairly penalize women for years of absence for child-rearing. Unless and until there are dramatic changes in social attitudes towards the family responsibilities of men, many women will be able to combine work with child care only by requiring employers to make their policies more flexible in these respects. Since most employers are men, and therefore benefit from the imposition of family responsibilities on women, the demands of women that work should be reorganized in minor respects are hardly unreasonable.

The Government has not given much of a lead in these respects with regard to its own employment policies or by requiring Government contractors to make such provision for their employees. Perhaps in recognition of this, the Prime Minister announced in February 1984 that a series of steps would be taken in an attempt to ensure equal opportunity for women in the Civil Service. These steps included a new emphasis on part-time work where feasible to help women to combine a career with domestic responsibilities.[53] It remains to be seen how much political muscle is put behind such laudable aims, with what results.

In the absence of this type of measure being voluntarily adopted in industry and elsewhere, it is time to impose legal obligations on employers to take positive steps to enable working women to combine their family care duties with work by the provision of day-care facilities and by the recognition of flexible working hours, part-time work, paternity leave, and job-sharing. Promotion, pay, and other employment practices need to avoid penalizing employees who have had a break in service for family care reasons, or who work part-time, unless this is crucially relevant to the employment decision. A Code of Practice is needed to require large companies to educate their personnel staff about equal opportunity law, to monitor the sexual composition of their workforce, and regularly to assess their job requirements to remove unnecessary conditions which adversely affect women.

---

[53] 53 HC 718 (9 Feb. 1984: written answer to Parliamentary question). See Tess Gill and Larry Whitty, *Women's Rights in the Workplace* (1983), 177–80 on the concept of job-sharing. See ch. 2 n. 59 on the use of indirect discrimination law to secure part-time work and flexible working hours for women.

The State could provide special grants for employers who train women for occupations presently dominated by men.[54] The State should ensure that those with whom it contracts take positive measures to assist women. Schools should be encouraged to provide instruction in metalworking, domestic science, and child care, for example, for both sexes.[55] Colleges and universities should be encouraged, by financial incentives, to train more women for engineering and other sciences presently dominated by men.

The provision of such positive measures will encourage women more fully to participate in public affairs. True equality of opportunity will, however, still be fettered by the perception of men and women as to their social roles. The Preamble to the UN Convention on the Elimination of All Forms of Discrimination Against Women 1979 recognized that 'a change in the traditional role of men as well as the role of women in society and in the family is needed to achieve full equality between men and women'. In particular, 'the upbringing of children requires a sharing of responsibility between men and women and society as a whole'. The difficult question is to what extent (after amending the 1975 Act and validating or requiring affirmative action programmes) the State should attempt to alter the assumptions on which our society is based in order to secure equal opportunities for women.

VI

Men and women are, of course, different in obvious physical respects. In addition to physiological distinctions between all men and all women, there are physical distinctions between most men and most women, for example in relation to height[56] and weight.

---

[54] In 1982, Britain received only 5.4 per cent of the section of the EEC Social Fund that is set aside for training women aged more than 25 in non-traditional jobs such as engineering, electronics, and building. The Government explained that it did not tap this source because it 'contains a strong emphasis on positive discrimination' which was in conflict with Government policy. See *The Times* 27 Oct. 1983. The European Court of Justice wasted a good opportunity to further equal opportunity at work and to weaken stereotyped assumptions about the role of women by the decision in *Hofmann* v. *Barmer Ersatzkasse The Times* 24 July 1984 that an employer who grants maternity leave is not obliged to grant paternity leave: see ch. 5 nn. 33–8.

[55] See Hilda Scott, *Sweden's 'Right to be Human'* (1982).

[56] See Elizabeth Laidler, 'Why Women Look Up To Men' *The Guardian* 30 June 1982.

There are also differences of gender between most men and most women. These result from our culture, not from any inherent distinctions between the sexes.[57] They cover a wide range of attitudes and behaviour from dress to criminal conduct to mortality rates.[58] The differences of gender are learnt by us early in our lives, partly by the lessons our parents teach us about the way in which boys and girls should behave and partly by our own perception of the expected behaviour of boys and girls that we see around us or read in books.[59]

It is difficult to see how women can be given equal opportunities with men unless we can reduce the differences of gender which limit our perception of what it is appropriate for men and women to do. While we impose constraints—by way of criticism, discouragement, or ridicule—on women who take non-traditional paths in employment and other contexts, we cannot be surprised if few women overcome the barriers imposed by their gender.

When we have removed the evils of women being denied the vote, property, education, and employment because of their sex, when we have ensured that women have control of their own fertility, and when we have devised programmes to encourage women to take greater advantage of opportunities for education and employment in non-traditional areas, the only impediment to equality will arise from the stereotypes we adopt of the male and the female role in our society. As Richard Wasserstrom has lucidly explained,[60] we cannot know what a sexist society is unless we have a conception of what a non-sexist society would look like. To what extent should society treat a person's sex like their eye colour? Certainly sex should be so treated in the provision of basic political rights and obligations (including the obligation of fighting for one's country in time of war) and in the supply of other societal benefits and obligations such as employment and education. In these contexts, individuals should be considered by reference to their own specific attributes, not by reference to their sex (unless an affirmative action plan is required to compensate for past discrimination). But in personal decisions, relating to private conduct, friends, and relationships, most of us recognize and value

---

[57] See ch. 1 nn. 49–50.
[58] See *Sex Differences in Britain* (ed. Ivan Reid and Eileen Wormald 1982).
[59] See *Racism and Sexism in Children's Books* (ed. Judith Stinton 1979).
[60] Above, n. 34 at 603.

as vital to our conception of the good life the essential differences between men and women.

For radical feminists, however, equality can only be achieved by the creation of 'a new androgynous culture which incorporates the best elements of both the present male and the present female cultures . . .'.[61] They believe that, as the socialist revolution requires workers to seize control of the means of production, so the sexual revolution depends on women gaining control of the reproduction of the species and replacing it by, at the very least, the option of artificial reproduction.[62] The problem they face is that however one defines the present differences between male and female culture, to commit oneself to their abolition and to their replacement by a society which treats a person's sex like their eye colour for all purposes is a policy which will attract very few converts. Most of us would prefer the perpetuation of some injustice and inequality to joining the march towards an androgynous society. Many women consciously and deliberately choose to marry, to wear make-up, to enter beauty competitions. It is important not to remove their liberty to do so in the name of liberation.[63] The goal should be to enhance their opportunities to choose between different options irrespective of their sex.

Our desire to preserve, on a personal level, the differences between men and women should not validate stereotyped assumptions about what men and women can achieve. The State has the duty to recognize that personal decisions about male/female

[61] Alison Jaggar, 'On Sexual Equality' 84 *Ethics* 275 (1974).
[62] Shulamith Firestone, *The Dialectic of Sex: The Case for Feminist Revolution* (1979), ch. 1.
[63] See Janet Radcliffe Richards, *The Sceptical Feminist* (1982). She rightly emphasizes, at 188, that there is nothing inherently wrong with different dress, interests, and occupations for men and women, any more than it is wrong for different countries to have distinct characteristics. The evil is the undervaluing of female attributes and the refusal to allow women to adopt other attributes if they wish to do so. Many women will not wish to take up the opportunity to work away from home, rather than working with a family at home. They may appreciate that 'if you are going to make the same incomes from the same professions that those men make you will have to accept the same conditions that they accept. Even from an upper window and from books we know or can guess what those conditions are. You will have to leave the house at nine and come back to it at six. That leaves very little time for fathers to know their children. You will have to do this daily from the age of twenty-one or so to the age of about sixty five. That leaves very little time for friendship, travel or art . . . That explains why most successful barristers are hardly worth sitting next at dinner—they yawn so': Virginia Woolf, *Three Guineas* (1938), ch. 2.

arrangements are, like decisions on religion, a topic upon which reasonable people may reasonably hold different views. The State should, by its laws, seek to ensure that different personal arrangements may be made by different people, if they so choose, without any adverse consequences for their civil rights and obligations as members of society. We trust individuals, in a liberal society, to choose their own religions free from State control (other than in exceptional circumstances). Similarly, we are not entitled to compel individuals—whether by criminal law, tax law, employment or education policies, dress codes or any other means—to conform to one type of sexual pattern. If gender could be seen as analogous to religion, being at least partly a matter of conscious choice of the individual which is open to change without being fettered by irresistible social pressures but being none the less a matter of considerable importance to many people, the stereotyped assumptions and prejudices which limit the horizons of women could more easily be brought under control.

VII

Some feminists see equality as realizable only by the eradication of sex differences or by the segregation of men from women. Women who adopt the latter approach are themselves guilty of offensive sex stereotyping. They perceive men—all men, because they are men—as oppressors of all women. They find it difficult to see men and women living together in society without the subjection of one sex to the other. This pessimistic dogma is most loudly expressed in the proposals of militant feminists for radical reform of the law on rape and pornography.

Rape, according to this theory, 'is nothing more or less than a conscious process of intimidation by which *all men* keep *all women* in a state of fear' (italics in the original).[64] The enemy of equal opportunity, therefore, is the male, the conscious oppressor who is pathologically programmed to await the opportunity to degrade and possess women. There is little room here for the possibility that some men are not rapists, have no desire to be rapists, and are repelled by the thought of rape. Those women who see rape as the basic issue in male–female relationships mistake the isolated

---

[64] Susan Brownmiller, *Against Our Will: Men, Women and Rape* (1976), 15.

(though none the less repellent) crime for the norm. To support their case they need to redefine rape so that the term can cover the experiences of more than a tiny minority of unfortunate women, while utilizing the repugnance which the vast majority of people feel for the concept of rape. Feminist theories of rape tend to distract attention from the need for men and women to work together to secure better enforcement of the laws which are designed to deter and to punish the crime.

Feminist reaction to pornography is similarly misdirected. The conclusions drawn by Andrea Dworkin[65] are typical of the mistakes which can be reached in this area. Ms Dworkin spent three years looking at thousands of items of pornography. It made her physically sick, misanthropic, and very angry. Much of what she has to say about the subject is compelling. The multi-million dollar business evidently degrades the female sex by presenting it as an object existing solely for male gratification, there to be whipped, chained, or otherwise abused. Women, the pornographer implies, either welcome this role or have no right to complain about what is thrust upon them. Where one parts company with Ms Dworkin is in the meaning and the importance she attributes to the trade of the pornographer. For her, the items she has handled are not merely pathetic tools of the weak and unfulfilled. They constitute, rather, evidence to prove what all men really believe and desire. Hence, '[p]ornography reveals that male pleasure is inextricably tied to victimising, hurting, exploiting'.[66] Ms Dworkin ignores the fact that the disturbing examples of hard-core pornography that she vividly describes are bought by a minute proportion of men and are likely to have an emetic effect on most spectators, whether male or female. For these reasons, pornography may well have a less significant impact on the behaviour of individuals than the women's magazines which convey stereotypes of the 'proper' female role of housekeeper, cook, and nurse to millions of impressionable and devoted readers.

A lack of perspective and proportion weakens the opposition of militant feminists to pornography and rape. There is no answer to the claim that a wife should have legal protection against a husband who forces her to have sexual intercourse against her will.

---

[65] Andrea Dworkin, *Pornography: Men Possessing Women* (1981).

[66] Ibid. at 69. Similarly, at 176, she suggests that 'force leading to death is what men most secretly, most deeply, and most truly value in sex'.

Similarly, it is undeniable that rape laws should be administered with more concern for the victim. But these points become devalued by reference to 'Dachau brought into the bedroom'[67] and by the suggestion that females suffer 'rape most of the time'.[68] The offensiveness of the gynaecologically explicit pornography on sale cannot adequately be explained if one uses the same language about, and expresses similar anger at, female pin-ups in national newspapers or the use of undressed women to advertise cars. An author who sees Nazi gas ovens when she looks at a picture in *Playboy*[69] has exhausted the range of human disgust on the least unacceptable publications and is guilty, at the very least, of lack of judgment.

What is disconcerting in such writings is the sexual stereotyping adopted by the author. The Marquis de Sade is, apparently, 'Everyman'[70] (despite the fact that many men have no desire to mutilate or otherwise cause physical pain to women), and *men* understand 'love' to mean using women as objects.[71] This thesis, and similar theories of rape or pornography, are comprehensible only when one appreciates that for Ms Dworkin, and others like her, sexual intercourse between a man and a woman is, of itself, an evil, 'an act of possession . . . an act of ownership, taking, force'.[72]

Pornography and rape are disturbing aspects of any society. The former is a necessary evil in a liberal society which rejects censorship. The conservative (concerned with values) and the socialist (concerned to prevent exploitation) may decide to prohibit pornography. The liberal, while declining to give any approval to such publications, is not prepared to support restrictions on freedom of expression unless there is a pressing social need. The liberal is far from convinced that the suppression of pornography is possible or that, in any event, such suppression would materially improve the status of women. The female sex tends to be most oppressed in those Islamic States where pornography is most rigorously forbidden.[73] The liberal is committed to the reform of the rape laws to protect women and to deter, catch, and punish rapists. But he or she cannot accept that it

---

[67] Ibid. at 69.   [68] Ibid. at 51.   [69] Ibid. at 142–3.
[70] Ibid. at 100.   [71] Ibid. at 128.   [72] Ibid. at 23.
[73] In 1983 the Pakistani Ministry of Information ordered newspaper editors to stop printing photographs of women which had no news value: *The Times* 1 June 1983.

is other than unjustified sexism to apply a theory (whether in the context of sexual activity or in the context of who should be allowed to attend a peace rally organized by women) that all men, because they are men, are not to be trusted. Rape and pornography are irrelevancies (albeit ones that understandably cause anxiety and distress to many women, and to many men) in the effort to secure equality for women. Pornography and rape do not create or support the male dominance of society. They are minor consequences of that dominance in the minds of an insignificant proportion of people. Those who are concerned to enhance the status of women would be well advised to turn their main attention to more pervasive issues.

VIII

The 1975 Act covers action taken on the ground of a person's sex (and, in the employment context, on the ground that a person is married). The Race Relations Act 1976 prohibits discrimination on the grounds of colour, race, nationality, or ethnic or national origins. These are prohibited grounds for action because they are based on immutable characteristics which are generally irrelevant to the provision of employment and other important benefits but which have been and continue to be the subject of adverse action for reasons of prejudice to the disadvantage of weak sections of the community.

Discrimination on the grounds of a person's religion, sexual preferences, age, or physical handicap is also common. It is, in many cases, as reprehensible as discrimination on any of the grounds covered by the 1975 and 1976 Acts. Individuals are (except in the case of religion) no more able to control these attributes than they are their race or sex. Nor are these characteristics relevant to the provision of a wide range of benefits. Where religion, sexual preferences, age, or physical handicap is so relevant, anti-discrimination legislation would—as do the 1975 and 1976 Acts—provide exceptions to a general prohibition of action on such grounds. There is a need for a broader anti-discrimination law to cover less favourable treatment on the ground of a person's religion, sexual preferences, age, or physical handicap.

Religious discrimination is not specifically prohibited by the Race Relations Act 1976. Such conduct may be indirectly discriminatory against persons of a particular race and therefore unlawful under the 1976 Act.[74] Nevertheless, there will be many circumstances where domestic law gives no remedy for such treatment.[75] It is noteworthy that in Northern Ireland the Fair Employment (Northern Ireland) Act 1976 does prohibit discrimination in employment on the ground of a person's religious belief (or political opinion). It is anomalous that no similar provision applies to the mainland.

Homosexuals, and other persons whose sexual preferences are shared by a minority, frequently find themselves victims of discrimination on the ground of their sexual preferences. Several foreign jurisdictions have enacted anti-discrimination laws prohibiting such conduct in specific contexts.[76]

In the USA, the Age Discrimination in Employment Act 1967 (as amended) prohibits discrimination in employment on the ground of age against individuals who are at least 40 but are under 70. The employer does not act unlawfully if it can show age to be a bona fide occupational qualification. In Canada, the Human Rights Act 1977 and the legislation of several provinces outlaw age discrimination. The Anti-Discrimination Board of New South Wales, Australia reported in 1981 that age discrimination was widespread and should be made unlawful.[77] Persons who are adversely treated by employers because they are considered too old or too young for the job should have a legal right to require the employer to consider them by reference to their individual abilities and not by reference to a stereotyped assumption (based on an immutable characteristic) that their age disqualifies them for the job because most people of that age cannot do the job.[78]

The need for broader anti-discrimination legislation is further seen with regard to disabled people. Employers who normally employ 20 or more employees already have a duty to take specified steps to employ at least a defined quota of disabled persons under

[74] See, for example, *Mandla* v. *Dowell Lee* [1983] 2 AC 548 (House of Lords), discussed in ch. 2 nn. 89–94.

[75] See, for example, *Ahmad* v. *ILEA* [1978] QB 36 and *Ostreicher* v. *Secretary of State for the Environment* [1978] 3 All ER 82 (decisions of the Court of Appeal).

[76] See ch. 8 n. 30. See generally ch. 8 s. II on discrimination on grounds of sexual orientation.

[77] 7 *Commonwealth Law Bulletin* 1127 (1981).

[78] In 1983, a Labour MP unsuccessfully introduced a Private Member's Bill to prohibit age discrimination in employment: *The Times* 3 May 1983.

the Disabled Persons (Employment) Acts 1944 and 1958 and regulations made thereunder. These laws are, in substance and in enforcement, inadequate to deal with discrimination against the handicapped.[79]

The physically handicapped are, by reason of impairment of bodily functions, obviously less well equipped than others to compete for the benefits offered by society. Quite rightly, we attempt to compensate for such physical handicap by the provision of a variety of allowances and grants designed to ease the difficulties faced by the handicapped. But what causes particular concern among the handicapped is that their opportunity to obtain a fair share of society's resources, and their chance to make a contribution to society's needs, are often diminished not by their own disabilities but by the attitudes of the non-handicapped. The disabled are refused employment and services which they are, on their merits, well qualified to obtain and to use. The refusal occurs because of erroneous assumptions about the scope or effect of their disablement, or because of prejudice or embarrassment. The handicapped do not demand that they be given jobs *because* they are disabled. Rather, they object to less favourable treatment on the ground of their handicap when that is irrelevant to the job or service offered. The woman in a wheelchair who applies to work as a typist wants to be considered on her merits and not to be rejected because of a disability irrelevant to her competence to perform the job duties. The handicapped also suffer from indirect discrimination. Employers and others impose requirements or conditions which, though not expressly excluding the disabled, have a disproportionate adverse impact on the handicapped and are unjustifiable.

There is no doubt that discrimination against the handicapped is common. Nor is it possible to justify such conduct. The main issue is whether legislation should be introduced to deal with the problem. The arguments in favour of such a law are overwhelming. First, it would, like other anti-discrimination laws, provide a much needed, educative statement of public policy. Secondly, it is difficult to believe that such discrimination will be reduced without the intervention of the law. The handicapped (who are in the best position to evaluate the advantages and disadvantages of such a law) have no doubt that legislation would be of enormous

[79] For the content of those laws see Harvey, *Industrial Relations and Employment Law*, i, paras. 1–3214 to 3230.

assistance to them. New South Wales, Victoria, many Canadian provinces, the Canadian Human Rights Act 1977, and many States in the USA prohibit employers and others from discriminating against the disabled. These other jurisdictions have found anti-discrimination law to be a necessary and useful mechanism to assist the disabled. Thirdly, arguments from cost provide a weak basis for opposing any change in the law. Any cost to employers and others would be passed on to consumers as a minute fraction of what we pay for the relevant goods and services. Principles of social justice strongly suggest that it is a cost that the fortunately able-bodied should, and no doubt would, be prepared to pay. In any event, bringing the disabled forward as employees and consumers would have considerable economic advantages for the State. We already spend large amounts on the handicapped. Expenditure on an anti-discrimination law would be of especial value in restoring to the disabled a large degree of autonomy.[80]

Discrimination against people on the ground of illegitimacy is less widespread than it once was, but it persists and should be prohibited by law for reasons similar to those explained above.[81]

Article 2 of the United Nations Universal Declaration of Human Rights guarantees the enjoyment of the rights and freedoms set forth in that document 'without distinction of any kind, such as race, colour, sex, language, religion, political or other opinion, national or social origin, property, birth or other status'. Article 14 of the European Convention on Human Rights is in similar terms.[82] During the Committee Stage of the Race Relations Bill 1968, Quintin Hogg (prior to becoming Lord Chancellor Hailsham) tabled an amendment to widen the prohibited grounds of discrimination stated in the Bill to cover all those mentioned in the UN Declaration. He explained that otherwise there would be 'a privileged class of victims'.[83] Sex discrimination is only one type of discriminatory conduct which is

---

[80] Private Members' Bills have unsuccessfully attempted to prohibit discrimination against the disabled: see *The Times* 7 July 1982, 11 Feb. 1983, and 19 Nov. 1983.

[81] See *Family Law—Illegitimacy* (HC 98, Law Commission Report no. 118: 1982).

[82] It states that the rights and freedoms mentioned in the Convention shall be secured 'without discrimination on any ground such as sex, race, colour, language, religion, political or other opinion, national or social origin, association with a national minority, property, birth or other status'.

[83] See Anthony Lester and Geoffrey Bindman, *Race and Law* (1972), 97.

unfair to individuals, contrary to the interests of society and deserving of prohibition by the law. A general anti-discrimination law is required to make it unlawful to discriminate on the various grounds mentioned above in defined contexts and with defined exceptions. Bodies which act under statutory powers or which carry out statutory duties already have a public law duty to consider all relevant factors and to ignore all irrelevant factors in the exercise of their functions.[84] A more general anti-discrimination law would justifiably move towards the imposition of similar duties on employers (who already have a legal duty not to carry out unfair dismissals), suppliers of goods, services, and premises and on educational institutions. While most employers, suppliers, and educational institutions do not have statutory functions, they do play a vital role in the distribution of scarce and valuable resources. They should not be permitted to exercise their functions to the undeserved detriment of less powerful sections of the community.

The law against sex discrimination 'has in recent decades been a vital component of the trend toward a more general norm of non-discrimination'.[85] It is one aspect, albeit an important aspect, of a wider principle of equality based on tolerance and respect for other human beings. George Bernard Shaw explained that whereas in the nineteenth century 'it was believed that you could not make men good by Act of Parliament, we now know that you cannot make them good in any other way . . .'.[86] It is almost ten years since Parliament acted on Shaw's aphorism and brought the Equal Pay Act 1970 and the Sex Discrimination Act 1975 into effect on 29 December 1975. The experience of that decade confirms that anti-discrimination law remains an essential protection against those who would implement their prejudices in the distribution of the major resources of society.

---

[84] See *Associated Provincial Picture Houses Ltd* v. *Wednesbury Corporation* [1948] 1 KB 223 (Court of Appeal).

[85] Myres S. McDougal, Harold D. Lasswell, and Lung-chu Chen, 'Human Rights for Women and World Public Order: The Outlawing of Sex Based Discrimination' 69 *American Journal of International Law* 497, 509 (1975).

[86] George Bernard Shaw, Preface to *Androcles and the Lion*, in *Prefaces by Bernard Shaw* (1934), ch. XX, 553.

INDEX